CHECK SIX!

CHECK SIX!

A Thunderbolt Pilot's
War Across the Pacific

JAMES C. CURRAN *&*
TERRENCE G. POPRAVAK, JR.

CASEMATE
Philadelphia & Oxford

Published in the United States of America and Great Britain in 2015 by
CASEMATE PUBLISHERS
908 Darby Road, Havertown, PA 19083
and
10 Hythe Bridge Street, Oxford, OX1 2EW

Copyright 2015 © Terrence G. Popravak, Jr.

ISBN 978-1-61200-299-6
Digital Edition: ISBN 978-1-61200-300-9

Cataloging-in-publication data is available from the Library of Congress and
the British Library.

10 9 8 7 6 5 4 3 2 1

Printed and bound in the United States of America.

For a complete list of Casemate titles please contact:

CASEMATE PUBLISHERS (US)
Telephone (610) 853-9131, Fax (610) 853-9146
E-mail: casemate@casematepublishing.com

CASEMATE PUBLISHERS (UK)
Telephone (01865) 241249, Fax (01865) 794449
E-mail: casemate-uk@casematepublishing.co.uk

CONTENTS

DEDICATION

As the title indicates, this is Jim Curran's book. Had he lived to complete it he most certainly would not have dedicated it to himself. But I have been privileged to put it together for him, and I am not so constrained. So I can say, appropriately and with great satisfaction, that:

> *This book is dedicated to the memory of Jim "Jug" Curran, fighter pilot and gentleman, one of the founding members of the 460th Fighter Squadron, and to his squadronmates in the Black Rams. "Check Six!"*

And a hand salute to all the officers, non-commissioned officers and enlisted men of the 348th Fighter Group, who proved beyond the shadow of a doubt the outstanding combat capability of the Republic P-47 Thunderbolt in the Pacific War.

Terrence G. Popravak, Jr.
Lt. Col., USAF (Retired)

THUNDERBOLT (P-47)

Now what dark, Mars-begotten chrysalis
Could breed a titan dragonfly like this
That takes its stark siesta all alone
Beside THE TRIBUNE'S spire of startled stone?
Six tons of weight, eleven yards of length,
Ferried by twenty hundred horses' strength
To scour the heaven's starry fields and cloudy hedges
With eight death knaves astride its grim wing edges.
Wonder of all is how some mad young wag on
This sinister seven-miles a minute dragon
Can climb the zenith's ladder and demolish
Daredevils like himself with zest and polish;
Then, off for home, descend and nonchalant
As any casual looker-on could want,
And grin as he sets her down with scarce a jolt,
"Some baby, eh—this good old Thunderbolt?"

—LISTER ALWOOD

FOREWORD

J IM CURRAN AND I FIRST MET IN FEBRUARY 1943 AT DALE Mabry Field, Tallahassee, Florida where, as newly commissioned second lieutenants, we began training in the P-47 "Thunderbolt," the biggest, most powerful and arguably the best, multi-purpose fighter aircraft employed in World War II. After completing the transition course in July, we headed for Hamilton Field, California for further deployment to the Southwest Pacific Area and assignment to the recently formed 348th Fighter Group commanded by Colonel Neel E. Kearby, soon to become a leading fighter ace and winner of the Congressional Medal of Honor.

Initially, Jim and I saw little of each other as he was assigned to the 341st Fighter Squadron based at an airstrip 17 miles from Port Moresby, New Guinea, while I was sent to the 342nd Fighter Squadron at another primitive airfield just five miles from Moresby. We both flew the P-47 "Thunderbolt" on the same types of missions and endured the same unpleasant living conditions, and the almost changeless tropical and mountainous environment, that has defined New Guinea for centuries.

We were united again when a new P-47 fighter squadron, the 460th, was formed and added as a fourth squadron to the 348th Fighter Group. Both Jim and I were among the more experienced pilots selected to man the new unit and to provide leadership and guidance to the inexperienced and untested pilots being sent to us from the States. Major William D. "Dinghy" Dunham, already an ace and an inspirational combat leader, was chosen as our commander.

I can confirm Jim's comments about the food. It was pretty bad. We hit a low point during the days just after the landing at Leyte in the Philippines. Dozens of LST's were nosed onto the beach offloading cargo in scattered piles right onto the sand. Hungry? And we were. Go to the C-ration pile. Need eating utensils? Yes, we did. Use a stick. Want a hot meal? Love one. Build a fire.

I can confirm, too, Jim's comments about the diseases that were part of the New Guinea experience. He tells about some of them but not about the mysterious skin rashes. We had two standard treatments. Smear on a pinkish white Calamine lotion for a week. Then switch to a purple colored liquid called Gentian Violet, an old horse remedy. And then keep alternating until the rash disappeared.

I want to say something also about the rotation policy for pilots assigned to the 348th Fighter Group. There wasn't one. Except for down time when moving, sick, or on leave, we flew almost every day. That's why Jim and many others amassed more than 200 combat missions in an 18 to 20 month tour.

Finally, I think something should be said about the commander in chief, Southwest Pacific Area, General Douglas MacArthur. Jim had mixed views about him along with many others. And MacArthur was a very controversial figure. William Manchester, in the preamble to his book *American Caesar,* said that: "He was the best of men and the worst of men." And that "No more baffling, exasperating soldier ever wore a uniform." But he went on to say that: "unquestionably he was the most gifted man-at-arms this nation has produced." General Jonathan Wainwright, left behind when MacArthur departed Corregidor, said of him: "I'd follow that man—anywhere—blindfolded." And yet many of his troops and some of his officers referred to him disparagingly as "Dugout Doug."

There is no question, however, in anyone's mind, about his brilliant military leadership in Jim Curran's war. From Brisbane, Australia across the Coral Sea to Port Moresby. And then some 1200 miles up the northern coast of New Guinea, step by leap-frogging step, from one airfield to another: Port Moresby, Finschhafen, Saidor, Wakde Island, Biak and Noemfoor. In doing so he left nearly a quarter of a million stranded and starving Japanese troops in his wake. And Jim Curran was with him, or very close behind, every step of the way.

We know, for example, that MacArthur returned to the Philippines on

October 20, 1944, when he waded ashore at Leyte Island. Well, just 21 days later, Jim Curran landed his P-47 Thunderbolt on the unfinished runway at Leyte's Tacloban airfield while a construction battalion was still at work extending the runway with pierced steel planking. Another 1000 feet had to be laid before the field was fully operational. Jim took off the next day to attack troop transports and naval forces in Ormoc Bay as they tried to land the reinforcements needed to push us off the island.

Jim never considered himself to be a hero. He claimed no special merit for serving his country when so many others were serving. But he was of special merit. He performed a vital and dangerous task, under highly adverse conditions, in an outstanding manner. He took his place in a long, unbroken line of good, and brave, and unfaltering patriots who have never let this country down.

DeWitt R. Searles
Major General, USAF (Ret.)

PREFACE

THIS MEMOIR OF JAMES C. CURRAN'S AERIAL COMBAT IN World War II, in his own words, is based on his writings about his military experience during the war that he wrote to share with his family members. His efforts to add and elaborate continued with composition and editing assistance from family members, which formed the basis of the information I received in order to complete this story.

To it I have added information that is intended to detail or corroborate things that Mr. Curran wrote about, which is contained in the text and the endnotes supporting his writings. This additional information is not intended to distract from his account of his combat service.

And to those who might be surprised at seeing pejorative references to the enemy of the day, the Japanese, it was common in World War II to refer to this enemy in such a manner, and thus Jim's term of reference, also carried in many official histories of that era, is carried intact. Additional reference or supplementary material does not use these terms of reference.

ACKNOWLEDGMENTS

To Casemate Publishers, for seeing the promise in this work, my humble gratitude. Thanks to Mr. Steven Smith, Ms. Tara Lichterman and Ms. Libby Braden for all your superb coordination and work.

To the brave men of the 38th Bombardment Group (Medium), Mr. Michael Alex, Mr. Harlan Denning, Mr. Harry "Terry" Terrell and others, who flew your B-25s from Morotai to Ormoc Bay, Leyte, to stop a Japanese reinforcement convoy on November 10, 1944, I render a hand salute. Researching your inspiring mission, in which you successfully met the enemy in battle and sacrificed greatly, for which you received a Distinguished Unit Citation, is what lead to my contact with one of your 460th Fighter Squadron P-47 escorts that day, Mr. James C. Curran.

A warm thank you to Mrs. Mary Jean Curran, who shared many precious photographs, military records and documents of her dear husband Jim; and to Jim's son John for the look at a sample of his father's 16mm gun camera film, and grandson Bradley for sharing several pictures.

Many thanks to Black Rams Major General Dewitt Searles, USAF (Ret), Mr. Ed DeMeter, and Mr. John J. (J.J.) Smith, who endured countless emails and phone calls with questions about air combat in the South Pacific. Special thanks to General Searles for writing the foreword for this account; to Mr. Howard Minnick, Jr., son of Black Ram pilot Howard Minnick, Sr., and Mary Curran's son-in-law Mr. Wayne "of the Woods" Murray, who started development of this record with Jim Curran in 2005 and provided helpful feedback on the manuscript in its early stages; thanks to other Black Ram contributors such as armorer Nolan Machen with daughter-in-law Janet Machen for help with information and images; to Black Ram Mustang pilot Mr. Tim Frable for his wonderful memoir and Mr. Kirby Bennink, son, and his wife Nancy, of Black Ram pilot Mr. William Bennink, for support with information and images. To Mr. Ed Reinbold for the Black Rams website which was a great resource in the project's early stages. And thank you to Mrs. Margo Prudente, daughter of 460FS commander William D. Dunham, for her interest and support of this project.

And thanks to the Blackjacks, with appreciation to Mr. Gerald Excell and Mr. Tony Gibbons for their perspective of service in the 341st Fighter Squadron. Thanks to Mr. Roger Zeine, nephew of 341FS pilot and wartime commander Mr. Merle Zeine, who helped to locate additional sources of information and images for this work.

Down Under, thanks to Mr. Peter Dunn of Oz at War, for his support and interest. To Ms. Karen Reid Nunan at the MacArthur Museum in Brisbane for help with information on the arrival of the P-47 in Australia. For information on American aircraft deliveries to Australia during the war, thanks to Mr. David Jones for researching the Queensland State Archives.

To several kind people in the Philippines, mabuhay! As helpful now as your forebears were then in the great campaign to liberate your land and people from the clutches of militarism—maraming salamat to Mr. Tony Feredo in Antipolo City, for help with the Japanese air order of battle in the Philippines, 1944, as well as Philippine geography. Salamat po to Ms. Erlinda Rule, Librarian In-Charge at the Bohol Provincial Library & Information Center in Tagbilaran City, and her assistant for information about and the image of Governor Celestino Gallares.

Thanks to Ms. Tammy Horton, Ms. Maranda Gilmore and Dr. James M. Cloninger Jr., at the Air Force Historical Research Agency for their good help with unit histories and awards of the 348th Fighter Group.

Thanks to the sea services and historical shipmates Mr. Leonard Gardner, USS *Reid* (DD-369) Association, for sharing information on the role of *Reid* in the South Pacific. To Mr. Fred Willshaw, Manager, NavSource Destroyer Archive for *Reid* imagery support, and his colleague in the Patrol/Gunboat department, Mr. Joe Radigan for PT boat imagery help. Thanks to Mr. Curt Lawson, Mr. Joe Ezell, and the volunteers at the Emil

Buehler Library on duty 15 August 2014, all at the National Naval Aviation Museum, for assistance with Navy and Marine aspects of the air war in the Pacific.

Thanks to photo contributors to this work, Mr. Jack Cook, Mr. Jonathan Watson, Mr. Mark Mansfield and Mr. John Stanaway for their help in illustrating the P-47 in the Southwest Pacific Area. Special thanks to Mr. Air Defense, Marty Isham, for help with black and white color interpretation, and encouragement. Thanks to Mr. Justin Taylan at Pacific Wrecks for his help in networking with contributors.

To my dear family who allowed me all the time to research and to write this story, thank you very much, Edelina, Sean and Nathan, for your loving support of this journey to the South Pacific. Special thanks to Sean for his digital help to his analog father with the maps in this book.

A hand salute to the veterans of World War II, to whom we owe a debt of gratitude for your service and sacrifice, air, land and sea, who were victorious and preserved our freedoms in that titanic global struggle.

Thank you all, and regrets to any I may have unintentionally missed in these brief acknowledgments.

And finally, thanks be to God for allowing this wonderful opportunity to share this story, and for His blessing in Christ bringing this work to a successful completion— *"But they that wait upon the Lord shall renew their strength; they shall mount up with wings as eagles; they shall run, and not be weary; and they shall walk, and not faint."* Isaiah 40:31

INTRODUCTION

ALTHOUGH THE AIR WAR IN THE PACIFIC DURING WORLD War II has not seen as extensive a coverage in historical literature as has the air war in Europe, it was every bit as challenging and deserving of recognition and study. Jim Curran arrived as a P-47 Thunderbolt fighter pilot in the Southwest Pacific in the summer of 1943, at a time when Allied forces had begun to reverse the tide of Imperial Japanese expansion in New Guinea and the Solomon Islands. Following this reversal, efforts were made to push Japanese forces back across vast expanses of air, land, and sea. These efforts frequently required the cooperation and teamwork of joint Army, Navy, and Marine forces to accomplish that goal.

The Republic P-47 Thunderbolt was first introduced into combat in the Pacific in Jim Curran's 348th Fighter Group. The group's renowned commander, Colonel Neel Kearby, faced a daunting challenge not only from the Japanese, but also from skeptics in our own armed forces who doubted the capability of the P-47 to perform adequately in the Pacific theater. But Kearby and his group soon showed everyone what a terrific weapon the Thunderbolt was, and Jim Curran helped him prove that.

At first employed in defensive roles as the Allies expanded their footholds in the Southwest Pacific, the group soon began offensive fighter sweeps as Allied airpower clashed with Japanese Army and Navy air forces across New Guinea and in the upper Solomons. Jim Curran flew in the 341st Fighter Squadron, the Blackjack Squadron, and clashed with Imperial Japanese Navy Zero fighters over the Solomon Sea while defending a Navy convoy, and got the better of them.

As the Allies broke the back of Japanese airpower in the Southwest Pacific, MacArthur began his famous leapfrogging westward, and the P-47 Thunderbolts played their part to help him create and retain the momentum of those rapid, dramatic advances. This even involved some use of the P-47 in an air-to-surface role, expanding the combat employment options for Allied airpower in the Pacific. Nadzab, Finschhafen, Saidor, and Wakde were a few of the bases Jim Curran flew from in these operations.

In the summer of 1944, Jim volunteered to join a new squadron being formed in the 348th Fighter Group, the 460th Fighter Squadron, the Black Rams. The unit formed in theater, trained up at Nadzab, then moved west to Noemfoor Island from where it flew long-range fighter-bomber strikes on various Japanese bases in the Dutch East Indies.

From Noemfoor, the Black Rams deployed via Morotai and a combat mission en route to Leyte Island in the Philippines, where they played a key part in the defense of the beachhead as the Japanese military made all-out efforts to fight a decisive battle in the Philippines. Among many air-to-surface missions, Jim clashed with Imperial Japanese Army Air Force Tony fighters, and again got the best of the enemy.

Advancing to San Marcelino Airfield on Luzon in early 1945, Jim then played a role in the conversion of the unit to the P-51 Mustang fighter. Although a good fighter in its own right, the Mustang wasn't exactly welcomed by all P-47 veterans, who had to part with their beloved Thunderbolts. By this time Japanese airpower in the Philippines was eclipsed, and the Black Rams flew many missions in support of our ground troops fighting a still tenacious foe.

It was there on Luzon in the spring of 1945, after his third combat mission of the day and some battle damage, that Jim Curran received orders to return stateside; his combat tour in the Pacific was complete. He did his part to bring American airpower west some 2,500 miles, all the way from Port Moresby and back into the Philippines, virtually to the doorstep of the Japanese home islands. His story is one of dedication to country, military service, and to his squadron mates.

PART ONE

GETTING TO THE WAR

Chapter One

THE WAR BEGINS

I WAS BORN IN CHICAGO, ILLINOIS, AT THE LAKE SIDE Hospital, not too far from the University of Chicago, on October 6th, 1921. My first recollections of Chicago were at 5624 Prairie Avenue. My father, Patrick James Curran, used to take me to Washington Park on Sundays. We later lived at 7934 Ingleside (Chatham area). In 1933 we moved to 8135 Prairie Avenue which was my residence until 1946. I attended Leo High School on West 79th Street, Class of 1940. In the 1930'S I used to drive to Hammond, Indiana to get gas at eight gallons for a dollar.

I remember 1934 vividly. It was the second year of the "Century of Progress" Exposition on Chicago's lakefront. I visited it many times in 1933 and '34. The Hall of Science was my favorite place to visit; in '34, I saw myself on rudimentary television in that hall.

During the first part of summer, 1934, I went to Ashkum, Illinois, to visit my grandfather, David H. Chandler. He was living with his brother, Alfred, about nine miles west of Ashkum on Alfred's farm. I had fun with my cousins, the offspring of Charles Chandler, my grandfather's other brother. The two oldest sons of Uncle Charlie operated a blacksmith shop on the farm and I was fascinated with it. They allowed me to practice on an electric welding machine that they built from scratch. I actually learned to weld a little.

That same summer, in August, while preparing to start fifth grade at a brand new school, I came down with Infantile Paralysis (Polio), which almost did me in. My recovery was slow so I didn't start school until October. I had lots of time to read while recovering from my illness and I remember a cartoon in the newspaper about the Depression. It was a scary time. I remember asking my dad what would happen if he lost his job. His answer was he would walk east until his hat floated. East was Lake Michigan and the thought of my father walking there had no appeal to me. He did not lose his job and the Currans ate well during the Great Depression. In 2010, I thought, "I sure hope we are not in a repeat of the 1930s because I doubt if the present generation could hack it."

World War II started for me on December 7th, 1941, at about 1p.m. while I was awaiting the start of the Bears-Cardinals football game. I was in Chicago in front of the family Silverstone radio with my parents and maternal grandmother when the attack on Pearl Harbor was announced. We were nonplussed at news of the attack—everybody was numb. It was as devastating as 9/11. But the response to 9/11 was nothing to compare with what happened in 1941. This nation was unified like no other time. The reaction was the flooding of the recruiting facilities on Monday morning. I still have the chair that I was sitting in on December 7, 1941. It is in excellent condition.

I never hated the Germans or the Japanese. I abhorred some of the stories I heard, but hate was never in my personal feelings—it is not a part of my psyche. Pearl Harbor made me mad and I reacted by going to the recruiting facilities December 8, 1941.

I wasn't hatefully mad, but I wanted to get even.

Early in the month of December 1941, I was dating a comely natural blonde with the family name of Messerschmidt who resided on Champlain Avenue in Chicago. When I called on her later in the month, she and her family had completely disappeared. Rumor had it that the head of the family was a member of the German American Bund, a subversive organization. I never saw or heard from her again.

There was some tradition of military service in my family. My dad was a swabbie, stationed in Grant Park, Chicago, in 1917. He was later assigned to the USS *Wilmette*, which never made it out of the Great Lakes. The ship was formerly known as the SS *Eastland*, which capsized in the Chicago River with a load of Western Electric people on it. It was later scrapped at the Calumet Shipyard and Drydock Company in South Chicago. I worked there prior to World War II as a welder.

As a small boy I remember my great-grandfather James Gallagher, who served in the US Army in the Dakotas, fighting in the Indian Wars. I asked him how many Indians he killed. His sage answer was "just as many as killed me." Another great-grandfather, Major Thomas Chandler, formed the Livingston County Volunteers in Illinois. He served in the Grand Army of the Republic. His father was born in New Hampshire, but we have no military record on him.

My dad had eight brothers. He was number four. The youngest, Delaney Curran, five years older than me, served in the Marine Corps. The other brothers were spared military service.

My best friend from my high school days was John Peter Fardy, who was in the 1st Marine Division. He received the Medal of Honor posthumously from President Truman. I was at the presentation in 1945 in Chicago, and it was most impressive. I met several Marines from his unit who claimed John saved their lives by smothering a Japanese hand grenade with his body.

Monday, December 8th, I proceeded to the naval recruiting office on West Jackson Boulevard. My interest in aviation stemmed from my first flight in 1926, in Los Angeles, California, on my mother Rose Ann Mary Curran's lap in a World War I Jenny. I applied for Navy pilot training but was immediately eliminated because I didn't have the necessary college credits. This took all morning, so in the afternoon I proceeded to the Army recruiting station, same street, where I applied for pilot training. I was accepted, but had to have a parent sign off for me because I wasn't 21. My father refused, but I was able to coerce my mother into signing. By the time this was accomplished, a whole week had passed and I was becoming panicky that the war would be over before I got a chance to fight. The slow process of getting started finally got underway just before New Year, with arduous physical and mental tests.

The period from December 8th, 1941, to March 26th, 1942, encompassed many tests, both mental and physical, alongside those people desiring to become pilots like me, and there were a lot of us. In March, I received orders via the US Mail to report to the recruiting office on West Jackson Boulevard, for induction into the Army of the US.[1] I reported for swearing in. This process took almost all day because there were hundreds of us to be sworn in. After taking my oath, I was informed that I was now

James C. Curran, Army Service Number 16077163, Private, Unclassified, Army of the United States. My orders were to return home until notification of assignment by mail, at a pay $21.00 a month with Temporary Duty (TDY) pay allowed.

I, now Pvt. Curran, returned home and waited until finally a registered letter arrived in early June 1942, directing me to report to Dearborn Station for rail transportation to duty station (secret). I arrived at the specified date and time, 0700, and waited again all day for the train to depart. I was assigned with others to a car; little did I realize then that my train companions would be my associates for months to come, at least those who survived the training process.

Finally, after waiting all that June day, and with dusk approaching, the troop train got underway. We played cards all night because there were no sleeping accommodations. In the morning we determined that we were in southern Ohio heading south. By nightfall we were leaving Tennessee, heading west; speculation on where we were going was the main topic of conversation.

On June 9th, 1942, we arrived at Brooks Army Air Field, San Antonio, Texas, an adjunct to Randolph Field, the West Point of flyers. A group of non-commissions officers (NCOs) took charge of us after appropriate "short arms" inspection, a must at every change of station.[2] We were herded to the Quartermaster (QM) where we were issued two fatigue suits and an empty footlocker. We were assigned to a squad tent, already erected and located on a marked company street. Civilian garb was stowed with the exception of socks and underwear, which we were admonished to keep until the QM could furnish G.I. shoes, socks and underwear. We were finally fed at a mess tent and informed that our status was "zero," in cold storage until the next cadet class, and to hit the sack because tomorrow we would be very busy.

0530 came soon enough and the process of "fall in, fall out, attention, at ease, fall in, fall out," got underway full-steam. After breakfast, the first assembly was to march in ranks to the barber, where all excess hair was removed. By excess that meant anything beyond 1/4 inch. Next was a physical exam to determine if you were alive. We determined there were 3,000 of us in like circumstances and that's why everything took so long to accomplish. Sometimes, between appointments with the medics, dentist or barber, we would pick up rocks or other debris on the parade ground or company area. Having no hats, many of us were getting extreme sunburn.

After about a week we were beginning to resemble raw recruits. Our main physical exams finally got underway and my first encounter was with the oculist to determine if I was blind or not. Believe it or not I failed the color chart and the oculist examining me inquired how I ever got into the Army in the first place. Fortunately, I had my records from Chicago and they showed normal vision. Upon further examination the doctor wanted to know why I was so sunburned on my face and head. I informed him that we were not issued any hats and were forbidden to wear sunglasses. I was put on hold until several other doctors examined me. The end result was that we all had to report to the QM for hats, Ray-Ban sunglasses, shoes, socks, underwear, and everything else we needed. After a week I had to take the vision exam again and had no problem passing.

PREFLIGHT

On June 23rd, 1942, we were finally assigned to the Gulf Coast Air Corps Training Center, later redesignated as the Central Flying Training Command, Aviation Cadet Class 43-B, the second class slated to graduate in that year.[3] The preflight school was designed to teach us the basics of what you had to know to become a competent aviator. If one washed out one reverted to the rank of private, unclassified and were placed elsewhere at the discretion of the powers that be. We were assigned to a barracks building, issued new uniforms and all supporting paraphernalia, including an Enfield 98 military rifle.[4] This began the most arduous period of my life, eight weeks of preflight training, which kept us on the run. Literally, we ran everywhere, from 0530 to 2200. Then, gratefully, we collapsed into the sack. The Army crammed about four semesters of college into eight weeks.

We also had rigorous physical training, drill, and firearm instruction—the Enfield 98 came straight out of a wood box packed in Cosmoline, and I married this piece. I learned how to use it and qualified no problem. Drill was required daily with the Enfield rifle, and by the time I returned it to ordnance at the end of preflight training, I had added considerable muscle to both arms.

We learned how to become an officer. A typical requirement was to become proficient in Morse Code, sound and visual. We also studied aircraft identification as well as identification of ships, tanks, and submarines.

We walked sentry duty and marched on parade Saturdays. In other words, we had to learn in eight weeks what our peacetime predecessors had four years to absorb. At the end of eight weeks of preflight training, I had no loose skin. It was a tough row to hoe, but we somehow coped.

Along came August and those who survived Aviation Cadet Ground School were shipped to Oklahoma Air College at Cimarron Field, Oklahoma, a country club atmosphere after Brooks Field. Thus began the next eight weeks of hell and fun.

NOTES

1. James C. Curran was one of 66 men selected by Aviation Cadet Board No. 3 at Room 283, US Courthouse in Chicago Illinois, according to the board's Special Orders No. 28, March 26, 1942. Major Floyd M. Showalter, Air Corps, was the Board President. Paragraph 1 of the orders read as follows: "Pursuant to authority contained in Letter, Headquarters, Sixth Corps Area, Chicago, Illinois, File AG 341.2-1 (Rctg) Subject: Supplement No. 2, to 'Keep 'Em Flying' Requisition No. 2, dated 10 March 1942, the following-named civilian candidates for appointment as Aviation Cadets, having been enlisted at this station, this date, in the grade of Private, for Air Corps, Army of the United States, are hereby transferred to the 'Special' Corps Area Air Corps Detachment, 460 South State Street, Chicago, Illinois, and placed on furlough for the period March 26 to May 25, 1942 . . ."
James C. Curran, 16, 077, 163

   Paragraph 2 concluded the orders: "At termination of above furlough the enlisted men will report, in person, to the Commanding Officer, 'Special' Corps Area Air Corps Detachment, 460 South State Street, and transfer to an Air Corps Replacement Training Center."
2. A "Short arms inspection" was a physical inspection of a male's private parts by authorities in order to detect any signs of venereal disease. "The origin of the term "Short Arm Inspection" info," http://www.military-quotes.com/forum/origin-term-short-arm-inspection-t1161.html
3. The Gulf Coast Air Corps Training Center was established at Randolph Field, Texas, on 8 July 1940, and was responsible for Army flight training (basic, primary, advanced) conducted at airfields in the central United States. It was renamed the Central Flying Training Command on 31 July 1943.
   "Central Flying Training Command," http://en.wikipedia.org/wiki/Central_Flying_Training_Command
   "Randolph Field Historic District," http://www.nps.gov/nr/travel/aviation/ran.htm
4. This is probably a reference to the M1917 Enfield, the "American Enfield," an

American modification of the British .303 caliber P14 rifle that was mass-produced in 1917–1918 to help equip the American Expeditionary Force in World War I. The P14 had copied features of the German Mauser Model 98 rifle.

"M1917 Enfield Rifle," http://olive-drab.com/od_other_firearms_rifle_m1917en-field.php

"M1917 Enfield Rifle," http://en.wikipedia.org/wiki/M1917_Enfield

Chapter Two

PILOT TRAINING

PRIMARY

Aftertrain ride to Oklahoma City, we boarded buses to Oklahoma Air College located west of the city at a wide spot in the road called Cimarron.[1] The barracks were low-slung buildings laid out military style on company streets; it looked like a country club. This atmosphere quickly evaporated with the appearance of a new animal, upper classmen, whose sole object in life was to make life miserable for lower classmen. At ground school there were no upper classmen, only TAC officers to deal with. But now that changed. We had both tack officers and this new menace to contend with, plus instructor pilots whose powers were secondary only to God.

From the very start, it was double-time everywhere. There was no such thing as walking to a chore or class. The hazing we endured would try the patience of a saint.

In spite of all these distractions, I finally got to fly in a military aircraft as a student on August 10, 1942. The flight lasted 30 minutes and I did not get sick. The instructor even let me touch the controls briefly to get the feel of them. The aircraft selected by the Army was the Fairchild PT-19A, a low-wing, two-seat, single-engine monoplane made chiefly of plywood. It had a 39-foot wingspan and two open cockpits; the forward one for the student and the aft one for the instructor. It was powered by a Ranger 175-horsepower (hp), inverted, inline engine with eight cylinders. The propeller was made of wood and was fixed pitch. It had a wide landing gear and tail wheel which did not retract. The aircraft was very stable and ideal for training dummies like us.

Over the next four weeks of hell, due to the hazing of upper classmen, I accumulated 30 hours of flying time and a great deal of smarts. Then, for the next four weeks, we were the upper classmen and gave it to the 43-C cadets just like we got from the 43-A class.

One hurdle to be overcome was the final check ride one had to pass prior to graduating. In my case this was performed by a flying officer, First Lieutenant Schneider, whom everybody feared because of his propensity to wash out students who performed poorly. He put me through power-on stalls, power-off stalls, spins right and left where he demanded a certain number of turns in each spin, i.e. two and a half turns right and then flight recovery. No variance was allowed. The final part of the check ride was to make a three-point landing on a designated spot on the airfield, no bounce allowed on the touchdown. To this day I don't know how I got by this guy, but I do think he saved my life by making me pass this test at the end of primary.

We were congratulated by our instructors and wished good luck on our new assignment. We were also asked what our future ambition was in the Air Corps. Mine was to fly P-47s as a fighter pilot in the Pacific Theater. I accumulated just over 60 hours of flying time in my primary training.

BASIC

Straight north of Cimarron was Enid, Oklahoma, the flattest place on earth where we were assigned to do Basic Flying Training. Thus began the middle part of pilot flight training. The upper classmen were less severe at Enid Army Flying Field than at primary, mainly because their schedules were so intense.[2] Having gotten through preflight and primary, we were becoming more valuable to the military effort. In basic we were really considered an asset to be "cultured" as quickly as possible.

I was assigned a second lieutenant for instruction in the basic trainer aircraft, which came in two denominations: the Vultee BT-13 Valiant and the similar BT-15. The former was powered by a Pratt & Whitney nine-cylinder radial engine; the latter by a Wright Whirlwind nine-cylinder radial engine. The BT-13, also known as the Vibrator, was a two-seat, low-wing monoplane. My instructor and I didn't hit it off so well. I could feel him touching the controls when I was supposed to be flying the aircraft. This resulted in a bad mark for me and he suggested I take a voluntary washout, though I had already soloed the basic trainer by that time and knew I had no problem flying it. Upon reading my instructor's report, my squadron C.O. suggested I quit. I refused and stated that if I was to wash out it would be at the hands of the base commander on a check flight, as he was the final answer.

I was assigned a new instructor, a laid-back gentleman named Louie LaSheen, a civilian attached to the Army as an instructor. Louie and I immediately hit it off as friends. On my first flight with him, he never touched the controls once and after a touch and go landing he told me to go up and do some aerobatics. After about a half hour of fun flying, I turned to look back at Louie and found him sound asleep. That was my last check ride in basic. Nothing marred my Basic experience after that except for getting a "Dear John" letter from my high school sweetie who decided to marry a guy I went to high school with. That's a blow to your ego when you are 20, but it didn't stop my enthusiasm for flying.

The highlight of flying with Louie LaSheen was when I was invited to fly a formation cross-country with him to El Paso, Texas. I was informed that I would have a passenger on the reciprocal part of the journey; I had no objection. Three planes comprised the flight, with Louie leading without a student. At El Paso we had lunch at the officers' club while our aircraft were being serviced. Returning to the flight line, Louie admonished me to pay no attention to the passenger, which looked to me like freight under the seat belt.

The flight back was uneventful and upon landing, I was greeted by ground personnel who immediately removed the contents of the back seat while I was filling out the Form 1, Flight Record. The Form 1 was the flight log and report for maintenance for aircraft and pilot records. Later I got a call from Louie to meet him at his car in the parking lot, where he presented me with a fifth of bourbon whiskey, which, he informed me, was part of what I had brought back from El Paso. I was a bootlegger! Oklahoma was a dry state then. Thus ended Basic, on a happy note. After gaining another 82 flying hours in basic, it was now on to advanced.

ADVANCED

Upon the successful completion of Basic, we were assigned to Lake Charles Army Air Field at the town of the same name in Louisiana.[3] No troop train was involved on this move. We were authorized rail travel and used public facilities to get to Lake Charles where we reported for duty at the beginning of December, 1942.

On December 18th, I had my first flight in Advanced Flying Training in an "advanced trainer," the AT-6C, a low-wing, two-seat monoplane that resembled a fighter aircraft. It was powered by a 650-hp Pratt & Whitney Wasp nine-cylinder engine, and featured a hydraulically-retractable landing gear and hydraulic flaps to help slow the landing speed. The airframe was manufactured by North American Aviation. The United States Navy used an almost identical plane for advanced training called the SNJ; the main difference being the tail hook arresting gear on the Navy version to facilitate landing on an aircraft carrier.

The AT-6C is possibly the most fun-flying aircraft of all time—it was loved by all who flew it. Three days before Christmas I soloed the AT-6. Besides flying in the air, we continued to fly the Link Trainers (a flight simulator) for instrument proficiency. Link training was started in basic, but in advanced training we were preparing for actual instrument flying.

We had to be proficient in navigating the beam, which meant listening to radio signals that depicted the "A" sound in Morse code, "dit dah" and the "N" sound that was "dah dit." When you combine "dit dah" with "dah dit" you get a hum. "A" was the right-hand signal and "N" was the left-hand signal. When you heard the combined signals, you were on the beam and could navigate to a safe landing without seeing the ground. This is no longer used in flying; the latest systems are easier to use and much safer.

The Army decided that around the 14th of January 1943, they would move the class of 43-B to a new airfield at Victoria, Texas. On the day of the move from Lake Charles to Victoria, all planes were loaded with two personnel, an instructor and a cadet, or two cadets. The weather forecast left much to be desired. We all took off in the morning and headed west to the new base, called Aloe Army Air Field.[4] Our assigned altitude was 5,000 feet.

Soon after takeoff the ceiling began to drop and visibility was down to a mile. Instrument flight was not authorized for this trip so we had to keep the ground in sight, and as the weather continued to deteriorate, we found ourselves flying almost at ground level. This was extremely dangerous because one had to be alert for transmission lines and other high structures.

We literally flew the "iron beam" so to speak, the railroad tracks. Almost all towns along the tracks had water towers with the town name inscribed on the tanks. That was our only means of identifying where we were.

Fortunately Aloe Airfield had a railroad spur going right into the base; it lined up with the runway. We flew along the spur and dropped the landing gear as soon as the base was visible. Almost all the planes made it to Aloe. The ones that didn't make it landed at various other fields. No planes were lost. This was the beginning of our last four weeks of training as cadets.

The atmosphere had entirely changed for us. We were allowed to enter the officers' club with full privilege and were respected for our achievement of becoming pilots. We flew just over 50 miles southeast to Matagorda Island in the Gulf of Mexico for aerial and ground gunnery training. Ground gunnery consisted of shooting at six-foot square targets on the ground with a bulls-eye on them. We fired with a single Browning .30-caliber machine gun in the right wing, a fast-firing weapon that had considerable recoil.

The trick of hitting the bull's-eye was to approach the target with no slip or yaw and squeeze off the least number of shots possible and still have the target in range, approximately 300 yards. This sounds easy, but it took a lot of practice. Of course that was why we were there. I set the all-time record for bull's-eyes at this range, 100 out of 100 rounds of ammunition. It took me 33 passes at the target. We were severely admonished not to shoot any cattle because the Army was liable for cattle losses. There was no bombing training at all. There were no controllers involved in any of the gunnery, but we were urged to stick to the designed patterns for ground shooting in order to protect the target attendants.

Aerial gunnery, conducted over the Gulf of Mexico at about 10,000 feet, was entirely different. The target was a piece of heavy canvas, 10 x 30 feet, which was towed by an AT-6 with a long tow rope. The front had a heavy brass rod through it to keep it from furling, and the rod had a heavy weight on one end to keep it vertical. Six planes were assigned to shoot at the target with bullets tipped with wet paint. Each pilot had a color so that hits on the target could be identified as to whom they belonged. If the target survived they would count the hits and congratulate anybody hitting the target. Ninety-degree deflection shots were discouraged as well as zero-deflection shots, for the safety of the tow target pilot. All in all it was a

PILOT TRAINING • 33

farce, but we did occasionally hit the target as well as shoot it off, which happened from time to time. Hitting a moving target proved to be much more difficult than hitting a ground target. I think the tow target pilots and ground gunnery personnel all deserved medals of extreme bravery in the line of duty.

While at Aloe we were very close to the Goliad battleground of the famed battles for Texas independence from Mexico. It was a very wild place inhabited by the last remaining herd of horses for the cavalry. About 10,000 wild horses comprised the herd and it was an awesome sight to behold. But the town had only 10,000 inhabitants, making time off-base a pill. There was no such thing as having a date with a girl, so we were happy to stay on base most of the time.

LARGEST ARMY AIR CLASS TO GRADUATE

More than 100 men from the Chicago area will be graduated as fighter and bomber pilots at Randolph Field, Tex., today, in the largest single class ever to be graduated there.

The class, known as 43-B, has been divided among nine advanced flying training schools in Texas. All will receive pilot's wings and some will receive commissions as second lieutenants, while others will be appointed to the recently created rank of flight officer. Other schools in the list are (include) Aloe Field, Victoria, Tex. —The *Chicago Sun*, February 16, 1943, Page 4

February 16th, 1943, finally arrived and we were assembled for the graduation of Class 43-B. I had added another 84 flying hours to my pilot log at advanced. Graduation consisted of us aviation cadets being honorably discharged from the Army of the US, and for a few seconds we were civilians again. But that was followed by being sworn in and commissioned into the US Army as second lieutenants (2nd Lt.), rated as Pilots, and placed on extended active duty. Orders were issued to proceed to 3rd Air Force at Dale Mabry Field, Tallahassee, Florida for Transition Training. A ten-day delay en route was authorized which meant I could go home to Chicago, if I could find transportation.

Graduation day from the Aviation Cadet program meant getting new uniforms as well as starting a new chapter in life. The Army very generously provided funds for uniforms and even gave us a shopping list as a guide. After the severe discipline of the cadet program, no one even considered deviating from the guide furnished by the War Department.

The balance of February 16th was spent making reservations for travel and packing. Willis M. Cooley, a classmate, and I got reservations to fly to Chicago; home for me and a transfer point for Cooley who lived in Washington State. We flew to Houston to transfer for a flight to Love Field, Dallas.

We arrived on the 17th at Dallas and got bumped off our flight to Chicago by military brass who had priority for space over everybody. We were entitled to priority space for travel on a change of station, but not on a delay en route. American Air Lines had issued our tickets for the entire trip, mine showing passage from Victoria, Texas, to Houston, to Love Field, Dallas to Chicago, with a seven-day layover and then to Atlanta continuing on to Tallahassee, Florida. I was all paid and no one could bump me off from Chicago to Florida because that was a change-of-base journey. My problem was getting to Chicago.

American Air Lines offered little help and said we would just have to wait until they had space. This went over like a lead balloon, so I called my father at work in Chicago and told him of my dilemma. He had the vice-president of Cuneo Press, Incorporated, call Alderman Gralis of Chicago, who's ward encompassed Midway Airport, to prevail on American to get me out of Dallas. It worked. I got to sit in the baggage compartment of a Douglas DC-2 for the ride to Chicago; as a plus; they let me bring my friend Cooley. We arrived early on February 18th, and I had a delightful visit at home followed by my trip to Florida.

TRANSITION

Dale Mabry Field, my new base, was also the civilian airport for Tallahassee, so it was easy to report for duty when my plane landed in March 1943.[5] I was assigned to a Bachelor Officers Quarters (BOQ) in Building #483, which was a typical barracks except we were two to a room instead of an open-bay dormitory. Our meals were served in the officers' club; the food was outstanding, the head chef having been drafted from a fancy New York hotel. Physicals were again required and the Transition Training immediately got underway.

Initially, I was assigned to the 439th Fighter Squadron of the 338th Fighter Group, then on June 7th, further attached to the 312th Fighter Squadron. We had to make proficiency flights in AT-6 aircraft and fly around the field to familiarize ourselves with the area, which was heavily camouflaged. We were informed that we would soon be training in the P-47 fighter plane, the very latest aircraft in the Army's arsenal.

The Republic P-47 Thunderbolt was a huge fighter plane that weighed almost 14,000 pounds. It was powered by a 2,000 hp Pratt & Whitney radial engine with 18 cylinders, in two banks of nine. The engine was turbo-supercharged by a turbine device located behind the pilot. In 1943 this device could produce full military power for the engine at 32,000 feet, a stupendous advantage over any other aircraft at that time.

As candidates expected to operate this aircraft, we were required to memorize the cockpit and be able to touch every switch, button, and control while blindfolded. There were no two-seat P-47s, so the new pilot soloed on his initial flight. This was an awesome experience that left me gasping for breath. Having accomplished my first P-47 flight on March 14th, 1943, the next few months would bring a number of memorable times.

In the Aviation Cadet training schools, I accumulated just under 227 hours of flying time. Another 107 hours would be accumulated in Transition Training, mostly in the P-47 aircraft. My training included some test flying of early model P-47s that had trouble with the secondary counter-balancers in their Pratt & Whitney engines. Much time was accrued in Link Trainers (14 hours) as we honed our instrument skills. It was not apparent at this time why the Army was so insistent on our proficiency as instrument pilots, but the answers would become clear months later in combat situations.

There were other aircraft at Dale Mabry Field as I underwent training there, such as the Bell P-39 Airacobra. I never flew a P-39, though they were used extensively at Dale Mabry in 1943. A P-39 instructor told the story of a final approach at night when his plane hit prop wash and inverted just as he was about to land. He said he let go of the controls and shouted, "God, you got it!" The plane flipped upright and landed . . . so the story goes.

Speaking of fighters, I am truly sorry I never flew the twin-engine Lockheed P-38 Lightning. What I liked most about the Lightning was the counter-rotating propellers—no torque, which was a never-ending problem with single-engine aircraft. Remarkably, I did have a training mission in a Douglas B-18 Bolo at Dale Mabry, the purpose being a demonstration of instrument piloting. I was very grateful to have survived the flight because I was so unimpressed with the flight characteristics of the B-18: *a slow boat to nowhere!*

I saw one of the early North American Mustang fighters at Dale Mabry, and I haven't seen one of these "Razorbacks" since then. But in Tallahassee we had one that was designated as an attack bomber, the A-36, which was returned from North Africa for some reason beyond my ken. One of my classmates attempted to land it in a Jack Pine forest. Unfortunately, there was an incident with a cypress tree . . . adios, buddy. A P-47 pilot did the same thing in Okefenokee Swamp but came back without a scratch. Of course he had enough sense to avoid cypress trees. But we were impressed with the Mustang, also called the "Spam Can."

Florida was a great place to fly. There were no mountains to dodge and one altimeter setting was sufficient for the day. The Gulf of Mexico was close by, as was the Atlantic Ocean; thereby comes the first action against the enemy. The enemy's U-Boats were wreaking havoc along the continental shelf so we were armed with small depth charges when operating over the Atlantic in case we spotted a U-Boat. Of course it never happened, and we were admonished not to bomb whales or our own submarines. No one ever dropped a bomb, and with our lack of experience it is doubtful that under the most favorable circumstances we would have been able to hit any of them.

One spring day I was assigned to a solo, cross-country training flight. My flight plan called for me to fly from Tallahassee to Cape Canaveral, to Jacksonville, and back to Tallahassee. It was a beautiful Florida day, but there was a warning about an approaching cold front. As I turned north to Jacksonville a report on the radio said Tallahassee was closing due to the weather. I contacted control and they instructed me to land at the naval air station at Jacksonville. As I approached the alternate, they announced that they were closing and for me to return to Cape Canaveral. By the time I got turned around and headed back, Canaveral closed and Tallahassee opened. And there I was, trapped over the ocean with the whole east coast of Florida closed.

My only option was to penetrate the cold front and try to make it back to Tallahassee. This proved to be the acid test for my instrument flight abilities. No one can prepare you for what you get with a cold front with tops over 50,000 feet. I hit the front at about 10,000 feet and immediately went on gauges because there was zero visibility. I calculated myself to be over Okefenokee Swamp where I didn't want to be forced to bail out. The turbulence was extreme, with 60 mph up and down drafts. I finally popped out of the north side of the frontal storm at 5,000 feet, completely covered with ice, which sloughed off in great chunks as I hit warmer air. The rest of the journey was uneventful and I finally got home only about 45 minutes late. Never again would I challenge a thunderhead. This was a happy end to a frightful experience.

Fortunately there was no damage to my P-47 from ice during my "Bermuda Triangle Day." You must remember, the P-47 was built like a Sherman tank and a few tons of rime ice had no effect other than to slow it down a little. Some paint was taken off the leading edge of the wings, and that was actually an improvement.

We did have a problem with P-47 engines seizing up from time to time. The sound of a warm engine was beautiful, but you would have bailed out if you'd ever heard a cold start up—it sounded like an anvil chorus. Anyway, we were asked to do test flying to see if they could find out the cause of the engine seizures. The test was to fly the P-47 right over the air base at full military power for five-minute intervals for up to one hour. I was included in these tests with no failures. It was eventually determined that the failures were caused by a design flaw in the secondary, counterbalance of the Pratt & Whitney R-2800 engine, which was fixed. I never suffered an engine failure in a fighter aircraft, but did have a harrowing experience in a C-54 returning to the US at the end of my overseas tour—more on that later.

I didn't break any of Uncle Sam's airplanes and never even blew a tail wheel, even though I was in three aircraft accidents. But only in one was I the pilot of the plane involved, and that was when I made a wheels-up landing at night while in training at Dale Mabry, on April 16th, 1943, bending the prop and damaging the skin on the bottom of a P-47B. For this mistake, I signed a statement of charges for $25,000. Fortunately, they didn't deduct it from my pay.[6]

It wasn't all work and no play in Transition. Weekends were usually spent in Tallahassee or the neighboring countryside which was delightful, for instance, going to Wakulla Springs to swim. Along with my roommate, Jack Crandell, who had an automobile, we made a trip to Jacksonville one weekend and another to Valdosta, Georgia where we had great times. Valdosta was great because there was no military base close by and the locals were very kind to soldier boys. Not so in old Tallahassee where the civilian population was overwhelmed by the influx of military personnel looking for a good time.

Jack Crandell was a super-good handler of the Jug, as we came to call the P-47, and also a good drinking buddy. His mom and dad visited Tallahassee during our training and brought him a case of Canadian Club. My mom was visiting at the same time and Jack gave us a bottle out of his case. Now that's a buddy.

And although pilots were known for their singing songs at the bar, at this time we hadn't developed anything, fighter pilot song-wise, except the Army Air Corps song, "Off we go into the wild blue yonder." Chattanooga Choo Choo and Lilly Marlene were two of my favorites just then.

We had no tactical training comparable to the modern-day Air Force's Nellis "RED FLAG" exercises. There were no planes at Dale Mabry that could even be considered a threat to the P-47—we were considered the ultimate in flying machines. We had aerial and ground gunnery but no bomb dropping training. The P-47 was still considered a high altitude defensive weapon. You must realize that fighter pilots are a different species; we learned by the old trial and error system when we started dropping bombs later in combat.

As for information on the enemy, we didn't receive much data because very little had been amassed at this time. We had a few pilots with RAF and Flying Tiger experience who we listened to, who advised us about things like "don't turn or climb with a Zero." We studied aircraft silhouettes, photos, and sometimes used flash cards to identify planes.

March to June flew by and it was now payoff time. In early July, 12 of us were on a high-altitude cross-country training flight, between 35,000 and 40,000 feet over Florida from Dale Mabry to Cape Canaveral to Jacksonville and then returning to base. The USN and the USMC were making a demonstration beach assault for congressional big wigs at Daytona Beach near Cape Canaveral, again, a turning point of our training mission. We could see the operation easily from our high vantage point. Chatting back and forth on our radios, we decided to give them an unplanned fly-by. We accomplished this by making a mock attack at treetop level at about 600 mph. What fun! What a mistake! They got our numbers and reported us so we were accosted by M.P.s as soon as we landed. We were severely admonished by our C.O. and were told not to leave the base.

The next day, July 4, 1943, orders were issued sending all 12 of us, 2d Lt.'s Robert A. Ducharme, Gerald W. Excell, Robert L. Frank, Wallace M. Harding, Bernard M. Mahoney, Robert J. McNulty, Walter S. Monroe, Jr., Earnest R. Ness, DeWitt R. Searles, Harold E. Vandayburg, Edward B. Wade, and me, on a permanent change of station. We were released from assignment and duty with the 439th Fighter Squadron and ordered to proceed as the "2D LT'S of Shipment #FJ-902-AB" to Hamilton Field, California.

Looking back at my training experience, the aircraft that I flew were remarkable products of American ingenuity. The training I was blessed with worked for me, for which I am truly grateful.

NOTES

1. Oklahoma Air College was one of the Army Air Forces contract flying schools, and used Fairchild PT-19 trainers for primary flight training. It operated at Cimarron Field, about 14 miles west of Oklahoma City, beginning in October 1941. Today the field is known as Clarence E. Page Municipal Airport.
   "WWII Army Air Forces Contract Flying Schools Database," http://www.airforcebase.net/aaf/cfs_list.html
   "Clarence E. Page Municipal Airport," http://en.wikipedia.org/wiki/Clarence_E._Page_Municipal_Airport
2. Enid Army Flying Field is known as Vance Air Force Base today. It is one of the main pilot training bases for the Air Force's Air Education and Training Command (AETC).
   "Vance Air Force Base History," http://www.vance.af.mil/library/factsheets/factsheet.asp?id=6069
3. Lake Charles Army Air Field in southwest Louisiana served to train advanced single engine flight training until mid-January 1943, when that training shifted to the new Aloe Army Air Field in Texas. Thereafter Lake Charles served as a tactical

bomber training base and was closed after the war. It was reactivated during the Cold War as Chennault Air Force Base, closed again in 1963 and is now in use as Chennault International Airport.

"Guide to the Lieutenant General Claire L. Chennault/Chennault Air Force Base Collection 1953–1999," http://ereserves.mcneese.edu/depts/archive/pdfs/Chennault010.pdf

"Chennault Air Force Base," http://en.wikipedia.org/wiki/Chennault_Air_Force_Base

4. Aloe Army Air Field opened in January 1943, was closed after the war and served as the Victoria County Airport until 1960. It has not been used again for aviation, and today the field has been redeveloped into an industrial park and housing development.

"Aloe Army Air Field," http://www.tshaonline.org/handbook/online/articles/qca01

"Aloe Army Airfield," http://en.wikipedia.org/wiki/Aloe_Army_Airfield

5. Dale Mabry Field was dedicated in 1929 as Tallahassee's municipal airport. It became an Army Air Forces base in January 1941 and was used as a fighter training base during the war, training some 8,000 fighter pilots. Used by civil aviation after the war, it closed in 1961. Today the campus of Tallahassee Community College occupies the former flying field.

"Dale Mabry Field, Tallahassee, FL," http://www.airfields-freeman.com/FL/Airfields_FL_Tallahassee.htm#mabry

"Dale Mabry Army Airfield," http://en.wikipedia.org/wiki/Dale_Mabry_Army_Airfield

6. James C. Curran's 16 April 1943 landing accident involved P-47D-1-RA serial number 42-22305. It was one of the first P-47's produced at Republic's Evansville, Indiana, factory. In comparison to the cost of the damage which he mentioned in this accident, $25,000, the average cost of a P-47 in 1945 US dollars was $83,000.

"April 1943 USAAF Stateside Accident Reports," http://www.aviationarchaeology.com/src/AARmonthly/Apr1943S.htm

Baugher, Joseph F., "1942 USAAF Serial Numbers (42-001 to 42-30031)," http://www.joebaugher.com/usaf_serials/1942_1.html

Knaack, Marcelle Size. *Post-World War II Fighters, 1945–1973*. Washington, DC: Office of Air Force History, 1986, page 303.

Chapter Three

THE LONG JOURNEY TO THE PACIFIC

U PON RECEIVING OUR ORDERS, WE IMMEDIATELY BEGAN the required compliance actions. That meant getting shots and packing our gear as specified in the orders. We were to travel by rail to San Francisco, reporting to the 2nd Air Port of Embarkation at Hamilton Field, with everyday uniforms, a Val pack with a supply of daily necessities, plus our 201 File.[1] Spare uniforms, towels, bedding and auxiliary socks and undergarments were packed in our footlockers to be shipped by railway express to our next station. We were required to have a full complement of cold weather clothing packed. We were issued sidearms but no ammunition. There was no choice in sidearms; one received a .45-caliber pistol, standard Army issue. We were told to wear the sidearm in the holster provided in lieu of packing it in our luggage where it could be compromised. Thus began two years of toting a heavy automatic pistol. *(Note: For a full list of typical pilot issue equipment, see Appendix A)*

Departure day came and we boarded the Southern Pacific train in Tallahassee, heading west. Our accommodations were first class so we had comfortable beds to sleep in at night. We had no idea where we were heading other than Hamilton Field, so we speculated that we might be heading for Alaska, given the heavy clothes we were required to pack in our footlockers. There was not much to do on the train except party, so we did that at every opportunity. Our day was divided into breakfast, lunch, cocktails, dinner and then after-dinner libations and to bed, only to repeat the next day.

We proceeded without incident across the US, finally exited from Arizona then an unscheduled stop at Needles, California because of an air conditioning problem. Since it got very humid in the cars, soaking us all in sweat, we got off the train to try to cool off. What a blast; it was about 120 degrees in Needles and we dried off so rapidly that we got chilled. I had wired ahead to Los Angeles to my mother's sister who lived there to meet me at the train station because we had a few hours between train connections. We were scheduled to leave on the Southern Pacific Railroad's Night Lark from L.A. for San Francisco. The air conditioning repaired, we left Needles in comfort.

Arriving in L.A. only a little late, my aunt and my former girlfriend who had sent me the "Dear John" letter while I was in basic, met me at the train. It was a shock to see my former girlfriend since I had no idea she had moved to L.A. and become friends with my aunt. Nevertheless, it was fun to see someone from home and we had a nice visit while waiting for the next train.

The Night Lark was a super deluxe train, the best I experienced. At its rear was an articulated buffet lounge car, two cars long with every amenity one could imagine. Twelve flying officers, me in charge, literally took over the lounge. We romanced all the pretty girls in sight and celebrated until closing, about midnight. It was a blast, preparing for an assault on the Top of the Mark Lounge at San Francisco's Mark Hopkins Hotel. I never had more fun in my whole life.

In the morning we arrived in San Francisco and proceeded by bus to Hamilton Field. At Hamilton Field we were processed in and informed that we were free until the next day; we could report in by phone rather than make a trip to the base. We were also informed that we would leave the country by aircraft as soon as a plane was available. I immediately phoned my aunt to let her know that I would be in San Francisco that night, and she made arrangements for me to stay at the Alexander Hamilton Hotel where she and her husband resided. The accommodations were superb. We had a great dinner together that night and she even fixed me up with a date for the evening. The next day we were told by our base contact to enjoy San Francisco and report the following day. We were having the visit of a lifetime in one of the most glamorous cities in the world.

After several days of delay we were told to report for transportation at Hamilton Field. I told the people at the hotel to keep my room ready, assuming that I would be back in a couple of hours. But at seven that evening we assembled at the flight line and boarded a B-24 bomber that had been converted into a mail plane; the pilot, co-pilot, and engineer were employed by Pan American Airlines. Besides the 12 fighter pilots, there were 12 USO civilians as passengers. I headed the 12 pilots by virtue of my name being ahead on the alphabetical list. The USO team was headed by the actor Ray Bolger, best known for his role as the "Scarecrow" in the 1939 movie, *The Wizard of Oz.* We all greeted one another and took our places on the mailbags, getting underway at sundown, heading out over the Pacific Ocean.

July 16th, 1943, was departure day for the flying officers who received their orders on July 4th. At about 1900 hours, the B-24 lumbered down the runway as dusk approached, and swung out over San Francisco Bay. We could see San Quentin fading away to the east as we flew over the Golden Gate Bridge. The B-24 made slow climbing turns until reaching an altitude of about 11,000 feet. Planes were not pressurized then, so in order to keep the passengers from suffering oxygen shortage they were limited as to how high they could fly. The B-24 was capable of flying at high altitude but we weren't, so 11,000 feet it was. Though it was summer and we were flying at low altitude, we wore winter garb with A2 leather flight jackets. The USO personnel wore similar clothing.

We quickly ascertained that we were headed on a west-southwest course, and not heading for Alaska, which would have been north-northwest. We knew this by looking at the stars, which were very visible, and soon came to the conclusion that we were headed for Hawaii. Half the USO troupe was already airsick because it was very bumpy at the altitude we were flying. Smoother air was above, but we couldn't go there.

The plane did not have a restroom facility, only a toilet seat over a pipe hole looking down into the ocean, located aft of the bomb bay on the port side of the aircraft. It remained open all the time, having no door. The B-24 was equipped with two large waist gun ports on each side and both were also open, so you looked directly into the noisy slipstream. Smoking was prohibited in the middle of the aircraft, but one could smoke forward in the cockpit. The reason for the ban was because of the huge auxiliary fuel tanks hung in the bomb racks. The crew allowed the passengers to visit the pilots' office in small numbers to smoke and get warm. There was no heat in the passenger part of the plane.

After about four hours, the captain announced that we could open our orders once we passed the point of no return. Until this time we were in the dark as to what was happening. He also informed us not to worry about going down at sea because there were four ships on picket rescue duty between San Francisco and our destination. Sleep was almost impossible with the roar of the engines and prop wash; sick civilians constantly stumbling to the so-called toilet didn't help either. As the night progressed, it became colder and we really began to suffer. In spite of this discomfort I did finally get some fitful bouts of sleep.

Dawn finally approached, the stars began to disappear and a glorious sky appeared. We knew that Oahu was our destination and Hickam Field would be our landing spot. About 1000 hours Hawaii time, we viewed the carnage of Pearl Harbor as we approached to land. The sight of what had happened there was forever engraved on my mind. Upon landing, while taxiing to a parking spot, we could see first-hand the scars of December 7th, 1941. It was awesome.

The USO team came back to life as soon as we parked the aircraft. We were treated to fresh orange juice by the most beautiful Hawaiian lady I have ever seen, who had 12 immediate offers of marriage from our young fighter pilots. We were allowed to clean up and shave at very nice facilities, and then fed a sumptuous meal while waiting for our bomber-turned-mail-plane to be serviced.[2]

We again boarded the B-24 and at about 1400 local time, on July 17th, we took off for Johnston Atoll south-southwest of Hawaii. We arrived at Johnston about 1900 hours local time after a very bumpy daylight flight. Here we were thousands of miles from home already, on a chunk of sand barely big enough for an airstrip. The USMC was in charge of the atoll and they herded all of us, including the USO people, into barracks surrounded by sand bags three rows wide and ten feet high.[3] The isle had a contingent of four Bell P-39 Airacobra fighter planes with Army pilots and numerous anti-aircraft guns. They fed us and advised us to get some rest, as tomorrow would be a long day of flying.

Night had just fallen at Johnston Atoll when three very loud explosions were heard. A Marine noncom informed us it was an air raid warning. The garrison was equipped with 90 mm dual-purpose anti-aircraft guns which were fired to announce the red alert—why they used the AA guns I don't know. We assumed it was a drill because we were only 36 hours out of the United States and a mere 800+ miles from Hawaii. But our complacency was soon deflated when another Marine appeared and told us to report to the command post on the double. Upon arriving there, we were issued ammunition for our sidearms at the direction of the C.O. of the garrison, a Marine colonel. They had blips on the radar screen indicating that we were going to be attacked by surface vessels as well as aircraft. In other words there was a major invasion in the offing. They scrambled the four P-39 fighter planes and sent them up to 5,000 feet.

With that, three Kawanishi flying boats appeared in the searchlights, and the anti-aircraft guns began blazing with a deafening roar. As the flying boats passed over we heard a new, never heard before sound that was akin to what you would imagine a lost soul would make on its way to hell. It was the sound of bombs coming down; an eerie sound I will never forget, followed by earth-shaking explosions. Our fright knew no bounds as the Japanese aircraft disappeared into the night. We could hear the P-39s flying around the atoll. They had flown to 5,000 feet as directed by an artillery officer who was calling off the altitude in yards, so the enemy planes were really at 15,000 feet, two miles above the defending aircraft. Why the Marines called off the altitude of the raiders in yards is also a mystery to me.

All the bombs the Japanese planes dropped fell into the lagoon, killing thousands of fish, but doing no damage to the installation where we spent the rest of the night in total quiet. It was determined by the local command that the radar blips seen on the water were a mistake and what we'd had was only an air raid.

The next morning, the 18th of July, we again mounted the mail sack seats in our B-24 for the next leg of our journey. A boring, bumpy day ensued with nothing to do except wait for our next turn to visit the cockpit. Finally, Canton Island appeared, where we spent a quiet night. Just prior to arriving on Canton, we had a brief little ceremony conducted by the Pan Am first officer to mark the crossing of the equator, for those of us making it for the first time.

On July 19th, we took off on the next leg of the journey heading for Suva in the Fiji islands. While en route to Suva, we crossed the International Date Line, losing a whole day in the second it took to cross the imaginary line. We refueled and ate at Suva and then took off for Noumea, New Caledonia, where we were to remain overnight. The stops we were making were so our flight crew could get needed rest, but it was also for us, because flying on mail sacks wasn't the most comfortable way to spend one's time.

At Noumea we were billeted at a traveling officers BOQ with a nice club attached, where they served any amenity one could ask for. While enjoying the local atmosphere we were entertained by two Marine flying officers also passing through. They were expert at playing the piano and singing all the latest tunes, with a lot of stuff they had picked up in Australia and New Zealand. A great time was had by all into the late hours.

July 21st saw a relatively easy flight to Brisbane, Australia, where we landed at Eagle Farm Royal Australian Air Force (RAAF) base. We bid adieu to our Pan American crew and the USO team and reported to the US Army command on the RAAF base. We were billeted in squad tents arranged in typical company streets, with showers and toilets in conventional wooden barracks-type buildings. There was no heat in the tents and it was July in Australia, the middle of winter there. The daytime temperature was in the middle 50's and the nights in the 30's. The first night I could not get warm, even with all the clothes I could put on, besides every blanket available.

The next day, July 22nd, after I defrosted, I was informed that we would be here for a while doing some special work before we were sent to join our assigned squadrons in New Guinea. We received orders from HQ Fifth Air Force assigning us to the 348th Fighter Group, commanded by Lt. Col. Neel E. Kearby.

NEEL KEARBY ARRIVES IN THE
SOUTHWEST PACIFIC AREA (SWPA)

Kearby, a short, slight, keen-eyed, black-haired Texan about thirty two, looked like money in the bank to me. About two minutes after he had introduced himself, he wanted to know who had the highest scores for shooting down Jap aircraft. You felt that he just wanted to know who he had to beat.—General George C. Kenney in *General Kenney Reports, June–August 1943*

The following day, an aircraft carrier arrived at the quay adjacent to

Eagle Farm Airfield. The carrier's deck was loaded with P-47 fighter planes all wrapped up in protective covering for the long sea journey. The planes were quickly unloaded and towed to the airfield. Upon unloading its cargo, the carrier withdrew from the quay and hit full speed as it raced toward its next task. What a sight to see, awesome![4]

Civilian representatives from Pratt & Whitney, Curtiss Electric Propeller and Republic Aviation appeared as if by magic to supervise the preparation of the P-47's for flight. These were brand-new aircraft never before flown. Their propellers had to be installed along with ailerons, rudders and elevators. There were no US military people available to do this so RAAF personnel were drafted for the job. As the planes were readied for flight it was our job to make the first test flight and "slow time" the planes. Slow time was the break-in period for new engines. It was not a test period. Ten hours of flight were required for each engine, operated at reduced power, to break-in the engine. This was similar to driving a new car at reduced speed. The process was dull and time-consuming.

DOUBTS ABOUT THE THUNDERBOLT

. . . everyone in the 5th Air Force, from Whitehead to Wurtsmith down, except for the kids in the new group, decided that the P-47 was no good as a combat airplane.

Besides not having enough gas, the rumors said it took too much runway to get off, it had no maneuverability, it would not pull out of a dive, the landing gear was weak, and the engine was unreliable.—General George C. Kenney in *General Kenney Reports, June–August 1943*

Since we could not demonstrate the abilities of the P-47, we were the butt of jokes by the Australian fighter pilots with whom we shared the officers' club. The Aussies were flying Supermarine Spitfires, a very remarkable fighter that proved itself in the Battle of Britain. It was much better than the Brewster Buffalo, which is what the RAAF had in New Guinea—you had to be very brave to fly this aircraft in the vicinity of a Japanese fighter. Upon completion of ten hours of slow time, we gave the RAAF base an air show they would never forget. My friend, Bill Cooley, blew the radio antenna off the Aussie alert shack at 600 mph.

KENNEY COMMENTS ON THE P-47

No matter what objections there are to the P-47, it has eight guns and is faster than the Zero at any altitude so I will use it and gladly take all I can get.—General Kenney in *The Fifth Air Force in the Huon Peninsula Campaign, Jan to Oct 1943*[5]

P-47 slow timing proceeded morning and afternoon into the first week of August. One day, Bill Cooley and I were requested to go to the headquarters of the US Army in Australia to pick up some documents, and were furnished a jeep for transportation. Since we had just finished four hours of slow timing, we were still wearing our A2 leather flight jackets. As we approached headquarters on foot, who should walk out the door but none other than General Douglas MacArthur. We came to an immediate halt, popped to attention and saluted the general. He peered at us and turned to his aide de camp, saying ". . . put those officers on report for being out of uniform." He then disappeared into his limousine. The aide took down our names and asked us why we were out of uniform in Brisbane. We told him we were going to a warehouse to pick up material necessary to our assigned mission. We explained that we were on flying duty and had been pressed into this errand without the opportunity to change uniforms. MacArthur's aide directed us into the headquarters building to make a report to another aide. That was the end of the show and we never heard from MacArthur again. This was the first and last time I saw General MacArthur, thank heavens! He was not a very popular C.O. at that time.

The second week of August we were shipped to Townsville, Australia, to await our orders to fly up to Port Moresby, New Guinea. We had no specific duties while waiting, so Cooley and I borrowed a jeep command car and took a ride west into the Outback to a cattle station (ranch). We were furnished a guide and saddle horses and did a little exploring of the desert.

We met some nomadic natives who were still very primitive for that time. They were hunter-gatherers and armed with bow and arrows, and wore practically no clothes. Their skin was deeply tanned and wrinkled from the sun. They were not attractive but the children were beautiful, especially the babies whose skin positively glowed, their faces framed in gorgeous, brownish-auburn hair. We also met a white hunter of kangaroos who hadn't been to a single town since 1939. He was surprised to hear the war news.

HEADQUARTERS / FIFTH AIR FORCE
APO 925 / 23 July 1943
Subject: Letter of Commendation.
To: Commanding General, Fifth Air Force Service Command.
Commanding Officer, 348th Fighter Group (Through Command-
ing General, V Fighter Command)

1. The arrival, assemblage and delivery of the 348th Fighter Group to its combat station reflects great credit on the Fifth Air Force Service Command and the 348th Fighter Group. The ground echelon of this organization arrived from the United States on June 14. Upon its arrival an air echelon was established at Bris-bane and the remainder of the group proceeded to New Guinea to prepare a group camp. The first P-47-type aircraft scheduled for this organization arrived by boat June 27th and in less than one month 100 of these aircraft were completely erected and 80 of these aircraft delivered to New Guinea battle stations. The aircraft were erected at a rate in excess of six aircraft per day. These aircraft were test flown and received a minimum of 10 hours local flying prior to departure. The first squadron of the Group departed for combat station on July 12th or within two weeks of the date aircraft were received. The second squadron departed July 16th and the third squadron departed July 22nd. During these flying operations only two aircraft were damaged and that by a taxying accident.

2. The wholehearted efforts of the Service Command in erecting the aircraft and the efficiency of the tactical Group in receiving these aircraft and departing as a fighting organization reflects the greatest credit upon this Air Force. I desire to commend the officers and enlisted men responsible for this achievement.

George C. Kenney
Lieutenant General,
Commanding[6]

NOTES

1. According to Jim Curran, ". . . a 'Val pack' was a standard GI issue suitcase made of olive drab canvas for officers, with lots of zipper compartments. It was carry-on luggage, but too large to fit into the compartment in a P-47. I normally used my parachute bag for travel in the combat zone, like going on R&R to Sydney." The 201 File was an official military personnel file; it contained personal orders and records and documents showing military service history and was hand-carried by officers between assignments.
2. For an interesting discussion of the establishment of this aerial lifeline from the United States to the South Pacific, see *Development of the South Pacific Air Route, Army Air Forces Historical Studies No. 45*. Arlington, VA: AAF Historical Office, February 1946.
3. Research on the internet could find little indication of a Japanese air attack against Johnston Island, though this does not mean such an event did not take place. At this time, Johnston Island (sometimes referred to as Johnston Atoll) was defended by the USMC's 16th Defense Battalion. The P-39 Airacobras there were likely a detachment from a Seventh Air Force P-39 squadron stationed in Hawaii, such as the 72nd Fighter Squadron.

Melson, Charles D., Major, USMC. *Condition Red: Marine Defense Battalions in World War II*. Washington D.C.: Marine Corps Historical Center, 1996.

There is virtually no information readily available about Japanese air attacks on Johnson Island during the war, though shellings by Japanese submarines are fairly well documented. One passing mention to an air attack is as follows: ". . . But the looming spectre of war with Germany sealed its fate when President Roosevelt gave control to US navy for an air station. From this point on the island would become a magnet for the tools and products of 'war' as it suffered aerial bombings from Japanese fighter planes during World War II and would later become a pivot point for just about every nuclear, chemical and rocket testing program the U.S military could come up with. . . ."

Jason Stevens, "The Forgotten Island of Johnston Atoll," http://www.jason-stevens. com/2010/07/the-forgotten-island-of-johnston-atoll/

"Johnston Atoll," http://en.wikipedia.org/wiki/Johnston_Atoll

Other information indicates the Japanese conducted air attacks on these American islands between Hawaii and Australia, such as a 27 March 1943 attack on Canton Island which destroyed a US Navy PBY-5A Catalina seaplane of VP-54, and a 23 October 1943 aerial engagement between USAAF P-40's and an IJN Kawanishi H8K EMILY in which the Japanese seaplane was shot down, 70 miles south of Baker Island. The month prior, F6F Hellcat fighters from the light carrier USS *Princeton* (CVL-23), vectored with help from destroyer USS *Trathen*, clashed with the big Japanese Kawanishi EMILY seaplanes near Baker Island, destroying one on 1 Sep 1943 (the F6F Hellcat's first aerial victory) and another on 3 Sep 1943. All of these incidents serve to show some of the Japanese actions against these island stepping stones between Hawaii and Australia/South Pacific.

"Aircraft Lost in the Vicinity of Nikumaroro," http://tighar.org/wiki/Aircraft_lost_in_the_vicinity_of_Nikumaroro; "WWII Navy Pilot Grouping, Guadalcanal VP-54," http://www.usmilitariaforum.com/forums/index.php?/topic/96911-wwii-navy-pilot-groupingguadalcanal-vp-54/

"USS *Princeton*," http://www.history.navy.mil/danfs/p12/princeton-iv.htm

"USS *Trathen*," http://www.history.navy.mil/danfs/t7/trathen.htm

Tillman, Barrett. *Hellcat: The F6F in World War II*. Annapolis, MD: Naval Institute Press, 1979.

4. This ship was the US Navy escort carrier USS *Barnes* (CVE-20) which began unloading P-47 and P-38 fighters in Brisbane on 21 July at 1200 hours.

341st Fighter Squadron records indicate that P-47 aircraft arrived at Brisbane by 28 June 1943, but does not indicate which vessel(s) brought the 100 aircraft mentioned. 342nd Fighter Squadron records state that the first P-47's to arrive in the SWPA arrived by boat on 27 June 1943.

According to Mr. David Jones at the Queensland Maritime Museum in Brisbane, Australia, the USS *Nassau* (CVE-16) was the first aircraft carrier to bring aircraft to Brisbane, some three weeks before the arrival of USS *Barnes*. Naval history sources indicate that after taking part in Aleutian Island operations, *Nassau* returned to the US, and arrived at Alameda, California, by 8 June 1943 to onload 45 aircraft destined for Brisbane, Australia. *Nassau* delivered the aircraft by 2 July and returned to the US. Other ships in addition to escort carriers were used to deliver aircraft to Australia.

According to *The Fifth Air Force in the Huon Peninsula Campaign, January to October 1943, US Air Force Historical Study No. 113*, Chapter VI, Problems of Men and materiel, May–September, states on page 143: "By 3 July 79 P-38's and 59 P-47's, and a month later 36 additional P-38's and 56 more P-47's, had arrived."

The fighters were assembled at Eagle Farm, and then flown over to Archer Field SSW of Brisbane for ten-hour flight checks, boresighting, and final acceptance. The 342nd Fighter Squadron received its aircraft first, then the 341st and lastly the 340th, with order determined by coin toss. The 342nd flew its 25 P-47s in two flights, led by the squadron's commander, Maj. Raymond K. Gallagher and 348th Fighter Group commander Lt Col. Neel E. Kearby, on 12 July 1944 up to Port Moresby via Rockhampton, Townsville, Cairns, Cooktown, and Horn Island, and landed at Ward's Drome on 14 July 1943. By the end of July, the 341st had received 25 P-47D's, flown up to New Guinea and began orientation flights around the Port Moresby area and along the neighboring coastline.

History of the 341st Fighter Squadron, Chapter II, (January–July 1943), page 4.

History of the 342nd Fighter Squadron, Chapter II, (January 1st to June 30th, 1943), page 11.

History of the 342nd Fighter Squadron, Chapter III, July 1, 1943 to January 31, 1944, page 1.

"War Diary of USS *Massachusetts*," http://www.eugeneleeslover.com/USNAVY/USS_Massachusetts/War_Diary_2.pdf

"USS *Barnes* (CVE-20, CVHE-20)," http://navalwarfare.blogspot.com/2012/03/uss-barnes-cve-20-cvhe-20.html

"USS *Barnes* CVE-20," https://www.flickr.com/photos/dougsheley/5673502173/

"Escort carrier USS *Barnes* transporting P-38 Lightning and P-47 Thunderbolt fighter planes across the Pacific, July 1, 1943," http://ww2db.com/image.php?image_id=17848

USS *Nassau (CVE-16)*, http://www.history.navy.mil/danfs/n2/nassau.htm

USS *Saratoga (CV 3)*, *War Diary, July 1943*

5. General Kenney did his part to help bring the P-47 into a position to prove itself in the Pacific. He recalled in his memoir, *General Kenney Reports*, on page 264: "I then went out to Eagle Farms . . . and found that no droppable fuel tanks had come with the P-47s. Without the extra gas carried in these tanks the P-47 did not have enough range to get into the war. I wired Arnold to send me some right away, by air if possible. About a week later we received two samples. Neither held enough fuel, they both required too many alterations to install, and they both were difficult to release in an emergency. We designed and built one of our own in two days. It tested satisfactorily from every angle and could be installed in a matter of minutes without making any changes in the airplane. I put the Ford Company of Australia to work making them. We had solved the problem but it would be another month before we could use the P-47 in combat."

Kenney, George C., *General Kenney Reports*. New York, NY: Duell, Sloan and Pierce, 1949, reprinted by Office of Air Force History, Washington, D.C., 1987. (Hereinafter Kenney)

This was a 200 gallon belly tank, according to a more detailed discussion of P-47 external fuel tank development described in *The Fifth Air Force in the Huon Peninsula Campaign, January to October 1943*, 164–165.

6. History of the 342nd Fighter Squadron, Chapter III, (July 1, 1943 to January 31, 1944), Enclosure 1, "Letter of Commendation from Lt. Gen. Kenney, 23 July 1943."

PART TWO

WAR IN THE PACIFIC

Chapter Four

INTO THE FIGHT

DURAND AIRSTRIP—17 MILE DROME

W<small>E RETURNED TO</small> T<small>OWNSVILLE AND WERE ORDERED TO</small> board an ATC plane to Port Moresby, New Guinea, to join our squadrons. New Guinea is big, some 1,200 miles long by 500 miles at its widest point. It was 99% jungle, 75% mountains with zero navigational aids at that time. The only airfields were those built by the military—ours and the enemy's. The pre-war administrative dividing line was north and south between Australian-administered Papua New Guinea in the east of the big island, and Dutch-run New Guinea on the western part.

We were assigned to the 348th Fighter Group of the Fifth Air Force, which consisted of three fighter squadrons. A fighter squadron consisted of 40 flying officers, appropriate ground officers and about 250 enlisted men whose job was to keep us in the business of flying. The squadrons were designated by numbers as follows: 340th Fighter Squadron (340FS), 341FS, and 342FS. There were several airstrips around Port Moresby and the squadrons were dispersed to different strips.

On August 21st, I received orders assigning me to the 341FS along with Gerald W. Excell, Robert L. Frank, and Robert A. Ducharme. The other eight of us who flew to the Pacific were sent to the other two squadrons. Mahoney, McNulty, Monroe, and Harding went to the 340th while Ness, Searles, Vandayburg, and Wade went to the 342nd.

FIRST CASUALTY *It was at Port Moresby that the first casualty occurred. On 15 August 1943, while attempting to land on Durand Drome, Second Lieutenant John H. Schrik of Oak Park, Ill, was caught in a cross wind that sent*

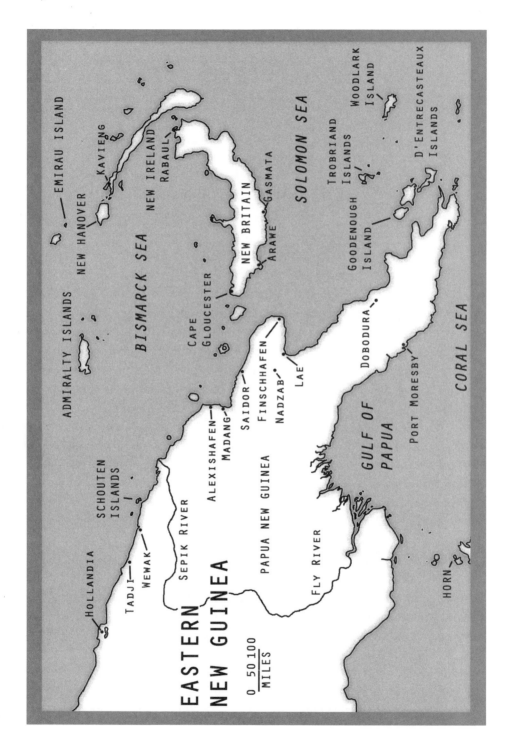

him into a fatal tail spin off the end of the strip.—History of the 341st Fighter Squadron, August 1943 through January 1944[1]

Robert Frank was a devout Jewish boy from New York City; Ducharme was a fireman on a coal-fired engine from Wisconsin; Excell is still alive and lives in Maryland. The 341st was assigned to Durand, or sometimes called 17-Mile Airstrip.[2] It was the farthest out of all the airstrips at Port Moresby. The other two squadrons were at airfields closer in to Port Moresby.

NEW HOME DROME *Because Major Campbell had served with the 35th Fighter Squadron while he was in New Guinea several months previously, the (341st) squadron was assigned to this old fighter squadron to learn the ways of the tropics . . . the camp area was built up and the men became acclimated to the tropical weather, especially the hot sticky days, and the cool, often rainy nights. The squadron was to operate off Durand Field, commonly called 17 mile.*—History of the 341st Fighter Squadron, August 1943 through January 1944

We arrived at Durand by truck transport in the late afternoon, reporting for duty to the C.O., Major David A. Campbell. We were introduced and assigned to a tent; it had a dirt floor and four cots equipped with a mosquito bar which completely draped over the cot. The cot had no mattress or pillow, or sheets. We were issued several standard military blankets and a flashlight. Two blankets were folded to the shape of the cot to form a rudimentary mattress. One kept the mosquito bar folded up when not in use. At bedtime I would get on the cot, lower the mosquito bar as quickly as possible and tuck it under the blankets all around so no mosquitoes could get in. I then turned on the flashlight to search for mosquitoes until it was safe to go to sleep. One had to lie in the center of the cot without touching the sides or be eaten by mosquitoes. This was the pits. But I guess we were lucky to even have a path through the jungle where we were.

ARRIVAL IN NEW GUINEA *At the end of July the squadron had received 25 P-47D's and already had begun orientation flights around Port Moresby and up and down the neighboring coast. When the 35th Fighter Squadron moved* *out, the 341st took over the old camp area and the new mess hall. Quarters were the standard pyramidal tents pitched along Malaria Lane, Atabrine Row, and Mosquito Drive. The entire squadron was being molded into a compact fighter squadron ready for action—which was to come in a few weeks.—His-*tory of the 341st Fighter Squadron, August 1943 through January 1944

We were also introduced to Atabrine, a yellow medication we had to consume daily to keep from getting malaria. We had a shower in which to bathe and sanitary facilities consisted of a bench with holes over a pit. Both the shower and toilet were open to the sky and everything else. The officer's mess abutted the general mess and meals were eaten out of a mess kit which one washed after each meal. Water was in a Lister bag and was near unpalatable. We had a screened-in building which we called an officer's club where we could spend time writing home or reading without being tormented by bugs. The area was carved out of a tropical rainforest by the US Army Corps of Engineers. How that was accomplished will forever remain a mystery. The food at Durand airstrip is a subject that could absorb a whole chapter. To put it in a nutshell, it was awful.

DURAND CAMP *The squadron's camp area was set up about two miles from the strip along the main road into Port Moresby. A permanent mess hall, a thatched enlisted men's club, and a modern officer's club were erected. The weather was pretty well mixed between rain and mud and sunshine and heat. To all the squadron personnel Port Moresby will always be remembered for its aggressive mosquitoes, which according to some tall tales formed there, were divided into various types of dive and fighter squadrons.—History of the* 341st Fighter Squadron, August 1943 through January 1944

On the 26th of August 1943, I flew my first combat mission.[3] It was called an escort of transports, and was to Marilinan Airfield, in the northeast of New Guinea. Operating out of Durand Airstrip in August and September, I flew 18 combat missions, but the squadron flew every day. Most of the missions were escort of transports over the Owen Stanley Mountains to Tsili Tsili, New Guinea, though I did also fly a bomber escort to Malahang (Lae) and an intercept against enemy planes reported near Yodda (near Kokoda) with nil sightings.[4]

AUGUST COMBAT MISSIONS *During the past month our missions have been top, medium and low cover escort for transports to Tsili Tsili.*—341FS Combat Evaluation Report for August 1943

When I joined the 341st, they were fully operational. The Army had taken a spot in the Ramu Valley called Tsili Tsili, on the east slope of the Owen Stanleys; it was remote enough that Japanese ground forces were no problem. The Japanese had numerous air bases on the northeast coast of New Guinea that were well-endowed with fighter planes.

STATUS OF AIRPLANES *Transferred 2 P-47D-2's to 374th Service Sq for repairs—one for main gas tank, other, for damaged fuselage, etc. caused by piece of wood from blasted stump near parking area.*—341FS Weekly Status & Operations Report (Form 34), Report, 5-11 September 1943[5]

Our Douglas C-47 transports carried both troops and supplies, with the latter sometimes dropped by parachutes. Making an airfield there was accomplished by airdrop from transport planes. After enough of a landing strip was cleared off by manual labor, the transports brought in air-portable mini-bulldozers to construct a full airstrip. Our mission was to discourage any attack by enemy fighters as our transports dropped supplies and brought construction materials to the ground forces. Our presence was very effective. After we returned for home, the Japanese would mount attacks on our forward base.

ON THE RECEIVING END *It was at Port Moresby, on 20 September 1943, that the squadron experienced its first air raid in the early morning hours. Two Betty type enemy bombers dropped 10 unidentified bombs in the jungle far from the airstrip which was their target. Of course the usual whinning [sic] sound of the bomber's engines left a distinctive impression carried by the personnel all through the subsequent months. The dense overcast covered their target.*—History of the 341st Fighter Squadron, August 1943 through January 1944

The transports would be loaded at night so they would be ready for takeoff at dawn, in order to cross over the Owen Stanley Mountains before the clouds built up. Cloud buildup in the afternoon posed big problems for the transports getting back to Port Moresby. Forty-eight C-47s was a modest number of planes for us to escort, with 16 fighters for protection while cargo was being dropped.

Upon completion of the drop we would escort the C-47s back over the hump for safety. Thus our mission was defensive. Tsili Tsili Airstrip was completed and a pincer was in place to take the Ramu Valley. Subsequently, on September 5, 1943, a vertical attack by paratroopers was made at Nadzab, which, in conjunction with an amphibious landing, secured the nearby port of Lae. MacArthur's forces were on the move.

SUPPORT TO SALAMAUA OPERATION *Some of the subsequent (to Nadzab) escort missions for the transports supplying the troops advancing on Salamaua finally saw the capture of that port on 12 September 1943.*—History of the 341st Fighter Squadron, August 1943 through January 1944

Our mission continued to be defensive in protecting these new bases from aerial attack. When the landing facility at Nadzab was completed, we were the first fighters to land at the strip, even as dozers and graders were still working on it.

SEPTEMBER COMBAT MISSIONS *During the month we have performed normal escort for transports. Also provided part of the protection for Nadzab strike and Finschhafen landing.*—341FS Combat Evaluation Report for September 1943

The Japanese watched us from afar, seldom challenging us to get at the transports. Consequently, our guns hardly ever got fired. Our ordnance people decided that the ammo was getting too old and should be expended, so we were requested to expend our ammo in practice on ground targets. The only place that looked safe to do this was at a huge rock jutting up from the sea floor at a place called Redscar Bay, about 30 miles northwest of Port Moresby.

On October 10, 1943, when returning from an escort mission to Nadzab, we took turns shooting at the rock to deplete the old ammo. John Lolos was firing his eight .50-caliber guns at the rock when a ricochet must have hit a vital spot on his P-47, causing him to have to ditch into the sea. Upon hitting the water he quickly got out of the plane, which sank almost immediately, and then inflated his Mae West survival jacket. We saw that he was OK because he waved at us, and since there was nothing we could do to help him, we returned to Durand Airstrip to report what happened. A rescue boat was dispatched from Port Moresby but it would take all night for the rescue craft to get to Redscar Bay where they hoped to find John floating in his Mae West. There was no such thing as a helicopter rescue because such an aircraft hadn't yet been invented.

In the morning, aircraft were sent to Redscar Bay to search for the downed pilot, but he was nowhere to be seen. As the days passed, hope for John was dimming. On the third day, tides washed John up to the shore, where natives found him comatose and barely breathing. Somehow they were able to contact the military and John was retrieved and brought to the hospital in Port Moresby. He was almost dead, completely dehydrated and almost rubbed raw from his experience. It took two months for him to get back on his feet and another month to get back to duty.[6]

John Lolos' experience prompted the powers that be to furnish us with emergency flotation gear besides the trusty Mae West. They produced an inflatable life raft which was incorporated into our parachute gear. It was folded into an 18-inch square about three inches thick, and was situated between the parachute and the pilot's rear end. A CO_2 inflation bottle was positioned right in the middle of the raft directly under one's crotch. When you sat on it, it pressed into your bottom and was very uncomfortable, to say the least. This caused a lot of trips to the flight surgeon due to the soreness it caused, and occasionally it resulted in infections of the urethra. It did, however, give us some peace of mind that if we went down in the ocean we might have a better chance of survival.

After getting the life rafts, one of our pilots had an engine failure over the Sepik River and he bailed out to land safely in the river. The Sepik is the longest river on the island of New Guinea, 300 miles west of Port Moresby. His wingman ascertained that he was OK and returned to base to report his whereabouts. A search was launched by a small aircraft, but he was never seen again.

STILL MISSING IN ACTION *On . . . the 22nd (of October 1943), First Lieu-*

tenant Harold Jacoby was reported missing from an escort mission for B-25s to Wewak. It was later learned that he lost his way, ran out of gas, and bailed out about 100 miles up the Fly River valley. He was seen to parachute into a large patch of kunai grass. He is still missing.—History of the 341st Fighter Squadron, August 1943 through January 1944[7]

Speaking of survival in the Southwest Pacific, we wore a jungle survival pack, which was attached to our parachute harness on the back and contained a folding machete. I also carried a 12-inch double-edged knife in my boot. Flying clothes consisted of khaki pants and shirt. The Jug was a very warm aircraft, needing no heat even at 35,000 feet.

For survival and recue training, we had zilch training stateside. Once we got life rafts we had some instruction on how to survive in a raft, which consisted of "save your parachute, if possible," and "catch a fish if you can." "Dice the flesh and squeeze out the juice," was another piece of advice, as it was purported to be fresh water. Not many pilots survived long after going down at sea. PBY Catalina seaplanes became active rescue craft, and later the Navy also used submarines to collect downed pilots.

As the year transpired, I was eventually given a 341st P-47 which I could call my own. When this aircraft was assigned to me it had a fuel leak that caused the smell of 100-octane fuel to permeate the cockpit. Nobody wanted to fly it, and me being the lowest grunt on the totem pole, I got the unwanted plane.

We had technical representatives from Republic Aviation attached to the squadron with whom I made friends. Besides the fuel odor, my new plane would do no more than 285 mph top speed without being in a dive. I complained bitterly to my crew chief and the tech reps, so they went to work on the plane. They found the fuel leak and fixed it, refitted the misfit engine cowling, put putty on some of the rivets and sanded for days on the entire airframe. Their efforts were very successful in improving the speed of the plane. It wasn't very pretty to look at after the putty work but it was very fast and that's the bottom line.

So I went from having the slowest Jug to the fastest. In a test at Port Moresby circa November 1943, she attained a top speed at sea level, full military power, no dive, of 335 mph, indicated air speed. But the fuel odor reputation never left the plane so I got almost exclusive use of it. I flew it for about a year, on approximately 65 to 70 combat missions, and finally gave it up when I moved to the 460th Fighter Squadron. I flew other aircraft in the 341st and later in the 460th. Most of my contemporaries flew 200 or more missions. I eventually closed out with 221.

My P-47 was painted in the standard olive drab and neutral gray. The paint on the aircraft had much wear from the sun and wind, plus damage from engine run-ups and testing prior to takeoff, like from "mag checks" by the aircraft in front of you. Our aircraft were not pretty airplanes like the privately-owned Thunderbolts or the USAF Thunderbirds at air shows of today.

For markings we had the standard white star and bar for the national insignia. The leading edges of the wings as well as the rudder and tail were also painted white. My Jug had no unique markings, such as mission hash marks, but it did have some nose art. My buddy, Lt. Robert Bagby, who turned out to be an accomplished artist, painted a Vargas girl from the September 1943 issue of *Esquire* magazine on the cowling. I named my Jug, "Windy City Kitty." Bagby was also a fighter pilot and flew Windy City Kitty on a few occasions, as did many other members of the Blackjack Squadron. He died years ago, but I still communicate with his family occasionally.[8]

As for the ultimate fate of "Windy City Kitty," she was eventually retired as war weary and probably went to the junk pile. I don't think anyone knows the ultimate fate of those early P-47s in New Guinea.

The Turbo-Supercharger on "Windy City Kitty" turned at a maximum rate of 18,500 revolutions per minute (rpm). You had to adjust throttle settings at about 33,000 feet to keep from exceeding the limits of the rpm. They were known to blow up if not manually regulated. A 12-inch disc turning over too fast could sling a "bucket" component so fast it could penetrate the 5/8-inch armor plate, killing the pilot. I did lots of flying over the critical altitude for turbo speeds. The bucket on the hot side of the turbo was made of cast tungsten and other metals. They could not be machined in the manufacturing process so they had to be precision cast. At ambient temperature they were so loose they would rattle. At operating temperature they were solid and unmovable.

The process for creating this bucket apparatus was very complicated. The factory, located on South Chicago Avenue in Chicago, Illinois, was super-secret. The name of the company was Austenal Dental Laboratories—yes, dental![9] They were the only people in the country with the knowhow to cast these high temperature buckets. The people who worked in the factory had absolutely no concept of what they were working on. The security must have been on par with the A-Bomb project. So I had some heroes in my backyard. Incidentally, I knew of this laboratory because I used to go to John's Bakery in the same area to get fresh bread for my Mom's table. I never knew of the facts described here until the 1990s.

Later in the war, my last Jug, a P-47D-23-RA, had a turbo redlined at 23,000 rpm. Coupled with alcohol/water fuel injection, the Pratt & Whitney engine delivered 60 inches of manifold pressure all the way to 40,000 feet. What a ride!

Getting back to flying, later in the same month I was outbound on an escort mission when I had an engine outage at 18,000 feet over the area John Lolos went down. Without power, the P-47 had the glide ratio of a brick and I was rapidly losing altitude over the worst wilderness in the world with no hope of rescue if I went down. I frantically attempted to restart the engine until 3,000 feet, when I slid the canopy back in preparation to jump out. Saying my prayers I hit the energizer one more time and the engine coughed to life. I was all alone but could still see my squadron flying away. My radio did not seem to work so I increased throttle and regained my position which was number 16 out of 16 planes, dead last.

This was the closest I came to aborting a mission for any reason and I continued not to abort for the rest of my combat experience (unless the whole mission for the unit was scrubbed). Not to convey the wrong impression, but our maintenance was super. The ground crews kept the planes in top-notch condition; how, I don't know, but they did. I never had a mechanical abort of a mission my whole tour. Hand salute to our support troops!

Some of the missions flown by the senior pilots in the group were a little different. The C.O. and some of the flight leaders went on fighter sweeps deep into enemy territory looking for Japanese aircraft to shoot at, missions that usually consisted of four planes. There was a reason for these incursive raids, having as much to do with shooting down Japanese as for boosting the reputation of the P-47.

We were in the Southwest Pacific Area (SWPA) Air Force under the overall command of General Douglas MacArthur. Under his command was Lieutenant General George C. Kenney, commander of Fifth Air Force; his deputy commander was Major General Ennis C. Whitehead, and Brigadier General Paul B. Wurtsmith was in charge of V Fighter Command. These generals were not too happy about getting a group of P-47s as reinforcements. They wanted P-38s because they had long-range capabilities and an excellent history of success in the theater. They deemed the P-47 to be too big and heavy, and too gasoline hungry. The latter might be true because the P-47 used 60 gallons an hour at cruising speed and 300 gallons an hour at full military power.

The displeasure expressed about the Thunderbolt was felt mostly by Col. Neel Kearby, the 348th Fighter Group commander who was a staunch advocate of the P-47. Dick Bong, a P-38 pilot, had already demonstrated the power of the P-38 by shooting down 16 enemy planes. Kearby felt that the P-47 was just as good as the P-38 and maybe even better, so he ordered fighter sweeps by his most experienced personnel (I didn't fall into that category so was never invited to participate). Kearby also flew these missions, soon amassing a score of victories to match Dick Bong. The result was more confidence in the P-47 by the commanding upper crust.

KEARBY PROVES THE THUNDERBOLT

Medal of Honor Citation for Colonel Neel E. Kearby, Air Corps, United States Army. For conspicuous gallantry and intrepidity above and beyond the call of duty in action with the enemy near Wewak, New Guinea, on 11 October 1943. Colonel Kearby volunteered to lead a flight of 4 fighters to reconnoiter the strongly defended enemy base at Wewak. Having observed enemy installations and reinforcements at four airfields, and secured important tactical information, he saw an enemy fighter below him, made a diving attack and shot it down in flames. The small formation then sighted approximately 12 enemy bombers accompanied by 36 fighters. Although his mission had been completed, his fuel was running low and the numerical odds were 12 to 1, he gave the signal to attack. Diving into the midst of the enemy airplanes he shot down 3 in quick succession. Observing one of his comrades with 2 enemy fighters in pursuit he destroyed both enemy aircraft. The enemy broke off in large numbers to make a mul-

tiple attack on his airplane but despite his peril he made one more pass before seeking cloud protection. Coming into the clear he called his flight together and led them to a friendly base. Colonel Kearby brought down 6 aircraft in this action, undertaken with superb daring after his mission was completed.

By Order of Secretary of War:

G.C. Marshall, Chief of Staff

General Orders No. 3, War Department, Washington, D.C. 6 January 1944[10]

In October we started some different types of missions—we now were escorting bombers. For escort we usually flew 16 planes in a four flights of four, vee formation. We were also doing intercept missions from Dobodura, about 90 miles northeast of Port Moresby near the Solomon Sea. The P-38s were operating out of the new airstrip at Dobodura on long missions to Rabaul, New Britain, and Kavieng Harbor in New Ireland. When this occurred we flew to Dobodura to sit alert as protection for the base. Our squadron had a ready shelter next to the aircraft parking area. Four pilots, sometimes eight, with eight more nearby, were kept on alert. We filled our canteens from the Lister bag. No food.

The Japanese frequently bombed Dobodura at night but avoided the area in the day because they knew we were waiting. How did they know this? By way of radio chatter and ground observers who could see the base from hidden points of advantage. Despite several scrambles to intercept the enemy, I was yet to get close to a Japanese aircraft. Our job was still 90% defensive.

Preparation for a combat mission was simple. The squadron's S2 (intelligence officer) created and issued a grid map, on 8-1/2 by 11 mimeographed paper, the blue ink barely legible and with zero information. Weather was an estimate, usually severe thunderclouds in the PM with tops of 60,000 feet—we flew at 25,000 to 30,000 feet. "Rain in the PM. Keep your eyes peeled for enemy planes," was the typical briefing.

Our aircraft recognition training started back in Ground School and continued, ad infinitum. In the Pacific we had silhouettes of enemy planes we had to learn to identify; the same with navy surface ships. Enemy bases were well known with lots of photos available, and there was a special emphasis on identifying anti-aircraft artillery; the Japs were very good shooters.[11]

We had no navigational aids at all. Navigation was entirely by dead reckoning, and you learned very fast to know your whereabouts. I never got lost, not even once! Flying was restricted to daytime only. The enemy harassed us nightly, and Tokyo Rose knew almost every pilot in the Fifth Air Force and entertained us nightly with the best music. The S2 would gather sighting information after missions if there was anything to report.

Once, when we were escorting bombers to Wewak, New Guinea, we met a similar force of enemy planes over the Ramu Valley heading toward our home base. The Jap bombers aborted and so did ours. A P-38 pilot shot down two enemy bombers and one B-25 in the snafu, where about 100 aircraft met head-on. We held formation with our bombers, which protected them from the Jap fighters, so we fired not a shot but lost no bombers. The S2 had a field day of reports, cross-examining the 16 pilots of my squadron.

With regard to the combat tactics we employed, training for combat really started for me in Primary in a PT-19. The exercise was called aerobatics. Basic involved formation flying, more aerobatics, cross-country, day and night, with navigation. Advanced was more of the same with aerial and ground gunnery. Transition was still more of the same.

The Flying Tigers did a lot of research on Japanese fighter planes which was passed along to us in training, i.e. never try to turn or climb with a Zero—amen! We changed formation flying from staggered close formations to spread out line abreast. This shift facilitated everybody having a total eyeful of the world around us. There was nothing in writing.

In the combat theater we were exposed to lots of instruction from our S2 officers as to what to expect if we engaged enemy aircraft. We were constantly advised to stick together in an engagement. But aerial engagements with the enemy for me were a rarity.

The dismal living conditions at Durand began to take a toll on my health. I had already lost twenty pounds. The food was abominable. We had no refrigeration at all. No fresh meat, veggies, or fruit. We had Aussie canned corned beef daily at two meals and some kind of canned concoction of meat and veggies that was sickening. The cooks made bread daily and I think that was our saving sustenance. The original members of the squadron who started combat the first of July had already lost so much weight that they were being sent to Sydney, Australia for rest and recuperation.

I had several combat missions before I got a chance to see Port Moresby on the ground. That event occurred when I got a registered letter in the mail that required a signature by me, and the local post office would not bring the letter out to 17 Mile. So I had to borrow the C.O.'s car and drive to town. The roads were not paved and it was an arduous task to drive the 17 miles to, and 17 miles from, the post office, which was located on a concrete two-lane street one block long. The letter was from my draft board on 79th Street in Chicago instructing me to report immediately for military service under penalty of law for noncompliance. My C.O. took care of the matter.

The next time I visited town was in a C-47 that we were using to cool beer at 12,000 feet. We invited some ladies from the local hospital to join us in the cooling operation. Fun, fun, fun! Later on, I made a third trip to Port Moresby, for military decorations.

Speaking of the C-47 and beer cooling, I should mention our squadron's "Fat Cat." Fat Cat was a term used by Pacific air squadrons to signify our auxiliary means of getting edible and liquid supplies. Our food situation was the pits and we needed a Fat Cat to fly to Australia for food. The first one we had in the 341FS was when our C.O. traded a P-47 from the squadron for a war weary Douglas P-70 night fighter, an adaptation of the Douglas A-20 Havoc light bomber. There was a night fighter squadron of these planes at Port Moresby, but I was way out at Durand so I never saw them. Night fighter pilots told me that because they flew sans illumination inside or out, when you pulled the trigger you went blind from the flash of the guns, temporarily, of course!

Our "new" P-70 was all black, ugly and slow, loaded to the hilt with night fighting gear. We got two brand new engines in the trade. Captain Dave Campbell was the guy who engineered the swap, a superb leader and fighter pilot who later commanded a P-38 group. He taught me many lessons on staying alive in a fighter aircraft. Unfortunately, he was killed in June 1944, on a mission against a place called Babo in western New Guinea.

Our line people went to work and attacked it with all their expertise to make it back into an A-20 twin-engine machine we could use to fly to Australia. We had three civilian tech reps, all engineers, who also helped in the refurbishing of the P-70. All the armor and guns were removed, along with a ton of ugly black paint, revealing a gorgeous aluminum surface. And once it was stripped down to bare necessities, it was much lighter. We installed the new engines and had a beauty contest winner, a magnificently beautiful plane that was not only good looking but with phenomenal performance, like hum along at 250–260 mph cruise at 30 inches manifold pressure and 2,400 rpm's. This was at sea level with no diving acceleration. I had one ride in it and remember seeing the beauty of the Coral Sea from the bombardier's window, which had the black paint removed by our fabulous ground crew.

It didn't stick around too long, only a few months, because it was too hot of an aircraft for our fighter pilots. Several trips were made to Australia for meat and other goodies before some hot rod fighter pilot busted it up beyond repair in Townsville. What a loss. It was cracked up coming back with a load of beer and meat, some of which was salvaged from the wreck. I think they were sampling the beer.[12]

That's when we got the C-47, a very dependable airplane even in the hands of fighter pilots, who once even ground-looped it with me in the cabin (I was unhurt in the accident). But it was no fun at all compared to the A-20. We got another C-47 later for the 460FS, but they wouldn't let me drive it because I was a known member of the "10,000 Feet Club," a distinguished organization from Port Moresby. Remember that cooling beer incident with the personnel from the Port Moresby general hospital, with no parachutes on board? We had great rapport with the hospital gals because we had beer.

With the beer there was song, and one that sticks out in my unmusical memory is a refrain from the early days in New Guinea:

By a Guinea waterfall, one bright and sunny day,
By the wreckage of his Thunderbolt, the young pursuiter lay
His parachute hung from a nearby tree, he was not yet quite dead,
Now listen here to the very last words this pursuiter said
I'm going to a better land, where everything is right
Where whisky grows on telephone poles, play poker every night
We haven't got a thing to do, but sit around and sing
Where all our crews are women, oh death where is thy sting?

Oh death where is thy sting, oh death where is thy sting?
The bells of hell will ring-a-ling-a-ling for you but not for me

Another song I remember was *"I wish all the girls were like girls down in Sydney."* Alas, we had no records or players, tapes were yet to be invented and the main ingredient of song, booze, was very scarce and non-existent at times. We did have a few radios and listened to Tokyo Rose most of the time. She really served up the most popular recordings of that day.

Life between combat missions was tedious to say the least. We sometimes had poker going 24/7 and bridge games too. The stakes in poker were enormous because we had no place to spend our money; nothing to buy, or sell. Later on at fields near the sea we spent lots of time shooting at floating objects in the ocean, just to pass the time.

I did organize a big party once at Durand. We got five gallons of medical alcohol and several liters of Aussie beer. We had the blowout at the officer's mess, also our club, and induced some nurses to come from the hospital. On the day of the party, however, I drew duty for Officer of the Day, so couldn't even have a drink—bugger! The next morning I had the unpleasant task of rousing out of bed pilots scheduled to fly for duty. This was a very delicate task in one case since one of the nurses had accidentally fallen asleep in a pilot's bed. This took a mountain of tact. You can easily visualize the trials and tribulations of a young second lieutenant fighter pilot in 1943!

AIR BATTLE OVER THE SEA

Part of the 341st Fighter Squadron had been put on temporary duty at Dobodura, New Guinea, in October to enhance the quick response capability of the base. We had an invasion of the Japanese stronghold on New Britain in the works. At noon on the 23rd of October we were sent on patrol duty with 14 Thunderbolts for a convoy of four troop transports and four destroyer-type escort vessels. They were positioned in the Solomon Sea north-northeast of Dobodura, about midway from Dobodura and the middle of the southern coast of New Britain, aiming towards the center of New Britain, approximately 100 miles from the obvious target. This was an invasion convoy heading for the breadbasket of New Britain. The Japanese knew all about what was happening because it was so obvious. This was a sham to divert the enemy forces, probably away from the imminent landings at Bougainville in the northern Solomon Islands, planned for the 1st of November. We were privy to the plan and knew the small task force would be diverted to another location.

Our mission was to cover the convoy for three hours and be relieved by the 340FS. The convoy's fighter intercept controller had the radio call sign "Duckbutt."[13] Ours was "Gambler." This day I flew on the wing of Captain Samuel V. Blair, my former flight commander and now the operations officer for the squadron. For three hours, we watched the convoy zigzagging across a placid sea from our assigned altitude of 25,000 feet. At about 1500 hours, the 340FS called Duckbutt to confirm that they were about to arrive to relieve us; Duckbutt acknowledged and told us our relief was on the way and thank you. We acknowledged the controller and anticipated our relief. We were on a north tack when we spotted about 15 aircraft to our left, flying south, and assumed it was the 340FS having overshot the convoy. As the planes drew near, they suddenly turned toward us. As they did, we recognized them as Jap Zeros.

The Japanese had timed it perfectly. We were asleep at the switch and so was the radar operator on Duckbutt, and about 15 Japanese Navy Zeros were on top of us with no warning. It was my first meeting with Japanese fighters. Captain Sam Blair, whose right wing I was flying, turned toward the Japanese fighters as soon as we recognized them. A lot of things had to be done within a few seconds: full throttle had to be applied, gunsight turned on, gun camera and gun switches activated, and most important, jettison the 200-gallon belly tank which caused great drag on the aircraft. All this had to be accomplished while staying next to the flight leader who was in a maximum left turn. Our turning ability was no match for the highly maneuverable Mitsubishi Zero, probably flown by top Japanese fighter pilots who also had the element of surprise.[14]

Woe to me, my belly tank, which had to be released by hand lever, refused to come off. In my dilemma, I had already lost sight of my flight leader and three Zeroes got the jump on me and were climbing up my tail—two of which were firing their guns at me. I could see the tracers whizzing by and my thought was "adios world!" The only defense was to try and escape by diving out of the fire, so I turned the plane over on its back and pulled straight down in a split-S maneuver to save my bacon while trying to make myself as small as possible behind my armor plate. In seconds the plane accelerated to maximum speed and I was already at 15,000 feet over the Bismarck Sea. A check of my six o'clock position determined that the Japs had broken off their attack on me, so I used my great speed to recover all the altitude I had lost. In my escape from the original Jap attack, my belly tank fell away, maybe prompting the Japs to break off their attack, thinking they had hit me fatally; of course, this is only speculation.

At the top of my recovery climb, I found myself at 28,000 feet and in a position to attack the Japanese. Lo and behold, there were three Zeroes beneath me, perhaps the three that had shot at me. I cleared my three, six and nine o'clock positions, could not see anyone in my squadron and seeing no one else, I pressed Windy City Kitty into a dive to attack them. Targeting the one on the right and furthest back, I attacked. My shots hit and the right wing of the Zero folded. Kill Number One.

Seeing the first Zero incapacitated, I adjusted to shoot the lead plane. This was a deflection shot so the target had to be lead—just like shooting at a duck at 90 degrees. As the bullets flew out to the Zero, they were barely visible over the center of my cowling; the camera got a similar view. I had to pull up to avoid the possibility of ramming the Zero. As I did, I noticed it was now in an uncontrolled tumble, almost sure death. Kill Number Two. The third Zero was now out of sight as my speed carried me out of the mix and I could hear over the radio the chatter of other pilots; the controller reported that the convoy was under attack by torpedo bombers. Maybe 90 seconds had elapsed by this time and I still could not spot any of my comrades.

Peering over my right side I could see nothing but flak. The Navy was firing at anything that moved, including me. Thousands of feet below, I spotted a torpedo bomber on the deck heading for the convoy, so I dove full-speed to try and intercept it before it could launch its weapon. I was already going about 500 mph and moving maybe three or four times faster than the bomber, so catching it didn't appear to be a problem. But the problem was I was going so fast that I would only have a millisecond to fire at the enemy plane. I positioned myself so that I would have a zero deflection shot with the pipper of the gunsight right on the bomber's tail. The 100-mil sight would indicate the correct time to pull the trigger. I had to wait until the wingtips of the enemy plane touched the outer ring of the sight.

As I was preparing to dispatch the bomber, the flak was becoming very intense. The Navy was throwing up everything they had. The bomber and I were on the same course heading right in the center of the eight-ship convoy. As I closed on the target and drew into range, the enemy plane began to fill the gunsight. Just then the navy gunners made a direct hit on it, wiping it out. They almost got me too. I had to traverse all the convoy flak coming up after streaming by the remnants of the torpedo bomber. They did not stop firing; I had to fly through the flak, but I came through untouched and quickly regained altitude and found some other P-47s which I joined to go back to base.

The attack appeared to be over. The fight lasted only a few minutes, and none of our ships were damaged. It appeared that the Jap attack was a failure, having lost seven planes for sure. After rejoining members of my squadron and flying back to Dobodura, the air was filled with chatter about the fight that had just taken place, in less than five minutes. Captain Blair, whose wing I was flying that day, expended all his ammunition immediately in the scrap and had to withdraw. I expended about one third of mine and returned with all guns in operating order.

Several pilots were already claiming victories over the radio. All 14 planes of the 341st were returning to base and several of us did a victory roll over the field to celebrate our aerial victories, including myself.

ACTION OVER FINSCHHAFEN *On October 23, fourteen P-47's from our squadron were patrolling shipping over Finschhafen at 20,000 feet, when they intercepted a dozen enemy fighters. In the ensuing combat five enemy airplanes were definitely destroyed without loss to our side . . . In this interception the enemy used the same four-ship element as our squadron. The enemy seemed largely inexperienced and most of them attempted no other evasive action than gentle diving turns to the left. A few of the enemy pilots seemed eager enough, but by keeping our speed well over 200 MPH, none of them was able to press home any attacks.*—History of the 341st Fighter Squadron, August 1943 through January 1944[15]

It was determined at the debriefing that five Japanese planes were shot down with four probables. Mine were two of the probables because I had no confirmation by other pilots. To get credit for an aerial victory, you had to have an eyewitness plus film.

The gun camera combat films were immediately rushed to development for the intelligence people. We were the last to see the films and intelligence was all agog because the films showed something unusual, which I will explain shortly.

My film was positive for two victories, but I had no witness to verify. My pictures showed the two Zeros getting hit and going out of control, but not the erratic tumbles that occurred after the attacks. Since I was on another attack pattern I did not watch their ultimate demise. My film was good enough to show the arresting hooks on them, which were not discovered until the gun camera films were developed and reviewed. When the tail hooks were detected on the film, it was confiscated by the powers that be and unfortunately never seen again by us—they never returned any of it. I never did get a confirmation on the two Zeros, but from what I observed, I have no doubt about their destruction.

CLAIMS FOR DESTROYED AND PROBABLES *On October 23rd, our squadron consisting of 14 ships intercepted 12 ZEKES and HAMPS at 20,000 feet over Finschhafen. In the ensuing combat 3 ZEKES and 1 HAMP were definitely destroyed and 3 ZEKES and 1 HAMP probably destroyed without damage to any of our ships.*—341FS Combat Evaluation Report for October 1943

What little film the Army let me keep was caught by the ravages of time and disintegrated many years ago, lost forever. I had only one surviving strip showing the destruction of a Sugar Charlie type vessel off the coast of New Guinea near Madang, destroyed by machine gun fire. We were on an escort mission with a PBY at the time we spotted the ship, practically flying on the deck due to inclement weather.

Speaking of film, Colonel Kearby had his own camera mounted on the dashboard next to the gunsight with which he got lots of color film shots. He used the latest Kodak color technology at that time and had phenomenal movies of combat. What happened to the film escapes me and is a mystery.

I discussed the fight with P-38 ace pilot, Dick Bong, because we were at his base at Dobodura. His comment on shooting down Japanese fighters was "get up close so you can't miss," and this about sums up our combat training. It must have been good because I am still here and the 348th did have a nice score at the war's end. With the Jug, we had a big advantage with its eight .50 caliber machine guns.

It was fall season and 1943 was drawing to a close. We had eaten our evening rations, which were not much different than what we ate at Durand Airstrip in Port Moresby: dehydrated potatoes, meat, and vegetable stew from cans, and bread. Dobodura, our temporary billet, did offer one amenity—an air mattress with a sheet to sleep on.

As I tucked my mosquito bar under the mattress my day's activities still rumbled around in my mind. My adrenaline rush from the day's battle had finally ceased and my body felt normal again. I started to realize what had occurred today. I had taken the life of another human being, possibly two. The gravity of this barbaric act was beginning to settle in. I had no opinion on the Jap Navy pilots other than they were doing their job, which was to protect their bombers, and which ultimately failed to hit any of our ships.

My thoughts turned to the families of the Japanese flyers who had perished that day. What were they going to feel when the sad news arrived? It would be just as bad for them as it would be for my parents if the situation was reversed. My feelings were really bad and no amount of reasoning seemed to alleviate my profound assessment of the events of the day. Sleep finally arrived and we got through the night without a bombing raid for a change.

Although Japanese air attacks were rare in the daytime, the nights were another matter. The Japanese did not mount night raids with a big number of planes, being more prone to keep us awake all night with a constant stream of one-plane raids. These raids were remarkably effective in causing stress as well as inflicting considerable damage to installations. Thus ended the day of October 23rd, 1943.

Combat with the enemy reminded me of seeing some Japanese prisoners, whom were seldom captured during the war. I recall one time when 12 were captured near Dobodura and turned over to the Aussie MPs. Their condition didn't look very good, and they had to be transported back to Port Moresby where there were interpreters. The Aussies loaded them onto a C-47 transport plane for the journey over the Owen Stanley Mountains. As the story goes, 11 of them escaped by jumping out of the plane as it crossed the mountains. So much for the Aussie MPs. I often wonder how the Japanese would have treated us if the situation was reversed.

The next morning, our intelligence officer told us the impact of our combat films. The chief thing was that the frames revealed that the planes were Japanese fighters capable of landing on an aircraft carrier. This revelation alarmed the high command, thinking there might be a Jap carrier task force out there undetected; it put the Navy and Army on a state of super alert. They now had reconnaissance planes searching everywhere, looking for the Japanese carriers that they suspected because of our combat film.

The high command was so concerned because we had numerous ships in the area poised for attack on a beachhead that was not disclosed to us. We knew the convoy with Duckbutt was heading for the middle of New Britain, where the Japanese had their huge naval base at Rabaul on the north end of the island. Reconnaissance had determined that the Japs were going all out to defend the area where our small task force was headed. As things turned out, no enemy task force appeared; we had no casualties on our ships during the very successful diversion by our combined forces. I sometimes think that we as a nation were very lucky to have survived World War II.

OCTOBER COMBAT MISSIONS *During the month we have performed normal escort missions for transports and medium bombers, convoy patrol, strafing missions and fighter sweeps to Wewak and Hoskins.*—341FS Combat Evaluation Report for October 1943

By the end of October I had flown another dozen combat missions. Soon November came around and our missions became more diversified. The high command had its eyes on New Britain, where we were called upon to strafe ground targets that were designated by a smoke marker. Since we didn't see any specific target, we saturated the area with heavy machine gun fire. The results were not visible to us, but the reports we got back from the infantry were satisfying.

NADZAB

On 7 November 1943, I was about to taxi out for takeoff on a local mission at Nadzab when a red alert sounded. The control tower called for a scramble, so we all raced as fast as possible to the takeoff end of the strip. I was about seventh in line to take off; I could see the tower blinking a green light at me, so I poured on the coal to my heavily laden plane.

As I was gathering speed down the runway, bombs started to explode all around with a deafening roar. Fortunately, none hit the runway so I was airborne with instructions to get the Jap bombers. With full military power applied, my P-47 clawed for altitude. The enemy was at 20,000 feet, heading for Rabaul, New Britain. There were eight of us in the chase, all flying at maximum power. We got to 26,000 feet so fast that many of us suffered bends from the rapidly changing air pressure. Try as we could, we couldn't find the Japanese planes. We searched all the way to Cape Gloucester, New Britain, where we exhausted our fuel and had to return to base.

On return to Nadzab, we found no damage to our living area but lots around the airstrip. This was the result of another radar goof-up. We had no warning of the raid so the Japs escaped unharmed, and they scared the crap out of us. Our radar was still very crude by today's standards. We then visited the flight surgeon. The discomfort from the rapid ascent was minimal, but had to be reported to the flight surgeon.[16]

DOBODURA

Sometime in mid-November, my flight was sent to Durand from our position at Dobodura. It was already late in the day so we were bound to have a tough time crossing the Owen Stanley Mountains. The flight leader got disoriented in the clouds, resulting in us flying between peaks with cloud cover all around. We got up some draws so steep that full power was necessary to keep from stalling. Several times I had to hang on my prop at full military power to negotiate canyons. At 300-gallons per hour, we were rapidly using up our fuel reserves. Things kept getting worse, and I was sure that this was the bitter end.

Fortunately, we finally broke out of the clouds in the Ramu Valley about a hundred miles north of where we should have been. There was no place to land other than Tsili Tsili, a very short dirt strip. We found it still under construction, and made an emergency landing. My fuel gauge was at empty as we approached the tiny strip, but as I was number four to land, I had to wait while the others got down. As the third plane touched down, my engine sputtered, signaling that I was out of fuel. I lowered my flaps to slow the plane down, but kept my wheels up to extend my glide, which looked like it might be a few hundred yards short. I had a good lineup so I prayed that I wouldn't stall.

At the last minute, I dropped the landing gear and as soon as it clicked and locked into position, I touched the very end of the runway for a safe "deadstick" landing. As my fuel was exhausted there on the runway, they had to call for a jeep to tow me to a parking area. I was so shaken by the experience that I had a difficult time filling out the Form 1. We had to rest overnight as it was too late to fly back to Port Moresby with the afternoon clouds over the Owen Stanleys, plus the plane had to be refueled; I slept in the cockpit.

Refueling was a problem because the fuel had to be pumped by hand from 55-gallon barrels. It took six drums, some 300 gallons, to fill the internal tanks, which was half the load of a C-47 that flew gas into Tsili Tsili. We had a hand pump designed for 55-gallon barrels, standard issue from the Quartermaster. The pump screwed into the top opening of the barrel, the nozzle end of the hose fit into the tank filler neck of the plane, and then with a manual back and forth motion on the pump, the contents were pumped into the plane. I had help from ground personnel who complained that the tanks were too big. I can't recall the amount of time the pumping took, but we took turns. Wrestling the drums took help.

We were soon back at the new 10,000-foot long airstrip at Dobodura. The flight leader got his rear chewed by the C.O., and his wingmen, including me, declined to fly with him again after getting us lost. My records do not reveal any of this experience, for reasons I do not know. I was pissed off at our flight leader for a long time for getting us into a mess, especially since it was never my habit to get lost. Negotiation of the Owen Stanleys always posed a problem because of the intense buildup of clouds in the afternoon; the tops of the clouds there are in the stratosphere daily.

In the month of November 1943, I was on temporary duty at Dobodura, when another pilot and I made a deal with a B-26 crew to fly to Port Moresby for a party. We made two takeoffs in the B-26, the second one being the trip to Port Moresby. It ended shortly after takeoff due to engine failure, resulting in an emergency landing at Dobodura that ended in a landing gear collapse and overshooting the runway with serious damage to the aircraft. No one was injured seriously. The event was entered into my records, but there seems to be an error in the typing of the date. I cannot recall the names of the B-26 crew but the squadron was part of the "Great Silver Fleet."[17]

Major David A. Campbell was the commanding officer of the 341st Fighter Squadron, followed by Captain John T. Moore. Campbell was a little older than most of us, about 26 or 27. He was very popular with all the squadron personnel and also with his contemporaries in the other squadrons and group command. He participated in fighter sweeps with Colonel Kearby, the Group C.O. and had shot down a few Japs.

A CHANGE OF COMMAND *A farewell party for Major David A. Campbell, Commanding Officer of the squadron, was given on 20 November 1943 at Port Moresby. Major Campbell left to become Executive Officer of the 49th Fighter Group. Captain John T. Moore succeeded Major Campbell as squadron commander.—341FS, August 1943–January 1944*

Our group commander, Neel E. Kearby, was a colonel who commanded the group from its start in October 1942, into mid-November 1943. He was age 32 when he was shot down several months later, on March 5, 1944. Many of us young whippersnappers thought he should have been grounded from combat; we were all getting old ourselves, like 24.

HEADQUARTERS
V FIGHTER COMMAND / APO 929
20 November 1943
TO: All Officers and Enlisted Men:
Headquarters, 348th Fighter Group
340th Fighter Squadron
341st Fighter Squadron
342nd Fighter Squadron

I would like to express my pride in, and appreciation to, every member of the 348th Fighter Group.

During the demanding months of organization and training, during the equally trying move overseas, and today in a combat theater, you have and are performing your duties as individuals united to form a combat team.

The pilots of the 348th Group have already written a battle record unique in any theater of war.

I am proud of them for an aggressive, determined attitude which has consistently overcome the difficulties of terrain, and of an enemy numerically superior wherever the enemy has been met.

I am equally proud of the officers and men who comprise our ground elements.

Your task lacks the glamour and constant action of the air echelon but your contribution to this organization cannot be over-emphasized.

Your individual will, loyalty, and cooperation has been one of the outstanding characteristics of the Group.

The combat record you have already established will be hard to better. But as I was once confident you could establish that record, now I am confident you will break it wide open.

Good luck to you all.

Sincerely,

NEEL E. KEARBY, Colonel, Air Corps[18]

By the end of November I had added another 17 combat missions to my credit. With the capture of Nadzab, the Ramu Valley was secure; the Tsili Tsili airstrip, which had served its purpose, was no longer needed. Finschhafen, on the tip of the Huon Peninsula across from Cape Glouces-ter, New Britain, was now in striking distance for our ground troops. Fifth Fighter Command started to send us up the northeast side of Dutch New Guinea.

NOVEMBER COMBAT MISSIONS *During the past month we have performed normal escort missions for medium and heavy bombers, strafing B-25s and A-20s, dive bombers and photo planes. In addition we have patrolled areas, shipping and flown intercept missions and strafed.*—341FS Combat Evaluation Report for November 1943

NOTES

1. The very next day after Lt. Schrik's loss in P-47D-2-RE, serial number 42-8108 (the first 348th Fighter Group casualty in the combat zone), 16 August 1943, the 341st Fighter Squadron claimed its first aerial victory on the first day of aerial combat for the 348th Fighter Group. While escorting C-47 transports, the squadron intercepted enemy fighters attempting to attack the transports as they landed at the forward airfield at Tsili Tsili. Second Lieutenant Wilburn S. Henderson destroyed one Oscar-type enemy fighter (according to squadron history, but not apparently officially credited). Second Lieutenant Leonard O. Leighton then destroyed one Zeke-type fighter (officially credited), but himself fell victim to another enemy fighter, becoming the squadron and group's first loss in air-to-air combat. "From this unfortunate loss, the all-essential lesson of staying in at least a two-ship element was impressed upon the other pilots of the squadron for their mutual protection." These two 341FS losses showed the need for a ready supply of replacement pilots in overseas combat units.

   History of the 341st Fighter Squadron, Chapter III, (August 1943 thru January 1944).

   Baugher, Joseph F., "1942 USAAF Serial Numbers (42-001 to 42-30031)," http://www.joebaugher.com/usaf_serials/1942_1.html

2. Durand Drome was named after 1st Lt. Edward D. Durand, USAAF, a P-39 Airacobra pilot in the 35th Pursuit Squadron, 8th Pursuit Group, who was lost in action during an attack against Lae Airfield on April 30, 1942. He is remembered on the Tablets of the Missing at the Manila American Cemetery, Manila, Philippines. He was awarded the Distinguished Service Cross and the Purple Heart.

   "P-39F-1-BE Airacobra Serial Number 41-7128," http://www.pacificwrecks.com/aircraft/p-39/41-7128.html

   "17 Mile Drome (Durand, Waigani)," http://www.pacificwrecks.com/airfields/png/17-mile/

   "Edward D. Durand," http://www.abmc.gov/search-abmc-burials-and-memorializations/detail/WWII_105420#.VB3f2hbLBOI

3. This was 341FS Mission Number 35, 26 August 1943, Escort cover for transports landing at Marilinan. Eight P-47D-2's that took off at 1148 in the morning on a mission that lasted one hour in duration. It was incomplete, likely due to weather. The next day, Curran took off at 0807 local time to fly on Mission Number 36, a 12 P-47-strong escort mission for transports going to Tsili Tsili Airfield (see description below in footnote 4). It was a successfully completed mission of three hours duration. Marilinan Airfield was a few miles southeast of Tsili Tsili. It was an emergency strip and also served to confuse the Japanese about Allied airfield construction and purposes. It was originally established prewar, but in June 1943, US Army

871st Airborne Engineers expanded and improved the facility.

341st Fighter Squadron (341FS) Weekly Status and Operations Report (Form 34), (Report for Period 8/22/43 to 8/28/43 Inclusive), page 2.

"Marilinan Airfield," http://pacificwrecks.com/airfields/png/marilinan/

4. Tsili Tsili Airfield was used as a forward airfield for operations against the Japanese stronghold in the Lae area, and was about 40 miles away from Lae. It was a quickly-constructed airfield, established by the 871st Airborne Engineers in mid-June, 1943. Curran's bomber escort was Mission Number 54, "Escort Bombers to Lae & Malahang" on 6 September 1943, 16 P-47's that took off at 0830 and flew a 3.3-hour mission, successfully completed. The intercept mission was Mission Number 59, 7 September 1943, with a takeoff at 1650 by eight Thunderbolts. The mission was of 50 minutes duration, with nil sightings of the enemy.

"Tsili Tsili Airfield," http://pacificwrecks.com/airfields/png/tsili-tsili/index.html

341FS Weekly Status and Operations Report (Form 34), (Report for Period 9/5/43 to 9/11/43 Inclusive), page 1.

5. The AAF Form 34 was a report that captured essential statistics about the missions a given air unit accomplished. For each mission it recorded such items as the number of planes employed, flying time, types and number of weapons and ammunition expended, fuel and oil consumed, as well as losses and mission results. The Form 34 replaced earlier fragmentary and uneven reports from combat theaters with a worldwide standard for recording vital operational statistics.

Wesley F. Craven and James L. Cate, Editors. *The Army Air Forces in World War II, Volume VI, Men and Planes.* Chicago, IL: University of Chicago Press, 1955. (Hereinafter Craven, et al, *The Army Air Forces in World War II*), Chapter 2, "The AAF," page 38.

For a detailed discussion of the origins and use of the Form 34, see *Statistical Control in the Army Air Forces, Air Historical Studies No: 57.* Maxwell AFB, AL: USAF Historical Division, Air University, January, 1952. Chapter VI, The Statistical Control Reporting System, Combat Operations Report, pages 84–87.

6. This was 341FS Mission 97-3, seven P-47's that took off at 0808 on a mission to escort transports to Nadzab which lasted 3.6 hours. "On returning 1 plane made water landing. Pilot found OK on Tuesday 10/12."

341FS Weekly Status and Operations Report (Form 34), (Report for Period 10/10/43 to 10/16/43 Inclusive), page 1.

For more on this incident and survival experience involving John Lolos and the ditching of his P-47D-2-RE "Hi-Topper," serial number 42-8081, see the 2009 interview of him at "John Lolos—348th Fighter Group P-47 Pilot," http://www.pacificwrecks.com/aircraft/p-47/42-8081/index.html

7. It is unclear if what Jim Curran recalled describes the 22 October 1943 loss of 341FS pilot 1st Lt. Harold Jacoby, reported missing in P-47D-2-RE Thunderbolt serial number 42-8117 on an escort mission for B-25s attacking Wewak. Lieu-

tenant Jacoby, who entered the service from Oregon, remains missing until today. He is remembered on the Tablets of the Missing at the Manila American Cemetery in Manila, Philippines. Lieutenant Jacoby received the Purple Heart and the Air Medal for his service and sacrifice in World War II.

On the same day and mission, another 348FG pilot experienced a similar dire situation. Lt. Wynans E. Frankfort of the 342FS saw another P-47 ditch in a small lake on a B-25 escort mission that really stretched the Thunderbolt's endurance. A few minutes later, Frankfort bailed out of P-47D-2-RA serial number 42-22497 due to fuel exhaustion. He landed in a tall tree, then managed to get himself down with some injury, and trekked along the Fly River for two days before meeting some friendly natives, and a few days later was returned to friendly forces.

"Harold Jacoby," http://www.abmc.gov/search-abmc-burials-and-memorializa-tions/detail/WWII_114641#.VFL_tMnLBOJ

"P-47D-2-RE Thunderbolt Serial Number 42-8117," http://www.pacificwrecks.com/aircraft/p-47/42-8117.html

"P-47D-2-RA Thunderbolt Serial Number 42-22497 Nose 57," http://www.paci-ficwrecks.com/aircraft/p-47/42-22497.html

Jacoby was not the only 341FS pilot to go missing over New Guinea, albeit under very different circumstances. Probably the last one to go missing over the big island was 1st Lt. Harold F. "Junior" Wurtz, Jr. In May 1945, Lieutenant Wurtz, who appears to have been still assigned to the 341st Fighter Squadron in the Philippines at the time, was at Nadzab Airfield, where the FEAF Combat Replacement Training Center was located. In the afternoon of 12 May 1945, he took off in a P-47D from Nadzab with a passenger, Miss Harriet E. Gowen, American Red Cross nurse, for a local area flight. The two never returned, and a three-day search failed to find any sign of them. They remained missing until 1996, when Papuan natives found their crash site, five miles from the airfield they had taken off from in 1945. Their remains were recovered by the US Army Central Identification Laboratory Hawaii (CILHI) in 1998 and subsequently identified, and both were buried with honors at Arlington National Cemetery in 1999.

"Harold F. Wurtz, Jr. / Harriet E. Gowen," http://projecthomecoming.org/sto-ries_WurtzGowen.html

"Harold F. Wurtz, Jr. / Harriet E. Gowen," http://www.arlingtoncemetery.net/mys-tery.htm

8. "Windy City Kitty's" nose art was based on the Vargas work titled "Military Secrets," from the gatefold section of the September 1943 issue of *Esquire* magazine. Apparently this particular artwork, and some other Vargas pieces, was the basis for the Postmaster General of the US failed efforts in 1943 to deny *Esquire* second-class postage because of obscenity. The issue went all the way up to the Supreme Court, which decided in *Esquire*'s favor in 1946.

"Alberto Vargas: the Esquire Pinups," http://www.spencerart.ku.edu/exhibitions/

vargas/labels.shtml

"Esquire," http://www.britannica.com/EBchecked/topic/192802/Esquire

9. Chicago-based Austenal Laboratories, Inc., expanded from precision casting of dental and surgical appliances into aircraft engine superchargers with their superior castings after General Electric requested their help in order to improve manufacturing practices for greatly expanded wartime production demands.

Dempsey, Paul M., *Supercharger Development in the US During the Inter-War Period*, http://www.enginehistory.org/Piston/InterWarSCdev/InterWarSCdev.shtml

10. History of the 342nd Fighter Squadron, Chapter III, (July 1, 1943 to January 31, 1944), Enclosure 9, "War Department General Order No. 3," January 6, 1944.

11. As the war continued, some intelligence resources for aircrew improved. Subjects like this are not often well-covered in general histories, but are important to understand the various factors which contributed to American aircrew readiness in the air war. One example is found in the History of the 341st Fighter Squadron for October 1944, a year or so from this comment about aircraft recognition training with silhouettes of enemy planes. It was probably shared in the other squadrons in the group. As the 341st history relates: "The squadron intelligence section received seventy-eight discs, each showing kodachrome views of Allied and enemy aircraft as seen through a gunsight ring. The underlying principle of these views, part of Sawyer View-Master, is to combine training in range estimation and deflection (the main purpose) with recognition (secondary purpose). Each view of a particular plane is seen through a luminous ring representing the standard seventy mil ring sight. As the disc is rotated each view presents the plane at a different range and deflection. One disadvantage of the Sawyer View-Master is that all the views on each disc are of one particular aircraft, although at different ranges and deflections. It is felt that the views on each disc should be of a different plane, still with different ranges and deflection. Another drawback of the Sawyer View-Master gadget is that only one person can look at the view at one time. To overcome these disadvantages a theoretical combination of the above principle with the Renshaw slide and screen method of presentation has been worked out. If the views were taken off the discs and put on slides that could be projected on a screen, not one but many persons could be taught simultaneously. The Renshaw method of split-second identification of aircraft and ships has been tried and proved by both the Air Forces and the Navy. The Renshaw method, using a 35mm projector with screen, is designed for classroom work.

The first difficulty to be overcome in adapting the View-Master views to the Renshaw slides is that of transferring the 16mm kodachrome views to 35mm slides that can be used in the projector. Once the views of the planes are transferred from discs to 35mm 2" by 2" slides, a more thorough course of instruction in recognition and gunnery could be presented to a greater number of persons at the same time.

From informal interviews with the pilots of this squadron who have been trained in the Renshaw split-second method of aircraft identification and who have been in combat with the enemy aircraft, this proposed combination has found great favor. The pilots stated that it would be the best method of instruction in recognition and gunnery that they had seen or experienced. They hoped that something would materialize soon from the idea. Only technical difficulties, as having the facilities for transferring the 16mm views to 35mm slides, have prevented the squadron from carrying the idea through experiment to completion."

History of the 341st Fighter Squadron, Chapter XII, October 1944, pp. 2–4.

12. Jim Curran recalls the P-70 Fat Cat during his service with the 341FS. But it is possible that this recollection could be of the A-20 that was assigned to his later squadron, the 460FS at Nadzab in the summer of 1944. A later date might make more sense, in that by August 1944, the Northrop P-61 Black Widow night fighter entered service in the Pacific, replacing the P-70 in that role, thus making the P-70 an excess aircraft and available for something like "Fat Cat" service.

History of the 460th Fighter Squadron (SE), Chapter II, (1 August 1944–31 August 1944), p. 4.

McFarland, Stephen L. *Conquering the Night: Army Air Forces Night Fighters at War.* Washington, DC: Air Force History and Museums Program, 1988, page 36.

For additional information and images of a typical unit "Fat Cat" see the Douglas A-20 appropriately named "STEAK and EGGS" flown in the 3rd Attack Group in sources at:

"A-20A "Little Hellion / The Steak & Eggs Serial Number 40-166," http://www.pacificwrecks.com/aircraft/a-20/40-166.html

"Crash landing of an A-20 Havoc on a beach on Low Woody Island on 11 June 1944," http://www.ozatwar.com/ozcrashes/qld231.htm

13. "Duckbutt" was the radio call sign for the fighter direction team embarked on the US Navy destroyer USS *Reid* (DD-369). The *Reid* performed the fighter direction role in a number of operations in the New Guinea area in 1943 as part of "MacArthur's Navy," as the US 7th Fleet came to be called during World War II.

Reid began her aircraft lookout warning role after a suggestion from an Australian wing commander provided a solution to the air warning problem affecting the September 1943 amphibious landing near Lae, which was outside of land-based radar coverage. The Australian officer suggested a destroyer stationed in between Lae and Finschhafen would afford better radar coverage of the landing area and approaches than any land based station. *Reid* was selected to serve as the early warning picket at a position some 45 miles southeast of Finschhafen.

"On the destroyer were two controllers (one was a Capt W.M. Ball) and two signal corps enlisted men armed with radar and radio sets, two loudspeakers, two voice receivers, two voice transmitters, and two SCR-188 receivers. With this equipment the controllers were in a position to monitor the normal radio channels of the fighter sectors, including the one which transmitted information to "the General's Board at Moresby." In this way, they would be warned of the approach of aircraft picked up by (other) radar sets in addition to those on the destroyer. Then with grease pencils they could record all suspicious plots on gridded maps covered with plexiglass."

Reid repeated her Lae performance, which had resulted in successful intercept of Japanese raiders, for the Finschhafen landings of 22 September 1943. Captain Ball and his crew successfully directed elements of five fighter squadrons, including the 341st Fighter Squadron, to fend off Japanese raiders at Finschhafen.

On the day of Jim Curran's aerial engagement of 23 October 1943, USS *Reid* was escorting a convoy of three LST and fleet tug USS *Sonoma* (AT-12). Two YMS and four SC accompanied the ships and served as an inner screen while *Reid* and destroyers *Perkins, Smith, Mugford Drayton, Mahan,* provided the escort to ward off submarine and air attack. *Reid,* with embarked fighter direction team "Duck-butt," thus took part as the fighter controller in this air-sea battle. *Reid* fired on aircraft several times between 1050 and 1108 that morning, correlating to the time when Jim Curran engaged enemy fighters.

During *Reid's* three-month tour in the SWPA with the fighter direction team aboard, "Duckbutt" claimed credit for the destruction of 93 enemy aircraft via the fighter direction team embarked. *Reid* was "adopted" by Fifth Air Force and designated as the 25th Fighter Sub-sector.

Unfortunately, *Reid* succumbed to enemy air attack while escorting LCI's and LSM's to Ormoc Bay, Philippines, on 11 December 1944. With four Marine Corsairs above, she fought against a ten aircraft attack, but was crashed and bombed several times and sank with 103 members of the crew, guns firing, in two minutes time, taking seven of the enemy with her in the brief but violent fight. The landing craft in the convoy picked up her 150 survivors.

To consider the contribution of warships such as USS *Reid*, consider the following introduction from the summary of her wartime service: "During three years of war in the Pacific, she steamed 220,000 miles, fired nearly 10,000 rounds of five inch projectiles, participated in thirteen landings, sixteen shore bombardments, shot down at least seventeen planes, sank one Jap submarine and five landing barges, and captured eight Jap prisoners. The *Reid* roamed the Pacific from San Francisco to within 1,000 miles of Tokyo and from the Bering Sea to Botany Bay."
Email from Mr. Leonard Gardner, *USS Reid Association,* 22 February 2012, Subject: "USS *Reid* and fighter control in 1943."
The Fifth Air Force in the Huon Peninsula Campaign, January to October 1943, Chapter VIII, SALAMAUA TO FINSCHAVEN, 1 SEPTEMBER–2 OCTOBER, pp. 202–225.
USS Reid, *War Diary, October 1943*

Porter, R.C., Jr. *War record of the USS* Reid *(DD369), Narrative of.* 31 December 1944.

"USS *Reid,* History," http://www.ussreid369.org/History.htm

"USS *Reid,*" http://en.wikipedia.org/wiki/USS_Reid_%28DD-369%29

14. This incident involved land-based Japanese naval aircraft which James Curran encountered just before the first week in November 1943, when the Japanese Navy initiated Operation "Ro," a series of attacks against American forces invading Bougainville in the Solomon Islands. For this operation, Japanese naval aircraft from fleet carriers *Shokaku, Zuikaku* and *Zuiho* were sent from the Japanese base at Truk, in the Caroline Islands, to airfields on Rabaul, between 28 October and 1 November. The prospective movement of these Japanese aircraft carriers and their air groups would account for the alarm at the possible presence of carrier aircraft (and presumably their carriers too) in the combat zone. However, the Japanese carriers remained at Truk. Earlier in 1943, the Japanese Navy had conducted a similar operation (Operation "I" in early April 1943), sending aircraft from their carriers at Truk to land bases at Rabaul in order to conduct attacks on American forces at Guadalcanal and Allied forces in Papua New Guinea.

"IJN Zuikaku ("Happy Crane"): Tabular Record of Movement," http://www.combinedfleet.com/Zuikak.htm

Shaw, Henry I. and Kane, Douglas T., Major, USMC. *Isolation of Rabaul.* Washington, DC: Historical Branch, G-3 Division, Headquarters, US Marine Corps, 1963, Chapter 3, Knockout by Torokina, pp. 481–482.

15. This was 341FS Mission Number 111-1, 14 P-47's that took off at 0825 to patrol the Finschhafen area. The engagement occurred at 1040. The mission lasted a total of 3.5 hours. 341FS Weekly Status and Operations Report (Form 34), (Report for Period 10/17/43 to 10/23/43 Inclusive).

In this 23 October air battle, Captains Kenneth M. Briggs of Binghamton, N.Y., and Samuel V. Blair of Minneapolis, Minn., destroyed one (1) Zeke and one (1) Hamp respectively; Lieutenants Samuel Galik, Jr., of River Rouge, Mich., one (1) Zeke; Eugene F. Spencer of Highland Park, Mich., one (1) Zeke); and James L. Rowe, one (1) Hamp."

History of the 341st Fighter Squadron, Chapter III, (August 1943 thru January 1944), p. 4.

16. This description correlates with a raid on Nadzab Airfield by Japanese Army Air Force bombers and fighters. Jim Curran's flight log shows a 7 November 1943 intercept mission of two hours duration. The 341FS Form 34 covering that day recorded three scramble missions at Nadzab against enemy planes, the first being Mission 129-1, "Interception at Nadzab (Saidor)," takeoff at 0755 local time on a 2.4 hours flight reaching 22,000 feet with two aircraft, coordinated with another pair from the 342FS. They were vectored against five HAMP fighters, but the report, an abstract of Table III from the Form 34, says in the remarks "Attack on 5

Hamps over Saidor," with no indication of enemy or friendly loss on the mission. Next was 129-2, "Scramble at Nadzab—Enemy planes," with takeoff at 0755 local time by 12 P-47's which made it as far up as 22,000 feet with a flight duration of 2.1 hours. Time of (attempted?) engagement was listed as 0815. The remarks section is largely illegible on the AFHRA CD copy, but appears to end with ". . . no interception." The second recorded was Mission 129-3, "Scramble at Nadzab— Enemy planes," with a 1240 takeoff local time by 12 P-47's which made it as far up as 25,000 feet during a flight duration of 1.5 hours. Time of (attempted) engagement was listed as 1320. In difficult to read remarks, it said "15 Hamps sighted. No contact could be made."

341FS Weekly Status and Operations Report (Form 34), Report for 7 Nov. 1943 to 13 Nov. 1943 Inclusive).

A 342FS Narrative Combat Report of 8 November 1943 (Enclosure 15 to the History of the 342nd Fighter Squadron, Chapter III, (July 1, 1943 to January 31, 1944) described the aftermath of the raid as a flight of four P-47D-2's (two from the 341FS, two from the 342FS) took off from Port Moresby at 0715 for Nadzab, where they planned to refuel before making a sweep against Wewak. En route they observed the bombs exploding at Nadzab in the distance as they approached, and then pursued the retiring enemy aircraft and engaged enemy fighters in the vicinity of Saidor between 0855 and 0915 local time, landing at Nadzab at 0930L. Their report indicated the flight downed four enemy aircraft described as HAMPs, with Lt. Col. Robert R. Rowland claiming two, Capt. Samuel V. Blair one and Capt. Frank G. Oksala, one. Capt. Edward F. Roddy narrowly avoided taking a friendly P-39 under fire when he noted the white elevator on the aircraft and managed only a snap shot at a HAMP, which eluded his fire.

This 7 November 1943 Nadzab raid is described in some detail at the Pacific Wrecks website as nine Ki-21 SALLY with Ki-43 OSCAR and Ki-61 TONY fighters from several units as escort. Sixteen American aircraft on the ground were destroyed or damaged in the raid. This account did not give a time of day for the raid. The perspective of the personnel on the receiving end of the attack on the ground is covered in Edwards Park's historical fiction account of the air war in the Southwest Pacific *Nanette,* pages 180–182, as well as his memoir *Angel's Twenty: A Young American Flyer a Long Way from Home,* pp. 137–142.

"Japanese Missions against Nadzab, November 7, 1943," http://www.pacificwrecks. com/airfields/png/nadzab/missions-nadzab.html

Park, Edwards. *Nanette.* New York, NY: W.W. Norton & Company, 1977.

Park, Edwards. *Angel's Twenty: A Young American Flyer a Long Way from Home.* New York, NY: McGraw-Hill, 1997.

17. This may have been the aborted flight of 22nd Bomb Group, 19th Bomb Squadron Martin B-26-MA Marauder serial number 40-1368, which crashed on takeoff at Dobodura on September 8, 1943. The aircraft, flown by pilot Captain

Ralph P. Higgins, had an engine fire. Higgins was able to decelerate the aircraft before it cracked up and all aboard escaped without injury. While flying this same aircraft on June 4, 1942, then Lt. Higgins survived a collision with a Japanese Zero over Papua New Guinea. Jim Curran's flight record for November 1943, indicates a B-26 flight on 3 November, but the entry is made after the 14 November flight entry, suggesting perhaps it was a retroactive entry with a possibly erroneous date. The author could find no other B-26 mishap on 3 November 1943 such as Jim Curran described.

"Accident of B-26 serial number 40-1368 on 8 Sep 1943," http://www.b26marauders.com/Roster.aspx

"USAAF 40-1368 Martin B-26-MA Marauder," http://asisbiz.com/il2/B-26-Marauder/1940001368.html

"B-26 Crash 5th November 1942 at Maroondan near Gin Gin," http://lists.topica.com/lists/OzCrashes/read/message.html?sort=t&mid=813889381

18. History of the 342nd Fighter Squadron, Chapter III, (July 1, 1943 to January 31, 1944), Enclosure 18, "Letter from Col. Kearby," 20 November 1943.

Chapter Five

R&R IN AUSTRALIA

DECEMBER 1943 WAS UPON US AND I HAD LOST 30 POUNDS from my August weight. After flying 45 combat missions the flight surgeon deemed it was time for me to get out of New Guinea for a few days. Orders were cut for me to fly by ATC to Sydney, Australia on/about December 6th, for seven days of leave, excluding the travel time to and from. I packed my parachute bag with cigarettes, which we got for no charge, and headed for Australia.

Shortly before I went on R&R, one of our pilots had an engine failure on the first turn off Durand airstrip. I saw him bail out and disappear into the jungle. No word was heard from him prior to my leaving for Sydney. After my leave, I learned that he made it back to the airstrip in a little over a week. When he stumbled out of the jungle he was barely able to move. He was completely dehydrated, covered with sores, insect bites, with his clothes in tatters. He had lost all of his survival equipment except for his bolo knife which he had tied to his wrist with parachute cord. He had to chop every inch of his way out of the jungle. He related he could hear the planes on the strip all the time. It was estimated that he was only one to two miles from the strip when he went down. His terrifying experience earned him a trip stateside, and out of combat for the duration.

From Port Moresby to Townsville, we flew on to Brisbane, where we stayed overnight. C-47 transports were the north and south mode of transportation. Eagle Farm Airfield was the drop-off point. I had two parachute bags with me, loaded with cigarettes, which were trade items in Sydney. I recall the loadmaster beefed about my excessive luggage.

We renewed old acquaintances at Eagle Farm RAAF base and joined the Aussies for beer at their officer's club. We stayed with them until the beer ran out, about 2300 hours.

The next morning we were on our way to Sydney. The flight was long and bumpy, but Sydney Harbor and the city finally came into view. It was one of the most beautiful places I had ever seen. Upon landing we were bused to Kings Cross, where the headquarters for people on rest and recuperation could find guidance.[1] We got clothing coupons good for anything made out of cloth. My uniforms no longer fit because of the weight loss, so I needed new pants, shoes and shirts. A blouse wasn't necessary because in December, it was now summer down under. Bed sheets were a necessary find to take back to New Guinea, plus an air mattress to call my own.

The squadron had rented a four-bedroom apartment near Kings Cross, so we got our ration of beer, six liters, and taxied to the apartment. Four officers from the squadron were already there, so the first night I had to sleep on the couch. A party was in full swing when I arrived so I joined right in. The other men all had dates with charming young Aussie girls who seemed to be ultra-friendly. They told me to go to the Royal Australian Hotel next day where all the Aussie girls came to meet service men. The party, broken only by a quick visit to the nearest restaurant, lasted till the wee hours, when fatigue finally overcame me.

The next day I was up early in spite of little rest. First stop was a grill where I introduced myself to the great traditional Aussie breakfast of T-bone steak and eggs, pronounced, "Stike n eigs!" Next was the tailor who had me in new clothes in 30 minutes. Next, I got my sheets and made arrangements to meet the bootlegger to sell my cigarettes. This was not a cash transaction. It was a trade for Scotch Whiskey and champagne. With that accomplished, I headed in my new togs to the hotel to see if I could get a date with one of these attractive Aussie girls.

The Royal Australian Hotel was very modern in central Sydney, accessible by tram from eastern Sydney. It was already after noon when I entered the lounge to find it packed with military personnel and their prospective dates. Everybody seemed to be paired off, so I just ordered a beer and watched the activities.[2]

The beer we got in Sydney was made by the Sydney Brewing Company, in one-liter bottles with the sub-head "Triple XXX Bitter." It was the best beer I ever tasted and packed a wallop—one liter spun your top. That was the drink of '43 and early '44. After that, we got canned beer from the States which was wet—that's all I can say for it—and was rationed out in dribbles. Our main problem was getting it cold. We had no refrigeration in those days except in hospitals. War is hell!

Finally, I strode into the lobby and spotted a comely, exquisitely dressed young lady sitting alone. Summing up my nerve, I tried to make a conversation. She was not rude, but politely told me she was waiting for someone. I retreated to the lounge and had another beer. A little later on my way out of the hotel I saw the young miss again and she was obviously distressed. I asked her if I could be of any assistance. She said she did not think so, that her date was a Navy lieutenant with whom she had a firm date to meet for lunch. I told her I could call naval authorities to see if they could shed some light on his whereabouts, which I did. They told me he was shipped out on short notice and provided a mailing address, a naval post office; I related the news to the young lady, Kathy. I also sympathized with her and suggested dinner. After considerable hemming and hawing, she accepted the offer and we were off to dine. As the evening wore on we opted to go to the squadron apartment for the nightly jamboree.

The next day, I called Kathy to see if she could help me on a little shopping expedition. She agreed and we were off to look at a stone for my class ring, which I had broken while letting the landing gear down on a P-47 flight. I was in the market for an opal, a stone which Australia is famous for, and we succeeded in finding one which I then had installed in the ring. Later in the day, we went to the horse racing track where Kathy asked me for 50 Aussie pounds to make some bets. I was a little shocked because that amounted to a lot of American dollars, the exchange rate being 3.22 to 1 Aussie pound. There were two ways to bet at the racetrack. You could wager on the tote (paramutual) or with licensed bookies who operated under umbrellas all over the track area. Kathy took her scratch sheet and went around haggling with the bookies for odds. This was hysterically funny to watch even though I could not understand any of the Aussie lingo that was bantered between Kathy and the bookies.

Finally the race went off and Kathy was yelling loudly to encourage her selection. With shouts of glee, she informed me that we had won, and we tore off to find our bookie. On the payoff, she handed me back my 50 pounds plus another 25 and kept 25 for herself. Not a bad day at all. That night Kathy told me about her navy friend who was a torpedo boat commander that had been injured in a battle with the Japanese and was recuperating in Sydney. She was enthralled with him, saying she wouldn't mind if he asked her to marry him. She said that beside his good looks, he was wealthy. I told her that I worked a little with PT boats and was impressed with their crews. Kathy grew more comfortable with me and became my companion and tour guide for the rest of my R&R. The days in Sydney flew by rapidly and it was suddenly time to return to New Guinea. I stored my uniforms with Kathy, loaded my parachute bag with bottled spirits and was on my way to Brisbane, where on December 20, I picked up a new P-47 to fly up to Port Moresby.

The plane was the latest D-model. It was painted olive drab with only a serial number, and was already "slow timed" by Army pilots. My parachute bags were loaded with booze. When I got the new plane, I opened up the ammunition bays in the wings and loaded the booze in the bullet trays, as it was the only way I could transport the goodies. They would have been stolen by any other means. I flew the new plane to Townsville, a major stop-off point, where we landed for fuel and I remained overnight.

Someone determined that I wasn't smart enough to fly across the Coral Sea without a navigator, so on December 21 I was sent to Horn Island, at the very end of a long peninsula north of Townsville, to join with a B-25 crew who had a navigator. Arriving at Horn Island de la tarde, I had to remain overnight. An RAAF fighter squadron furnished us quarters and invited us to a pre-Christmas party, which was accepted with glee. They had only beer to drink and ran dry at about 2130. I felt bad about drinking up all their beer, so I encouraged them to drive me to the airstrip where I could get some goodies out of the wings of my P-47. I got a dozen bottles of champagne, and the party resumed until midnight when we ran dry again.

In the morning I had a huge hangover, but had to fly to Port Moresby with the B-25 as navigator. The following day, December 22, along with several other pilots from the group, we flew the new planes over the Great Barrier Reef and the Coral Sea to New Guinea. There were four P-47s flying on the wings of the B-25 bomber for the long flight from Horn Island to Port Moresby. The flight over the reef was incredibly beautiful. The colors were beyond imagination.

Halfway across the Coral Sea we ran into a stationary tropical front. The B-25 captain opted to fly under the front. As we descended to a hundred feet over the sea it became unbearably hot so I opened the cockpit ventilator full open, which was a two-inch tube between the rudder pedals. I recall we also had a pilot relief tube. It required dexterity beyond my ability. If it was used, it was suggested you not engage in inverted flight at the same time.

As we entered the storm, the rain came down so heavily that I could hardly see the B-25, even though my prop was just behind his left wing. To make matters worse, water started spewing out of the vent tube until the cockpit floor had a foot of water. How I got through this mess is a miracle, and was the last time I ever used a navigator. Lesson—booze will make life difficult at times.

If I had been making the flight plan I would have flown directly from Townsville to Port Moresby at 30,000 feet, thus avoiding messy clouds and rainstorms. The same holds true for the Horn Island jaunt. It was always easy to find holes in fronts at high altitude.

New Guinea did not present too many reasons to celebrate Christmas; it was just like any other day of mosquitoes, heat, and humidity. The support contingent of the squadron attempted to give us a good meal, but we had no refrigeration, so it was the same old chow line with a 55-gallon barrel of boiling water to dunk the mess kit in.

BIG AIR BATTLE *Another big day for aerial combat was on 27 December 1943. Sixteen (16) P-47s from this squadron were patrolling Cape Gloucester, New Britain, when attacked by twenty (20) to thirty (30) Zekes and Oscars . . . eleven Zekes and two Oscars were destroyed . . . Unfortunately, in this engagement our planes did not get away without losses. One pilot belly-landed his plane near a PT boat and was rescued . . . Another plane piloted by Lt. Wilburn S. Henderson failed to return from this mission. When last seen, a few miles south of Arawe, New Britain, Lt. Henderson was in no apparent difficulty. He may have been the pilot, believed American, who was seen parachuting out a few miles west or [sic] Omoi. This is a region of reefs and the possibility of capture there was strong.—*History of the 341st Fighter Squadron, August 1943 through January 1944[3]

On December 28th, 1943, I resumed combat missions.

DECEMBER COMBAT *Combat activity for the squadron continued on an increased scale during December as the enemy made some effort to stem the tide of Allied advances up the New Guinea and New Britain coasts.*—History of the 341st Fighter Squadron, August 1943 through January 1944

NOTES

1. During and before WWII, the Kings Cross district of Sydney was known for its music halls and grand theaters.
   "Kings Cross, New South Wales," http://en.wikipedia.org/wiki/Kings_Cross,_New_South_Wales
2. The co-author could find no information on a Royal Australian Hotel in Sydney. It is unclear whether the Royal Australian Hotel which Jim Curran recalled was either the Royal Hotel or the Australian Hotel in Sydney, which actually exists.
3. First Lieutenant Wilburn S. Henderson, who was lost while flying P-47D-2-RE, serial number 42-8099 (MACR 2603), was from Missouri, and is remembered on the Tablets of the Missing, Manila American Cemetery, Manila, Philippines. He was awarded the Distinguished Flying Cross, Purple Heart and Air Medal for his service in World War II.
   "Wilburn S. Henderson," http://www.abmc.gov/search-abmc-burials-and-memorializations
   Baugher, Joseph F., "1942 USAAF Serial Numbers (42-001 to 42-30031)," http://www.joebaugher.com/usaf_serials/1942_1.html

Chapter Six

FIGHTING WESTWARD

BACK TO NEW GUINEA

Returning to New Guinea after Christmas brought many changes. Upon returning to New Guinea from R&R, I delivered the new P-47 to the proper aircraft pool and motored to Durand to pick up my gear. While I was in Australia, the squadron moved to Finschhafen.

ON TO FINSCHHAFEN *This squadron moved from Port Moresby to Finschhafen, on 17 December 1943, with most of the personnel and equipment coming by air and only the heavy equipment and vehicles by LST . . . The main body of the squadron had barely moved to Finschhafen and set up camp area when the planes arrived on 20 December 1943. During the stay at Finschhafen operations were directed by the 308th Bombardment Wing (H) (then known as the First Air Task Force) and the Fifth Fighter Command.*—History of the 341st Fighter Squadron, August 1943 through January 1944

The convoy that we were protecting on its mission to the center of New Britain, in late October, was a decoy for the real strike. As the convoy approached central New Britain, it changed course and headed west to the western tip of New Britain. At the same time, the Army pushed along the coast of New Guinea to Cape Finschhafen, driving the Japanese forces to retreat as fast as possible. In New Guinea, the scattered Japanese troops were having a difficult time holding any ground because their supply lines were severely compromised by Allied forces. On December 26, 1943, the 1st Marine Division landed at Cape Gloucester on New Britain directly across from Finschhafen. The Japanese were really out-foxed by the maneuver, having sent their forces to the center of New Britain where they thought we were going to assault the island.

There were a few squadron personnel at Durand who were packing up items to be shipped to Finschhafen. I was surprised to see two Cocker Spaniels that were the property of Operations Officer Sam Blair.[1] Taffy was a reddish color and Terry was dappled black and white. Blair had purchased the dogs in Australia and flew them up to New Guinea in the squadron's "Fat Cat." As you will recall, the "Fat Cat" was an aircraft we acquired to use in ferrying supplies for the mess from Australia.

The two dogs were the squadron mascots so had to be brought along to Finschhafen. That job fell to me, so I leashed them up and put them aboard a transport on December 28th, headed for the new base. After that I flew a P-47D-4 up from Wards Drome to Finschhafen the same day. The next day, 29 December, I was back at it, flying an uneventful (nil sightings) three-and-a-half-hour patrol over to Cape Gloucester, which was my last combat mission of 1943.

After getting the two animals to Finschhafen, they adopted my tent for a place to sleep at night. Terry became very attached to me and would not leave my side and had fits when I took off on a mission.

FINSCHHAFEN

Finschhafen was a brand-new airstrip carved out of a Balsa wood tree forest by the Seabees. The airstrip was a deluxe one-mile long runway of impacted coral covered with metal. At this new airfield we were able to hit targets throughout New Britain, New Ireland, Saidor, Madang, Alex-ishafen, Wewak and Hollandia in New Guinea, and as far north as Manus Island. We were now semi-offensive in our objective. We were beginning to strafe ground targets as well as escort medium and heavy bombers.

Our ready tents and sleeping areas were separated, and we kept pretty much to ourselves. We didn't even have much communication between squadrons of the group, although we worked well in the air on group missions.

FINSCHHAFEN CAMP *The squadron was still stationed at Finschhafen atop a small hill overlooking the ocean, about a mile or two from the coast road* *and about three miles from the strip. The tents were pitched in company street formation and were built up off the ground with wooden floors. The climate was hot and humid for the most part, especially during the middle of the days. When the rains came, they turned the whole post, roads, and camp area into a sea of mud. The roads were slick and slippery like wintertime. In the hills overlooking Kangmak Bay (poss Langemak Bay) there had been a Luthern [sic] mission consisting of two European type buildings, painted red. Around this mission the Japs had been dug into the hillside until dislodged by the landing at Finschhafen. Ample evidence was available in the form of trenches, gun emplacements, grass huts, abandoned clothing, and equipment to indicate that the enemy had been well established once. On the ocean side of the camp area, about a mile away, there was a fine green sand beach ideal for swimming.—* History of the 341st Fighter Squadron, February 1944

Anyway, we had a brand-new airstrip at Finschhafen and were reinforcing the area at top speed. The Japanese tried their best to make things difficult with nightly bombing raids and some in the daylight also. I can't recall any increase in enemy air attacks because of our advanced locations. We had the usual "Washing Machine Charlies" interrupting sleep, and an occasional day incursion. The bombing raids on Japanese bases were very effective and our whole military effort was moving the enemy back toward Japan.

FINSCHHAFEN RAIDS *The second night after arriving at Finschhafen, 1 Betty enemy bomber dropped ten (ten) unidentified bombs against shipping, causing no damage. Indeed Finschhafen was destined to be a station with numerous red alerts and air raids. On the 19th, two (2) Bettys dropped four 150 kilogram daisy cutters during the night with nil damage, and the following night two (2) Bettys dropped six unidentified bombs harmlessly in the jungle.—*History of the 341st Fighter Squadron, August 1943 through January 1944

Prior to moving to Finschhafen from Durand, we were occasionally assigned to cover for bombers on raids to Japanese ground installations. We were still defensive in our tactical role, but now we were included on an offensive mission with the bombers. We also started the interception scramble from forward fields like at Nadzab, which was a new role for us.

MORE RAIDS ON FINSCHHAFEN *It was on 27 December 1943 that the enemy began his nightly bombing attacks after a week's rest. That night four (4) Bettys dropped ten (10) 150 kilogram daisy cutters on the Finschhafen strip damaging a single P-47 parked there (not from this squadron). The next night, the 28th, two (2) Bettys dropped four (4) anti-personnel bombs in a camp area some distance from ours. On the 30th, a single Betty dropped seven anti-personnel and three (3) incendiary clusters (32 duds were counted later), causing slight damage to local installations and knocking out a searchlight. This single Betty was shot down by ack-ack.*—History of the 341st Fighter Squadron, August 1943 through January 1944

1943 was a year of great achievement by the US military. In January of 1943, the Japanese were pushing their war plan, called the Greater East Asia Co-Prosperity Sphere. They controlled the Solomon Islands, the north coast of New Guinea, New Britain, New Ireland, Biak, the Philippines and most of China, Burma and the East Indies. They were threatening to take Port Moresby, with full intent to establish a beachhead in northern Australia. Townsville, Queensland and Darwin, Northern Territory, were in danger. The bulk of Australian troops were dispersed in North Africa and the balance was committed to the defense of Port Moresby. Things looked very bad for the Allies. Our crème de la crème offensive strike force, the USMC, was committed to trying to maintain a foothold in the Solomon Islands.

But the Japanese were denied a foothold in Australia. The Marines held their ground in the Solomons, and MacArthur's forces started taking back control of the northeast side of New Guinea. Taking control of Nadzab led to the capture of the deep-water port at Lae, setting the stage for a foothold at Cape Gloucester, New Britain and the capture of Finschhafen, New Guinea.

It became clear to us in early 1944 that we would be moving often from here on out, because the Japanese forces were no longer able to reinforce their ground troops and we controlled the daylight skies. The Japs continued to harass us at night, but not with the effect they had in 1943.

DECEMBER COMBAT MISSIONS *During the past month we have performed normal escort missions for medium and heavy bombers, B-25 strafers and*

PBYs. In addition we have patrolled area, shipping; also strafed and flown intercept missions.—341FS Combat Evaluation Report for December 1943

One night, after we shut off the generator that provided electricity for the lights, Taffy and Terry got in their favorite spots to sleep when something disturbed them. They started to bark and whimper so bad that someone turned on the generator so we could see what was bothering them. When we looked out of the tent we spotted a huge constrictor snake, a Python. It was 30-feet long and almost a foot wide, and it was apparently looking for a meal, the dogs. By this time the whole camp was awake and an enlisted man shot the snake with a Thompson sub-machine gun.

After ascertaining that it was dead, we retired, waiting until morning to figure out what to do with the carcass. To our amazement, in the morning there was a contingent of natives from the hills observing the giant snake. After conversation we determined that the natives wanted the snake, to which we agreed. The big mystery was how did they know about the snake being in our campground? We never found out. Many strange things occurred with these primitive people. The natives quickly dressed out the snake, preserving the skin and disposing of the unwanted parts. They asked if they could have some vessels to cook the meat in. The enlisted men furnished them with some cleaned out 55-gallon barrels. They put the cut-up snake, about 300 pounds of it, in the drums and built a fire around the bottoms and cooked the snake all day.

The natives in the coastal area had been coached by missionaries not to eat each other. I found them to be delightful people, full of fun. Certain young men were designated as police and were issued an Enfield rifle as a symbol of authority. They were not issued any ammunition.

NATIVE REFLECTIONS *For security reasons, little has been said of the invaluable aid rendered by the local natives in rescuing our downed pilots. This is due to the excellent achievements of the British and Dutch missionaries who in pre-war days had sacrificed their own comfort to come into the jungles and try to educate the primitive people. Suffice it to say, that of all the airmen forced down, either in friendly or enemy territory, a majority of those rescued owe their lives chiefly to the efforts of these natives, Papuans, who speak a jargon known as Pidgin English. Naïve, uncultured, and relatively poor, the na-*

tives proved their loyalty in appreciation of the benevolence shown them by the missionaries compared to the barbarian treatment of the enemy, risking their lives and working untiringly to effect the rescues. There were still head-hunters in the area and tribes who had been won over by the Japanese, but these were in the minority."—History of the 342nd Fighter Squadron, July 1, 1943 to January 31, 1944[2]

That night the whole tribe descended from the hills to partake of the feast. They ate every last morsel, plus a few cases of corned beef, meat, and vegetable stew from our kitchen. Things like this event made life bearable for us. The natives invited us to participate in the feast, but we declined. The cooked python closely resembled chicken breast. We found out later from the Australians assigned to govern the area that the only meat these people ate, after being trained not to eat each other, was fish, birds, and an occasional snake or crocodile. All meat they acquired had to be consumed immediately; otherwise it would rot in the intense tropical climate.

It is indeed unfortunate that we didn't have film to record these unusual events. It seems that film was not very high on the priority list and was very hard to keep in the tropics due to heat and humidity. My Brownie camera had long since bitten the dust in New Guinea, so to speak. My camera lasted less than a year in the tropics, so my photo album is very short.

JANUARY AIR RAIDS *For the first three weeks of January 1944 the enemy made no air raids over Finschhafen, although red alerts were still frequent. On the 23rd, with six Bettys dropping ten (10) unidentified demolition bombs, five men were killed in a direct hit on a liberty ship. The next night two unidentified enemy dive-bombers dropped two (2) unidentified demoli-tion bombs causing no damage. On the night of 25 January, a single Zeke dive bomber made a near miss on an LST in the harbor. During the middle of the afternoon of the 29th, a single Zeke dive bomber slipped in over the harbor without causing a red alert and dropped one unidentified demolition bomb near a liberty ship. Finally, to close out the month, a single Zeke dive bomber dropped his bomb harmlessly in the water at night.*—History of the 341st Fighter Squadron, August 1943 through January 1944

In January 1944, I flew 17 combat missions, mostly patrol and escort.

Our combat missions were in support of the invasion of Cape Gloucester, New Britain, and the consolidation of the Finschhafen area in the Huon Peninsula of New Guinea. We were operating out of Finschhafen the whole month. Our ground troops were approaching an area called Saidor, where the Japs had a small airstrip.

JANUARY COMBAT MISSIONS *During the past month we performed search missions, normal escort missions for medium and heavy bombers, A-20s, transports and B-25s. In addition we have strafed, flown intercept missions and provided area and shipping cover.*—341FS Combat Evaluation Report for January 1944

In February I flew a total of 23 combat missions, again largely a mix of patrol and escort. We extended operations northwest to Madang and Wewak, which was the key Japanese air base in the western part of the Commonwealth portion of New Guinea. New Guinea was divided by treaty between Great Britain and the Netherlands, north to south, west of Wewak. The landing by the First Marine Division on Cape Gloucester went very well, with minimum casualties, mostly due to the feint landing described previously, which sucked the main Japanese defending force away to the south-central coast of New Britain.

BATTLE TESTED *The period from August 1943 to January 1944 . . . saw this squadron grow from a new squadron lacking the battle test to a squadron that had grown and matured through several encounters with the enemy and through unfortunate losses. The variety of missions carried out—escort, patrol, bomber cover, fighter sweeps, and interception—were all part of the purpose of this squadron as a P-47 fighter squadron. Experience gained at Port Moresby and on the move to Finschhafen was indeed beneficial in the many month(s) yet to be spend [sic] in the New Guinea jungles.*—History of the 341st Fighter Squadron, August 1943 through January 1944

One day in February 1944, the Reccos (reconnaissance aircraft) found a concentration of Japanese shipping at Kavieng Harbor in New Ireland. A raid of B-25 bombers was staged to assault the harbor. The North American B-25 was the bomber of choice for the Fifth Air Force. Colonel Pappy

Gunn of the V Bomber Command was very innovative in hanging .50-caliber machine guns over every conceivable place on these twin-engine bombers. Pods of two machine guns were hung on each side of the cockpit. Guns were also in the tail, sides, nose, and a pair of .50s were also displayed in a turret atop the plane. Internally, the bomber carried a host of different bombs.

These bombers would approach targets at treetop height with all guns blazing and dump their lethal load of bombs equipped with tiny parachutes to slow the bombs down enough so the bombers could escape the blast. This was most effective against ground installations because nothing was left after the attack.

On February 15th, 1944, four members of our sister squadron, the 342nd, were assigned to escort a Navy PBY Catalina flying boat supporting the mission to Kavieng. The flying boat was virtually defenseless against fighters so had to be protected in its mission, which was to recue any airmen downed on the raid.

The P-47's arrived with the slow-moving flying boat just as the bombers were concluding the raid. The flak put up by the defenses was sky-blackening. Five bombers were hit so badly they had to ditch right in the harbor. The Navy PBY pilot proceeded right into the flak and landed the huge flying boat near the first crew they spotted in the water. The Thunderbolts provided top cover and called out positions of survivors while the intrepid PBY pilot went about his business of picking up the downed B-25 crews. The crash survivors of five planes were hoisted aboard the PBY, all the time under fire from shore batteries. The PBY turned toward the open sea at full throttle attempting to take off. The plane did not seem to have enough power to get airborne or break the surface tension of the placid sea, which was at dead calm. Upon exiting the harbor, the PBY pilot performed a 270-degree turn on the water and came back over his own wake. The wave was enough to break the surface tension and the PBY was airborne. He immediately set a course for Finschhafen and very gradually gained a little altitude, but he seemed to be having a problem getting up to cruising speed, about 90 knots.

The fighters stuck with him until their fuel supply became critical and they reluctantly had to head for the base at Finschhafen. They arrived home in about an hour and spread the news of the rescue plane. We all went to the harbor where the PBY was expected to land in the water—some Navy PBYs had no ground landing gear. Hours passed and the PBY finally appeared and prepared to land, much to our relief. He touched down flawlessly and began to taxi to the beach. A few yards from the water's edge the venerable flying boat, full of holes from enemy gunfire, began to sink. Fortunately the water was shallow, so his keel kept him from sinking. Rescue people quickly got the crew and precious cargo of B-25 crews to safety. We hugged every member of the PBY crew, which had just accomplished the most amazing rescue of the war that we were aware of. Every member of the PBY crew was awarded the highest medals of both the Navy and Army. I can't remember if our guys we were mentioned for any award since they didn't fire a shot.[3]

I think escorting a PBY was considered a dumb mission by the hot shots. I was impressed with the rescue mission because of the bravery evidenced but I also considered it all in a day's work for all involved. In other words, that's why we were there.

Weather interfered one time on an escort mission we had for a PBY going to the Bam Island area. As we were searching along the coast for the seaplane, we spotted a Japanese cargo vessel pulled up to shore. This was definitely a target of opportunity, but we were very cautious. The flight leader laid out an attack plan over the radio. He and his wingman would go in first and strafe the beach; the other element, me and my wingman, would provide cover. If it didn't look like a trap, we would then shoot at the Japanese ship. The bow of the ship was pointed at the beach and our pattern was from land to sea.

UNFORTUNATE VESSEL *On February 16th, four planes observed an enemy freighter of around 1500 tons apparently aground near the Sepik River. Each plane fired approximately 1,000 rounds; the ship was thoroughly strafed and set afire in several places.*—341FS History, February 1944

The initial pass on the beach set off a lot of fires but no ack ack. As the leader pulled up, my wingman and I attacked. My heart was pounding. I aimed for the engine room of the ship, hitting the port side, pouring in the maximum of the eight .50-caliber machine guns. We were now equipped with armor-piercing incendiary (API) ammo; the devastation to the ship was awesome. A huge internal explosion took place followed by an enormous ball of fire. My wingman hit the bow of the ship and more explosions took place. Seeing no enemy fire coming our way, we all made another strafing pass which left the ship burning from bow to stern, plus many fires on the shore. We got a "good job, well done," from the C.O.[4]

FEBRUARY AIR RAIDS *Alerts during the month were frequent, sometimes several in one night. The enemy seemed to be going after either the air strip or the boats in the harbor. However the damage done by the raids was small.—* History of the 341st Fighter Squadron, February 1944

Bombers and PBY's weren't the only thing we escorted or that was affected by the weather. One late afternoon, my flight was tasked to provide air cover for some PT boats going out on a night raid along the coast. The weather deteriorated to a fog, which gave great cover for the PT boats but made it hard for us to keep them in sight. They were traveling at slow speed so as not to show a tell-tale wake, which would be visible for miles, and we finally lost them in the fog.

January and February passed quickly and it was obvious that we would soon be moving on from Finschhafen to Saidor, New Guinea.

ON TO SAIDOR *By the middle of the month the squadron had prepared to move from Finschhafen. On February 16th an advance water echelon left by LST with most of the squadron's vehicles and heavy equipment for Saidor. Six days later a supplementary advance detail was flown up to Saidor. When the advance detail arrived at Saidor, the strip was under construction, usable for transports, cubs, and P-40's. An open kunai plain about two miles up the Nankina River and about five hundred yards inland from the western bank was selected to be the squadron's new camp area. The advance detail set to work in clearing the new area and constructing a mess hall. Lumber was available from virgin forests back in the hills about three miles away up the valley.—*History of the 341st Fighter Squadron, February 1944

As March drew near my body weight was again approaching the 140s, so the flight surgeon sent me to Sydney to fatten up. The day I left for R&R, John Wayne came to Finschhafen with his USO team. My tent was confiscated to house the USO people. My buddies told me that John Wayne used my bunk. It turned out that John Wayne had such a good time with the Blackjack Squadron he stayed a week. We had one short pilot named Jim Nixon who offered to take the actor up in a P-47. Wayne agreed so they both got into the P-47; Wayne first, and then Jim Nixon on his lap. They flew without benefit of parachutes. Jim even gave John a demonstration of the .50-caliber machine guns. Wayne commented that if it were in his power, he would be part of the 341st Fighter Squadron. This event has been documented by many members of the Black Jack Squadron.[5]

FEBRUARY ACCOMPLISHMENTS *The majority of the squadron and all the planes remained at Finschhafen all month. In the operations conducted out of that base six hundred twenty-three (623) combat sorties and 1554:20 hours of combat time were flown. Slightly over half these sorties were in convoy cover and patrol in the Saidor–Cape Gloucester area, while two hundred thirty-four (234) were flown in covering B-24's, B-25's, and A-20's on their numerous strikes against Alexishafen, Madang, Marienberg, Bogia, Hansa Bay, Wewak, and New Britain.*—History of the 341st Fighter Squadron, February 1944

R&R IN AUSTRALIA

On March 1st, after completing 88 combat missions in the SWPA, the Flight Surgeon deemed it necessary for me to go to Sydney again to restore my body weight, which had fallen again to less than 150 pounds. My normal weight at that time was 180. I hopped a C-47 to Port Moresby and then on to Townsville, where I remained overnight. On March 2, 1944, I was promoted to 1st Lt., and proceeded to Eagle Farm RAAF Base at Brisbane.[6] Travel was difficult because I was toting two parachute bags full of cigarettes, plus toiletries and clothing changes. The cigarettes were for trade with suppliers of goodies in Sydney. The US government supplied troops in the combat zones with free cigarettes as a perk (much different thinking then). We were also doled out two ounces of spirits after each combat mission.

I finally arrived in Sydney after the long journey and got bused to Kings Cross Reception Center to get my ration of beer. The squadron had acquired an automobile of dubious quality and improved quarters in a beautiful four-bedroom house in Double Bay, an upscale portion of Sydney. We had daily maid service and the goodie sellers arrived about 1000 every morning. Piper Heidsieck 37 Champagne and Johnny Walker Black and Red were available in exchange for cigarettes. The latter item was better than cash.

LOSS OF COLONEL KEARBY *On March 5th, the entire 348th Fighter Group was stunned by the news that Colonel Neel E. Kearby, our former Group Commander, was missing in action from a fighter-sweep over the Japanese bastion at Wewak. At the time Colonel Kearby had twenty-two enemy planes to his credit and was Chief of Staff for the V Fighter Command. Colonel Kearby was awarded the Congressional Medal of Honor by General MacArthur for shooting down six enemy fighters on one mission in the face of overwhelming odds. Every man in the Group knew Colonel Kearby as a man as well as a leader. He had been with the Group since activation and was an inspiration to everyone. A man of his caliber is seldom found and he will always be remembered for what he was rather than for what he did.*—Narrative of Squadron History, 340th Fighter Squadron, March 1944[7]

My lady friend Kathy from my previous R&R was on hand for my arrival, having been notified by telegram of my arrival time. I was greeted with hugs and plans were immediately formed for activities, which included Bondi Beach and the racetrack. Mornings started with steak and eggs with hash brown potatoes, the premium Aussie breakfast, and then off to activities. Time went fast and I gained about two pounds a day. I got back to the squadron March 20th, about 25 pounds heavier, with my two parachute bags full of canned ham and booze, mostly Gilbey's Gin which went well with canned grapefruit juice. We did get canned things, thanks to rationing at home.

Shortly after returning from R&R, we moved from Finschhafen to Saidor in Papua New Guinea.

Recalling my hectic flight across the Coral Sea, it was comforting to get back to combat flying where you know what the dangers are; well, at least most of them.

SQUADRON MORALE *Enlisted men must be given some hopes of furloughs on a definite schedule, and pilots must have a goal to shoot for in the matter of returning home.*—Medical report, History of the 341st Fighter Squadron, April 1944

Finschhafen was a very busy air base, being our most forward, operational airstrip. We could now hit Wewak with ease. Hollandia, New Guinea and the Schouten Islands were also in range of the P-47s and P-38s, and Rabaul, Kavieng, and Manus Island were now easy targets. The three squadrons of the 348th Fighter Group, three squadrons of P-38s and three squadrons of P-40s, were using the base, as were bombers, many ATC planes, air evacuation and some Australian aircraft. With this big of a load, takeoff and landing operations were tight, so the fighters had to be squeezed in between all the others.

Since the runway was narrow, we took off single file about 30-seconds apart and tried to simulate that time schedule on landing. We were usually critical on fuel upon returning, so the flight commander would warn the controllers of our arrival time to the nearest minute in order to get all the runway hogs out of the way. C-47 and multi-engine aircraft took a lot of runway time compared to us. We wasted very little time on takeoff and landing, in spite of the zigzag taxi necessary to the Jug.

We would usually approach the field at about 400 mph and the leader would watch the tower for a green light to land. When it was time to get back to the house we never wasted any time, and would use our altitude depreciation to get the most speed. The Jug was a real blast at high speed compared to the standard cruise of 190 mph. Seeing a green light, a flight leader would chop throttle and peel to the left in a tight turn of 360 degrees, constantly killing speed and altitude, flaring out at the last second to land. All of us would emulate this pattern to get our planes down as fast as possible. As soon as we slowed down to under 200 mph, we dropped the landing gear and flaps. After the landing gear locked we had to equalize hydraulic pressure with an equalizer valve located on the cockpit floor. This allowed our flaps to come down at the same time and at the same rate, a very important function.

One time while returning from a long flight, I followed this procedure, but on my flare-out just prior to touch down my right flap did not come down. I was about to crash sideways. Somehow I was able to get full power back up, but the plane had the left flap full down and the landing gear was causing drag. I pushed the joystick full right and did the same to the rudder pedal. Somehow I found time to operate the landing gear to up, and the plane began to fly again. I could not dump the flap because that would have plummeted me into the ground. With full power on, the prop wash literally blew the left flap up. This hairy adventure took all of 30 seconds and somehow my guardian angel pulled me through this life-threatening event. We never did find out what went wrong with the flap sequence. I ran it three times before I landed and it worked just fine each time. We had a flap equalizer valve that worked well. This was an unusual occurrence, which nearly cost me my life. So much for Finschhafen.

SAIDOR

In late March 1944, we moved to the new field at Saidor, in Papua New Guinea. My flight records show a one-hour flight from Finschhafen to Saidor on March 27, along with three other combat missions that month. The new strip lay parallel to the ocean, which meant you always landed crosswind. The wind blows either onto the land or off the land. The runway was also hundreds of feet higher on the south end than it was on the north end, so we always had one-way traffic with a crosswind. Our living quarters were laid out by the Corps of Engineers and the QM had our tents built on platforms several feet off the ground. The tent area was a thousand feet higher than the strip, next to a rushing river whose soft water was replenished by daily downpours. The engineers had erected a huge canvas holding tank for water which was pumped out of the river. It sat in tropical heat all day so we had hot showers in the evening. The strong ocean breezes made life bearable here and kept the mosquitoes to a minimum, but we still had to take Atabrine for malaria protection.

MARCH COMBAT MISSIONS *During March, 1,011:40 hours were flown on 404 combat missions. Of these combat missions slightly over half (240) were flown in convoy and area patrols. Other combat missions were on fighter sweeps, interceptions, bomber cover, and reconnaissance.*—History of the 341st Fighter Squadron, March 1944

With Rabaul neutralized, our efforts were again concentrated on the north coast of New Guinea, including the Dutch part. With these small moves forward, our range of operations increased in kind. We also phased out the 200-gallon belly tank which caused a lot of drag. It was an aerodynamic mess, being very wide, thick, and too close to the bottom of the plane. The drag effect was awful. Also, it had to be dropped manually, which caused me a serious problem once (see pages 72–73).

In place of the belly tank, we received 165-gallon wing tanks that were also used by the P-38 Lightning's. They could be jettisoned electrically in an instant, though most of the time we returned to base with the wing tanks in place. They were very aerodynamic, caused very little drag and would lift their own weight at 100 mph. You can easily see this was a great advantage. When we got the P-38 tanks, the old belly tanks were cut up for various purposes, one of which was a boat that I never chose to try out. I presumed they would not float very well. Art Cronk made a water landing with the wing tanks which I witnessed at close range—more on that later. Some people thought the Jugs wouldn't be able to handle the P-38 tanks but we disproved that in no time at all.

IMPROVED THUNDERBOLTS *During the month of April, the Squadron was almost completely equipped with P-47D-15's and subsequent model airplanes. Previously the equipment consisted of P-47D-11's and prior models. The major difference is that the P-47D-15's and subsequent models have wing adaptations suitable either for wing tanks or bombs . . . Due to the overheating of the guns from the gun bay heaters in the P-47D-16 and D-21 models, a metal disc has been placed over the gun bay heater hole in the gun bay to stop the overheating of the guns.*—S-4 Supply and Materiel, Engineering report, 341FS History, April 1944[8]

There was an added bonus of gas with two wing tanks over one belly tank which equaled about one and a half hours of air time available. This equaled another 150 miles of operational range, a huge plus-factor. The P-47, when operating at 30-inches of manifold pressure at 2,000 rpm, gobbled 60 gallons an hour. This was one of the reasons the P-47 was not popular with MacArthur.

NEW P-47 WING TANKS *Wing tanks presented new problems. The tanks themselves are P-38 tanks and much easier to install than the formerly used Australian-made belly tanks. The main problem on the tanks was that 3 out of 4 airplanes would come back with damaged flaps or ailerons after dropping the tanks. The trouble was traced to the kick-off braces. These braces were factory installed so that when the tank was not installed they would fold up snug against the wing, being pulled out by shock cord. These braces had short stubby arms, about 2 inches long that more or less fitted the contour of the tank at the point of contact. It was found that when the tanks were released that the nose dropped first, imparting a tumbling motion. Consequently the kick-off brace would fold up against the wing as soon as the tank went past a perpendicular position to the brace. This left the tank free to float into the flaps and ailerons. To remedy this situation, the shock cords were removed and a metal brace installed, resulting in the kick-off brace being held rigidly in position at all times. There was also trouble with the tanks rolling off the shorts arms on the kick-off braces. This was cleaned up by welding an extension of each side, thus increasing the length of the braces from 2 inches to 10 inches. Now the wing tanks give very little trouble.*—S-4 Supply and Materiel, Engineering report, 341FS History, April 1944

With this extended range, we were able to start missions as far away as the Schouten Islands. Little did we realize at the time that Biak, which was in the Schouten Islands, would be MacArthur's coup, bypassing the enemy stronghold of Wewak. We seldom flew multiple sorties in a day, except for June of 1944, and during our time at Leyte. The increased air time of our missions seemed to have no negative effect on us; we had plenty of time between combat missions for rest.

SQUADRON ORGANIZATION *Operational and combat missions were carried out by 45 assigned pilots . . . Pilots are divided into two major flights, A and B. Pilots of "A" flight go on duty the noon of one day and are relieved the following noon by pilots of "B" flight, who take over for a similar period. This alternating schedule tends to lessen combat fatigue and to reduce flying load of pilots for any one day of sustained activity. Upon receiving the scheduled missions from higher headquarters, the Operations Officer informs the heads* *of engineering, armament and other departments immediately to facilitate and coordinate the work in carrying out the planned assignment.*—S-3 Operations report, 341FS History, April 1944

After getting settled down at our new base at Saidor, some interesting things happened. The first one was [because of] my promotion to first lieutenant, which came with additional flying duties. The promotion made me an Element Leader. A fighter squadron was normally composed of four flights. Flights were composed of two elements, and an element was composed of two aircraft. An element leader could also be a flight leader at the discretion of the squadron C.O. I got to be both in my promotion, but was also saddled with the training of new replacement pilots. For this increased responsibility there were no check rides, no ceremonies; I was just assigned a new position.[9]

Shortly after my promotion, two new guys were assigned to fly my wing. One of the first lessons was learning the protocol for takeoff from Saidor airstrip, which was always to the north due to the runway being much higher on the south end; traffic was one way all the time. Takeoff was parallel to the ocean. We were admonished to always turn right, over the water, and never to the left over the mountainous land. I tried to drill this advice into my two recruits. On our second or third takeoff together, one of my trainees had engine trouble. He was alert enough to jettison his wing tanks, but forgot the rule about always turning toward the ocean. He left-turned and ran into a mountain and was instantly killed. The rest of us continued the mission and did not hear about his demise until we returned. This was a devastating shock to the rest of the pilots. His body was recovered from the wreck and buried in a casket donated by a plantation owner. This was our first burial of a comrade; others that were lost were never recovered. The casket was made of Mahogany and was so heavy it took eight of us to lift it.[10]

We lost pilots for a variety of reasons and they were replaced from the fighter pilot pool in Port Moresby. There was no special training and we didn't have any two-seaters to check out replacement personnel.

REPLACEMENT AIRCRAFT *The silver P-47's model D-21 are coming over with a heavy protective coating on them. Since we do not have facilities for* *removing this, it is recommended that the Service Squadrons remove it before releasing the ship to a fighter squadron for combat duty.*—History of the 341st Fighter Squadron, April 1944

Another incident that happened at Saidor was a low-level night attack by a Japanese light bomber. He caught us by total surprise. We had our lights on, making us an easy target. I was walking to the shower when the plane roared over the tent area releasing phosphorous bombs. The explosions were deafening and glowing embers of the chemical were strewn all over the place. Fortunately no one was injured, despite being scared to death. Everybody revamped their foxholes the next day and the C.O. made us turn lights out shortly after dark.[11]

APRIL COMBAT MISSIONS *During the past month we have performed escort missions for B-24's, B-25's, A-20's, PBY's, and transports. We have also dive-bombed, flown intercept missions, and provided area and shipping cover. On the above escort missions, we have encountered very little ack-ack, and this was easily avoided by slight diving or climbing turns. Resistance to bombing in the WEWAK area seems to be decreasing each day.*—History of the 341st Fighter Squadron, April 1944

In April 1944, I flew 13 combat missions, mostly patrol and escort. We also started dropping bombs from the P-47s, which was new for us. We had lots of close-by targets to practice on, so we carried bombs under the wings in lieu of wing tanks. My first bombing mission was 1 May 1944, to Hansa Bay, which I bombed again the next day, followed a few days later by another bombing mission to a target near there, at Aris Island. If we had wing tanks, we were limited to one 500-lb bomb carried on the belly.[12]

GLIDE BOMBING *On April 27th four P-47D-16's participated in the first glide bombing mission assigned to the Squadron. Each of the planes carried two 500 lb. demolition bombs, one under each wing. The flight attacked personnel targets at BUNABUN HARBOR with unobserved results. The briefing for this mission (and subsequent missions) covered a detailed description of the terrain surrounding the target, outstanding landmarks, and the location of possible ack-ack fire. Two passes were made on the target, the planes drop-*

ping one bomb on each pass . . . The results of these glide bombing missions are often unobserved by the pilots because of the pull-away from the target . . . The pilots are gaining vital training and valuable experiences in the glide bombing art through actual enemy targets.—S-2 Intelligence and S-3 Operations reports, 341FS History, April 1944

There was lots of speculation on what MacArthur would do next. The Japanese base at Madang was seized and everybody thought MacArthur would attack Wewak next, but that didn't happen. Instead, we attacked Wakde, a small island about 100 miles northwest of Hollandia. The island was long enough for an airstrip. At nearly the same time, MacArthur attacked Biak in the Schouten Islands. This proved to be one of the bloodiest battles of the Pacific War.

BOMBS USED IN GLIDE BOMBING *Several size bombs were employed, notably 250, 300, and 500 pound general purpose demolition bombs, fitted with the AN M103 nose fuze and M101 A2 tail fuze. After the first few missions, tail fuzes were no longer used as several fin assemblies had become unscrewed from the bomb while the plane was in flight, causing the tail fuze to become armed. This problem was overcome by staking the fin retaining nut to the thread on the bomb body, thus preventing the loosening and turning of the fin. The AN M103 S-1 nose fuze was used after several days' use of the AN M103, and is now used exclusively. With this type fuze the bomb will detonate about a foot above the ground, throwing shrapnel out parallel to the ground. The use of this fuze is for daisy cutters and is believed more suitable for the specific targets of supplies and personnel.*—S-4 Supply and Materiel, Armament and Ordnance report, 341FS History, April 1944

NOTES

1. A P-47D flown by Samuel V. Blair, P-47D-2-RE, serial number 42-8130, named "Frankie," and in which he reportedly achieved at least three of his aerial victories, was written off in an accident late in 1943. But the heavily damaged aircraft was eventually recovered from New Guinea and is reportedly now in storage awaiting

restoration at the Pima Air & Space Museum in Tucson, Arizona.

"P-47D-2-RE "Frankie" Serial Number 42-8130 Nose 67," http://www.pacificwrecks.com/aircraft/p-47/42-8130.html

2. See Appendix 2 for a list of Pidgin English Phrases created for pilots to use in case they came down in Papua New Guinea.

3. This description matches that of the famous rescue flight of 15 February 1944 by US Navy LT (JG) Nathan G. Gordon, PBY Catalina seaplane commander who made four water landings with the "Arkansas Traveler" off the enemy held shore at Kavieng, New Ireland, in order to rescue 15 downed airmen from Fifth Air Force bombers that had attacked Kavieng. LT Gordon was awarded the Medal of Honor for this outstanding rescue mission. It correlates with 342FS Mission 2-181, flown 15 February 1944, with takeoff at 0955. Four P-47's flew on this five-hour mission to "Escort P-BY at Narago Island to Kavieng." Results: "P-BY landed 5 times at various points in Kavieng Harbor to pick up survivors of A-20 and B-25 strike. Landings were made under fire from dual purpose guns on shore & .50 cal guns. Our flight & one B-25 called positions of survivors in area to PBY. Sea marker dye & mirror flashes helped in locating survivors."

At least one member of the P-47 escort received a decoration for participation in this outstanding rescue mission. 342FS pilot 1st Lt. Wynans E. "Flip" Frankfort was nominated and approved for the Silver Star after his aircraft was holed in the tail by enemy fire during the mission. Unfortunately, Wynans went missing in action from Wakde in P-47D-16-RE serial number 42-75940 on a combat mission to Biak on 27 May 1944, before he was ever presented the award. His crash site and remains were discovered in 1991, and in 1995, the US Army recovered his remains. Only then did the Frankfort family learn of his Silver Star award, and Lt. Frankfort's older brother Philip went to Ft. Eustis, Virginia, to receive the award on behalf of his younger brother.

342FS Weekly Status and Operations Report (Form 34), (Report for Period 11 February 1944 to 20 February 1944 Inclusive), page 4.

"Lieutenant Commander Nathan G. Gordon, USNR, (1916-2008)," http://www.history.navy.mil/photos/pers-us/uspers-g/n-gordon.htm

"P-47D-16-RE Thunderbolt Serial Number 42-75940," http://www.pacificwrecks.com/aircraft/p-47/42-75940.html

4. This recollection appears to correlate with an event noted in the squadron's history. Jim Curran flew two missions on February 16, 1944; a three hour and twenty minute mission as escort of a PBY to Bam Island, the southeastern-most of the Schouten Islands; and a three hour local patrol. From the unit's Weekly Operations and Status Report, this is Mission 1-173, "Escort PBY to Bam Is.," by four P-47's that took off at 0920 on a mission of 3.5 hours duration. The Form 34 remarks on the right side of the form are unintelligible due to poor quality of the print CD copy of the history.

History of the 341st Fighter Squadron, Chapter IV, (February 1944), page 2.

341FS Weekly Status and Operations Report (Form 34), (Report for Period 13 Feb 1944 to 18 Feb 1944 Inclusive), page 2.

5. John Wayne was part of a three-month USO tour to the Southwest Pacific in early 1944. He visited Army and Navy units in New Guinea and Arawe, New Britain. From the History of the 348th Fighter Group, Chapter IV (February 1944): "The local theater was an achievement of "art" being in the shape of a natural amphitheatre. Many enjoyable evenings were passed there—particularly one in which the master-of-ceremonies was none other than that rip-roaring, two fisted hero of the screen, John Wayne." Wrote John Wayne of his experience: "When you look out and up into a natural bowl that only recently was jungle and see 5,000 and 6,000 men sitting in the rain and mud, you wish you had the best show on earth . . . They are wonderful guys when the going gets tough. They get back to the fundamentals out here. It's the greatest thrill and privilege anyone can ever have to see them yell and relax in front of a show."

Davis, Ronald L. *Duke: The Life and Image of John Wayne*. Norman, OK: University of Oklahoma Press, 1998, page 114.

"History of the 348th Fighter Group, Chapter IV (February 1944)," http://www.ww2f.com/topic/37324-history-of-the-348th-fighter-group/

6. According to HQ 5AF SO No. 34, Curran was promoted from 2nd Lt. to 1st Lt., effective 3 February 1944.

7. Colonel Neel E. Kearby's remains were recovered in 1949. Natives reported that he had apparently bailed out of his stricken P-47, but died of wounds. He was buried with full military honors at the Hillcrest Memorial Park Cemetery, Dallas, Texas, on 23 July 1949, next to his older brother, Army Major John Gallatin Kearby III, who also died during the war, in an airplane crash stateside on 2 August 1943.

The wreckage of Kearby's "Fiery Ginger IV" remained undisturbed at the original crash site until the 1990's. In 2004, the tail section bearing the aircraft serial number was donated to the National Museum of the USAF, at Wright-Patterson AFB, Ohio, where the tail is on public display next to a P-47 painted in the colors and markings of "Fiery Ginger IV."

Since that fatal day, additional information has come out to help complete the picture of what happened, though the definitive account is perhaps yet to be written. Stanaway, author of *Kearby's Thunderbolts*, describes Kearby's final combat in some detail on pages 89–92 though it does not resolve the ultimate fate of the American ace. Another source (Dunn) indicates that a IJAAF Sgt. Major Shironushi Kumagaya, of the Ki-43 Hayabusa (Allied codename OSCAR)-equipped 33rd Fighter Regiment, shot Col. Kearby down after the Thunderbolts shot down three IJAAF Type 99 light bombers, also known as Kawasaki Ki-48 LILY bombers (as opposed to the Mitsubishi G3M NELL bombers mentioned in American accounts based on after action statements from Capt. Sam Blair). This was the 33rd Fighter Regiment's first aerial victory after arriving in New Guinea in late February 1944.

In another article by Dunn, he elaborated on Kumagaya's victory over Kearby, and includes another level of detail in assessment of the day. The actual location of Kearby's crash site is some 100 miles from where the low-level action of 5 March occurred. Dunn assessed that Ki-43 pilots Warrant Offocer Mitoma and Sgt. Hiroshi Aoyagi of the 77th Fighter Regiment may have hit and damaged Kearby's aircraft, and that later, as Kearby strove to return to an Allied airfield, Sgt Major Kumagaya engaged his lone P-47 at 4,500 meters (just under 15,000 feet) and shot it down in flames, according to native sources on the ground.

Dunn reported that native sources indicated Kearby bailed out but died upon hitting the jungle trees below. Another source (Baugher) indicates that Col. Kearby successfully ". . . bailed out but became tangled in a tree . . ." after parachuting from his stricken aircraft, and that "he was shot and killed," presumably by Japanese soldiers on the ground. The cause(s) of Col. Kearby's ultimate demise may remain a mystery, but there is no doubt he was a successful combat leader and proved the capability of the P-47 in the Pacific.

"Colonel Neel Kearby: Fire and Ice and the Race to Become First Top Gun," http://www.homeofheroes.com/wings/part2/11_kearby.html

"Kearby, Neel Earnest," https://www.tshaonline.org/handbook/online/articles/fkevv

"John Gallatin Kearby III," http://www.cadetcorps.org/PDFs/JGKearbyHOHbio_final.pdf

"Fiery Ginger IV Vertical Fin," http://www.nationalmuseum.af.mil/factsheets/factsheet.asp?id=15612

Greinert, Robert, "Donation of P-47 Tail Section and Machine Gun from Neel Kearby's Thunderbolt to USAF Museum," http://www.pacificwrecks.com/aircraft/p-47/42-22668/donation.html

Dunn, Richard L., "248th Hiko Sentai: A Japanese "Hard luck" Fighter Unit, Part 3," http://www.j-aircraft.com/research/rdunn/248th/248th-3.htm

Dunn, Richard L. "Double Lucky? The Campaigns of the 77th Hiko Sentai, Part 9," http://www.warbirdforum.com/lucky9.htm (Hereinafter Dunn, "Double Lucky?")

Baugher, Joseph F., "1942 USAAF Serial Numbers (42-001 to 42-30031)", entry for serial number 22668, http://www.joebaugher.com/usaf_serials/1942_1.html

8. The 342FS history for April 1944, amplifies this arrival of newer versions of the P-47 at Saidor: "During the latter part of the month, we received sleek looking silver Thunderbolts, with the camouflage paint removed. The lack of paint decreased the weight of the ship thereby increasing its speed by 10 to 20 miles per hour, using the same manifold pressure. These newer model P-47s came equipped with wing

tanks instead of belly tanks, which increased the fuel capacity from 100 to 330 gallons of 100-octane gasoline. The added weight of additional gas increased the wing loading of the plane, making it more difficult to handle on takeoff. Therefore, other than for exceptionally long-range missions, we did not fill the wing tanks to capacity, but only enough for maximum efficiency."

9. One should be careful not to confuse the use of the term "flight" between tactical and organizational applications. In the tactical sense, aircraft in the air on a mission, a USAAF flight of fighters, was composed of four aircraft, divided into two elements of two aircraft each. On a given mission, a squadron could generate several flights of aircraft from the 25 fighters typically assigned to a fighter squadron. Organizationally, to fly those aircraft, the squadron had between 40 to 50 pilots assigned, with a few in the command section (commander, operations officer and assistants) with the bulk of the pilots assigned to four lettered flights in the squadron, typically "A Flight," "B Flight," "C Flight," and "D Flight. A lettered flight had more than four pilots assigned to it, so as to allow it to schedule personnel appropriately in the squadron's missions, allow for any temporary absence for other duty or leave, account for any attrition, as well as allow enough capacity to train up new pilots to replace those lost or returned to the US after they finished their combat tour. It is unknown how long the 341FS two flight organization scheme mentioned earlier was used in the unit.

10. This was probably Lt. Robert M. Stroud, lost on April 13, 1944, in an operational flying accident. He is buried in the Salem Baptist Cemetery in Lake, Mississippi.
   Stanaway, John C. Kearby's *Thunderbolts: The 348th Fighter Group in World War II*. Atglen: Schiffer Military/Aviation History, 1997, page 177. (Hereinafter Stanaway, *Kearby's Thunderbolts*)
   "Robert M. Stroud," http://billiongraves.com/pages/record/RobertMStroud/9765122

11. Stanaway, *Kearby's Thunderbolts,* page 95, mentions an undated nocturnal phosphorous bomb attack on Saidor and that the next night, Tokyo Rose claimed Japanese forces had bombed a secret underground hangar at Saidor. Group members were amused, as they hadn't seen an aircraft hangar since leaving Australia in the summer of 1943.

12. During March 1944, the 342FS's history noted an experiment with the P-47 as a dive-bomber, which made it the first squadron in the 348th Fighter Group to drop bombs. There is no indication that this experiment was carried out in Jim Curran's 341FS—the squadron's first glide bombing was noted in its April 1944 history as taking place on 27 April 1944. Nor is there mention of any bombs being dropped by the 340FS until April 1944. But over in the 342nd, almost routine missions over Wewak in the period gave the bombing idea to Major William M. Banks, squadron commander, who noted how enemy activity on the ground at the fortified base continued even when Thunderbolts were overhead; perhaps the enemy

was confident in their anti-aircraft defense capability against the possibility of any low-flying fighters strafing. He gave his idea to T/Sgt Iddings, technical inspector, S/Sgt Bowen, crew-chief, and S/Sgt Katz, sheet metal man, and they blueprinted plans for installing bomb shackles on the P-47. It took them a week to prepare Major Banks' aircraft for a test run. Two 100-pound demolition bombs were loaded for the test, which Major Banks flew against some coral reefs just offshore in Lange-mak Bay. It was a successful test, and soon Major Banks and Lt. Orr conducted dive-bomb attacks against Japanese forces in the Hansa Bay area, coming into the area at 8,000 feet, diving to 3,000 feet without throttle and releasing their bombs with good effects notes, fires and evident damage. The Major then scheduled fighter sweeps to New Britain, coming within 100 miles of Rabaul, and dropping these bombs on enemy locations. Fifth Air Force was surprised when bomb expenditures started appearing on the squadron's reports, and asked them to list the results on mission reports. Soon all the 342FS planes were modified to carry bombs, and could mount missions as four, eight, or sixteen-ship formations, using either 100- or 250-pound bombs with which they hit Japanese targets in Hansa Bay and Wewak. Squadron statistical reports indicated 100-pound bombs were used in March, and 300-pound bombs expended in April 1944.

History of the 342nd Fighter Squadron, Chapter V, (1–31 March 1944), pages 3–5.

History of the 341st Fighter Squadron, Chapter V, (March 1944), Appendix 1, Squadron statistical report for March 1944.

History of the 340th Fighter Squadron, Chapter 5, March 1944, Enclosure 1, Statistical data for month of March.

Chapter Seven

WAKDE

BLACKJACK ON THE MOVE *The rapid Allied advances along the northern coast of New Guinea in taking the enemy bases at Tadji, Hollandia, and Wakde Island, placed the P-47 fighters of this Squadron beyond their effective range, and out of the sphere of probable enemy action. While operating from Saidor, combat with the enemy was out of the question completely. Subsequently, two echelons, a water and an air, were formed to carry the Squadron to a station within effective striking range of the enemy bases in the Geelvink Bay area of western New Guinea and the Schouten Islands.*—History of the 341st Fighter Squadron, May 1944

As soon as Wakde was secured, the Seabees put down a metal airstrip 40-yards wide and a mile long. We were shipped there immediately so we could provide cover for the next beachhead at Biak. I had another R&R down from Saidor to Sydney in mid-May after flying six combat missions at the start of the month, and brought another new P-47D back up to New Guinea on May 31, getting to Wakde shortly thereafter. Wakde stunk so bad of rotting bodies we could hardly stand the smell. There wasn't a square foot of the island that didn't have military gear on it. It was the most crowded place I ever experienced. Our planes were jammed into revetments at the end of the runway and there was no place for us to sleep. What did we do? We commuted to nearby Insoemanai Island, another island a couple miles away, by landing barge. The island was about as big as a city block and the members of the whole group were quartered there; everybody commuted by barge. We lived on such an island since there was no room on Wakde.

WAKDE ARRIVAL *On 22 May the water echelon of the Squadron (11 officers, 134 enlisted men, vehicles, equipment and supplies by LST) arrived on the beach of Wakde Island, just 5 days after the initial invasion landing. . . . the airplanes were operating out of Saidor until the 25 May . . .*—History of the 341st Fighter Squadron, May 1944

We were back to square one as far as accommodations went; tents and cots on the ground and food out of mess kits. Everybody got diarrhea and half of the pilots were too sick to fly. There were so many people sick we had difficulty manning 16 planes for patrol missions to Biak.

THUNDERBOLT WEAR AND TEAR *Normal maintenance and inspection work at Wakde have been reduced to a bare minimum due to the crowded conditions and the dusty, sandy conditions of the strip. The dust and sand blowing in off the strip are expected to shorten the life of the Pratt and Whitney engines by at least 33 1/3 per cent. On the other hand, the main landing gear casings are lasting better here than at any previous station. Apparently the sandy coral strip proves easier on this structural member than do the metal strips.*—S-4 Supply and Materiel, Engineering report, 341FS History, May 1944

A more pleasant Wakde surprise was that we got two pays, one from Uncle Sam and one from the Netherlands government in exile. On payday we were paid in Dutch Guilders rather than Aussie Pounds, receiving what a Dutch officer of our rank would have received. It was a small sum compared to our pay, but nevertheless very welcome. Money was no problem because we had no place to spend it, so we just held it until R&R time and then changed it into Aussie money. I didn't have to pay any income tax on it.

FRIENDLY FIRE *At Wakde Island on 28 May S/Sgt Charles J. Charlier met accidental death by friendly gunfire.*—S-1 Personnel report, 341FS History, May 1944

June 1944 was a very busy month for the 348th Fighter Group at Wakde Island in Dutch New Guinea. We assembled all three squadrons of P-47 fighter planes, the 340th, 341st and 342nd. Our main objective was

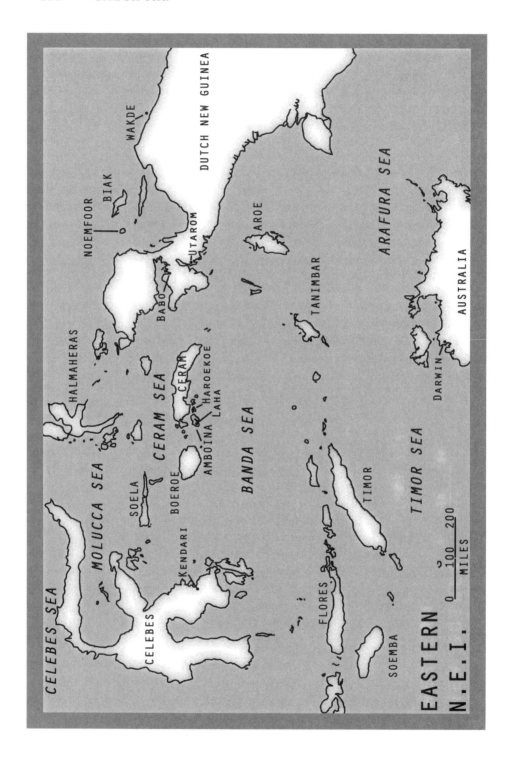

to maintain air superiority over Biak Island. I resumed my combat missions on June 3, with a bombing mission over to Baffin Bay. Four bombing missions were accomplished, two to Baffin Bay and one to Noemfoor Island which will be important to discuss later on. The fourth mission was to bomb Kamiri. We also had two strafing missions. But mostly I flew patrols in the Biak area, 19 of them during the month, for a total of 25 combat missions in June.

NEW BELLY TANK *The glide bombing missions during the month used the new two-point suspension 200-gallon belly tank with wooden sway braces. No unusual difficulties were encountered by its use.*—S-4 Supply and Materiel, Engineering report, 341FS History, June 1944

On the 10th of June the entire group, all three squadrons, with 48 fighters total (48 planes was our operational maximum) was scheduled to go on a fighter sweep to Biak. We loaded up with 5,000 rounds of the new .50-caliber A.P.I. ammunition. This ammo exploded on contact similar to an artillery shell on a small scale. We were using four API to one tracer. All 48 planes of the group were equipped with two 165-gallon wing tanks of 100-octane aviation fuel, 12,960 US gallons total.

As the last planes were airborne, orders came through that the mission was scrubbed, and we were to proceed to the New Guinea mainland where the Tor River dumped into the ocean. This was across the water from, and within sight of, Wakde, where there was a fierce ground battle taking place between our Army ground forces and a contingent of the Imperial Tiger Marines of the Japanese forces. The Tiger Marines were akin to our special forces; they had to be at least six feet tall and, of course, dedicated. According to our ground forces, they were very tough opponents.[1] Our artillery fired smoke shells on the north side of the river to mark an attack area for us. Our radio orders were to drop our wing tanks in the smoke shell area and then strafe the area, setting the fuel afire. The ensuing conflagration was awesome. It took several strafing passes to expend all our ammunition.

On my last pass, I peeled up to my left and was looking right over my left bank of guns when I had a cook-off of one gun due to overheating. Firing the fifties for too long could make a round "cook off," according to our armament officer. It was the first time I ever saw a .50-caliber go off at an oblique angle, and the blast terrified me—I thought I had been hit with a cannon shell. The fire from the muzzle blast was at least three feet wide and eight feet long. Somehow one does not see this when looking through a 100-mil gunsight, so it was an unnerving experience. The sight was fixed with no adjustment.

NEW GUNSIGHT *The 'Mark 8' gun-sight is a great improvement over the old 'N-3-A' type, since it gives better lead for moving targets and is mounted higher, thus giving better visibility for strafing.*—S-3 Operations report, 341FS History, July 1944

This was the first time we used the P-38 wing tanks as an offensive weapon. Incidentally, this was the first 348th Fighter Group close support mission for ground troops, to my knowledge, and was reportedly extremely successful. It put the Imperial Tiger Marines in full retreat and they began a total withdrawal subsequent to the raid. I often wonder if we were really effective in helping our ground troops on this unplanned mission. This mission was the precursor to the greater use of the P-47 as an offensive weapon of great value and devastating to the enemy.

GLIDE BOMBING IN SUPPORT OF GROUND FORCES *For the first time, the glide bombing missions of the Squadron were coordinated closely with the ground forces in the Maffin Bay-Sarmi sector by attacking enemy personnel and supply dumps. Briefing the pilots for these glide bombing missions required particular attention as to the bombing and strafing restriction boundaries, and also to the terrain and target identification features. In a few of the early missions target identification proved difficult because the target selected on the map was actually hidden beneath the thick cover of the jungle foliage. The artillery was called upon to lay smoke shells on the desired target, making identification possible from the air. Since no enemy ack-ack was encountered during previous missions in this sector, the flights were able to go in low over the target, thereby increasing their accuracy. Commendation has been received from the Commander of the ground forces in the Sarmi sector on the effectiveness of the bombing and strafing missions against the enemy's installations, equipment and personnel.*

Similar glide bombing missions were carried out against enemy personnel and installations around Kamiri drome on Noemfoor Island. Here the bombs were released from an altitude of about 5,000 feet because medium and light ack-ack was expected, although never received.—S-2 Intelligence report, 341FS History, June 1944[2]

Before that mission, the Japanese had tried to invade our tiny island one night with eight landing barges. What they didn't know was that the US Navy had put two PT boats at anchor between Wakde and our small island. As soon as it got dark, the Navy PT's would go on the prowl looking for any enemy ships or boats. They caught the eight barges about to make a landing on our tiny little island. The PTs had blinding lights to accompany their .50 caliber machine guns, 20-mm cannons and even a 40-mm cannon. In less time than it takes to describe it, the battle was over. The barges all sank and the survivors made a huge repast for the sharks that lived around the islands. The Japs lost eight barges and all personnel to zero loss on our side. We just loved our PT boys. The PT guys liked us too, because we provided cover for them in daylight hours when they were most vulnerable.[3]

AIR-SEA COOPERATION *With the establishing of a PT base nearby liaison was made with the PT intelligence office and arrangements were made for the interchange of information, maps, etc.*—History of 348th Fighter Group, June 1944

The rest of June's missions were to provide protection for our forces on Biak, which had turned into a real nasty fight. Our casualties were running into the thousands due to the terrible terrain of Biak, and the Japs had all the high ground. The missions were boring because the Japs would not come out and fight. We amused ourselves by looking for the remnants of the Tiger Marines who were fleeing up the coast of New Guinea. Returning from Biak, we would have two planes fly low as possible along the beach looking for the enemy, and if they spotted anyone they would peel up and the rest of the squadron would zero in on the spot, guns blazing. We once caught a whole company in waist-deep water where they couldn't run away.

JUNE COMBAT MISSIONS *During the past month the squadron has performed chiefly area cover. Some dive-bombing and strafing was done during the end of the month. . . . The dive bombing was confined to personnel and stores in the Maffin Bay area and Kamiri airdrome area, Noemfoor Island. Good results were obtained in the Maffin Bay area on pin-point targets by low-level bombing, using 500 lb. demolition bombs and 8–10 second delay fuse. This type of bombing for the P-47 enables much greater accuracy. It has been found that in glide-bombing, slower diving speeds and shorter diving runs provide better accuracy.*—341FS Combat Evaluation Report for June 1944

June at Wakde was also a very busy month due to the unexpected arrival of an upper-respiratory virus, which struck all personnel on Wakde Island. Pilots were grounded in large numbers, making double duty for those who didn't fall ill.

The patrol missions to Biak were long and boring. The Japs were nowhere to be seen. But they came out after dark and raised hell at Biak and Wakde as well.

BATTLE DAMAGE REPAIR *This month the squadron had its first experience in producing airplane patches en mass [sic]. A number of the planes were holed by flying shrapnel from enemy bombs dropped in the strip area in the early part of the month. In the interest of speed, small holes were smoothed out with a file and covered with dope and fabric. The larger holes required considerable sheet metal work, which was difficult due to the lack of supplies and proper tools.*— S-4 Supply and Materiel, Engineering report, 341FS History, June 1944

One night during a raid, I got a coral scratch on my left cheek from jumping into my foxhole; I was left with a bump that took 30 years to go away.[4] I think that was the night I dove head first into my foxhole. This small bump mysteriously disappeared in the 1970s, but reappeared a couple of years ago as a melanoma which was excised without any damage.

ENEMY RAIDS ON WAKDE ISLAND *The losses given are not those of this squadron, rather they are the total Allied losses sustained in the area. June 5/6, raid lasted all night, harassing carried out by three enemy airplanes. Seven Allied airplanes destroyed. A/A engaged without result . . . June 8/9, two red* *alerts during the night. During the last alert, two enemy airplanes dropped bombs hitting revetment areas, destroying 10 Allied airplanes, damaging three others, and also damaging some trucks and refueling units.*—History of the 341st Fighter Squadron, June 1944[5]

I remember a B-24 taking off from Wakde one day—it ran off the end of the runway and blew up. The whole ammo load must have gone off. TNT bombs didn't seem to do this so easily in my memory. It may have been that the ammo was the new RDX formula of high explosive that was not as stable as TNT. How unstable it was I later found out. We did not know anything about RDX at the time.[6]

MORE BOMBS AND FUZES *With the glide bombing mission of the Squadron continuing on an increased scale during May, the supply of bombs available at the bomb dumps was often limited; when 500 pound bombs were not available, three and one hundred pounders were substituted. On the three hundred and one hundred pound bombs nose fuzes were used alone until a few duds were reported by the pilots. In addition, then, to the M-103 nose fuze, the M-100A1 and M-113 type tail fuzes were used. With the use of two fuzes no duds were reported.*—S-4 Supply and Materiel, Armament report, 341FS History, May 1944

My tent had four residents, Robert Ducharme, Sam Galik, Bob Frank, and myself. We all had been friends since entering the service. Sam Galik was from Detroit and was the only married man in our flight. Sam, like most of us, gambled in his spare time, for lack of anything else to do. Prior to Wakde, Sam was due for R&R in Sydney, but had lost a bundle and was practically broke. I loaned him a few hundred dollars for his R&R; he insisted I accept his personal firearm as security—a 9mm German Luger pistol from WWI. When he returned from leave I gave it back to him, and he said if anything ever happened to him, the pistol was mine.

One day in early June, we were returning from a patrol mission to Biak. I was in the lead when one of the flight leaders back in the formation aborted his landing, and came around for a second landing attempt behind Sam Galik. Unfortunately, this flight leader had no flaps and didn't slow down; he ran right into the back of Sam's plane. I had already landed and was standing very near, so I saw the whole thing occur. The planes were telescoped but didn't catch on fire, and without thinking I jumped up on the wing of Sam's plane to assist him. He was unconscious. I released his seat belt, shoulder harness, and parachute and somehow lifted him out of the cockpit onto the wing where others got him to the ground. Speed was of the essence since there was a big danger of fire. No fire occurred, but Sam was dead with a crushed skull. The flight leader was not injured but both planes were a total loss.[7]

I don't remember if there was an explanation as to why the flight leader's flaps were not down, but I was very mad about what happened next. Later in the evening, we returned to our bivouac island and Sam's empty bunk to assemble his personal effects for shipment home. Unfortunately, when we went through Sam's footlocker we discovered his pistol was missing, which meant some officer in the 341st had raided Sam's locker and violated his stuff before we could get transportation to the island. We did not lock our footlockers at that time.

This was a devastating blow to our morale. We had a thief in our midst and no idea who it might be. This preyed on my mind so much I volunteered that day to join the new fighter squadron that was being formed in the 348FG. The Luger I didn't miss, but having a thief in the flying cadre really did bother me. We never found out who the perpetrator was. I can't imagine what kind of low life rat would have stolen Sam's pistol. That kind of event can really affect trust in a unit. I was very happy to join the newly established Black Rams and didn't talk to anyone from the 341st for many years.

HIGH-TIME PILOTS *At the close of June a summary check reveals the following number of pilots in the categories of missions performed: 1 pilot over 200 missions (222), 9 from 150–200 missions, 15 from 125–150 missions, 3 from 100–125 missions, and 11 less than 100 missions. With respect to number of combat hours flown; one pilot over 500 hours (517:10), 8 from 400–500 hours, 19 from 300–400 hours, 2 from 200–300 hours, 8 from 100–200 hours, and 1 less than 100 hours.*—S-3 Operations report, 341FS History, June 1944

In June, despite the shortage of able-bodied pilots, I did not have to fly continuously, so there was time to explore the area. The Japs had heavily defended the island of Wakde, but our forces quickly overcame their defense because the island was so small, only a mile long by three-quarters of a mile wide. The ocean side of the island had lots of caves due to wave action on the coral composition of the terrain; the Japs used the caves as their last defense. Our G.I.s didn't let this disturb them very much, and used flame throwers to kill the enemy. The flame thrower does not necessarily incinerate the foe—most died from suffocation due to the available oxygen being consumed by the flames. There were hundreds of bodies along the shore. By the time I was able to view the area, the stench of the corpses was beyond belief. This didn't deter some enterprising infantry boys from mining gold. Yes, gold teeth from the cadavers; one G.I. had a bag with about two pounds of gold.

SOUVENIRS *With so much movement through captured enemy bases, the men in the squadron acquired a fair share of Japanese souvenir material. The men showed their willingness to cooperate in turning over this souvenir material to the Intelligence Officer for translation and censorship.*—S-2 Intelligence report, 341FS History, May 1944

At other times of leisure we practiced with our .45-caliber sidearms, shooting at bottles and cans in the surf. We got pretty good at sinking cans. I had no problem with the .45 and found it to be an excellent weapon. The only thing I ever shot with it was a land crab which invaded my bed at Wakde's sleeping area.

But there was something else useful which became available at Wakde. Until 1944, we were advised to keep radio silence since the enemy monitored our HF radio conversation. But of course, there were times when communication was necessary, so they knew who I was, as well as who many other pilots were. We knew this from Tokyo Rose's broadcasts.

With the introduction of VHF radios in 1944, our line-of-sight communication was not restricted. If I recall correctly we had HF and VHF, the latter being line-of-sight, air-to-ground and air-to-air, a big plus since the enemy could no longer effectively monitor our communications.

When we switched to VHF, the radios were equipped with a self-destructive device to prevent the components from falling into enemy hands.

We had several radios blow up due to hard landings. I never had this landing problem since I made it a habit to "grease them in." I lived in fear of a Check officer pilot in Primary Flight Training who terrorized me so badly I always made perfect landings in the three-point position, whether he was aboard or in sight. His name was Schneider, the same name as my father's superior where he worked. I never blew a tire or a tail wheel in my entire flying career. But for this you don't get the DFC.

HF TO VHF RADIO TRANSITION *The high frequency radios in all of the squadron's planes were removed and replaced with VHF. A group of VHF radio personnel from the Service Squadron aided the section's personnel in the changeover. The training in maintenance of the SCR-522 radio received at Hillsgrove as part of the overseas training program came into good use. A work shop has been set up to test all sets and two spare radios are kept on hand at all times.*—S-4 Supply and Materiel, Communications report, 341FS History, June 1944[8]

The Japanese must have been out of their box when our HF radio transmissions stopped. Nothing was ever said about it in their broadcasts to us. Tokyo Rose continued with great music, loaded with Japanese propaganda that was really entertaining for us, and we took it all with a grain of rice.

One day while returning from a patrol of Biak, we were flying parallel to a tropical storm front when a most remarkable event occurred under the edge of the front. Seven waterspouts—the equivalent of a cyclone at sea—were observed at one time. From the surface to the clouds was a column of water hundreds of feet wide and about 1,000 feet high; some of these lasted for five minutes. For an aircraft to hit one of these would be like running into a mountain. We avoided getting too close to this phenomenon.

By this time in the war, the Army had also come up with a new device, a very large crash rescue boat powered by two diesel engines. It was about the same size as a PT boat, but not as powerful. One day I was invited to go on a test run of the boat, and included among the passengers was the flight surgeon. We motored to an island about 15 miles north of Wakde where it was rumored there were some natives from the island of Bali who were being abused by the Japs. We did find them, and they were in deplorable condition. The flight surgeon gave them what medical supplies we had on the boat, and ordered the sergeant to get us away ASAP. The refugees were all young women who had been severely abused. So much for the grandeur of the South Pacific.[9]

WESTERN NEW GUINEA *The month of June 1944 saw a consolidation of the areas already captured from the enemy on Biak Island and in the Maffin Bay-Sarmi sector. Planes from this squadron were used on patrol and cover missions over Biak Island and convoys in the area, until other fighter squadrons were stationed on Biak during the last half of the month. When the number of patrol missions was cut down, glide bombing missions were instituted against enemy ground installations in the Maffin Bay–Sarmi sector and around Kamiri Drome on Noemfoor Island, 100 miles to the West of Biak.*

The offensive activity of the Fifth Air Force during the month has been so effective that the enemy was pushed back to his western-most bases in New Guinea and in the Halmaheras. This withdrawal of the enemy's air force made it impossible for the Squadron's planes to engage in combat, since the active enemy bases are beyond effective military range of P-47's.—History of the 341st Fighter Squadron, June 1944

With the taking of Wakde, we also captured Hollandia, New Guinea, about 125 miles east of Wakde. The Japs had three airstrips there, and the enemy was so confounded by MacArthur skipping over their stronghold at Wewak that they fled the airfields in a panic. We were rewarded with the capture of several brand new fighter planes that had just been flown down from Japan, including a couple in mint condition. Captain Weiks of the 341st, a graduate engineer, opted to fly the Jap Zero. He was so overwhelmed with its performance that he volunteered to fly it to Brisbane, Australia for a complete evaluation. The other was a radial engine aircraft but I can't recall the code name.[10]

Captain Weiks returned to the group about the first of July and gave us a detailed, first-hand report on the aircraft, saying it was a fighter pilot's dream. His assessments of the quality of the fighter shook us to our very bones. As an example, it could climb 20% faster and turn twice as fast. We had 3/8-inch armor plate; they had 5/8-inch armor. Their range was 30% better than the P-47, which made them a formidable foe. The Zero had about 40 pounds of camouflage paint compared to 300 pounds of the same on a P-47. On top of that, the Zero was harder to see than the Jug. This report was very depressing, even for a P-47 pilot who felt he was flying the leading edge of our fighter aircraft.

With all this bad news came something new and exciting involving Charles A. Lindbergh, a true American hero. Besides his crossing of the Atlantic in 1927, he flew with members of the Fifth Air Force during World War II as a civilian advisor. Lindbergh gassed up a P-47D equipped with two 165-gallon wing tanks at Brisbane, Australia and flew nonstop to Hollandia, New Guinea. This was a phenomenal feat of flying, eclipsing his historic crossing of the Atlantic.

The flight was accomplished by using the "Lindbergh Fuel Economy System," which was a radical departure from what we were using. Our normal throttle setting for cruise was 30-inches of manifold pressure at 2,000 rpm. At this setting, recommended by Pratt & Whitney, the P-47 consumed about 60 gallons an hour at any altitude and maintained an indicated airspeed (IAS) of 190 mph. Our propeller pitch was interlocked with the throttle advance.

Lindbergh's theory was that the Pratt & Whitney R-2800 Double Wasp aircraft engine used in the P-47 was designed to operate continuously at very high manifold pressure, 52-inches of pressure. This abnormal high manifold pressure was obtained with a combination of blowers and a turbo-supercharger. Full takeoff power was 52-inches manifold pressure and 2,700 rpm of the engine, which in turn produced 900 rpm of the propeller. At this setting one achieved a maximum power of 2,000 horses with a continuous rate of climb of about 2,500 feet per minute. With this setting, the plane consumed 300 gallons an hour, which would limit our flight time to one hour using internal fuel. Obviously, this was not the thing to do if one desired to stay flying very long.

Lindbergh theorized that if one disengaged the propeller control from the throttle, one could cut the rpm's and still maintain lots of torque on the propeller. The result of this simple maneuver was a reduction in engine rpm's to the range of 1,300 to 1,500 rpm's while still being able to have 35-inches of manifold pressure. One could achieve much better gallons per hour in fuel consumption in the P-47, as well as in the P-38 and P-51, by using the Lindbergh system.

The idea was to fly the plane at this speed using the propeller pitch as a control. This all worked beautifully, except for the lead build-up on the 36 spark plugs in the engine, which would lead to rapid engine failure. The crafty Lindbergh figured out how to avoid this unfortunate condition. After 30-minutes of flight he put the propeller pitch at maximum rpm for 30 seconds. This high power setting literally blew the lead deposits of the grade 130–100 octane gasoline off the spark plugs. He would use this surge in power to gain altitude. Each cleaning project resulted in huge gains in altitude where the air is thinner and cooler, both conditions resulting in higher true airspeed. Every degree drop in temperature resulted in greater true airspeed. Flying at 190 indicated airspeed at 35,000 feet would equate to a true airspeed of 335 mph, considering the factors of temperature and altitude.

The system was not difficult to employ. After reaching the desired altitude, one manually disengaged the throttle from the prop pitch control. The throttle was then advanced to max and the prop pitch was adjusted so that the plane flew at 190 IAS, standard for many fighters of that time. The rpm would drop dramatically, reducing the fuel consumption as much as 40%. One had to monitor the cylinder head temperature under these conditions. Slower speeds caused excessive temperatures so bombers could not use the system.

Lindy made the trip from Brisbane to Hollandia at night, crossing over the most unexplored part of New Guinea at dawn, letting him experience never before seen snow covered mountains in the wilderness. His safe arrival at Hollandia set off a buzz in the V Fighter Command that we had a new secret weapon. Lindy visited Wakde Island, but we did not get to see him. He was busy with the P-38 outfit, training them in the use of his fuel economy system.[11]

Unknown to many people, he also flew some combat missions and engaged enemy forces. He went on a night combat mission with three P-38 pilots to Palau, considered out of reach for a P-38. Flying at night, they used dead reckoning navigation, but were aided the last 250 miles by Jap welders working at night in the shipyards. The flashes of their welding machines were easily seen for that distance in the dark Pacific night. As dawn approached, they found themselves over the Japanese airstrip, undetected because the Japs never expected an attack at this base, which they considered secure from land-based aircraft. Several Jap planes were spotted taking off. The P-38 flight leader opted to attack, including Colonel Lindbergh. Lindy, the ultimate aviator, shot down two aircraft in the ensuing attack. This never happened officially because Lindy was a civilian; but in real life, Lindy was an ace that day, a true American hero. His fuel economy system contributed to extended range for our fighter aircraft, which helped save the lives of American service personnel. We owe him deeply.

One night at Wakde the Japs got lucky and hit the fuel dump starting a fire that looked like it would consume all of the island. We had fuel stored in 55-gallon drums which the Japanese bombs set off; we watched as they exploded one at a time all night with huge geysers of flame that turned night into day. The devastation was phenomenal; the fire raged from midnight until dawn. Luckily, we lost only a few planes, but a lot of sleep. However, the raid did not interrupt our flying schedule. They must have been working 24/7 in the States making 55-gallon drums as we had no fuel shortages.

SCORCHED THUNDERBOLTS *Two of our airplanes were scorched in the June 30/July 1 raid between 2105K and 2215K when a single enemy plane dropped six fragmentation bombs on the strip and set fire to 700 drums of aviation gasoline. The two planes from our squadron were dispersed within a hundred yards of the fire. One plane had to be transferred out, and the other was repaired by the engineering personnel.*—History of the 341st Fighter Squadron, July 1944[12]

July 1st, 1944, was a day off. July 2nd was a mission to Noemfoor Island, some seventy miles west of Biak. Our task was to keep enemy planes from attacking our naval forces that were about to soften up Noemfoor, where MacArthur wanted an air base. Upon our arrival at Noemfoor, we observed a large contingent of US Navy warships approaching the island. There were three cruisers and a number of destroyers all lining up to shell the area where the landings would take place. We watched from our high vantage point for two hours while the Navy shelled the target.[13]

NOEMFOOR COMMENDATION
TO: GEN WHITEHEAD

FROM: ADM FECHTELER
QUOTE THE AIR SUPPORT FURNISHED BY FIFTH AIR FORCE
ON NOEMFOOR ISLAND DOG DAY (2 July) COMMANDED
BOTH THE ADMIRATION AND APPRECIATION OF NAVAL
FORCES PRESENT X THANK YOU X ADMIRAL FECHTELER
UNQUOTE.
Message from HQ Fifth Air Force to all Fifth
Air Force Unit Commanders, 4 July 1944

It was positively awesome to watch as they poured salvo after salvo into the target. Watching from overhead, we could see the warships move sideways as they fired their guns. All at once, we could actually observe the projectiles of the larger vessels arcing through the air on their way to the island. Not one tree was left standing in the target area.

Since no enemy planes appeared, our mission was one super-duper 4th of July celebration. When our relief arrived, we were actually sorry to have to leave. We did not know it at the time, but this island would be the first combat base for the proposed 460th Fighter Squadron, which would be my new assignment in the near future.

SKIP-BOMBING EXPERIMENT *In a recent skip-bombing flight, an experiment was made using 1,000 lb. demolition bombs with 8–11 second delay fuse. Excellent results were obtained. On take-off, the ship handled the same as if carrying full wing tanks. In the air, control of the ship was a little better with the bombs than with the full tanks. The bombs can either be released singlely [sic] from an altitude of 100 feet. The I.A.S. on the bombing run was between 230 MPH and 250 MPH.—*341FS Combat Evaluation report for July 1944

The health of my comrades in June and July, plus bad living conditions and poor food, had a deleterious effect on everyone, including me. My weight had again dropped below 140 pounds.

SQUADRON FARE *For the most part the morale was fairly good, although the food and incoming mail situations were generally poor. The only relief from the tasteless diet of bully beef, "C" rations, canned salmon, dehydrated* *potatoes, strained spinach, and pancakes came during the middle of the month when enough fresh beef arrived to provide for three meals. At the same time enough fresh creamery butter arrived to last about a week when used sparingly. Whenever incoming mail did not arrive for periods, ranging from five to ten days and even two weeks, the morale slumped noticeably.*—History of the 341st Fighter Squadron, July 1944

My transfer to the newly-formed 460th Fighter Squadron was in the paper heap, though I flew with the 341st until July 23rd. Shortly afterward, I was officially reassigned to the 460th Fighter Squadron, effective July 27th. The last week in July, Biak was declared secure by MacArthur. That didn't end the fighting there, but it did lighten the work load for the 348th Fighter Group enough that R&Rs were resumed. My final assignment with the 341st was to go to Sydney for R&R. They cut the orders on July 22. I flew my last of seven combat missions for the month on the 23rd, and a few days later I was on my way.

JULY COMBAT MISSIONS *Since conditions are moving so fast, there has been little to do for the squadron this month. Our work consisted chiefly of patrols. Some glide-bombing, skip-bombing, and strafing were done. No enemy contact was made. Anti-aircraft fire was not encountered in the period . . .*—History of the 341st Fighter Squadron, July 1944

R&R IN AUSTRALIA

I was sent to Sydney from Wakde and my gear was sent to Nadzab for the newly formed 460th Fighter Squadron. My first stop in Australia was Townsville where I bunked the night at the BOQ. Townsville was famous for its ant population. The legs of the steel cots were set in cans of coal oil to keep the insects out of your bed. Unfortunately, one of these ants took up residence in my bed and proceeded to chomp on sensitive parts of my body. The Aussies dubbed these man-eating creatures "piss ants" because their target was always one's penis. In the morning I awoke with severe itching and swelling, but proceeded on my way.

It took the better part of a week for me to get to Brisbane where I renewed acquaintance with the Aussies at Eagle Farm RAAF Officer's Club. Too much beer flowed that night and when dawn occurred, I had to get on an old Douglas DC-3 for a bumpy low-level flight to Sydney. Needless to say, I was one sick puppy all the way so I just lay on my parachute bag on the floor at the rear of the plane and suffered.

Much to my discomfort, I itched all the way to Sydney. I was so discomforted upon landing I went straight to the Army hospital, where, much to my amazement, they accused me of having intercourse with a diseased person. I explained that this scenario was impossible due to my location where there were absolutely no partners available. Upon further examination the doctor discovered an ant's head under the skin, which was promptly removed without the benefit of anesthesia. I was required to stay at the hospital until all my tests came back and the swelling subsided. A few days' bed rest and good food did wonders and after three days I was ready for anything. In the hospital I saw many wounded veterans from island battles; their wounds were horrendous.

I was a total mess when I arrived in Sydney, so I hired a cab at great expense and went directly to Kathy's apartment; she was expecting me. As soon as she saw me she ordered me to shed and I was soon in a hot tub of water getting back to being a human being. A nice bath and a few hours of rest rejuvenated me. My weight was down to 135 pounds and I was ravishingly hungry for some decent food. As soon as I was rested we went out to a steak house where I ordered everything I wanted; soup, salad, shrimp and a porterhouse steak. Thus began a super leave at Sydney, which included a train ride down the coast to visit Kathy's relatives, about 100 miles south of Sydney. They were most friendly and fed me real good. I can still remember the soup they served. It was some local concoction that I liked, but the name escapes me. Being away from the hubbub of Sydney made the stay most pleasant, kind of like being home.

REST AND RECREATION *Ten enlisted men departed for furloughs to Mackay, Queensland, Australia, during the month, while fourteen enlisted men returned from furloughs. Three enlisted men were granted convalescent furloughs to Koolangatta, Queensland. Of the officers, eleven spent leaves in Sydney, New South Wales, and three returned.*—S-1 Personnel report, 341FS History, July 1944

My stay in Sydney was very restful. Time flew by swiftly and I was soon bereft of funds, so I had to start back to my new assignment with the 460th Fighter Squadron. By the end of August, I was on my way back to New Guinea, my new squadron, and new duty as a Flight Leader.

TRANSFER TO THE BLACK RAMS *On 2 August the following officers were relieved from assignment with this organization and assigned to our newly activated sister squadron, the 460th Fighter Squadron: Captains Charles A. Cronk, Jr., Frank B. Morrison, Jr. First Lieutenants James C, Curran, and George Della. These officers were joined on 20 August by Sergeants Russell D. Eide, Harry M. Kronewitter, and William K. Maclees.*—History of the 341st Fighter Squadron, August 1944

NOTES

1. The "Tiger Marines" were not an Imperial Japanese Navy formation, but the Imperial Japanese Army's 36th Division, Amphibious, commanded by Lieutenant General Tagami Hachiro. It was one of three Army divisions which were ordered reformed into amphibious-capable formations in late 1943 with the addition of a sea transportation unit, though as things turned out shortages of landing craft and personnel adversely affected the amphibious capability part of this reorganization. *"The 36th Division to the West New Guinea,"* http://forum.axishistory.com/view-topic.php?f=65&t=192783&sid=02636aca6e520a48e9993c63b2ac3c63

2. The development of close support for troops on the ground by the Army Air Forces in the Pacific developed in different ways as compared to the experience in other combat theaters. For a detailed discussion on the subject, see *Close Air Support in the War Against Japan, USAF Historical Studies: No. 86.* Maxwell AFB, AL: USAF Historical Division, Research Studies Institute, Air University, February 1955, (Hereinafter *Close Air Support in the War Against Japan*) Chapter IV, From Lae to Morotai, and the first section, Development of Air-Ground Liaison in the SWPA, pages 57–62.

3. Research by the co-author could find no specific report by a PT Boat unit that correlates to the description of this action. It is possible it is a description of an action in the area near Wakde. For example, on the night of 23/24 May 1944, PT 362 and PT 363 of Motor Torpedo Boat Squadron Eighteen on patrol between Wakde and the New Guinea coastline attacked enemy barges at Vandoemear Island (probably today's Vandumuar Island, about 17 miles west-northwest of Wakde, and just east of Sarmi). On the night of 25/26 May, PT 194 and PT 364 of MTB Squadron Twelve conducted a similar patrol and engaged enemy barges on the east side of

the Sarmi Peninsula. Later on the morning of 26 May, PT-194 set out for Hollandia for Wakde and ran across a small raft under sail with three Japanese soldiers aboard at 0815K. The crew attempted to take them prisoner but when the Japanese resisted with rifle fire they were killed.

"Motor Torpedo Boat Squadron Eighteen, War Diary—May 1944" and "Motor Torpedo Boat Squadron Twelve, War Diary, May, 1944."

4. Imperial Japanese Navy Mitsubishi G4M "Betty" bombers raided Wakde several times in early June 1944, and may have caused this foxhole injury Jim Curran incurred at Wakde. Details on some IJN air raids against Wakde as follows:

Japanese raid of June 6, 1944. Three G4M Betty bombers of the 732nd Kokutai took off from Wasile on the night of June 5th. Led by Ensign Isao Sunayama, the three bombers encountered very heavy weather. One bomber became separated and dropped its bombs in the Biak area. Sunayama and the other bomber continued to Wakde and were rewarded by a break in the clouds that allowed them to sight the field. The two bombers swooped down low over the field. Each bomber took one side of the runway along which American aircraft were parked. Releasing their bombs in a string over the parked aircraft, the Japanese flyers estimated they had destroyed dozens of American aircraft. In total, six planes are destroyed (one B-24, four P-38's and one L-4B) and 80 damaged. This June 6th attack stands out as a singularly successful Japanese effort at this stage of the Pacific War.

Japanese raid of June 8, 1944. Three G4M Betty bombers return to bomb Wakde Airfield.

"Japanese missions against Wakde Island and Wakde Airfield," http://www.pacificwrecks.com/airfields/indonesia/wakde/missions-wakde.html

5. Wakde was a rather unpleasant experience for the 348FG, as its small size and lack of space made it an easy target for Japanese bombers. The sister squadron of the 341FS, the 340FS, appears to have suffered a lot of damage from air raids on Wakde. In its June, 1944 history, the 340th reported that on June 9, 1944, two medium bombers dropped 12 unidentified bombs and destroyed ten Allied aircraft, five of which were P-47s of the 340th. The four air raids on Wakde during the month put a total of eight more 340FS P-47's out of commission, damaged so severely they had to be transferred to a service unit. Eleven others were repaired by the squadron's sheet metal department after being damaged by flying shrapnel. Four refueling units and a small ammunition supply were also destroyed in the June 9 attack.

In addition to the two raids on June 8–9 described in the 341FS history (see ENEMY RAIDS ON WAKDE ISLAND, page 127), other Japanese raids on Wakde in June 1944 did not inflict as much damage. On June 6–7, enemy reconnaissance; four red alerts during the night, but no bombs were dropped. On June 7–8, one twin-engine bomber made a run from east to west at minimum altitude in an early morning attack, dropping five bombs in the water. On June 10–11, a single enemy airplane made a pass over the island during the night, dropping three bombs in the water. On June 12–13, six small bombs were dropped at 0155K, causing slight damage to installations and one Allied vessel. Three men were injured. The 340FS had one P-47 damaged in this raid by a single medium bomber.

The 342FS also suffered a lot at the hand of these Japanese raiders at Wakde, as compared to the 341FS The 342FS history for June 1944 showed 24 P-47's on hand at the start of the month. During June 1944, a net decrease of 20 P-47's took place, accompanied by a net increase of 23 P-47s. In this airframe shuffle, the 20 losses were attributed as follows:

Lost or transferred due to combat: 2

Lost or transferred on the ground due to enemy action: 7

Lost or transferred through accidents: 3

Transferred due to major repairs or parts not in stock: 8

Thus the 342FS ended the month of June 1944 with 27 P-47's on hand, a net plus of three aircraft. In comparison, Jim Curran's squadron started June with 25 aircraft, lost none in combat missions, 1 on the ground from enemy action and three in accidents, and ended the month with 28 P-47's on hand.

History of the 341st Fighter Squadron, June 1944, Appendix I, Statistical Data for June 1944 and Appendix VII, Enemy Raids on Wakde Island.

History of the 340th Fighter Squadron, June 1944, Outline of Squadron History and Narrative of Squadron History.

Squadron History, June 1944, 342nd Fighter Squadron, page 1.

6. Research was unable to find a specific B-24 crash on takeoff at Wakde to correlate with this recollection, which is not to suggest that it did not happen. Anecdotal accounts do exist from personnel assigned to units on Noemfoor Island later in 1944, during the intense, long-range series of Far East Air Forces missions against the Japanese-occupied oil facilities in and around Balikpapan, Borneo. A 460FS Squadron Armorer, Nolan Machen, noted such in his war diary:

Oct 12th . . . A B-24 of the Long Rangers outfit taxied into a gas trailer by our revetments. Both burned completely within 20 minutes.

October 17 . . . This morning at three o'clock a B-24 crashed during takeoff. The unusual sound of the engines cutting out woke me up. A red alert was sounded. The bombs exploded while the plane was burning."

The Royal Australian Air Force also noted this terrible phenomenon at Noemfoor, as B-24's took off on long-range missions westward. "Liberator squadrons were soon operating (from Kornasoren Airfield on Noemfoor) on distant targets in Indo China, crossing Borneo and unloading any remaining bombs on Labuan Airfield, North Borneo. They would take off at dawn and return at dusk, sometimes coming in with motors faltering, running out of fuel. The heavily bombed up aircraft would run down the strip in the dim morning light with a crew of eight or nine men; sometimes, the load was too much for the heavily laden aircraft, and they would run off the over run into the jungle and blow up. At those times, the men would go very quiet, listening to the exploding ammunition, knowing that nine men had just sacrificed their lives."

War Diary of Nolan Machen, page 4

"The Noemfoor Island Operation," http://raafacs.homestead.com/5ACSNOEM-FOOR.html

7. First Lieutenant Samuel Galik Jr. was killed in a landing accident at Wakde on June 4, 1944. He is buried in the Manila American Cemetery in Manila, Philippines, at Plot D, Row 10, Grave 84. Lt. Galik was awarded the Purple Heart and the Air Medal for his service and sacrifice in World War II.

Stanaway, *Kearby's Thunderbolts,* 177

"Samuel Galik Jr.," http://www.abmc.gov/search-abmc-burials-and-memorializa-tions/detail/WWII_108479#.VBPeMhbLBOI

8. This radio upgrade took place throughout the 348th Fighter Group in the June, 1944 timeframe. "A detachment of experts arrived from Command to aid our communications in installing the new secret VHF equipment. Upon completion of the work a much more efficient and workable radio network will be available and it should do much to increase the safety of flying."

The new radio also required the removal of a 42-gallon fuel cell from the fuselage located to the rear of the pilot's seat (the Christmas Tree Tank). This procedure was to take place before the conversion to the new Command VHF radio installation. A directive to this effect, Service Memorandum No. 4, 16 June 1944, was sent out by HQ, Far East Air Service Command. According to the 342FS History for July, 1944, "This eliminated 131 pounds of superfluous weight, decreased the fire hazard to the pilot by the elimination of this vulnerable spot, and also facilitated the installation and replacement of VHF radio sets."

One other aspect of the conversion from HF to VHF radio in the Pacific is worth note. "Aside from the supposedly better communications thus afforded, such a change was essential in order to be able to communicate with naval aircraft."

"The History of the 348th Fighter Group, June, 1944," http://www.ww2f.com/topic/37324-history-of-the-348th-fighter-group/

History of the 342nd Fighter Squadron, Chapter IX, (1–31 July 1944), pp. 3-4 and Enclosure No. 4, "Service memorandum No. 4," 16 June 1944.

Close Air Support in the War Against Japan, Chapter IV, From Lae to Morotai, page 111.

9. Army Air Forces rescue capability grew significantly in 1944, and included a seaplane capability with the OA-10A Catalina and various types of crash rescue boats. In the Pacific, on 10 June 1944 the Fifth Air Force's 1001st Quartermaster Boat Company (Aviation) was redesignated as the 14th Emergency Rescue Boat Squadron (14ERBS) and soon received high-speed crash rescue boats. The movement of

these craft is not very detailed in the unit history, making it difficult to correlate to Jim Curran's recollection. First mention of the 85-foot crash rescue boat in the unit history was August 1944 when crews were sent to Milne Bay in eastern New Guinea to commission these boats. These were the closest in size to a PT Boat, though the 63-foot boats the unit also operated could have been the craft he remembered, given their physical characteristics. The unit sent two 85-foot boats from Dreger Harbor near Finschhafen on to a forward base on Biak Island in October 1944. One of these boats diverted to Wakde where it underwent wheel repairs. This was the only mention of Wakde in the 14ERBS history.

USAAF air-sea rescue capabilities continued to build through to the end of the war. On 24 September 1944, Fifth Air Force's Rescue Service became the 5276th Rescue Composite Group (Provisional) on 24 September 1944, with the 3rd Emergency Rescue Squadron (OA-10A seaplane) and the 14th Emergency Rescue Boat Squadron. In October 1944, Thirteenth Air Force activated the 5230th Rescue Composite Group (P) which included the 2nd Emergency Rescue Squadron and the 15th Emergency Rescue Boat Squadron. These squadrons were widely deployed around the SWPA into numerous small detachments in support of ongoing missions.

"History of the 14th Emergency Rescue Boat Squadron," http://scottdavis61.good-luckwith.us/14th.htm

Air-Sea Rescue, 1941-1952, US Air Force Historical Study No. 95, Maxwell AFB: USAF Historical Division, Air University, 1953, Chapter V, The Pacific Theaters and CBI, pages 66–99.

10. Hollandia was a major air base complex for the Imperial Japanese Army's Fourth Air Army, a major opponent of Fifth Air Force. Several abandoned Ki-43 OSCAR fighters were rebuilt to flying status by various units. The Allied Technical Air Intelligence Unit evaluated at least one of these aircraft. In the air war in the Southwest Pacific, Japanese Army OSCAR fighters were frequently mistaken as Japanese Navy Zero fighters, and this may be the case in this particular recollection.

Pluth, Dave, "The Captured Oscars of Hollandia," http://www.j-aircraft.com/re-search/dave_pluth/hollandia_oscars.htm

Dunn, "Double Lucky" http://www.warbirdforum.com/lucky12.htm

Trojan, David, "Technical Air Intelligence Wreck Chasing in the Pacific War," http://www.j-aircraft.com/research/David_Trojan/Technical%20Air%20Intelligence%20Wreck%20chasing%20in%20the%20Pacific%20during%20the%20war.pdf

11. Stanaway, *Kearby's Thunderbolts,* page 113, also wrote of Charles Lindbergh's visit to the 348th Fighter Group. Lindbergh arrived at Wakde on 16 August 1944 after a flight from Biak aboard a P-61 night fighter. "Lindbergh found the Headquarters area and Major John Moore's tent. He and Moore discussed fuel economy in the P-47. The men of the 348th had already heard of his nonstop flight in a P-47 from

Brisbane, Australia, to Port Moresby, New Guinea—without external fuel tanks (*author note:* This distance is about 1,130 nautical miles). So, there was a guaranteed audience when he spoke to the squadrons the next day."

The 342FS history for August 1944 also mentions the Lindbergh visit: "During the month, Colonel Charles A. Lindbergh, technical representative for one of the aircraft corporations, made numerous test flights in the P-47 in this area. As a result of these tests, he lectured our pilots on his theories of how to get the maximum efficiency in high-altitude, long-range flying. Notes on his speech were taken by Lt. Knapp, Assistant Operations Officer and are included as enclosure 2." This Enclosure 2 is included in this book as Appendix 5, Operations Memorandum dated 18 August 1944. Subject: Tactics on Operating P-47.

12. In this same 30 June 1944 raid by an unidentified bomber which damaged two 341FS Thunderbolts, the sister 340FS lost one P-47 destroyed and two more P-47's damaged.

History of the 340th Fighter Squadron, June 1944, Outline of Squadron History

13. The invasion of Noemfoor was called Operation Cyclone. Jim Curran flew top cover over warships conducting the pre-landing bombardment, which included the Australian heavy cruiser HMAS *Australia* and American light cruisers USS *Phoenix* and USS *Boise*. The Navy was appreciative of the air support it received from units like the 348th Fighter Group, as indicated in a 4 July 1944 commendation passed along to all Fifth Air Force unit commanders from Major General Ennis C. Whitehead, Commander of Fifth Air Force "(see extract on page 135, NOEMFOOR COMMENDATION).

"*USS Fletcher* DD-445, Noemfoor Action Report, July 2, 1944," http://www.ussfletcher.org/history/noemfoor.html

History of the 342nd Fighter Squadron, Chapter IX, (1–31 July 1944), Enclosure No. 3 "Commendation," 4 July 1944. CD A0778 / p. 1199

Chapter Eight

WITH THE BLACK RAMS

NADZAB

ON SEPTEMBER 1ST, 1944, I PICKED UP A NEW P-47D-21 at Townsville, Australia, flying it nonstop to Nadzab, New Guinea, about 880 miles, in 4:15 flying time.[1] Nadzab was the training site for the 460th. I did not use the Lindbergh fuel economy method at the time, because we were not all indoctrinated into the process as yet.[2] Nadzab was fairly neat by the time we started training with 40 pilots, four ground officers, and about 250 enlisted men.

The V Fighter Command deemed it a good move to expand the 348th group to four squadrons, thus the 460th Fighter Squadron was born. Major William D. "Dinghy" Dunham was selected to ramrod this new squadron.[3] This was a deal between Hap Arnold, Dunham, and some of the brass at group. The way I heard it, Dunham promised General Arnold he would train an elite cadre of pilots with an oversized number of aircraft to be ready for any eventuality on 15 minutes' notice. Dunham sold this concept to the powers that run things, and the 460th came about.

With Dunham in command, he in turn selected seasoned pilots from the other three squadrons as a nucleus of fighter pilots and got the balance of the pilot roster filled from the Combat Replacement and Training Center pool at Port Moresby. We had about three experienced pilots from each squadron of the 348th. With Dunham plus nine, we needed about 30 recruits. An airdrome squadron at Nadzab was integrated into the unit as the necessary ground crews.[4]

RESTLESS RAMS *Patience with delay was an unwelcome counterpart of the month of August. Capt. William D. Dunham . . . Squadron Commander, and his cadre of 15 veteran pilots restlessly awaited the assignment of planes and new pilots.*—History of the 460th Fighter Squadron (SE), August 1944

I was fortunate to be invited to join the squadron by Dunham, for what reason I haven't got the slightest idea, except I never snafued a mission. All the other squadrons remained at 16 planes for maximum operations. I haven't got the vaguest idea how a number for the designation of the 460th was selected. It would be of interest to know.

Major Dunham came from the 342nd Fighter Squadron. He brought key personnel with him, one of whom was my buddy Willis "Bill" M. Cooley. Bill Cooley and I were together from preflight through advanced and transition training. He went to the 342nd FS, flying wing on Bill Dunham many times. We immediately bunked together in the same tent, just like old times. We began the process of selecting pilots from the reserve pool. Each flight leader was allowed to nominate trainees from the replacement training center pool, subject to approval by Bill Dunham.

We had a variety of veteran pilots in the 460th. Otto Carter was an original member of the group when it was formed stateside in 1942, assigned with the 340th FS. Wallace Harding was also assigned to the 340th, but he was shipped overseas at the same time as me. All three of us were selected by Bill Dunham for the 460th. Of note, a P-47 flown by Otto Carter and crash-landed by Wallace Harding on 1 October 1943, has been recovered from the South Pacific, and I hope it can be restored.[5]

All new candidates were personally interviewed and informed about the aspirations of the squadron. We had no dual training aircraft, so recruits were put right into P-47s for training.

HAND-PICKED PILOTS *The last day of the month brought news that was reassuring. Twenty-four new pilots were on their way to the squadron from FEAF Combat RTC, Port Moresby. Many of these pilots had been personally selected by Capt. Dunham, who had made several trips during the early part of the month to Port Moresby, for that purpose.*—History of the 460th Fighter Squadron (SE), August 1944[6]

Intensive training began in late July at Nadzab. Two weeks were spent breaking in new pilots. New aerial tactics were taught as well as ground support tactics and low-level bombing. This was the transition from high altitude protective tactics to a new kind of offensive warfare for P-47 fighters.[7]

A SHORT TIME TO PREPARE *Time, before the squadron moved into the combat area, was even shorter than was expected. That the squadron would remain at Nadzab until its new pilots had been indoctrinated into the technicalities of flying in the South West Pacific Area was an accepted conclusion, but, that the time for accomplishing this objective was so limited was beyond even the most eager hopes of Captain Dunham and the old pilot cadre. For this reason, it was fortunate that the assignment of new pilots was not delayed another day. Twenty four pilots were assigned, and joined the squadron on 1 September, 1944.*—History of the 460th Fighter Squadron (SE), September 1944

Finally, by September 1st, we started to fly again. Everybody was rusty; but by the middle of the month we were starting to look like a fighting unit.

SENSE OF URGENCY *No time was wasted. On the very evening of their arrival Captain Dunham called a meeting of all officers for the purpose of introducing the new men, and acquainting everyone with the intensive schedule that he and Captain Orr, Operations Officer, had mapped out. An average of 100 flying hours a day, weather permitting, was their goal. It was a big bite, but all personnel were keyed to it. There was little doubt the squadron would meet, or at least come close, to its objective.*—History of the 460th Fighter Squadron (SE), September 1944

All pilots at the time had been trained to fly close formation, but Bill Dunham was of a new school of outstanding fighter pilots who advocated a "spread out" formation. Dinghy always stressed flying a "line abreast" formation versus the "staggered" formation, on the premise that it would be very difficult to attack because everyone could turn into the attackers. This required the pilots to learn how to navigate and stay in place while spread out in a line close to all abreast. This formation used in the combat zone allowed all pilots to have a view of everything going on and spread way out where anyone could turn inside of their companions. No one could sneak up on you with so many eyes looking on. This was a defensive posture.

TRAINING THE BLACK RAMS *The intensive training, ordered by Captain Dunham, began the following day in earnest, and continued to within three days of the actual movement into a more forward area. Training consisted of basic combat formations, aerobatics, aerial gunnery, and two recco missions to Rabaul. The record of these activities shows a close approach to the goal that had been set.*—History of the 460th Fighter Squadron (SE), September 1944

After the training process of the new 460th was complete, there was a rapid rotation of the older pilots stateside so we were soon blessed with some more new pilots. And all the original recruits didn't last through the training, so many were replaced, which made for a very fluid cadre of pilots. The above rotations started even while we were in Nadzab.

EXPEDITED *On the 11 September 1944, far earlier than had been expected, official announcement of the squadron's move to a more forward area was received . . . To this radio Captain Dunham replied that given the planes, estimated time of arrival of air echelon would be 18 September 1944.*—History of the 460th Fighter Squadron (SE), September 1944

Most of the training was not in the active combat zone, but on September 16, the 460th had its first combat mission, a four-hour reconnaissance over to the Japanese bastion of Rabaul, New Britain. Although this stronghold had been bypassed, it was still a very dangerous place to visit. We operated out of Nadzab, and as I remember, it was an escort mission. I don't think we hauled a bomb at that time and I don't remember firing guns, which usually stands out in my recollections. We did get shot at but suffered no damage, while inflicting some on the Japs.[8]

Some exciting things occurred in our short stay at Nadzab, which was now a huge Army base with a general hospital recently moved up from Sydney. A nurse from the medical facility was assaulted one evening by two troops. They left her on a road where she was discovered by MPs. She was physically OK but badly beat up. She had snatched the dog tags off one of her assailants, who were immediately rounded up by the MPs. A court martial proceeding was arranged for the next day; the following day, the trial occurred. In 1944, the penalty for this crime in the military was death by hanging. The two soldiers involved were found guilty and sentenced to death ASAP. There existed no facility for the sentence to be carried out so the culprits got two days reprieve while the Corps of Engineers built one. All available troops were ordered to view the punishment, including us. Thousands of troops sweated in the hot tropical sun while the sentence was carried out. Justice then was much different than it is now.

In August 1944, an aircraft carrier dropped anchor in Lae Harbor, some 25 miles southeast of Nadzab. It looked huge to me. It had anti-torpedo nets deployed all around the waterline to deflect any possible torpedo attack and was swinging at anchor. What it was doing in Lae Harbor was unknown to us, possibly in for repairs. I know the Navy performed miracles of maintenance in the war zones; it was the only time I ever saw a carrier not moving, except for the carrier at the quay in Brisbane unloading P-47s in the summer of 1943.

While training our new pilots, we flew over the carrier and noticed the anti-aircraft gun crews were tracking us for practice. I decided to give them a little air show, which attracted a large audience on the deck of the ship. As a finale, we came in over the stern and made like a landing pattern, letting wheels and flaps down. I guess they thought we were really going to attempt to land because they started to blink red lights, shoot flares and run the "Tilly" tractor into the middle of the deck. No harm was done and we had a good laugh.

The next day on a training mission, Art Cronk took his flight over to see the carrier. I watched from afar, not wanting to push my luck with the Navy. What occurred next was a once-in-a-lifetime event. Cronk's engine quit without warning when he was flying by the carrier. He had wing tanks on from a previous mission. He was too low to jump out so he flew his plane into a water landing a short distance from the carrier. The wing tanks acted like pontoons until his speed decreased enough to have the prop dig in. The plane sank instantly and it seemed like an eternity before Art popped up to the surface. The carrier crew watched the event and a small craft rescued Art immediately, so he got a free trip to the carrier.

He later related how worried the carrier people were when they saw us put down our landing gear. His water landing was very smooth. Cronk said he was 30 feet under before he could get his straps and belt off so he could escape the plunging plane. Art Cronk passed away in 2005.[9]

In keeping with the squadron's mission, we all had to be ready at all times to move on short notice, like a constant readiness posture. This included all our gear.

NOEMFOOR

On September 26, 1944, the entire 460th Fighter Squadron exited Nadzab for our first tactical base, on the island of Noemfoor, west of Biak in the Dutch part of New Guinea. It was a four hour and fifteen minute flight. This was the same place where we earlier watched the US Navy soften up the area for a landing of Allied troops.

GETTING TO NOEMFOOR *Finally, at 1500 hours, 22 September 1944, the air echelon received the information it had been awaiting. Twenty planes instead of the twenty-seven originally planned were allotted for the movement. By late afternoon of the day following receipt of movement orders, the air echelon had arrived at Noemfoor, Netherlands East Indies and was well advanced in the initial routine of establishing a camp. . . . On the fourth day after the main body's departure from Nadzab, the twenty-five pilots, who had remained behind to ferry the squadron's planes to the new base, arrived as well as seven additional planeloads of personnel and equipment.*—History of the 460th Fighter Squadron (SE), September 1944

The Corps of Engineers had built two beautiful runways out of compacted coral. There was no sign of the terrible devastation previously wrought by the warships—by the time we got to Noemfoor, everything was neat as a pin and the place looked like an Army base. Our squadron area was all laid out with streets of coral, and our raised-floor tents erected in neat rows with covered commodes and bathing facilities. We had a screened-in mess and club with electric lights and cooling fans. The latter was a big plus, as was the squadron refrigerator, which was opened daily for a cold drink for all, while it lasted. Needless to say, this was not a long period of time. It took 24 hours for the gas refrigerator to do its thing.

NOEMFOOR AIRFIELD *The new camp area was located some one half to three quarters of a mile inland from the southeast end of Kornasoren strip. As the revetments assigned to the squadron were located at this end of the strip, the camp was located very conveniently. The camp, itself, was in the 348th Group area, along with the other three squadrons of the group. . . . squadron morale was still high. Group facilities for coca cola, movies, ice cream and a public address system broadcasting daily the latest news and music, added greatly to their spirit. The commencement of operations furnished them the activity and interest necessary for good morale.*—History of the 460th Fighter Squadron (SE), September 1944

The other three squadrons were fully operational and snug as bugs in a carpet. All four of the 348th Fighter Group's squadrons were separated widely, as was Group HQ. As a consequence, we didn't get to mingle very much. Noemfoor was about the best base we had; San Marcelino, which came later in the Philippines, would run a close second.

REFLECTIONS ON NEW GUINEA *A campaign in its own right, New Guinea was at this moment proving itself to have been as well a great strategic training ground for the more exacting requirements of the grapple in the islands to the north.*—348th Fighter Group History, November 1944

On September 27, I was released from duty as an Assistant Flight Leader and, along with Willis Cooley, Wallace Harding and DeWitt Searles, was designated as a Flight Leader as my principal duty. The next few days we familiarized ourselves with the area and continued training flights and combat missions. We conducted long-range missions to Ambon in the Moluccas Islands and other places west of New Guinea. We flew bombing and escort missions into these areas of the Dutch East Indies.

INTRODUCTION TO COMBAT OPERATIONS *October can be considered as the maiden introduction of the squadron into combat, for it was the first month in which the great majority of all flights were of a combat nature and over enemy territory. It was not combat as the old, veteran pilots of the squadron knew at Salamaua, Finschhafen, Lae, Wewak and Wakde when the Nips* *were constant, hostile challengers to air superiority, and ack-ack over the target area was as common as it was heavy. Yet, it was combat, and a welcome change from the routine of training at Nadzab.*—History of the 460th Fighter Squadron (SE), October 1944

Meanwhile, the other three squadrons of the group were also running missions to targets in western Dutch New Guinea and across the Ceram Sea. Beyond Celebes Island was Borneo, where the Japanese controlled the oil fields at Balikpapan, Borneo. The oil was so good they could power their naval ships without refining it. The Thirteenth Air Force, with some help from Fifth Air Force, flew a series of B-24 bombing missions to destroy the oil fields in Borneo between September 30th and October 18th, 1944. The distance to Borneo was at the extreme range for the P-47s of another group based at Morotai.[10]

The first mission with fighter escort was set up for that P-47 group to take the B-24s in and out of the target area. One squadron went in prior to the bombers, one with the bombers and one squadron was to extract them. That's all good on paper, but it didn't happen that way. The first squadron scattered the Japanese fighter opposition, but the bombers had trouble on their approach in establishing their initial point; the bombing run was delayed so much that the extracting squadron was out of gas before the bombs were dropped. The bombers attacked and dropped their loads on the target successfully, but were without friendly fighter cover while heading for home. It was a disaster for the bomber crews who suffered many casualties from the Japanese fighters.

BALIKPAPAN AND BEYOND *While the "heavies" of the 13th Air Force were heard nightly as they took off from nearby Kornasoren strip for their long distance strikes against the oil fields and refineries of Balikpapan in Borneo, the fighter groups at Noemfoor were staging daily raids against nearer objectives in the Ceram Island Area, Dutch New Guinea, and the Kai Islands, or carrying out weather and search missions in the Noemfoor area.*—History of the 460th Fighter Squadron (SE), October 1944

While the Balikpapan raids were going on, we kept up the pressure on enemy airfields in the Dutch East Indies. I flew five combat missions that month, all glide bombing against these airfields. On October 6, I flew a morning mission as one of 11 of our P-47's (six armed with a single 1,000-pound bomb) were sent to glide bomb Utarom, also known as Kaimana Airfield, just south of Utarom in Irian Jaya of the Dutch East Indies. It was about 200 miles south-southwest of Noemfoor. "Results of bombing unobserved due to bad weather," according to squadron record.[11]

A BLACK RAM'S FIRST TIME TO RECEIVE *Oct. 8th at three o'clock in the morning I underwent my first bombing. Near three o'clock the red alert was sounded by three blasts of a siren, three red flares & three shots. About four minutes later we heard a plane. A few seconds after that they cut loose. The bombs made a woobling racket very unlike the movies. I only saw two flashes but some say there were more bombs. Yours truly was scared. I didn't pray as they usually say. I could only think where will they hit. Not in this truck rut I hope because that's where I was. Just as close to dear old earth as I could get.*—War Diary of Nolan Machen, Armorer, 460th Fighter Squadron[12]

On October 11, we launched a morning mission ranging almost 500 miles, 16 P-47's with one 500-pounder each, to glide bomb Kairatoe Airdrome on the western end of Ceram Island, in the Moluccas Island group. "Target was bombed through cumulus clouds which layed [sic] over target. Results were unobserved due to cloud formation," according to the squadrons mission results, but no doubt it was an unwelcome delivery for the enemy as we kept him on the defensive.[13]

OPPOSITION IN THE N.E.I. *No air opposition was met by the 460th's fighters, but ack-ack was frequently encountered. Weather was by far the most consistent and effective enemy. The high, frontal storms and sudden heavy squalls common to this region were a constant threat to the pilots. The thousand mile round trip to the target area left only a small safety allowance for gas which made detours for bad weather extremely hazardous. It was due to weather that the commander of the 348th Fighter Group, Major John T. Moore, AC, while flying with the 460th squadron, was lost somewhere over Haroekoe strait.*—History of the 460th Fighter Squadron (SE), October 1944[14]

On the 14th of October, I flew a nearly 500-mile glide bomb mission toting a single 500-pounder along with 14 other Jug pilots against Haroekoe Airdrome on Pelauw Island, in the Moluccas. Results weren't great and only six planes dropped bombs on the target.[15] Later that day, we were sitting around our evening cup of cocoa and jawing about what the next move by MacArthur might be. We used the chocolate K-Ration bar to make the cocoa. The bar was inedible in its solid form, sort of like plaster, maybe a little harder. It made a decent drink and didn't bother your sleep like coffee.

Anyway, Cooley and I had been awarded with an R&R in Australia earlier in October and attended a party in Sydney where we heard from a young lady that Leyte Island in the Philippines would be the next big landing target. We related this bit of gossip to our cocoa companions in our tent quarters. Our squadron intelligence officer (S-2), John R. Whitney, was sitting in on the conversation and almost had a stroke at our revelation. He arose to his feet and announced that no one was to leave the tent, on orders.

All hell broke loose with this revelation. In no time we had a host of heavyweight intelligence people all over the place. Within 15 minutes we were surrounded by counter-intelligence agents, the Counter-Intelligence Corps or whoever they were, embedded in the group. We had never seen these people before. They grilled Cooley and I as to where we got the info on Leyte. Neither Bill nor I knew where Leyte was, but we did remember the girl who divulged the landing secret, and Bill gave them her name.

After lots of questions, everybody in the tent was grounded, sworn to secrecy, and we were restricted to the squadron area, isolated from the rest of the group. The girl in Sydney was arrested within 24 hours and her boyfriend, a full colonel, was also arrested. Nobody would tell us what was going on; we were not allowed to fly because of the possibility of being captured by the Japanese and spilling the beans under duress. We heard later that the unfortunate officer who spilled the beans to his girlfriend wound up in Leavenworth, but I have no documentation of that.

We didn't have to wait very long before finding out we had the right place—Leyte. On October 20, Dugout Doug MacArthur walked ashore at Tacloban, Leyte, Philippine Islands. Those of us who were grounded started flying again.[16] The squadron was now up past full strength, with 48 pilots and 35 P-47 fighters. The reason for the over-strength in pilot numbers and planes was never revealed to us, but I think squadron commander

Bill Dunham knew what it was all about. He was chomping at the bit for an assignment for his specially-trained pilots and crews. It didn't take long for our fiery leader to get his wish.[17]

DUNHAM'S WISH *The Major went further than mere vocal wishing, and paid a visit to V Fighter Command Headquarters in an effort to persuade then [sic] that his squadron should be sent in first. In this plea there was much logic since on 23 October 1944 the squadron's water echelon had departed Nadzab for the Philippines, and it, bolstered by a small air echelon from the Noemfoor echelon, could be prepared to commence operations weeks before the 348th group could be moved to the new station.*—History of the 460th Fighter Squadron (SE), October 1944[18]

Bill Dunham was an inspiring leader but also a no-nonsense one. He expected every pilot to be just like him and we did try to emulate him. He was also a great and understanding friend. Fiery is a description I copied off of "Fiery Ginger," the name on Neel Kearby's airplane, because it fits Dunham to a tee.

We soon resumed our combat missions. On October 22nd, I flew on a mission to glide bomb the airstrip at Kairatoe in the early afternoon, with 16 Thunderbolts carrying a single 500-pound bomb each. We were able to bomb fairly well this time.[19] On a particular five-hour, 1,000-mile round-trip mission to Ambon on the last day of October 1944, we carried one 500-pound bomb each on 14 P-47's, aiming to disable Laha Airfield in the late morning.[20] After dropping our bombs, with results unknown due to weather, I got a call from Bill Cooley saying he was having control problems, "Jim, would you come over and inspect?" I detached from my flight and joined Bill's flight. Bill thought he had been hit by ack-ack, but a close inspection of his plane revealed nothing. In our radio communication Bill complained the plane wanted to roll left. I got up real close to take a look but could see no damage. I slipped my right wing under his left wing about two feet under and in—and presto, the complication eased. After some experimentation, we decided to fly that close formation back to the base at Noemfoor. I had lots of practice on close formation flying in school as well as the first six months in combat, before we started using the spread out style of formation.

As we neared Noemfoor, we called the controller, announced our problem and requested a straight fly-in approach. As we neared the runway we slowed down, dropping our flaps on cue together. Bill dropped his landing gear and I kept mine up. Just before touchdown I slipped out from under Bill's wing and he made a successful landing. We were both exhausted from the tedious formation flight but celebrated a safe landing.

The problem was solved immediately by our trusty ground crews. What had happened was the bolt holding the trim tab on the left aileron had worked loose and jammed the trim tab in a position that made the plane want to roll left. The air pressure of my wing under Bill's wing made it possible for Bill to maintain control.

KEEPING UP WITH THE TEMPO *On the ground, maintenance and service personnel were hard pressed to keep pace with the missions scheduled. Owing to the absence of the squadron's water echelon which comprised approximately 40 percent of squadron personnel, each section of the ground echelon was operating on a minimum basis. Despite this handicap, missions were never limited by the number of planes available, and only .08 percent of the missions were forced to return because of engine difficulties.*—History of the 460th Fighter Squadron (SE), October 1944

In early November 1944, I voted in a presidential election for the first time, absentee from the island of Noemfoor. My first vote was two years prior, also an absentee ballot, from Lake Charles, Louisiana, while in the Advanced AAF Flying Training School. I have not missed an election since that date. My first presidential memory, by the way, was of Herbert Hoover who was the signer of the congressional declaration that made the Star Spangled Banner our national anthem.

Also in early November, disaster struck in the Philippines in the form of a massive typhoon that devastated all our airstrips and turned the roads into mud piles. Our air forces in Leyte were decimated, with planes stuck in the mud. On November 4th, the 460th was alerted and ordered to reinforce the beachhead in the Philippines, with zero hours' notice.

THE TREK BEGINS *It was on the fourth that the anticipated orders which would get the squadron into the Philippines fight, already 15 days old, were* *received. Within two hours after the news was passed around, 35 P-47's manned by the unit's pilots were lined up at the North end of long, yellow Kornasoren strip. Major William D. Dunham . . . led the squadron off, and in record time all planes were airborne. Ground crews watched approvingly as the planes climbed and circled the field, joined formation and laid a course toward Morotai Island . . . Airplanes from other squadrons of the Group were assigned (to) the 460th for this mission as the total previously assigned was an insufficient number for operations in the Philippines.*—History of the 460th Fighter Squadron, November 1944

We quickly gathered everything we could pack into the tiny baggage compartment of our P-47s, and 35 pilots immediately took off for Morotai Island, south of Mindanao, P.I. We had only what we could stuff in the tiny luggage compartment of the Jug: Toiletries, spare socks, underwear, shirt, and pants. All else was in transit with the squadron personnel and equipment. One pilot could not be located during our rapid departure, so was left behind.

Morotai was to be a refueling stop on our way to Leyte. We all knew where Leyte was now and we had some decent charts with which to navigate. Our arrival at Morotai, a Muslim sultanate, was done with precision. We were warned not to visit with or talk to any females we might see. The penalties spelled out were severe, like maybe losing your head, literally, a local custom!

MOROTAI

It was still early in the day when we landed to refuel at Morotai. Confusion reigned as we climbed down from our P-47s. We knew no one and the ground crews had to be instructed as to what to do for our aircraft. The volume of gasoline being pumped into our thirsty planes astounded the ground service people. By the time the refueling was accomplished, we were informed that the continuation of the mission was to take place the next morning. The airstrip was a madhouse, with loads of C-47 supply planes coming in to land. They were flopping down so fast there had to be an accident.

Cooley and I were standing on a taxi strip waiting for transportation to wherever we were going to sleep for the night, when we saw two C-47s trying to land in the same airspace. The one on top mushed down in front of the lower aircraft so close that the bottom plane stalled in the prop wash. We thought it was going to hit us, but it fell short by about 100 feet. It burst into flames immediately and was close enough for us to see the pilot and co-pilot burning alive. It was a ghastly thing to watch. We were shaken but unharmed, and finally trucks arrived to take us to our temporary quarters. The sky was literally black with planes trying to land in the evening. Some were critical on fuel after the long haul from Biak.[21]

The whole area was a madhouse, we soon perceived. There were artillery units all over the place and we could feel their gunfire without letup. The airstrip and surrounding area was all that the Army invasion force held. We were surrounded on three sides by Japs. Our temporary sleeping area was 50-yards from a battery of howitzers. We each got one Army blanket and were assigned a tent half shelter to keep the rain off and get some rest. Dinner consisted of cold rations and coffee in a mess kit. The water from a Lister bag was awful. Darkness and rain came all too soon. The artillery shot all night without stop, but we were too busy dodging scorpions and monster centipedes to worry about the noise. All kinds of terrible insects came with the dark and we battled them until morning finally came. At sunup we longed for some breakfast but none seemed to appear.

We were finally transported to our planes where we had to do our own pre-flight checks, e.g. bleed the gas tanks to remove any condensation and push the props through to get the oil out of the bottom cylinders. There were some qualified ground personnel to help us. We finally got some coffee, bread, and more cold C-rations, just enough to survive. After the pre-flight and chow, we had our briefing, which was to fly the squadron to Tacloban Airfield on Leyte Island. We were issued a silk map of the Philippines which was the best map I had seen since leaving the US.

At last the order to man our planes came; we started our engines and taxied out to the runway. All 34 of us arose into the cloudy morning sky to assemble and start our flight to Leyte.[22] We donned oxygen masks at 10,000 feet and proceeded to climb to 35,000 feet. I never had any trouble with the A-2 oxygen system. It was a demand type and kicked in circa 10,000 feet, and gradually enriched the mixture as one flew higher. It was hot at lower altitudes, at least in the tropics.

Dunham led the squadron for our intended target to the north, but we faced towering clouds thousands of feet higher than us. We could find no break in the cloud cover and it was obvious we could not fly through them. A typhoon had command of the sky so we had to abort the journey and return to dreadful Morotai. We landed and taxied back to our parking area.

THE REST OF THE FLIGHT ECHELON *The flight echelon, still not sure if their destination would be Morotai or Leyte, left early as scheduled (0430, 5 November 1944 from Noemfoor) in the transport planes which were as heavily overloaded as ever. They all landed at Anguar Island in the Palau Group after a routine and uneventful trip. Fighter belly tanks had been installed forward in the C-47's enabling them to carry an extra supply of gas for the long over-water hop, and all hands were ordered not to smoke or light a match for any purpose because some of the planes on previous flights had been lost, and it was believed that a leaky connection of the fuel lines caught fire in flight.—* History of the 460th Fighter Squadron, November 1944

We spent the rest of the day with our aircraft making sure that all servicing was accomplished. By this time I was starved for some food. As we milled around waiting for something to happen, my nose detected the smell of cooking beef. Cooley and I discussed this at length. He said he couldn't smell anything, but I persisted that my smeller never failed me so we took steps in the direction my nose told me to go. When your navel gets close to your backbone, your sense of smell improves.

After about a two-mile hike, we entered an infantry area; sure enough, the cooks were preparing steaks. This was unheard of in the islands. We prevailed upon the mess sergeant for some food, but he told us that the Air Corps had all the good food. I was persistent and finally got a T-bone steak which was tougher than shoe leather; that made not one iota of difference. I devoured it from left to right and polished the bone. The mess sergeant was impressed, and I think he finally realized how hungry we were. Bellies full, we thanked our host with all our hearts and offered him what money we had, but he refused, admonishing us not to come back, or send any more pilots.

On November 6, the typhoon was in full blast and we didn't even try to fly. On the 7th we tried to penetrate the storm again, without success. We stood down on the 8th until the 9th of November, when we tried to punch through the typhoon, again without success. The living conditions were beginning to tell on all of us including our leader, Bill Dunham, who was getting frustrated.

Speaking of typhoon troubles, my best friend, Captain Henry Woessner, USMC, was a gunnery officer on the heavy cruiser USS *Baltimore* at the time. The *Baltimore* was in the Philippine Sea during a typhoon in December, 1944. A wave hit the bow of the cruiser so hard that it was bent down. They had to retire from the task force and go home for repairs; I didn't find out about this until he was my best man when I got married in August of 1945.[23]

THE TRANSPORTS ARRIVE FIRST *At about 0900 hours (on) 6 November, the first members of the 348th Fighter Group disembarked from transport planes on busy Tacloban strip. At that time, Tacloban airdrome consisted of enough steel matting to accommodate heavy bombers in an emergency, a control tower, and clusters of tents here and there where the three squadrons of the 49th Fighter Group housed their engineering and operations. The peninsula upon which the strip was constructed was at its highest point no more than four feet above sea level . . . no taxiways had yet been completed, though engineers with heavy equipment were hard at work constructing them. This meant that all of the airplanes the strip was handling had to be parked along the sides of the runway.*—History of the 460th Fighter Squadron, November 1944[24]

NOTES

1. Production batches from the block D-20 onward were fitted with a "universal" wing that could carry a variety of drop tanks or bombs. These batches also introduced the R-2800-59 engine with an improved ignition system. The power was the same as that of the -63, with a war emergency power output of 2,300 hp. "Major P-47 Thunderbolt Variations, Serial Numbers, & Production," http://www.368thfightergroup.com/P-47-2.html
2. Information on the Lindbergh Fuel Economy technique and a connection to the 348th Fighter Group can be found in Appendix 5 as well as at the following sources: "Charles Augustus Lindbergh helps the 5th Air Force during WW2," http://www.ozatwar.com/ozatwar/lindbergh.htm

Monday, Travis. *Wings, WASP & Warriors.* Raleigh, NC: Lulu.com, 2005.

"The Otto Carter Story," excerpt http://www.pacificwrecks.com/people/veterans/
carter/otto_carter_story.html

3. The name "Dinghy" apparently comes from an incident that occurred during the
war, when Dunham, after shooting down a Japanese aircraft over the sea and noting
a survivor in the water, came around and dropped him his own life raft. It is unclear
exactly when this occurred, although an aviation artist depicting the event rendered
Dunham in his 460FS P-47D "Bonnie," in natural metal finish with black recognition stripes, suggesting it was during the Leyte campaign, in which Dunham
downed several enemy aircraft. This painting is in the Boeing Museum of Flight
in Seattle, Washington, in the Personal Courage Wing.

Telecon with 460FS pilot J.J. Smith, October 2014.

Telecon with Margo Prudente, daughter of William and Bonnie Dunham, November 2014.

"2013 American Fighter Aces Reunion in Seattle ," http://ehangar.com/forum/col-
lecting-aviation-art/fuzzys-travels-2013-american-fighter-aces-reunion-seattle

4. General Orders (G.O.) No. 396, Headquarters Fifth Air Force, dated 14 July 1944,
truncated here, ordered as follows in Section I:

   I. REORGANIZATION, REDESIGNATION, AND AUGMENTATION
   OF THE 1st AIRDROME SQUADRON.

    1. a. Pursuant to authority in radiogram XR 5695, Headquarters Far East
    Air Force (P), dated 12 July 1944, the 1st Airdrome Squadron is re-
    designated as the 460th Fighter Squadron (SE) and will be reorganized
    in accordance with T/O and E 1-27, dated 22 December 1943, with-
    out change of station. (Note: The 1st Airdrome Squadron was then
    assigned to Gusap Airfield; as the new 460th Fighter Squadron, it
    began movement to Nadzab Airfield on 27 July where better training
    facilities were available, completing the 95-mile move by 23 August.)
    b. The authorized strength of this unit as augmented will be fifty-one
    (51) officers and two hundred and forty-seven enlisted men.

    2. The 460th Fighter Squadron (SE) is placed under the administrative
    and operational control of V Fighter Command.

    3. Personnel required for this reorganization will be obtained from avail-
    able sources, shortages of personnel to be requisitioned in the usual
    manner.

    4. Equipment will be supplied from available sources. Such equipment as
    is rendered surplus will be absorbed in other units under your control
    and any excess equipment reported to this headquarters for disposition.

    5. No individual will be reduced in grade as a result of this action.

    6. Date of completion of reorganization will be reported to this head-
    quarters without delay.

By command of Brigadier General WURTSMITH

/t/ MERIAN C. COOPER

Colonel, GSC, Chief of Staff

Under Special Orders (S.O.) No. 208, Headquarters V Fighter Command, dated 26 July 1944, Captain William D. Dunham was relieved as 342FS Commanding Officer and appointed C.O. of the new unit.

S.O. No. 209, Headquarters V Fighter Command, dated 27 July 1944, transferred three officers of the 340th, four officers of the 341st and five officers of the 342nd Fighter Squadrons to the 460th Fighter Squadron to act as a "flying cadre."

By 1 August 1944, the 460th Fighter Squadron was in possession of one P-47 and one A-20, and had the same aircraft when the month ended, awaiting additional aircraft and pilots. On 31 Aug the squadron numbered 10 ground officers, 17 pilots and 229 enlisted men for a total of 256 personnel.

"Captain William D. Dunham was relieved as 342nd Commanding Officer and appointed C.O. of the new unit. The place of activation was Nadzab and the unit is expected to remain there for at least 60 days so that it may work itself into a smoothly running squadron," according to the "History of 348th Fighter Group, Narrative History, July 1944,"

http://www.ww2f.com/topic/37324-history-of-the-348th-fighter-group/

History of the 460th Fighter Squadron (SE), Chapter One, 14 July 1944–31 July 1944, Enclosures 1 (GO No. 396), 3 (So No. 208) and 4 (SO No. 209)

History of the 460th Fighter Squadron (SE), Chapter Two, (1 August 1944–31 August 1944), p. 4.

5. Information on Otto Carter's surviving P-47D lost in a mishap on 1 October 1943 is at "P-47D-2-RE "Carter's Li'l Pill" Serial Number 42-8066," http://www.pacificwrecks.com/aircraft/p-47/42-8066.html

6. The Far East Air Forces Combat Replacement Training Center was the place where, in the words of General Kenney: ". . . the newly arrived replacement crews got a lot of gunnery and bombing training against bypassed Jap holdings at Rabaul and around Wewak. Their operations also assisted the Australian ground forces, who were investing Jap positions and mopping up isolated enemy garrisons all over New Britain and New Guinea." Kenney, 522.

The 460th FS History for August 1944 indicated the CRTC was at Port Moresby, where it was established on 15 June 1944 as the Far East Air Force Combat Replacement & Training Center (Provisional) under Col. Carl A. Brandt. The 8th Service Group, the V Bomber and V Fighter Command Replacement Centers, and miscellaneous service units came under this new organization.

Craven, et al, *The Army Air Forces in World War II*, Volume IV, The Pacific: Guadalcanal to Saipan, August 1942 to July 1944, Chapter 19, Final Victory in New Guinea," 649–650.

The FEAF CRTC moved to Nadzab on 4 September 1944 and was reorganized on 16 October 1944. The Pacific Wrecks website has information indicating that on 16 October 1944 the 360th Air Service Group was redesignated as the FEAF CRTC. The organization was relocated to Clark Field in the Philippines during the summer of 1945.

"FEAF Combat Replacement and Training Center," http://www.pacificwrecks. com/units/usaaf/crtc/index.html

7. An excellent and detailed discussion of Fifth Air Force fighter tactics used across the Southwest Pacific can be found in a late war booklet titled *Fighter Combat Tactics in the SWPA*, reprinted and accented with images and biographical information by Osprey in 2004 under the title *'Twelve to One' V Fighter Command Aces of the Pacific*. It is a gathering of combat insights and experience from ace pilots across V Fighter Command. Included in this report are the recommendations of five 348th Fighter Group pilots, including 460FS commander William Dunham, group commander Robert R. Rowland, William M. Banks, Marvin E. Grant (the sixth cousin of General U.S. Grant, Civil War leader and President of the United States) and Walter G. Benz, Jr.

8. "The 460th Fighter Squadron flew on the first P-47 mission over Rabaul on New Britain without meeting any aerial opposition," according to the September 1944, History of the 348th Fighter Group, http://www.ww2f.com/topic/37324-history-of-the-348th-fighter-group/

9. This aircraft landed in the water by Capt. Charles A. Cronk, Jr., may have been P-47D-21RE serial number 42-25402, which was shown as an undated 460th Fighter Squadron operational loss in the squadron's September 1944 history.

The September history shows this aircraft was administratively "transferred" from the 460FS to the 479th Service Squadron, APO 713-1. This APO is correlated to the Nadzab/Lae area and in one source to Nadzab Airfield No. 4 as APO 713, Unit 1, or APO 713-1.

"Nadzab No. 4 Airfield (Newton Field)," http://www.pacificwrecks.com/airfields/ png/nadzab_no4/

10. Noemfoor was a bit too distant for 348th Fighter Group operations against Borneo. However, P-47 Thunderbolts of the 35th Fighter Group did operate against Borneo in September 1944 from their base on the island of Morotai, about 500 miles west northwest of Noemfoor.

Birdsall, Steve, *Flying Buccaneers: The Illustrated Story of Kenney's Fifth Air Force*, Garden City, NY: Doubleday & Company, Inc., 1977, 216-219.

11. Mission 164-3-15, 6 October 1944, Glide Bomb—Kaimana, Time Over Target (TOT) 0845I. Six of the aircraft were armed with one 1,000-lb bomb each (Author note: likely one bomb under one wing and a drop tank under the other). Three planes returned early and jettisoned their bombs before recovery. The results of bombing were unobserved due to bad weather. 460th Fighter Squadron (460FS)

Weekly Status and Operations Report (Form 34), (Report for Period 1-10-44 to 10-10-44 Inclusive).

The 460FS history for October 1944, described the mission as follows: "6 OC-TOBER. 11 P-47's glide bomb KAIMANA, DUTCH NEW GUINEA. Incomplete due to weather. Other targets chosen. Results: 3 bombs were dropped through cloud in the UTAROM-KAIMANA vicinity. 3 were dropped through clouds in the BABO area. Remainder of bombs were jettisoned, and no results were observed due to weather."

12. 460FS Armorer Nolan Machen's recollection of the squadron's first air raid continued: ". . . Then the anti-aircraft cut loose. Along with caliber fifty ground institutions (or installations). The fire works was beautiful but I didn't stay to watch it long. I made a dash for my helmet for all that goes up has to come down.

Intelligence reports that only one plane came over while three others stood off to see what happened. The one that came over was shot down.

The next night I had a fox hole. About 8:30 we had another red alert. But the plane identified itself as friendly. However the next day the hole went still deeper."
War Diary of Nolan Machen, 3–4.

The 460FS history for October 1944 described the raid as follows: "The single raid of 8 October 1944 by one lone Jap night raider was no more than a token in comparison with some of those the older men had experienced, but it provided a sufficient threat to provoke a number of new excavations in the squadron area."

13. Mission 169-3-25, 11 October 1944, Glide Bomb Kairatoe Airdrome, TOT 0940I. One bomb was returned to base because it would not release.

460FS Weekly Status and Operations Report (Form 34), (Period 11–10–44 to 20–10–44 Inclusive).

The 460FS history for October 1944 described the mission as follows: "11 OC-TOBER. 16 P-47's glide bomb KAIRATOE AIRDROME, CERAM. Results: target was bombed through cloud. 1 bomb was seen to explode in the personnel area, 3,000 feet north of the strip. Other results unobserved due to weather."

Of note, one of the targets the 460FS flew against in this time period was Babo Airfield; the squadron sent missions against it on October 19th, 22nd, 24th, and November 1st. An IJN Mitsubishi Zero fighter wrecked at Babo during the war was recovered and restored in the 1990s. It is once again a flying aircraft in the Flying Heritage Collection in Everett, Washington, and regularly flies.
"Mitsubishi A6M3-22 Reisen (Zero)," http://www.flyingheritage.com/Template Plane.aspx?contentId=20

14. On 28 May 1944, Major John T. Moore, former commander of the 341st Fighter Squadron, Jim Curran's first combat squadron, was made acting deputy commander of the 348th Fighter Group. "Major John T. Moore of Group Headquarters flew his last flight on the 8th of October. Flying in bad weather over Ceram

Island, he attempted to let down through low cloud cover in search of an assigned bombing target and was not heard from again."

"The History of the 348th Fighter Group, October, 1944," http://www.ww2f.com/
   topic/37324-history-of-the-348th-fighter-group/

"There was some sign of antiaircraft fire and Moore may have fallen victim, but no sign of him was seen after he entered the cloud." He flew in P-47D 42-27596 on this mission, according to Stanaway, *Kearby's Thunderbolts*, 119, 177. On 8 October 1944, the 460FS was assigned Mission 166-3-18, Glide Bomb supply Dump at Binnen Bay. Sixteen P-47's with a single 500-lb each. Two planes returned early. Mission incomplete due to weather. Fifteen bombs were jettisoned; one bomb was returned to base.

460FS Weekly Status and Operations Report (Form 34), (Period 1–10–44 to 10–
   10–44 Inclusive).

Major John T. Moore is remembered on the Tablets of the Missing at the Manila American Cemetery, Manila, Philippines. He was awarded the Silver Star, the Distinguished Flying Cross with oak leaf cluster, the Purple Heart and the Air Medal with four oak leaf clusters.

"John T. Moore," http://www.abmc.gov/search-abmc-burials-and-memorializa-
   tions/detail/WWII_123712#.U8nFkrEuR4M

15. Mission 172-3-30, 14 October 1944, Glide Bomb Haroekoe Airdrome, TOT 1015I. Four bombs landed in water, nine P-47's returned early and jettisoned their bombs. The pilots cleared their guns over the target.

460FS Weekly Status and Operations Report (Form 34), (Period 11–10–44 to 20–
   10–44 Inclusive).

The 460FS history for October 1944 described the mission as follows: "14 OCTOBER. 15 P-47's glide bomb HAROEKOE AIRDROME HAROEKOE I. Time over target: 1015/I-1020/I. Results: 13% successful. 4 bombs landed in the water north of the strip, one landed 2,000 feet north of the strip, one landed 800 feet north of the runway. 9 bombs were jettisoned when 9 planes returned with mechanical trouble. Sightings: One small boat, apparently a lugger, was seen off the south shore of CERAM ISLAND."

16. Jim Curran's flight record for October 1944 shows that he flew combat missions on 6, 11 and 14 October. The next entry is for two local training missions on 19 October, followed by another local training mission on 20 October. He resumed combat missions after a weeklong break on 22 October and flew one more on 31 October to finish out the month. In the Philippines, preliminary operations for the Leyte landings began on 17 October 1944, with the main forces arriving on the beaches on A-Day, 20 October 1944.

It would appear from this record that Curran, if not completely grounded in the period between these combat missions, may have been restricted to flying in the local area. The Black Rams, however, or at least the non-affected pilots, continued to fly combat missions, as the Form 34 for the period shows combat missions flown on 15 (G/B Laha Airdrome), 16 (G/B Timoeka Airdrome) and 19 October 1944 (G/B Babo Airdrome), before the main landing at Leyte.

There is nothing in the squadron or group records reviewed to indicate there was such an incident, but given the sensitivity of the matter it is possible it could have been deliberately omitted.

History of the 460th Fighter Squadron, Chapter Four, (1 October 1944–31 October 1944) 460FS Weekly Status and Operations Report (Form 34), (Period 11/10/44 to 20/10/44 Inclusive).

"The History of the 348th Fighter Group, October, 1944," http://www.ww2f.com/topic/37324-history-of-the-348th-fighter-group/

17. The November 1944 narrative history of the 348th Fighter Group indicates why the 460th Fighter Squadron was chosen as the first squadron of the group to be sent to the Philippines. "For one thing, it had a complete ground echelon at Nadzab ready to be shipped north on vessels which happened to be more immediately available in New Guinea than at Noemfoor. In the second place, the strongly voiced and efficiently placed persuasion of Major Dunham . . . was not without its influence in those places where final decisions were made in such matters."

Squadron records show the 460FS was equipped with 25 to 26 P-47's (there was one operational loss during October 1944) before being ordered to the Philippines. Once the squadron was ordered to deploy to Tacloban, additional aircraft from the other flying squadron's reinforced the 460th, giving it an increased mission capability with 35 P-47s which also provided a ready source of attrition replacements.

460FS Weekly Status and Operations Reports, September and October 1944; History of the 460th Fighter Squadron (SE), Chapter Four, (1 October 1944–31 October 1944) and Chapter Five, (1 November 1944–30 November 1944).

18. HQ Fifth Air Force Movement Order No. 566 dated 15 September 1944 directed the water echelon of the 460th Fighter Squadron to move via the first available water transportation to STATION SECRET (Leyte), and upon arrival to be under the operational control of the 308th Bomb Wing. Logistical data (approximate) for the whole 460FS included 50 officers and 224 enlisted men, 77 vehicles, and 30 days of supplies in various categories, as well as two weeks of voyage rations. The water echelon accounted for about 40% of the squadron's personnel, and each section of the ground echelon that remained was operating with minimum staff. Despite this handicap, the squadron was able to accomplish its assigned missions.

History of the 460th Fighter Squadron (SE), Chapter Three, (1 September 1944–30 September 1944) and Chapter Four, (1 October 1944–31 October 1944).

19. Mission 180-3-39, 22 October 1944, Glide Bomb Kairatoe Air strip, TOT 1225I. Thirteen bombs were dropped on the target, and three other bombs were jettisoned for no noted reason.

460FS Weekly Status and Operations Report (Form 34), (Period 21/10/44 to 31/10/44 Inclusive).

The 460FS history for October 1944, described the mission as follows: "22 OCTOBER. 16 P-47's glide bomb KAIRATOE AIRDROME, CERAM I. Results: 68% successful. Bombs were dispersed over most of the target area, hitting dispersal areas, one direct hit on center of strip. 3 bombs jettisoned due failure release over target. Anti-aircraft: One heavy, inaccurate, burst over the north shore of MCCLUER GULF. Sightings: Small column of smoke were seen rising near the center of KAIRATOE STRIP."

20. Mission 189-3-47, 31 October 1944, Glide Bomb Laha Airdrome, TOT 1145I. Thirteen of 14 bombs were dropped on the target, and one bomb was jettisoned in the water for no noted reason. Ibid, 460FS Weekly Status and Operations Report (Form 34).

The 460FS history for October 1944, described the mission as follows: "31 OCTOBER. 14 P-47's glide bomb LAHA AIRDROME, AMBON ISLAND. Results: bombs dropped on target, but results unobserved due to local cloud cover."

21. With regard to the C-47 crash on Morotai that Jim Curran recalled, James Hilburn, an armorer with the 41st Fighter Squadron of the 35th Fighter Group, described an accident which may be the same event:

"Controlling Incoming Aircraft. As the American force was growing there, the traffic was very heavy. Two C-47's were making landing approaches one over the other. Many troops were waving frantically and the tower was shooting red flares. When the impending tragedy was recognized by the pilot of the upper plane, his obvious reaction was to pull the wheel into his stomach. This caused a stall and he crashed about 40 feet from our "D" flight. The craft exploded into flame, and all of our crew ran for safety in the palm trees along the runway. The one man whose name was Pearlstein went with a pry bar and was able, with the help of others inside to open the cargo door. They all got out. He was never recognized for an act of bravery and courage, nor was the others of us court-martialed for escaping the danger."

"James Hilburn, 41st Fighter Squadron," http://www.pacificwrecks.com/people/veterans/hilburn.html

22. There is no explanation in the squadron history or supporting documents (e.g. Form 34) for the change in number from 35 to 34 aircraft between Noemfoor and Leyte. Presumably it was due to a mechanical breakdown of some sort at the intermediate stop at Morotai. Given the squadron's transient status on Morotai, any substantive or timely repairs to an aircraft may have been too much to ask for at such a forward location, where parts availability may have been an issue as well.

23. Jim Curran's friend Captain Henry J. Woessner, USMC, was a crew member aboard the heavy cruiser USS *Baltimore* (CA-68). His ship was damaged by the infamous Typhoon Cobra on December 18, 1944. Deck plates were buckled, 20

and 40 mm gun mounts damaged, both observation planes were damaged and her two motor whaleboats destroyed. Three destroyers were sunk in this storm and many other ships damaged.

"Baltimore" http://www.history.navy.mil/danfs/b1/baltimore-v.htm

"Typhoon Cobra (1944)," http://en.wikipedia.org/wiki/Typhoon_Cobra_%28194 4%29

According to the 1946 cruise book for the USS *Baltimore* (CA-68), Captain Henry J. Woessner is listed as present aboard the ship from October 16, 1944 to June 4, 1945.

US Navy Cruise Book, USS Baltimore (CA-68), 1946, 220, http://www.fold3.com/image/#301704719

24. The 460FS's movements by air and sea to the Philippines were rather complex, but all parts reached their destination. The water echelon of the squadron from Nadzab arrived off Leyte on 4 November, and waited in San Pedro Bay to unload. Fortunately, the Liberty ship it traveled on was not struck by Japanese bombs and/or kamikazes before the squadron disembarked on the docks at Tacloban on the afternoon of 8 November, just as a typhoon passed over the area. They were billeted in the Mercedes Theater and stayed there the following day and night before they made their way over to Tacloban Airfield to join the flight echelon just before the squadron's aircraft arrived.

The squadron's second water echelon, those left behind to close out operations at Noemfoor, loaded up and departed with the 342FS aboard *LST-668* on 6 November. The vessel experienced an engine problem, dropped out of convoy on 11 November and put into Woendi Island near Biak. There it laboriously offloaded and transferred personnel and cargo to *LST-775,* which then joined a convoy that reached Leyte on 19 November, debarking at Orange Beach, at Dulag.

The two water echelons were ultimately rejoined with the two air echelons, described in this chapter, into one complete squadron at the same installation, once the unit moved to Tanauan Airfield in December 1944.

History of the 460th Fighter Squadron, Chapter Five, (1 November 1944–30 November 1944).

War Diary of Nolan Machen, 5–6.

Chapter Nine

LEYTE

D
AWN BROKE TO CLEAR SKIES ON THE MORNING OF
November 10, 1944, after another dreadful night on Moro-
tai. After a terrible breakfast mess, we assembled 34 pilots, ready to exit
Morotai, but the whole mission was changed. The new mission was described in the preflight briefing as an escort for a group of B-25 medium
bombers flying to attack barges and transport vessels at low level in Ormoc
Bay, on the southwestern side of Leyte Island. We were to provide high altitude cover to prevent any attacks on the bombers by Japanese fighters.
After the B-25s did their thing and extracted, we were to attack any remaining shipping by strafing. We were loaded with two 165-gallon external
drop tanks, one per wing, 5,000 rounds of .50-cal ammo, and soon we
were on our way to Leyte.

With the sun up, we were off to the Philippines, our 34 P-47s escorting
the B-25s of the 38th Bomb Group. The skies were finally clear and visibility was maximum. The bombers flew at about 12,000 feet and we flew
higher, finally achieving 35,000 feet as we cruised at 190 mph. This was
the Jug's best altitude to do its thing; of course, it was a great advantage
combat-wise to be higher than the enemy's fighters. All remnants of the
typhoon had disappeared from the skies except for some wispy ice clouds
that surrounded us, but did not impair visibility. I don't recall that we had
any radio communications with the bombers we were escorting. Bomb
groups never seemed to talk on the radio. We kept a standard lookout for
enemy fighters, but no enemy appeared. Perhaps they were suffering from
the effects of the storm also.

George Barry flew on my wing, while a chap named McClendon was in fourth position. McClendon was a substitute for a pilot who could not be found the day we hastily departed Noemfoor. The plane McClendon was flying on November 10 was assigned to this pilot. His non-availability at Noemfoor saved his life, because McClendon developed engine trouble right as we approached Ormoc Bay. He radioed his dilemma to me just before the Japanese ack-ack started tracking us at 35,000 feet. I instructed him to head for the nearby airstrip at Tacloban, Leyte. After he left, we assumed a big zigzag flight pattern to avoid heavy ack-ack.

Unfortunately, P-38 Lightning fighters made contact with McClendon as he headed for Tacloban. McClendon was losing speed and at about 15,000 feet altitude when he was spotted by P-38 Lightnings who took no time to identify his aircraft. McClendon did not have the power to maneuver to avoid the P-38s and they shot his crippled P-47 down in flames, killing him. J.J. Smith, who also had an aircraft problem and was diverting to Tacloban, saw the P-38's as they pounced but was able to maneuver to avoid their attack and land solo at Tacloban to tell the story of the attack.[1]

J.J. Smith made the following statement in the Missing Aircrew Report filed after the incident: "Backfire Squadron took off at 0800 on a mission to cover a flight of B-25s that were to attack shipping. I was flying Wing on Backfire 1 leader. Over target, my right wing tank seemed to fail to release. I was behind and to the right of Backfire 1 leader and noticed a lone P-47 with yellow tail and number 40 on it. It has since been established that this is the plane Lt. McClendon was flying. He had evidently been separated from his flight and joined us. I crossed in front of Lt. McClendon to Backfire 1 leader's left to have him check my right tank. He motioned for me to release it. When my tank failed to release, Backfire 1 leader told me to go home. At this time, Lt. McClendon was directly behind me. I broke sharply to the left and off my left wing, saw a flight of three P-38s, two of which were firing and to the best of my knowledge, it is very possible Lt. McClendon was in their line of fire. I did not see Lt. McClendon at the time because he was directly behind me. The P-38s were told those were P-47s they were firing at, and although I did not see them, they must have immediately broken off. This is all I know of what happened as I climbed for altitude and came to this field and landed."[2]

Our numbers now reduced to 32 P-47s, we approached the target area and started receiving heavy anti-aircraft fire from the Ormoc Harbor area.

The attacking bombers dropped down to low level and were on the deck approaching the enemy shipping, and we were at 35,000 feet. We could see the harbor and lots of surface vessels. The B-25s were using three small islands as a shield, masking them from being spotted by the Japanese ships. At the last second, the bombers popped up over the islands and began their attack on the Japanese ships, which had their anti-aircraft guns pointed at us. Radio silence was broken as soon as the bombers struck. They had a field day getting right on top of the enemy shipping.

Initially, the Japs had all their heavy weapons aimed at us. This was very fortunate for the bombers because they could not depress their guns fast enough to get a shot at the bombers. In spite of this stroke of luck with masking their approach, the bombers lost several planes in the attack. In the harbor at Ormoc were several destroyers, transports, barges, and a large warship that looked like a heavy cruiser. All the ships were hit. We lost five B-25s in the bay, all of them ditching, but we didn't have any air rescue aircraft accompanying us for this mission.

Those bomber guys made an outstanding attack on the enemy, but I don't think they knew what they were getting into. We sure didn't expect to see an enemy task force that well-armed and filling the whole harbor. The ack-ack blackened the whole sky. There was no mention of a Japanese task force in the pre-mission briefing; we expected to see barges, which the Japanese extensively used in New Guinea.

As the bombers pulled away to go back to Morotai, we descended to strafe. We found several destroyers, transport ships, and one heavy cruiser plus many barges. Some ships were sinking, others were on fire. We attacked the ships that were still operational in the harbor with our machine guns. We approached at very high speed because firing eight .50-caliber machine guns slowed one down considerably.

I chose to strafe a vessel that was burning on one side and moving very fast. As I passed over the target and looked back, I saw it was the heavy cruiser, the really big one.[3] As I exited over the side that wasn't burning, I was met with unbelievable flak from this ship, which was firing everything they had at us. This was not what we expected to see. Dunham ordered us out—which we did with gusto and without delay. Fortunately, no one was hit or shot down by the flak and we headed for Tacloban Airfield. Ten minutes later we were preparing to land on Leyte.

TACLOBAN AIRFIELD

Upon landing at Tacloban, I was steered into a slot right on the south end of the runway. There was limited parking space and the ground crews lined us up with our propellers just off the runway. As I shut down the engine and was filling in the Form 1, my plane was literally attacked by a horde of soldiers. The ground crew was ecstatic to see the 460th because the only defense the beachhead had was four P-38s. They swarmed all over the plane and immediately pumped it full of gas, oxygen, oil, and cleaned the canopy. My ammunition trays were filled to the brink with .50-caliber ammo and they were busy strapping 500-pound bombs under my wings. There were people on both wings trying to hug me, telling me how happy they were to see me. As I went to exit the cockpit they shoved me back and said "Don't get out!" I insisted, telling them I had to pee, so they let me descend to do what I had to do, and right back into the cockpit I went.

TACLOBAN TURMOIL *P-38's and P-40's were continually on the runway landing or taking off; fuel trucks, bomb trailers and jeeps were necessarily on the move, servicing the planes as they landed. Occasionally a B-24 would come rolling down the mat, its wingtips barely missing the planes which lined the strip. Flying sand was everywhere, and the entire area seemed alive with whirring propellors [sic] and roaring engines.*—History of the 460th Fighter Squadron, November 1944

There were so many people talking at once I could understand no one. I put on my helmet and asked the airfield controller what was going on. My instructions were to fire up the engine and lead a flight of four to return to Ormoc to bomb anything that moved; then, to return to Tacloban and fly cover over the strip and the adjacent San Pedro Bay until relieved. With that, we were airborne, 15 P-47's all in all, and on our way back to Ormoc. There we saw hundreds of people in the water of the harbor, but we could not strafe because we knew there were downed B-25 crews amongst the swimmers. We found some departing Japanese vessels and dropped our bombs; we garnered four near misses on one destroyer, and hit the water with the rest, Composition "B" 500-pound bombs, according to squadron records.[4] We then returned for picket duty over our new airstrip.

After about an hour we were relieved, but before we landed, we had a good opportunity to observe San Pedro Bay. There were hundreds of ships in the bay vying for a place to unload. This wasn't easy because the typhoon had devastated all the roads on Leyte and there was limited space to store equipment and supplies. Our infantry had already started to move around the north side of Leyte and were aiming to head south on the western side of the island toward Ormoc Bay. The Japanese were equally determined to block that maneuver, so there was heavy fighting going on to our west. There were also pockets of Jap infantry back from our beachhead that caused lots of trouble.

THE FIRST TACLOBAN MISSION . . . *that afternoon 15 planes were assigned to bomb the remainder of the (Ormoc) convoy. This was the mission that began a series of "Thunder-bomber" attacks which sank approximately 50,000 tons of Jap shipping, aided ground forces considerably in their tough Ormoc Valley campaign, and dropped a record-breaking tonnage of bombs for fighter squadrons in this theatre.*—History of the 460th Fighter Squadron, November 1944

Upon landing we were greeted again by ground crews who amazed us with their enthusiasm to see us. This welcome should have been a clue that something was amiss on the beachhead. As I debriefed with the intelligence officer, it began to dawn on me what the tactical situation was in Leyte. The Japs had successfully landed enough provisions and troops at Ormoc despite our successful attacks. This made the situation very difficult for Lieutenant General Walter Krueger, who commanded our ground troops on Leyte.

It was obvious that the situation here was very precarious for the US forces. I learned of our air defense, which consisted of four operational P-38 fighter planes. The rest were mired in mud on other airstrips that were lakes of mud due to the typhoon that had held us up from going to Tacloban earlier. We also had several orphaned Navy fighter planes that had a limited ability to start due to a shortage of the shotgun shells they used to start their engines. Jugs had 24-volt battery-operated energizers which wound up the starting system. You pushed the engaging button when it was fully energized. This system allowed an easy way to start the engine without running down the battery.

The addition of an overstrength squadron of P-47s to the defense force was the factor that made us so welcome. The defense was critical and Tacloban airstrip was maxed out with planes taking off and landing, plus no parking space. There were no revetments at all. So we lined up right along the runway the first few days we were there, until the Corps of Engineers built some parking areas.

The airfield was literally a beachhead, with LSTs lining the beach right next to the runway. As soon as they were empty, they would retract and another would take its place. The only saving factor in this mess was that there were no enemy ground forces shooting at us, but we were under constant threat of aerial assault.

At the post-mission debriefing, I learned of McClendon's demise at the hands of an overzealous P-38 pilot. I could not restrain myself from visiting the P-38 outfit to chastise them. At the P-38 ready tent they were apologetic, but would not produce the guilty pilot. I gave a stern warning to those present that they had better stay clear of us in the air or suffer the consequences—a hostile move against us from any P-38 would be met with maximum defense.

Ironically, shortly after the incident, I was approached during another mission in an unfriendly manner by four P-38s. As they swung into attack pattern the four of us turned into them for a head-on confrontation. I fired a short burst while out of range. They got the message and sheared off big time. They had been warned to stay clear of us by yours truly prior to this incident. I don't know what a P-47 looks like when all the guns light up, but it must be an awesome sight.

After this, we started to assess our own situation on Leyte. We had no support for living at all. We were already starved for something to eat, and no vittles were in sight. We all needed a shave and a bath. We had no clean clothes so it was bathing in the ocean and rinse out what clothes we had. Fortunately, I had an extra pants and shirt. We cleaned as best we could and then started our quest for food and a place to sleep. The best we could find was some bread and black coffee. We scrounged some C-rations to supplement our bread and coffee. Finally, someone found some jungle hammocks for us to sleep in.

A short distance from where we parked our aircraft, we found a coconut plantation where we set up camp. I found two sturdy coconut palms and erected my jungle hammock between them. Four ropes were used to suspend the hammock; two for holding up the body part and two to support the roof and mosquito bar, which was equipped with a zippered entrance. After getting it set up, I had to resolve the problem of getting in and out of it. This was no small task and took hours of practice and a lot of falls to the ground. By the time I had mastered the entry and exit, it was time to hit the sack. I removed all my clothes save my underwear and got in the sack. After positioning myself and closing the mosquito bar, I fell into an exhausted sleep listening to the rain hitting the roof of the hammock. I slept soundly through the night despite all the activity going on all around me.

TACLOBAN CAMP *The camp area which was assigned the squadron after the airplanes arrived and the air and Nadzab water echelons joined, was no improvement over the 96th Service Squadron area 9 (initially assigned). Though it was comfortably further away from the strip. It was so small that tents could not be arranged according to any system at all. It was located a few yards back from White beach, the site of Allied naval shelling before D-Day. Torn and blasted palm-tree stumps and trunks were scattered about; the shelling had been so severe that a large bowl of sand had been scooped out of the beach just large enough to accommodate all the tents. During the heavy almost incessant rains, this bowl filled with water whose level rose many inches above the floors of the tents and stayed that way sometimes for weeks at a time.[5]*—History of the 460th Fighter Squadron, November 1944

Nature finally called at daybreak and I exited my hammock for day number two in the Philippines. The first thing on the agenda was to look for food. The day we arrived at Tacloban we saw the Red Cross people assigned to our area had a tent set up on the strip on the center of the west side. They had coffee, but we could not locate any food, so we were out for a bad start of day two.

We assembled by our aircraft, parked on the west side of the runway, and were briefed by our squadron commander. Later we set up our ready tent on the east side. The whole area was subject to attack by enemy aircraft, and they made their presence known all night with nuisance raids from very high altitude. We suffered no damage and could see no evidence of any hits by bombs. It being very difficult to exit from the jungle hammock the previous night, I chose to take my chances and stay in bed during the raids.

The next weeks at Tacloban were a nightmare for all of us. Food was scarce and we had no living quarters. Sleep was impossible with night raids and all the ships in the bay heaving ack-ack into the sky. If the Japanese only knew how weak we were after the typhoon, it might have been a different story. Having just 33 P-47s and four P-38s was a pitifully small defense. Somehow the enemy never found out, and so we survived. But it could have been much worse. We were so adrenalized I don't think we had time to fret about what we were doing. We devised an escape plan in case of disaster from attack by enemy ships or ground assault. To save the planes, we would fly back to Morotai or back to Australia if necessary.[6]

We had very limited parking space. I remember two P-61 night fighters that took up space in the daytime when it was most needed for cargo planes that were being unloaded during daylight hours. Since night flying posed many obvious hazards to everyone, it was curtailed to the minimum. This is probably why we had only two P-61s. We all looked them over with great interest since they had no ailerons—they had spoilers instead, and looked impressive when they took off.[7]

The assessment by the brass was that the squadron would assume a defensive role until more reinforcements arrived. The rest of the group was at sea on the way to Leyte as fast as the slowest ship in their convoy could go. The aircraft were poised to fly to Leyte as soon as the landing facilities became available. At this point our total air force in the Philippines consisted of a squadron-plus of P-47s, a handful of P-38s, and a few Navy aircraft: three or four Grumman fighters and a lone TBM torpedo bomber which were stranded when their carrier was damaged so badly they could not return to it. The Navy planes were limited by how many blank 12-guage shotgun shells they had to start their engines; when they got to their last shell, it was goodbye or go into the ocean with a bulldozer pushing them in. Any plane that wouldn't start met this fate because there was no space to park them if they weren't operational.

Tacloban airstrip was the busiest place I had ever seen. Planes were either landing or taking off all day long. There was a constant stream of transports bringing in supplies and personnel and evacuating wounded.

The fighter planes had top priority for landing and taking off. We had eight planes parked in a position to scramble and four planes aloft over San Pedro Bay at all times from sunup to sundown. My job on November 11 was to glide bomb and strafe a barracks area at Valencia, Leyte, about thirty miles west-southwest of Tacloban. Fourteen of us dumped pairs of 500-pound bombs (Composition "B" types, with 1/10 second fuzing) and strafed the target, which was some seven miles north of Ormoc.[8] On return to base we assumed a patrol position until relieved by another flight. Upon landing, our aircraft were immediately serviced and re-armed so they were always ready for a scramble.

Having completed a mission, my flight was allowed to retire from the ready tent. As we scrounged for some food, we began to realize what a hazardous position we were in. The Japanese controlled most of the island. We controlled about 12 miles of the San Pedro beach and our forces had penetrated deep enough to keep us out of artillery range. Every inch of the beachhead had ships unloading the weapons of war. It was the most hectic scene that I had ever witnessed. Deuce-and-a-half trucks plowed through mud, 6 x 6 axle-deep, over what was once a highway; it was really slow going for all. There was no system, trucks everywhere and mud up to your neck. The only place that was dry was the Tacloban airstrip runway.

THE 348TH FIGHTER GROUP AT LEYTE *Leyte, to all who arrived there, meant mud, water, and flooded foxholes. It meant sleepless nights and exhausting days, bad food and long latrine lines. And it meant consciousness of real war, a realization of the hitherto unplumbed potentialities of every man, an admiration for the ragged Filipino patriots.*—348th Fighter Group History, November 1944

Late on the night of the 11th we were attacked by a new weapon, a kamikaze bomber, called by the Japanese "the Divine Wind." Although this attack occurred only a few hundred feet from where we were sleeping, we weren't aware of it until the next morning. So ended day two in the Philippines for the 460th Fighter Squadron.

On the morning of November 12, I arose from my night of fitful sleep feeling hungry. We headed for the Red Cross tent near the airstrip for some coffee and whatever else they had. Arriving at their facility, we were disappointed to find out they had abandoned it in the middle of the night, scared out of their wits from the bombing activities that lasted all night and the crash of a kamikaze aircraft right on Tacloban airstrip. They left without leaving a forwarding address and I never saw them again, but we found their coffee supply and made our own.

After checking in with operations, we were informed that we were not scheduled for anything and were free until the noon briefing. Rumor had it that the wrecked kamikaze airplane was in the taxiway at the middle of the strip; Bill Cooley and I decided to go look at the wreckage. The Japanese plane was a twin-engine, low-wing aircraft about the size of a Lockheed Electra, but it had a single rudder. Its code name escapes my memory. The wreckage was fairly well intact in a ditch just off the taxiway alongside the center of the runway. We could see the huge bomb, about a 2,000-pounder, still in the bomb bay behind the pilots office which, for some reason, did not go off. The body of the dead pilot was visible still in the left-hand seat with his hands taped to the control wheel with surgical tape. The co-pilot's hands were free, but his feet were shackled to the rudder pedals. Why it didn't explode and burn remains a mystery.

CAMP HAZARDS *Situated on one side of this area was a large heavy-artillery and howitzer ammunition dump, and on the other was a gas dump. Though the chances of a bomb landing in this area was infinitesimally less than they were at the 96th (camp area), the thought of what would happen if one did was as disconcerting as living closer to the strip.*—History of the 460th Fighter Squadron, November 1944

As Bill and I were contemplating what we saw, all hell broke loose; anti-aircraft guns started going off all around. We quickly scanned the sky to see Japanese fighter planes on a strafing run and coming right at us. I quickly dove headfirst for the only cover in sight, the wheel strut of a B-25 parked at the edge of the taxiway. I think it was one of the bombers damaged from the November 10 Ormoc raid that made it to Tacloban and was parked just off a taxiway in soft earth. The B-25 left a deep rut behind the wheel on the starboard side of the plane directly under the engine nacelle. I could hear the rattle of the enemy plane's machine guns as I lay face down in mud.

As the attackers sped off, I felt all wet. I finally opened my eyes and saw my hands were all red. I felt no pain, but I was sure I had been hit. As I stared at my hands, I felt wet on my head. Finally moving to a sitting position, I ascertained the source of the red fluid. I was under the engine nacelle of the B-25 and the Jap strafer's bullets had hit a hydraulic line on the plane directly over me. We returned to the ready tent where I was excused for the rest of the day to clean up. I found some saltwater soap to wash my clothes and body in the ocean, as we had no fresh water for bathing, only water for drinking.

ENEMY OPPOSITION *The squadron operated against opposition the intensity of which the Jap had been unable to show for more than a year. Tacloban received many daylight air raids and almost nightly alerts if not actual raids. The efficiency of the fighter-bomber was proven . . . The first victory for the squadron was scored at 1440 hours 12 November when Captain Richard C. Frost . . . shot down a Zeke 32 in Leyte Gulf, just offshore in view of the Tacloban beaches. Big Days were virtually consecutive except when frequent torrential rains grounded all air effort.*—History of the 460th Fighter Squadron, November 1944

We begged for food from other organizations who grudgingly shared after they learned we had no support personnel. The food was the canned variety that we had grown used to, not very palatable, but filling. My weight was again falling very rapidly and I was sure the flight surgeon would have a fit when he saw me next, which wouldn't be for some time.

The 13th and 14th of November, I flew patrol missions as did most of the squadron. The first was a local patrol for two and a half hours, and I did not see one enemy aircraft. Of course, the squadron had planes aloft all day. November 14th was the same; a three hour flying patrol in the Buri area, about five miles south of Tacloban. I encountered no enemy planes on my mission.[9]

VALOR DURING TACLOBAN AIR RAID *During the raid of 14 November a parked P-38 received a direct hit, injuring personnel who had been working on it just prior to the action. In spite of the attack still being in progress with enemy planes bombing and strafing the airstrip, ammunition and blazing* *gasoline tanks exploding violently, these medical corpsmen who were on line duty at the time (Cpl James D. McClain, Jr. and Cpl Ira W. Merriman), rushed out to the injured men and carried them to an ambulance thence away from the strip . . . Had it not been for the action of these two men, it is believed the lives of the wounded would not have been saved.*—History of the 460th Fighter Squadron, December 1944

We found it difficult to believe the enemy wasn't aware that we were so weak defensively. Any kind of enemy air offensive would have been devastating to our military effort. Little did we know that day what the Japanese had in store for us in the coming weeks on Leyte.

Since we were on the defensive, our objective was to keep the enemy from assaulting our positions on the beachhead and the shipping anchored for off-loading in San Pedro Bay. We had help from the ships, which shot at anything flying, including us. We were fairly successful in keeping the Japanese planes away during the daylight hours, but as soon as the sun went down, the Thunderbolts were not effective due to the blindness pilots incurred the second they fired their eight .50-caliber guns at night. The blast of light, even for a short duration of firing, completely ruined night vision for several minutes. The Japs only had to worry about our flak after dark, though the mortality rate of enemy aircraft from our ground fire was almost nil.

TACLOBAN CASUALTY *Bombing raids . . . cost the life of one crew chief, Richard N. VanNostrand, S/Sgt, who died of shrapnel wounds (on 14 November 1944) from one of the hundreds of small, hand-grenade-like anti-personnel bombs which the Nips had a fad for using during this time.*—History of the 460th Fighter Squadron, November 1944

Later on the 14th, Bill Cooley and I had our first trip into Tacloban. We obtained a jeep from somewhere and put it into four-wheel drive and waded into Tacloban. There were many nice structures in the town and it had not been harmed by the Japanese occupation or withdrawal when the Allied invasion took place. The town had little military value except for the airstrip, which the Japanese had used mostly for supply flights. We wandered around town and spotted a barbershop where I treated myself to a haircut and shave. The shave was a disaster. The barber shaved me so close I had skin rash for a week.

While cruising around town we heard a piano playing and the sounds of people having fun. Thinking it might be a party, we knocked on the door. We were greeted by a Filipino gentleman who introduced himself as a medical doctor and said he was having a bridal party for his niece. We tried to excuse ourselves, but he would have no part of it. Instead he insisted we join the festivities, which we did and had a great time. Dr. Pascual was a great host and his wife and family were a joy, but the food left a bit to be desired. They did have one rice dish that I enjoyed and the tuba (beer made of coconut juice and brown sugar) had a wallop. The doctor had trained at the Mayo Clinic in Minnesota and was overjoyed to meet some of the liberating forces. We became friends with him and his extended family, one of whom was a former governor of the island of Bohol, P.I. (more on the governor later). We returned to our dark camp full of Filipino food and beer, happy to have made some new friends.

On November 15th, we bombed an area called Ipil, about three miles southeast of Ormoc along the shores of Ormoc Bay. Eight Jugs lugged 16 500-pound GP bombs with 1/10th second delay fuses to the target area in the morning: "1 bomb landed in field, 3 bombs were unobserved, several buildings were hit," according to the squadron's Weekly Status and Operations Report.[10] On November 16th, I flew a quiet local patrol again, then in the morning of November 17th, we bombed and strafed shipping in Ormoc Harbor with eight aircraft and 16 500-pound bombs fused at 4 to 5 seconds. We also expended 8,000 rounds of .50 caliber ammunition, all of which resulted in "Many fires started on luggers and beach positions," according to the squadron records.[11] Ormoc was still an important enemy supply area, despite the bombings we made on the Japanese task force earlier in the month. The Japanese used the night to reinforce and supply their forces in Leyte.

About day five at Tacloban, I spotted an officer on a Navy LST landing ship on the beach who looked familiar. He turned out to be Ronnie Maloney, Lieutenant, USN, who lived at 82nd and Champlain in Chicago, a close friend; he was the captain of the vessel. While there, he made sure I got some good chow before his LST had to retract.

THE LEYTE ENVIRONMENT *Rain and mud immobilized transportation, rations were slim, and even drinking water was difficult to haul from the distant water point to the area. Red alerts and air raids were frequent, and water-filled foxholes were used only at the last minute. Clothes would not dry, feet were wet 24 hours a day.*—History of the 460th Fighter Squadron, November 1944[12]

November 19th was more local patrol for me, without incident. As November 20th was a day off for me, some of us made it out to visit our new friend, Dr. Pascual in Tacloban. Bill Cooley and I arrived in Tacloban de la tarde to find a house full of guests and relatives, some of whom came from the island of Bohol in the Japanese-occupied area. The uncle of Dr. Pascual, an elderly gentleman, was also the former governor of the island of Bohol.

Dinner was served early, which consisted of many local foods. One was a small, cured fish with the head attached. As the plate went around all the heads were saved for Cooley and me. They were double ugly and we couldn't understand why we were so honored to have the fish heads. Cooley and I passed on the option of the heads, only to find out that they were considered to be the best part of the fish, especially the eyes, which were very large. Oh well, we were only stupid Americans! The other foods were very tasty; after dinner, I inadvertently belched, much to the titillation of Mrs. Pascual, our hostess. Belching after dinner in the P.I. is considered the ultimate compliment to the hostess.

As mentioned, among the guests was Governor Celestino Gallares of the island of Bohol, which was about ten miles from the southwestern end of Leyte.[13] The governor, about 65 years old, was an uncle to Dr. Pascual and had canoed over from Bohol to where we were at on Leyte with a contingent of Boholians to get arms from MacArthur so they could combat the Japanese forces on Bohol. Governor Gallares was a very gracious gentleman. The governor and his companions travelled in sea-going, outrigger canoes over a hundred miles of ocean to get to Leyte to obtain arms to fight the Japanese, only to be ignored by the high command. Cooley and I sympathized with the governor and invited him and his entourage to visit our camp area to see if we could help them.

It was agreed that they would come as soon as possible. In the meantime, we asked Dr. Pascual if he could recommend someone to help improve our camp area. He furnished a young man who had some building skills. He had limited understanding of English, but was very responsive to our needs. Our tent and gear had arrived from their long sea journey and were ready to be erected.

LIFE ON LEYTE *At camp meals were eaten in the dark; pilots, ground officers, and ground crews, standing about in ankle-deep water, drenched in the downpour, would eat "C" rations from mess kits half-filled with rain water, cracking jokes, laughing, and enthusiastically re-hashing the events of the day.*—History of the 460th Fighter Squadron, November 1944

The young Filipino arrived the morning of November 21st with a cadre of male and female help. The women were assigned to help with clearing our camp area and washing our clothes and bedding. The men, after much time trying to understand our tent requirements, commenced building a platform about four feet high for our tent base. They used bamboo for the whole construction. They cut four large poles for the four corners, then used large poles to make the sides. To the sides they added bamboo rafters which they covered with split bamboo. The entire structure was accomplished sans nails. Everything was tied together with wet strands of plant fiber, which dried rapidly making a super-tight fit. They then erected the tent over the platform and tied the sides almost straight out. Our cots were then installed with mosquito bars and we had the best housing in the Pacific to date. The women returned in the afternoon with our bedding and clothes all neatly ironed and folded. Life was sweet! All this was dirt cheap, so we hired our young man as a permanent fixture. His staff from then on attended to all our needs.

THE FILIPINO PEOPLE *The Filipino people furnished a new aspect to the environment of the 348th Group. It was a source of amazement at first to see how consistently the Filipinos could deform the English language and still make themselves understood. But the Filipinos were good natured, intelligent, and clean. There was a new, refreshing good will and humor wherever American soldier and Filipino citizen met.*—348th Fighter Group History, November 1944

On November 21st, we were still in the defensive mode because we still had no backup forces. It was still the 460th and a few P-38s defending the Tacloban beachhead. The morning briefing indicated some surface vessels were observed in Ormoc Bay. Due to our defensive mode, only four aircraft were sent over to investigate. I was "elected" to the job and was scheduled for the mission with Lyman Peck (later a PhD in Math) as my wingman. We initially had our four planes on picket duty over Tacloban, and when relieved of picket duty we were to go over to Ormoc Bay to hunt for targets of opportunity.

Upon arriving at the target area early in the morning, we observed a sizeable transport ship laying idle some distance from the beach, far away from the Ormoc docking area. It looked very vulnerable, but also suspicious. We also spotted some very small surface craft not too far from the transport vessel near the shore. We flew low to identify what they were. The individuals on board the craft waved frantically when we approached, so we didn't shoot because we were aware that there were many Filipinos living in the area and Filipino fishermen too, and the vessels didn't fit the description of any enemy craft.

Being very suspicious of the larger ship, a medium-size freighter which was not moving and appeared to be at anchor, I decided to attack with supreme caution. I gained several thousand feet altitude keeping the vessel in view but not making any threatening moves. I informed my flight that I would attack it without support at very high speed and instructed them not to follow close—in other words to stay back and observe what happened after my initial attack.

Getting into a favorable position I armed my guns and proceeded to let down in a steep dive, attaining a speed of about 600 mph. At the last minute I made a sharp left turn to approach the ship broadside. Approaching at mast-head height, as the target grew in my 100-mil sight I fired my eight .50-caliber machine guns while still a bit out of range. As the cone of fire started to converge on the ship, I began scoring hits on the vessel. A half-second later, my plane was jolted with a monstrous shock wave. As I peeled around to the left and recovered altitude, all I could see was fire and a gigantic column of smoke already higher than I was.

I spotted my second element but not my wingman. I rejoined with the second element and they told me that my wingman was last sighted following me and disappeared in the blast. I lost radio communication with Lyman and was unable to spot him after rejoining my second element. We searched for him without success for over an hour. There was no trace of the ship at all. It had vaporized completely. Considering the blast, it must have been an ammunition ship.

My second element, still being fully armed, selected a suspect area of the harbor to strafe which started several secondary fires on some vessels, and we returned to Tacloban airstrip. We reported the loss of Lyman Peck, assuming that he flew in to attack too soon and got caught in the subsequent explosion of the vessel.

But we were relieved to find out that Lyman had survived, managing to fly his severely damaged, but still flyable plane to Baybay, in the isthmus of southeastern Leyte. There he crash-landed, wheels up in a rice paddy, in an area controlled by a Marine 155 mm "Long Tom" artillery unit.[14] Lyman was back with us the next day, unharmed. He had followed me a little too close and got caught in the blast of the ship as it disintegrated, causing a huge amount of damage to his P-47. Back around 2003, Lyman returned with friends to Leyte to the scene of the crash. He is still alive and lives in Ohio, and has attended some of our reunions held in Dayton, Ohio and Louisville, Kentucky.

In my opinion, the Jug was not suited for dive bombing in the classic sense because of speed build up. We had two methods of dropping bombs. One was glide bombing for troop support, which was done with a strafing approach, and the other was triggering the bombs when the "cone of fire" from the machine guns converged on the target. We used the same approaches with shipping, except employed maximum speed when attacking enemy ships.

On November 22, US Army troops were in northern Leyte, pushing south from Carigara Bay and enveloping the town of Limon on Route 2, the north-south road that goes down to Ormoc. After fighting the battle for Breakneck Ridge, just to the north of Limon, our troops were poised at the northern end of the Ormoc Valley.

On this day, I had a two hour and fifteen minute combat mission when we glide-bombed a place called Palompon, a small port town on the west coast of Leyte. It was a location the Japanese sent smaller ships and numbers of reinforcements to, as compared to the bigger port and town in

Ormoc Bay. Fifteen P-47's toting pairs of 500-pound bombs hit the target at 0915 in the morning. The squadron history recorded 28 bombs and 4,500 rounds of .50 caliber expended, two hits on a cement jetty in the harbor and one hit on a cross road at the base of a cement jetty. It also said six bombs were delivered on houses in Ormoc town, which means we attacked a secondary target on this mission, as well as the primary.[15]

I wasn't required to fly on the 23rd, but on the 24th I was on a scramble, without contacting the enemy. Also on the morning of November 24, our intelligence section revealed that a reconnaissance aircraft spotted Japanese ships taking on cargo at Port Cataingan on the island of Masbate, just northwest of Leyte. Four ships were seen, which included three cargo vessels and an escort. Intelligence suspected that this small task force was bound for Ormoc Bay to reinforce the garrison on Leyte. Only eight planes were armed for the mission, with pairs of 500-pound bombs and 5,000 rounds of .50-cal Armor Piercing Incendiary (API) ammunition, led by Bill Dunham.[16] The rest of the squadron had to be kept in reserve because we were still a very limited resource. None of the new airstrips were ready to accept aircraft which were still waiting outside the Philippines for places to land. I was on strip protection when this occurred, so I do not have eyewitness recollections.

Two of the cargo ships, LST types, were caught retracting from the beach and were totally destroyed. The other was Bill Dunham's duck soup. His flight of four hit it with eight 500-pound bombs, sending it to Davey Jones locker in minutes. One destroyer was hammered and left unable to move. This is the best I can remember of this battle.

Then on November 25th, I patrolled over Carigara Bay. From this position, we protected the northern flank of the Leyte operation. Ground forces had taken the Carigara port town in early November, then wheeled to the south to push on towards Ormoc.

When we got back to base, the press was already there to find out what we did. The Chicago Tribune correspondent Walter Simmons asked me what my hometown was, and I was delighted to give him my address in Chicago. A summary of my Leyte missions, dateline November 25, Leyte, was reported in the *Chicago Sunday Tribune*'s front page on November 26, 1944 under a huge banner which said "SMASH FOURTH JAP CONVOY"—"Lt James Curran of 8135 Prairie Av., Chicago, a Thunderbolt flight commander, today totted up his score after two weeks on Leyte. He had destroyed two small towns infested by Japanese. He had sunk a thousand ton freighter. He had sunk a 200 ton freighter, a 100 tonner, and a 50 ton sailing lugger."[17]

The *Chicago Tribune* reporter who interviewed me also quoted Major Dunham, Nez Perce, Idaho, who shared credit with Lt. Gerald Economoff, Gary, Indiana, for sinking a big transport: "I saw my bomb hit . . . and a Jap came cartwheeling up in the air as high as the ship's mast." The reporter continued with this description of the action at Port Cataingan: "Lt. David Singleton of Hammond, Ind., strafed the destroyer escort, then loosed his bomb. It missed. He swung over to the LST type ship and hit it squarely with his second bomb. The ship dropped its ramp and Jap soldiers in full field packs started bailing out. The Thunderbolts strafed them with pass after pass as the ship settled into the water." He concluded with another quote from Dunham: "All the ships were jammed with troops . . . It probably would be fair to say that at most 6,000 men were killed or drowned in the attack."[18]

Things did not let up much and on November 26th, I flew a combat mission to Legaspi, Luzon. DeWitt Searles recalled this about the Legaspi mission: "In late November, 1944, one or more Navy carriers were damaged to the point that they could no longer recover aircraft returning to land. Many of them were diverted to Tacloban. The strip was already overcrowded and we had to park the Navy aircraft, wingtip to wingtip along both sides of the runway. Also, additional Army Air Corps combat aircraft were scheduled to arrive every day. But we were out of space.

It was decided that the Navy aircraft would fly with us until such time as they could return to their carriers. The first such joint mission . . . was against the Airfield at Legaspi. And we did provide cover for the Navy dive bombers. All Navy aircraft returned to their own or other carriers within a day or two."[19]

On the 27th, Governor Gallares and his staff visited the airstrip at Tacloban. While they were with us, the Japs attacked by air in large numbers. I grabbed the governor and hustled him into a dugout while the raid was in progress. The sound of anti-aircraft guns was overwhelming.

When the shooting finally stopped we emerged from the dugout in fine shape; but the governor was still shaking from the experience and was hugging me with all his might. Later in the day, we furnished Governor Gallares with ten .50-caliber machine guns and about a 100,000 rounds of ammunition, which they took back to Bohol much to the demise of the Jap garrison in Bohol City. We heard that they were victorious in eradicating the Japs from their island. Months later I received a letter from the governor inviting me to Bohol as a guest of the government. I was never able to cash in on the offer.[20]

The rest of November was spent on hitting targets in and around Leyte. On November 28th, we had an afternoon mission to bomb and strafe shipping west of Leyte. But some enemy fighters attacked our formation of 16 P-47's just as we started our bomb run at about 1615 local time, and frustrated our attack.[21]

As we popped out of a cloud we saw the ships in the distance, but at the same time, some Jap fighter planes passed a few hundred feet over our heads. Disaster, I thought, we are loaded with bombs, enemy fighters are near, and we can't see them. I opted to commence an attack on the ships immediately. The aerial encounter upset our approach enough so that when we descended out of the overcast we were too close to make a low-level masthead height attack and the Japs were unloading with all their flak on us. Committed to a run at the ships, we wound up with a lot of near misses, inflicted minimal damage with our machine gun fire, and wound up with no casualties. We could not find the Jap fighters that we all saw prior to the attack. We returned to Tacloban, but it was too late in the day to load up and go back to finish the job.

The next day, November 29th, I flew another combat mission to glide bomb that enemy shipping now at Ormoc. Our commander, Bill Dunham, opted to lead the mission of 16 P-47's armed with 500-pound bombs. I cannot remember who had the third flight, but I led the second. We approached the target area at high altitude in order to be alert for enemy fighter planes. Fortunately, none were spotted and we were able to keep our bombs on board.[22]

As reported, there were the enemy ships, consisting of a destroyer, a liner-type vessel, and an LST-type ship that was retracting from the beach. The destroyer immediately started throwing up a heavy flak barrage. Dunham attacked the destroyer. The third flight selected the LST and my flight went for the liner, which was underway at high speed. With the targets all spread out, we were able to mount our attack all at once. The destroyer was hit immediately and disabled, and also attacked with machine guns. The third flight plastered the LST with eight bombs, sinking it in shallow water.

As we approached the liner, we could see the flashes of fire from small arms from bow to stern. The side of the ship was loaded with soldiers shooting their weapons at us. We closed on the ship with all guns firing and triggered our bombs, scoring eight hits of 500-pound high explosives. The ship was still going forward when it sank to the bottom. The whole fight was over in seconds with three ships sunk or damaged by bombs and machine gun fire with no losses to our side. We were very fortunate that no Japanese fighter planes appeared, which must have been a screw up on their part. If Jap fighters had appeared, we would have had to jettison our bombs to defend ourselves because one can't maneuver with bombs on board. We all returned to base and a lot of celebration took place.

Also on this morning shipping attack Flight Officer Robert P. Smith unloaded his bombs into a destroyer at close range. Unfortunately, they didn't explode, and just passed through the ship's hull, but severely damaged it and it lost headway. But the Japs hit his plane, disabling it. He bailed out and landed in the ocean far enough away that the Japs couldn't shoot him. All the Jap ships we found were sunk or disabled, with the loss of only one of our planes.[23]

This time, though, we had a Navy PBY rescue plane in on the mission and they gathered R.P. from his life raft and flew him to a hospital ship in San Pedro Bay. Flight Officer Smith was very popular with the squadron and we fretted for his safety. During the post-mission debriefing we got a signal from the hospital ship that he was O.K. and would be returning to the squadron before night. R.P. appeared before sundown, attired in his uniform, neatly pressed, and his stomach oddly distended. We were overjoyed to see him, but asked him what was wrong with his stomach, to which he replied that he had gobbled half a gallon of ice cream while waiting for his clothes to be dried and pressed. R.P. was happy to learn that his two bombs had hurt the Jap destroyer.

As the war traveled west in the Pacific, we also had submarine support for rescue of downed pilots. Some months later, circa March of 1945, we had a P-51 go down off of Hainan, China, and the rescue sub, cruising submerged on patrol with its radio antenna above water, vectored the pilot to its area. Since we had more advanced VHF radios in 1945, communication with such rescue forces was possible. The pilot ditched next to the sub as it surfaced. It was fresh on duty so the pilot had a long stay with his rescuers. With the good food served on the sub, he grew right out of his uniform. I was stateside by the time he returned to the squadron via Perth, Australia, which was the sub's base, but heard about it later, in June or July.

The loss of those vessels did not deter the Japs from trying again to reinforce Ormoc. A day later, 30 November, we had an early morning signal that Jap ships were once again heading for Ormoc. We loaded bombs as fast as possible after our planes returned from a morning mission, and the Black Rams took off in the afternoon to look for the enemy. There was about a seven/tenths broken overcast with the bottoms at about 5,000 feet, so they had to stay below in order to see the enemy as they approached their target.

But the attack was spoiled when enemy fighters jumped the squadron, forcing it to jettison bombs and fight it off, described in the squadron's December history as follows: "Sent to Port Carmen on the east coast of Cebu Island, the squadron was jumped from behind by a formation of six Oscar fighters just as the P-47's started their bomb run. 2nd Lt. Perry A. Tubre . . . was killed by the first enemy pass and many Jap shells were seen to strike in and around the cockpit. In the fight that followed, 2nd Lt. Samuel P. Denmark . . . and 1st Lt. DeWitt R. Searles . . . helped to avenge his loss by knocking down two of the Oscars."

My combat flying for the month, 21 missions altogether, concluded earlier the same day, on November 30, with a flight to bomb and strafe a target in Kananga, Leyte. Sixteen P-47's deposited 32 500-pound general purpose bombs at 1030 in the morning, which hit the target, a school house being used by the enemy.[24]

NOVEMBER 1944 COMBAT RECORD *During the month of November, in addition to damage done to the enemy by bombing and strafing troops and convoys, the squadron destroyed its first 10 Jap planes, chalked up three probable, and gained for itself the reputation for avid, efficient operations under trying circumstances . . . The first victory for the squadron was scored at 1440 hours 12 November when Captain Richard C. Frost shot down a Zeke 32 in*

Leyte Gulf, just offshore in view of the Tacloban beaches.—History of the 460th Fighter Squadron, November 1944

The next day the enemy ships were nowhere to be seen. This misfortune on our part might have encouraged the Jap command because they made more efforts to reinforce Ormoc, Leyte.

BLACK RAM STATISTICS FOR NOVEMBER *It had sunk an estimated 50,000 tons of enemy shipping. Contributing to this tonnage were nine large vessels, freighters, or freighter-transports. It had dropped on enemy targets 428,500 pounds of bombs, destroyed one float plane in the water and ten enemy planes in aerial combat.*—348th Fighter Group History, November 1944

NOTES

1. The mission results were described as follows in squadron reporting: Mission 3-50, 10 November 1944, Escort B-25's striking shipping at Ormoc Bay. Strafe shipping at Ormoc Bay, TOT 1110I. 34 P-47D's. Results: "Missing P-47 was last seen leaving target area, heading for Tacloban Strip."
   460FS Weekly Status and Operations Report (Form 34), (Report for Period 1–11–44 to 10–11–44 Inclusive).
2. According to Missing Air Crew Report (MACR) 11295, dated 17 November 1944, 2d. Lt. Adrian A. McClendon was flying P-47D-23-RA 42-27637 on 10 November 1944. The incident occurred at 1200 over Ormoc Bay, Leyte Island, at 10 degrees 48 minutes north and 124 degrees 40 minutes east. The yellow tail marking noted by F/O J.J. Smith indicates it was an aircraft borrowed by the 460FS from the 341FS. In paragraph 3 of the MACR, weather conditions at the time were CAVU, Ceiling And Visibility Unlimited. Paragraph 5 expressed aircraft loss resulting from: "Exact circumstances not known but believed to have been shot down by friendly fighter. P-38's attacked a flight of four (4) P-47s. Leader saw them and called on radio and the P-38's broke off. It cannot be stated that aircraft was shot down because of violent evasive action of the rest of the flight, which prevented anyone from seeing the results of action. Testimony of Flight Officer John J. Smith (see attached eyewitness report) indicates only that missing aircraft may have been on P-38's line of fire. Para 13, on whether the pilot may have survived, said to "See par. 5. A categorical statement cannot be made." Testimony of Major William D.

Dunham, (see attached eyewitness report) indicates only that a fire was sighted on the water after the action and that at that particular location, the waters looked as if a plane may have gone in. Neither of these statements offers conclusive evidence that (1) a plane went down (2) that Lt. McClendon's plane was shot down in the action." Major William D. Dunham, 460FS commander, made the following statement in the MACR "Statements in par. 5 and 13 of above report were made on the basis of my personal knowledge of the action. I was the leader of the flight mentioned in F/O Smith's testimony as the one which Lt. McClendon joined prior to the action. I cannot state that Lt. McClendon's plane was in the line of the P-38's fire, nor can I state that his plane went down. I can only state that I saw a brief flame on the water directly under the place where the action occurred, and that it appeared at that spot a few moments later as if a plane might have gone under at that point. I further state that an unsuccessful attempt was made to ascertain the pilots of the P-38 flight and secure from them information pertinent to the action. No further testimony from officers of this squadron could be found." MACR Para 16 indicated that "PBYs and flights of P-47s searched area and area fifty to one hundred miles around target for signs of life raft. The search was carried on for two days.

3. This "heavy cruiser" Jim Curran recalled was most likely the *Wakatsuki,* a large Japanese destroyer of the *Akizuki* class, a type frequently mistaken for cruisers because of their size and heavy anti-aircraft armament. In "Japanese Naval Vessels of World War II, as seen by US Naval Intelligence," Naval Institute Press, 1987, the official publication "ONI 41-42 Japanese Naval Vessels" specifically advised of the possibility of mistaking the identity of this type of destroyer with Japanese cruisers of the *Mogami* and *Yubari* classes, among other vessels.
   Nevitt, Allyn, "AKIZUKI Class Notes," http://www.combinedfleet.com/akizuk_n. htm

4. Mission 3-51, 10 November 1944, Glide bomb shipping north of Ormoc Bay, TOT 1530I. Fifteen P-47's with thirty 500-pound bombs. Results: "4 near misses on one Destroyer. 26 bombs landed in water in target area."
   460FS Weekly Status and Operations Report (Form 34), (Period 1–11–44 to 10–11–44 Inclusive).

5. In addition to the air echelon flown into Tacloban, the 460FS also had a water echelon from Noemfoor, embarked aboard LST-668 with the 342FS around 8 November. After three days in convoy on one engine, the LST dropped out and proceeded to Woendi Island, near Biak Island, where all aboard had to transfer over to LST-775 and after some transloading difficulties, including the need to build a 50-foot ramp in order to offload the heavy equipment and vehicles, the vessel headed to Leyte. It arrived at Dulag's Orange beach on 19 November and was sent along traffic-jammed and mud-rutted roads and on through abaca and banana palms to a muddy camp location on the Dogami River near the miserable,

rain-sodden Burauen and San Pablo airstrips. From there, some were sent to bolster exhausted personnel at Tacloban, which was essentially filled to capacity for
personnel and equipment.

History of the 460FS, Chapter Five, (1 November 1944–30 November 1944).

6. The 348th Fighter Group's history for November 1944, described this difficult period at Tacloban, when the Black Rams, ". . . the 110th Recco Squadron, and the
depleted Forty Niner Group were the sole representatives of American air power
in the Philippines. Indeed the 49th Group had suffered so severely in losses in the
air and on the ground that during the latter part of the month the Black Ram
squadron was flying near half of the missions which took off and landed at
Tacloban strip."

7. The P-61 Black Widows probably belonged to the USAAF's 421st Night Fighter
Squadron, which arrived at Tacloban on October 25, 1944. Due to some performance issues related to intercepting Japanese single-engine fighter-bombers involved
in dawn and dusk harassing attacks, the P-61s were replaced by USMC F6F-5(N)
Hellcat night fighters of VMF(N)-541 in early December 1944.

Maurer, Maurer, Editor. *Combat Squadrons of the Air Force, World War II.* Maxwell
AFB, AL: Office of Air Force History, 1982, entry for the "421st Fighter," page
517.

Chapin, John C., Captain, USMC. . . . *AND A FEW MARINES: Marines in the
Liberation of the Philippines.* Washington, DC: Marine Corps Historical Center,
1997, pages 1, 4–5. (Hereinafter Chapin, . . . *AND A FEW MARINES.)*

Boggs, Charles w., Jr., Major, USMC. *Marine Aviation in the Philippines, USMC
Monograph.* Historical Branch, G-3 Division, Headquarters, US Marine Corps,
1951. CHAPTER 2 Leyte and Samar Campaigns, pp. 29–30. (Hereinafter
Boggs.)

8. Mission 3-58, 11 November 1944, G/B and Strafe Barracks area at Valencia, TOT
1615I. Results: "Five buildings were destroyed, four bombs missed target area."

460FS Weekly Status and Operations Report (Form 34), (Period 11–11–44 to 20–
11–44 Inclusive).

9. These two missions appear to correlate to the following two missions in squadron
records: Mission 3-68, 13 November 1944, G/B Geyon DePatag (possibly Cogon
de Patag, Ormoc, Leyte), Fighter sweep to Legaspi, TOT 0925I, 8 P-47's with two
500lb G/P bombs each. Results: "2 Bombs were jettisoned. Nil sighting on fighter
sweep." Mission 3-77, 14 November 1944, G/B road intersection N. of Valencia
and Patrol Buri, TOT 0940I, four P-47's with two 500lb G/P bombs each. Results:
"8 bombs landed in the General area just S. of target."

Ibid.

10. Missions 3-86 and 3-87, 15 November 1944, Bomb Ipil and Patrol, TOT 0950I.

460FS Weekly Status and Operations Report (Form 34), (Period 11–11–44 to 20–
11–44 Inclusive). Ibid, 2.

Right: A youthful aviation cadet James C. Curran, 21 years old, from Chicago, Illinois, is pictured in flying attire, 1942.—*Mary Jean Curran*

Center: A Fairchild PT-19A Cornell, which served as the primary flight training aircraft for the USAAF during WWII, and was introduced into service in 1940. This picture was featured on the cover of the *Cimarron Chief Class 43A* book. Jim Curran underwent his primary training at Cimarron from August to October, 1942.—*Mary Jean Curran*

2nd Lt. Curran, assigned to the 341st Fighter Squadron of the 348th Fighter Group in August 1943, sitting in the cockpit of his P-47, possibly at Durand Airfield (17-Mile Drome) near Port Moresby. Note the aircraft crew chief's rank and name on the fuselage, S/Sgt T.C. Medlen.— *Mary Jean Curran*

Left: Jim Curran proudly wears his pilot wings in this photo taken with his mother Rose Ann in 1943, probably during his P-47 transition training in Florida at Dale Mabry Army Air Field in Tallahassee. Curran accrued over 100 hours, mostly in the P-47 Thunderbolt, during this phase of his flight training from March to June, 1943.—*Mary Jean Curran*

Right: Aviation cadet Curran in flying gear poses for a photo during his pilot training, ca 1942–1943. Note what appears to be the Army Air Forces Training Command patch on his left shoulder.—*Brad Curran*

Below: Aviation cadet Curran gives a thumbs up in a PT-19A during his primary flight training at Cimarron, Oklahoma, ca September 1942. The aircraft was powered by a 175-horsepower six cylinder inline inverted inline Ranger engine.—*Mary Jean Curran*

Curran, standing at the end of the middle row at far right, wears his dark color wheel cap, along with his Eastern Flying Training Command P-47 transition course classmates at Dale Mabry Army Airfield in May 1943.—*Mary Jean Curran*

Moored portside to Brett's Wharf at Brisbane, Australia, on the afternoon of 21 July 1943, the escort carrier USS *Barnes* unloads its cargo of 15 P-47's and 36 P-38's, along with 35 wing boxes, 20 propeller boxes and 47 radio equipment boxes. This was the same day that Jim Curran arrived in Australia. It is likely that Jim Curran was involved in the slow-timing of some of these P-47's before he joined the 348th Fighter Group up in New Guinea.—*David Jones, Queensland Maritime Museum, from US National Archives (NARA)*

2nd Lt. Curran (left) and 2nd Lt. Robert L. Frank, possibly at 17-Mile Drome (Durand Airfield), Port Moresby, late 1943, after assignment to the 341st Fighter Squadron. They were among a dozen replacement fighter pilots assigned to the 348th Fighter Group in the summer of 1943, shortly after the group arrived for combat duty as the first P-47 Thunderbolt unit in the Pacific theater of operations.—*Mary Jean Curran*

Left: P-47D-2-R serial number 42—"HI-TOPPER," was the mount of 341st Fighter Squadron pilot John S. Lolos. Note the wheel hub painted with concentric rings.—*Jack Cook*

Below: Undated photograph of key 348th Fighter Group combat leaders enjoying a jovial moment in the SWPA. *From left to right:* Commander Neel E. Kearby, with David A. Campbell (341st Fighter Squadron commander), Robert R. Rowland (group executive officer), William D. Dunham (342nd Fighter Squadron) and Raymond K. Gallagher (342nd Fighter Squadron commander), in front of a Martin B-26 Marauder medium bomber, probably taken at a Port Moresby area airfield in New Guinea, late 1943.—*Mary Jean Curran*

Colonel Neel E. Kearby climbs into the cockpit of his P-47 for another mission in this undated photograph. With 15 victories marked on his aircraft, this photo was taken sometime between 3 December 1943, after he achieved his 15th victory, and 22 December 1943, when he scored his next one. —*Jack Cook*

Center: Colonel Kearby, second from left, meets with men of the 348th Fighter Group at his P-47 named "Fiery Ginger IV" after his red-haired wife, Virginia. The man standing to Kearby's left is possibly the 342nd FS flight surgeon, Doc Weddel. Kearby flew this aircraft in the period when he scored his final ten victories, between 3 December 1943 and 5 March 1944.—*Jack Cook*

Below: A pair of 341st P-47 pilots relax for a picture at a wartime base, possibly Wakde Airfield, 1944. The pilot on the left is unidentified, and on the right is Merle Zeine, who became the 341st FS operations officer in June 1944, and then the squadron's commander. Note the drop tanks beneath the wings, 165-gallon types adapted from the P-38 Lightning for Thunderbolt use, increasing the reach of the P-47 across the expanses of the Pacific.—*Roger Zeine*

View of Colonel Neel Kearby's ship, "Fiery Ginger IV," being serviced, possibly at Finschhafen, 1944. On 5 March 1944, Col. Kearby flew this aircraft on his final, fatal combat mission, on which he achieved his 22nd and last victory before he was shot down by an enemy fighter. The wreck was discovered after the war and today the tail with serial number is in the Museum of the Air Force at Wright-Patterson AFB, Ohio. Why the aircraft has 22 victories depicted on it before the last mission is not explained. Perhaps the 22nd is the Ki-21 SALLY bomber he was given probable credit for on 9 February 1944.—*Mary Jean Curran*

341st Fighter Squadron P-47D pilot Robert W. Anderson stands on the wing of his aircraft "My Baaaby II," probably at Finschhafen Airfield, with his aerial victory seen below the cockpit, from his engagement with and defeat of an A6M Zero over Arawe on the morning of 27 December 1943. Note the extensive weathering of the paint on the propeller after several months in rough conditions.—*Jack Cook*

A P-47D-4-RA Thunderbolt of the 348th Fighter Group in the early markings of the group, with the white tail and white paint along the leading edges of the wing. A squadron number and color adorn the tail surface. Jim Curran flew P-47D-4s from late-December 1943 through February of 1944, according to his flight records.—*Jonathan Watson*

A Douglas P-70 night fighter, of the type Curran described as the 341st Fighter Squadron's "Fat Cat," used for the squadron's supply runs to Australia during his time in New Guinea. The P-70 was a conversion from the A-20 Havoc light attack bomber.—*U.S. Air Force*

A Mitsubishi A6M5 Zero, code-named ZEKE, captured during fighting in the Marianas Islands in 1944, is shown on a test flight. Jim Curran encountered Zero fighters like this during his dogfight over the western Solomon Sea on 23 October 1943.—*National Naval Aviation Museum, Robert L. Lawson Photograph Collection*

Late war aerial view of Elco class PT Boat *PT-601* completed in June 1945, and seen underway at speed, her roll-off torpedo racks empty but with a full gun armament including

.50 caliber machine guns, a 20mm, 37mm and 40mm cannon. Friendly fighters were used to provide them with air cover during daylight operations in proximity to enemy forces. Once night fell and friendly fighters returned to base, the PTs did much of their work against the enemy. —*NavSource*

"Windy City Kitty," a P-47D-2, was Curran's first "assigned" combat aircraft, which he flew for some 74 combat missions while assigned to the 341st Fighter Squadron. This picture was likely taken with Curran's Brownie camera, possibly at 17-Mile/Durand Airstrip, 1943.—*Mary Jean Curran*

A 348FG P-47D rests at Finschhafen Airfield, 1944. Note the 200-gallon belly tank beneath the fuselage, which enabled the Thunderbolt to engage in longer-ranged operations, a vital requirement in the Pacific—*Jack Cook*

Damaged U.S. Marine Corps F4U-1A Corsair of VMF-115 at Tacloban Airfield, Leyte, 1944 after a Japanese air raid on the strip the night before. Note the Army P-61 Black Widow nightfighter in the background, right, soon to depart Leyte in exchange for Marine Hellcat nightfighters.—*Mark Mansfield*

Pilots of the 341st Fighter Squadron pose for a squadron picture in 1944, perhaps at Wakde Airfield. Jim Curran is seen standing third from the left beneath the propeller.—*Mary Jean Curran*

Fighter pilots of the Black Rams take a moment for a group photo at Leyte, December 1944. From left to right are Willis M. Cooley, George Della, Richard C. Frost, DeWitt R. Searles, James C. Curran, William O. Carter, Vernon N. Turner, William D. Dunham and Frank G. Russo. Sitting on the wing is Wallace M. Harding. Note this photo was taken before the addition of black recognition stripes on the wings and fuselage of this P-47.—*John Stanaway*

Left: Part of Japanese convoy TA No. 3 trying to reinforce Leyte under air attack by some of the 350 US Navy warplanes of Task Force 38, 11 November 1944.—*NARA*

Center: View of Tacloban Airfield from north looking south, November 1944, after a month of improvements during the Leyte campaign. The Black Rams were based here from 10 November 1944 into mid-December, 1944, when they moved down the coast to Tanauan. —*NARA*

Below: Tanauan Airfield, Leyte Island, looking to the south, became the home of the 348th Fighter Group from mid-December, 1944 to early February, 1945. —*National Naval Aviation Museum*

A Kawasaki Ki-61 Hien TONY/Army Type 3 fighter of the Imperial Japanese Army Air Force sits forlornly after the battle at Clark Field in early 1945. This aircraft bears the markings of the 19th Sentai, with a stylized unit number 19 marking on the tail. This was the type of fighter Jim Curran shot down in an aerial encounter near Leyte on 10 December 1945. This and the other captured Japanese aircraft seen behind it are roped off, probably under technical study by the Allied Technical Air Intelligence Unit, SWPA, possibly to be restored to some type of operational status.—*National Naval Aviation Museum, Robert L. Lawson Photograph Collection*

Major William D. "Dinghy" Dunham, commander of the 460th Fighter Squadron, smiles from the cockpit of his well-employed P-47D-23 on Leyte, shaking hands with a member of the ground echelon, possibly his crew chief, J.A. Matisz, or armorer, Sgt. Albert Liedigk.—*Roger Zeine*

460th Fighter Squadron Armorer Sergeant Nolan Machen admires his squadron commander's tallies. He wrote: "This is what makes an armorer feel his work is doing good. My C.O.'s plane and his record: 15 Jap planes, 30 bombing missions, two 10,000 ton freighters."—*Nolan Machen*

Sign indicating the 460th Fighter Squadron area at San Marcelino Airfield, Luzon, 1945. The 460th Fighter Squadron flew from San Marcelino from early February to mid-May, 1945, when it moved to Floridablanca Airfield some 12 miles south of Clark Field. Information indicates that the name Black Rams and emblem originated during the squadron's time at San Marcelino.—*J.J. Smith*

Center: Pilots of the 460th Fighter Squadron next to an armed P-47D at San Marcelino Airfield in early 1945, during the waning days of the Thunderbolt's service in the 348th Fighter Group. Left to right, standing, are Orville R. Moderow, Herbert F. Cass, J.J. Smith with the goggles, Howard K. Minnick; kneeling are Raymond J. Huntkowski and James A. Hamilton, Jr. The aircraft's name appears to be "Duchess" with two aerial victories seen beneath the open cockpit.—*J.J. Smith*

Left: Captain DeWitt R. Searles, 460th Fighter Squadron pilot at San Marcelino, Luzon, in 1945. Capt. Searles commanded the Black Rams from December 1944 to April 1945 and made the Air Force a career, eventually attaining the rank of major general.—*Mary Jean Curran*

Right: Black Ram P-51 Mustang "Snow Job," flown by Howard Minnick, armed by Nolan Machen, on Luzon in 1945. Note the Black Ram insignia on the fuselage.—*Courtesy Nolan Machen*

Center: A US aircraft, which appears to be a Marine Corps SBD Dauntless, placed a high explosive bomb atop Hill 1700 west of Bamban, Tarlac, in central Luzon, on 23 February 1945. The 460th Fighter Squadron and 348th Fighter Group, in addition to other USAAF and USMC aviation units, provided much close support to friendly ground forces during the Luzon campaign. —*US Army*

An unidentified airman stands in front of a Catalina flying boat, possibly a Navy "Black Cat," at San Marcelino Airfield on Luzon, 1945. The Catalina is perhaps from the VPB-34 detachment with the seaplane tender USS *Orca* at Lingayen Gulf, 1945. Note the drop tanks lined up behind the aircraft, probably empty and perhaps ready to be filled with Napalm, then in use by American combat aircraft in the Pacific.—*Nolan Machen*

A Black Ram P-51D Mustang over Luzon, 1945, flown by 2nd Lt. Howard K. Minnick. Note the canopy is slid back slightly.

The Black Rams converted from the P-47 to the P-51 while at San Marcelino Airfield on Luzon beginning in February 1945.—*Nolan Machen*

Though Jim Curran's war across the Pacific ended in April, 1945, the 460th Fighter Squadron fought through the end of the war in the P-51. This Black Ram Mustang, "Six Shooter," flown by Capt. Sam Denmark, rests at Ie Shima Airfield in the Ryukyu Islands of Japan, late summer, 1945.—*Jonathan Watson*

Plumes rise from high explosives bombs dropped by four fighter-bombers at the foot of Mount Pearl, Philippines, in this 7 June 1945 photo. The fighters appear as mere silver specks above and

to the right of the smoke. This picture gives an idea of the rugged terrain in Luzon as well as the extensive cover on the mountains which the enemy took advantage of. Pilots were often unable to provide any feedback on results in such close support missions. —*NARA*

On 4 April 1945, Brig. General Frederic H. Smith, Jr., commander of the V Fighter Command, officiated at an awards ceremony for officers and men of the 348th Fighter Group at San Marcelino Airfield, Luzon Island. Here an unidentified NCO is being decorated by General Smith with the Bronze Star for gallantry in action at Leyte. 348th Fighter Group commander Col. Robert Rowland stands at attention to the left. In the back row, left to right, are Captains Jim Curran, George Orr, Ed Poppek and an unidentified man.—*Mary Jean Curran*

Enlisted men of the 460th Fighter Squadron pose for a picture with the Black Ram squadron insignia on the fuselage of a P-51D, possibly at San Marcelino Airfield in early 1945. In the background is a Mustang named "YUMPIN YIMINY."—*Nolan Machen*

Some of the Black Rams who flew with or supported Jim Curran gather for a group picture at San Marcelino in early 1945, in front of the P-51D "FARGO EXPRESS." From left to right: pilot Thompson, an unidentified man, pilots R.P. Smith and J.J. Smith with the holstered combat look, Reid O. Tait, Armaments Officer Lloyd Cuneo, and a playful pilot, Ed DeMeter.—*J.J. Smith*

The 28 "war weary" P-47D Thunderbolts seen here are being prepared for the voyage back to the United States aboard the escort carrier USS *Nassau* on 25 May 1944 at Dreger Harbor, Finschhafen, New Guinea. *Nassau* retrieved a total of 43 P-47's and one P-40 on this voyage, bringing them to the Naval Air Station San Diego.—*Peter Dunn, from NARA*

11. Mission 3-105, 17 November 1944, "Bomb shipping in Ormoc Bay," TOT 0925I. Ibid.

12. The typhoon season played havoc with military operations in Leyte, on both men and materiel. The 341FS History, December 1944, reflected that: "Under rugged conditions the Army Air Forces cletrac (Cleveland Tractor) proved completely unsuited for the combat conditions in the forward area. Rain, with attendant mud, is the adverse factor. Cletracs will operate and give good service when only used on dry hard surfaced roads and taxiways. Seldom, if ever, is this the case in forward area. The tracks of the cletrac become quickly clogged with mud and the tracks break. The squadron lost both its cletracs during the month for this reason." It continued: "The problems encountered by the transportation section all had their roots in the rain and mud. On the 10th of the month, 10 vehicles were grounded and required third echelon maintenance. However, although the ordnance channels were due to get the parts in several weeks, the parts were obtained somehow . . . The status of vehicles remains . . . very shaky. It is questionable if the majority of vehicles will be able to go through another move as demanding and grueling as the one from Noemfoor to the Philippines and the ensuing conditions."
History of the 341st Fighter Squadron, Chapter XIV, December 1944, page 11.

13. The Honorable Celestino Gallares was the Governor of Bohol from October 16, 1931 to October 15, 1934. Email from Ms. Erlinda Rule, Bohol Governor's Office and the Tagbilaran Provincial Library head, 12 May 2014.

14. Mission 3-135, 21 November 1944, "Tacloban patrol & strafe Sugar Charlie & gen'l barge sweep," TOT 1615I. Four P-47's expended 4,000 rounds of .50 caliber ammunition to obtain these results: "1 P-47 bellied in rice pattie 2 miles inland from Baybay. Pilot Recovered." In the Form 34 Table V—Remarks and Recommendations, it continued: "Mission 3-135. One Sugar dog, 1 large barge, 1 sugar Charlie and 1 large lugger left burning off Linao. Plane was hit by small arms fire."
460FS Weekly Status and Operations Report (Form 34), (Report for Period 21 Nov 44 to 30 Nov 44 Inclusive), page 1.

The summary for this mission does not indicate any tasking to bomb nor is there any record of bombs being employed by the aircraft on this mission. This was not unusual as several other 460FS missions on this very day were similar, aerial patrols without bombs, and then a shipping sweep around Ormoc Bay in an effort to remain vigilant about the presence of any Japanese reinforcement or resupply activity. It should be noted that USMC ground and air units made vital contributions in the Leyte campaign. Marine V Amphibious Corps (VAC) Artillery with 155 mm howitzers provided the Army divisions with corps-level fire support from October into December. Marine air units arrived in early December at a critical time in the campaign to boost airpower capabilities against continued Japanese resistance.
Garand, George W, and Strobridge, Truman R., "History of US Marine Corps Operations in World War II, Volume IV: Western Pacific Operations, Part IV:

Marines in the Philippines, Chapter 2. The Leyte Landings," Historical branch, G-3 Division, Headquarters, US Marine Corps, 1971, on Ibiblio HyperWar website, accessed 24 July 2014 at: http://www.ibiblio.org/hyperwar/USMC/IV/USMC-IV-IV-2.html

15. Mission 3-138, 22 November 1944, "Bomb Masbate Airdrome Primary Target;" and "Glide bomb Pavompon [sic] Harbor. Secondary target," TOT at Palompon 0915I. The Masbate attack was "incomplete due to weather," hence the attack on the secondary target at Palompon. The recording of damage in the Ormoc Bay area on the Form 34 suggests Ormoc was designated as a tertiary target, which makes sense given its important role as the primary receiving point for Japanese reinforcements in the Leyte campaign.
460FS Weekly Status and Operations Report (Form 34), (Report for Period 21 Nov 1944 to 30 Nov 1944 Inclusive), page 2.

16. Mission 3-145, 24 November 1944, "Bomb Shipping at Port Cataingan," TOT 1455I. Eight P-47's went on the mission and one returned early. Results of the bombs and 10,500 rounds of .50 caliber ammunition were: "A/A south end of strip. 1 plane returned early. A/A from Domorog. 14 (500-lb) bombs dropped on target. 2 jettisoned. One large freighter in Port Cataingan section 4 direct hits, left burning and exploding. One large freighter hit in stern and straffed [sic], fires and explosions. 1 ship similar to LST, one direct hit. Ramps were lowered an [sic] Japs straffed [sic] by the score. Ship left burning."
Ibid.

17. *Chicago Sunday Tribune*, Sunday, November 26, 1944, page 1.

18. The remarks by Bill Dunham were in the same *Chicago Tribune* article that mentioned Jim Curran, on Sunday, November 26, 1944, page 1. On the morning of 24 November, the Black Rams flew a 16-aircraft mission against Masbate Airdrome, on Masbate Island, off the southeast tip of Luzon. On the way back to Leyte they noticed the presence of enemy shipping in Port Cataingan, on the southeast part of Masbate Island. Joined by P-40 Warhawks of the 110th Tactical Reconnaissance Squadron, eight 460FS P-47s flew a combat mission against this shipping in the afternoon, effectively destroying Echelon 1 of Japanese reinforcement convoy TA-5, the fifth organized convoy the Japanese sent to reinforce their garrison on Leyte. Actual Japanese ship losses at Port Cataingan, Masbate on 24 November 1944 were three LST type vessels, *T.111, T.141* and *T.160*. Their escort, *Subchaser 46*, not a destroyer as initially reported, barely escaped with some survivors and attempted to return to Manila, but was sunk en route the next day by Navy carrier aircraft. Major Dunham received an Oak Leaf Cluster to his Silver Star while each of the other six flight members were awarded a Distinguished Flying Cross for their achievement on this mission.
348th Fighter Group Narrative History for November 1944, page 3.
Nevitt, Allyn D., "The TA Operations to Leyte, Part III," http://www.combined-

fleet.com/taops3.htm (Hereinafter Nevitt, "The TA Operations to Leyte, Part III")

19. Email correspondence with Major General DeWitt Searles, USAF (Retired), on 19 March 2013. The Form 34 for this period indicates this was Mission Number 3-159, 26 November 1944, "Strafe enemy aircraft on Legaspi, Masbate, San Jose and Bulan. Fourteen P-47's were over the target at 0700, and expended 9,100 rounds of .50 caliber ammunition during the mission." Results: "Destroyed one Betty on ground. Other Bettys hit, results not observed. One aircraft was damaged by flying rocks and mud thrown up by own machine gun fire." There is no mention of operating with US Navy aircraft on this mission, though other sources indicate this was the case on this Legaspi mission.

On 25 November 1944, Japanese kamikaze aircraft damaged several US Navy aircraft carriers operating east of Luzon, Philippine Islands, including the USS *Intrepid* (CV-11). Aircraft of Air Group 18 from the *Intrepid* which were airborne could not return to their ship because of her damage, and were diverted to Tacloban Airfield. On the afternoon of 26 November 1944, *Intrepid's* land-based aircraft flew a mission against Legaspi Airfield, and the next day began a journey eastward to the advanced naval base at Ulithi, via Peleliu, arriving there 28 November. "Balancan Harbor Bombing November 25, 1944," http://www.ulongbeach.com/balanacan_bombing.html

20. Though Jim Curran never made it to Bohol, several aircraft from his former squadron, the 341st Fighter Squadron, did so in January 1945, among other air units that found reason to use the emergency strip at Ubay during the Philippines campaign. On 8 January 1945, a Tanauan Airfield, Leyte-based P-51 Mustang flown by 2nd Lt. Kenneth A Steel, Endicott, NY, developed a fuel system leak while covering a convoy in the Mindanao Sea. He made a successful belly landing at Ubay, which was an emergency landing strip that Filipino guerrillas had prepared and guarded over. The friendly Filipino guerrillas took care of Steel until he was rescued and returned to Tanauan six days later by an L-5 liaison aircraft.

This was the prelude to a more spectacular unplanned visit to Ubay strip on 24 January 1945, when poor weather over Leyte forced a flight of seven P-51's of the 341FS to make an emergency landing at Ubay. They had to remain overnight until the weather cleared again, and in the meantime enjoyed some of the famous Filipino hospitality thanks to the people of Bohol who ". . . held open house for our pilots, entertaining them with five tasty, filling meals and a dance into the wee hours of the morning." The aircraft successfully returned to Tanauan the next day, after some aircraft were serviced with the field expedient of clean water in lieu of non-available inhibited glycol for their engine coolant systems. History of the 341st Fighter Squadron, Chapter XV, January 1945, pp. 4–5.

21. Mission 3-175, 28 November 1944, Bomb and strafe shipping West of Leyte, TOT 1615I. 16 P-47D "Formation was attacked by enemy aircraft as they started

bomb run." Two Zekes and two Oscars are noted in the report.

460FS Weekly Status and Operations Report (Form 34), (Report for Period 21 Nov 1944 to 30 Nov 1944 Inclusive), page 4.

22. This was likely one of several 29 November 1944 air attacks on elements of Japanese reinforcement convoy TA-6, including the *Shinso Maru* (2,880 tons), sunk at Ormoc and *Shinetsu Maru* (2,211 tons), sunk westward off of Camotes Island. *Subchaser 45*, an escort of this convoy and also sunk this day, was likely misidentified as a destroyer/destroyer escort. Although Jim Curran recalled no enemy air opposition prior to the attack, after making his bomb run, 460FS P-47 pilot 2nd Lt. Thomas Sheets destroyed one Oscar type fighter.

History of the 460th Fighter Squadron, Chapter Five, November 1944.

According to his flying records, it appears Jim Curran flew several combat missions against the Japanese efforts to reinforce Leyte, apparently including his 10 November 1944 arrival into the Philippines against convoy TA-4 (Ormoc Bay), 28–29 November against TA-6 (Ormoc), 2 December against TA-7 (vicinity of Pacijan Island southwest of Ormoc) and 8 December against TA-8 (San Isidro Bay). He also covered attacks on Convoy TA-9 on 11 December. Although his description doesn't neatly match some of these air-to-surface engagements, the battle situation on the land, in the waters around, and in the skies over Leyte at the time was truly chaotic. For a full description of these Japanese TA reinforcement convoys, see Mr. Allyn Nevitt's excellent account in the "The TA Operations to Leyte, Parts I, II and III," http://www.combinedfleet.com/lancers.htm

23. This was possibly Mission 3-176, 29 November 1944, Bomb and strafe transports and escort N of the Camotes Island, TOT 0900I. It was one of three shipping missions flown that day by the squadron. Sixteen P-47's with pairs of 500-pound bombs achieved these reported results: "4 direct hits, 23 very near misses, 2 bombs jettisoned, one bomb would not release . . . one P47 was hit by A/A and pilot bailed out receiving no injury. The pilot was picked up by P-BY. One P-47 crashed landed in Bay at Tacloban receiving no injury."

460FS Weekly Status and Operations Report (Form 34), (Report for Period 21 Nov 1944 to 30 Nov 1944 Inclusive), page 4.

From the 460FS history for November 1944, page 9: "On another shipping strike in Camotes Sea, also led by the Squadron Commander, one destroyer escort and two 5,000 ton transports were sunk. After making his bomb run, 2nd Lt. Thomas M. Sheets . . . destroyed one Oscar type fighter. Captain Lynn O. Parsons . . . with 2nd Lt. Robert P. Smith . . . flying his wing, led an attack in the face of accurate, intense, anti-aircraft fire on the destroyer escort. The warship was hit directly by heavy strafing, and missed closely by bombs. Lt. Smith's airplane was shot down by the ship's guns, but he was able to parachute safely into the water where he was later picked up by a rescue seaplane."

The aircraft appears to have attacked Japanese convoy TA No. 6, composed of five vessels, including two cargo ships escorted by two subchasers (probably mistaken for destroyers) and a patrol boat. PT boats sank a subchaser and the patrol boat near midnight on 28 November, whilst aircraft sank the rest of the ships the next day, 29 November; fighter-bombers sank a freighter and a subchaser, while the last ship, a freighter, succumbed to air attack the next day. Nevitt, "The TA Operations to Leyte, Part III."

Page 5 of the war diary of the seaplane tender USS *Orca* (AVP-49) for the period 1 November 1944 to 30 November 1944, dated 29 December 1944, indicated that on 29 November 1944, "Daylight two picked up 1st Lt. Robert P. SMITH, 460th Fighter Squadron, at the northern tip of Cebu Island." According to page 2 of the war diary, VPB-11 reported aboard for temporary duty in connection with air/sea rescue work on 9 November 1944. Also present aboard, from 4 November 1944, were two Army Air-Sea rescue crews on temporary duty to conduct rescue missions from *Orca*.

The other two combat missions of November 29 are described as follows. Mission 3-178, Bomb and strafe transports & destroyer escort N of the Camotes islands, takeoff at 1245 or 1345, TOT illegible on CD, mission duration 1.5 hours. Fifteen15 P-47's with 500-lb GP bombs. Results: "6 direct hits on transports; 22 bombs near misses. Two bombs were jettisoned. Mission 3-179, Bomb and strafe shipping in Cebu City, takeoff at 1540, TOT illegible on CD, mission duration 1.6 hours. Formation also bombed Ormoc." Results: "5 direct hits were scored. 24 bombs hit in target area destroying many houses and a bridge. 3 bombs failed to release over target."

460FS Weekly Status and Operations Report (Form 34), (Report for Period 21 Nov 1944 to 30 Nov 1944, Inclusive), page 5.

24. Mission 3-180, 30 November 1944, Bomb and strafe Kananga School House, TOT 1030I. Sixteen P-47's with 32 x 500-lb GP bombs. Results: "All bombs hit target area; school house was hit; 1 bridge was hit."

Ibid.

Chapter Ten

INTO DECEMBER

*T**he first weeks of December were an accelerated continuation of the intense activity of the last weeks of November. The Ormoc Valley battle had developed into a serious campaign. Though many enemy convoys had been sunk, and thousands of Japanese soldiers and sailors killed, the Imperial High Command's decision to make Leyte the critical effort for the Philippines was adhered to by the defenders . . . It was a fierce struggle and was fought on a greater scale than any other battle in the Southwest Pacific Area to date.*—History of the 460th Fighter Squadron, December 1944

The start of December 1944 found that food was still a major problem for us despite the arrival of our support people. We were living on C-rations, coffee, and bread made by our baker, Richard "Dick" Demirjian, also known as a photographer. Demirjian's specialty was bread. He still has strong hands from kneading. He lives near the Reagan Presidential Library in California and was host for a reunion there a couple of years ago.

Rumor had it that the United States Marine Corps, stationed about 15 miles south of Tacloban, had some new rations called "ten for one." Translated, that meant a package of this ration could feed one man for ten days, or ten men for one day. Our hunger was so great we decided to try to get some of these rations. We got a couple of enlisted men and two officers into a six-by-six truck and started down the road to the Marine's station. The road was almost impassable in four-wheel drive; we were axle-deep in mud and could only advance about two miles per hour. After half a day of driving, we finally spied the supply dump where the rations had been unloaded from the ships.

The area was well-guarded by Marines with their guns loaded and pointed at us. We begged for some of the food only to be told to scram or be shot. They were too much for us, as we were only armed with .45-caliber pistols. Crestfallen, we returned to our base and mulled over our options.

By this time, my footlocker had arrived from Noemfoor; in it, I had several fifths of Gilbey's Gin. This cache was more valuable than gold. The next morning I selected two bottles of gin, and we drove back to the dump of rations and were met by the same no-nonsense Marines from the day before. Upon seeing us, they reiterated their previous warnings. But this time, I said we have the password, and I brandished two fifths of gin before their eyes. They answered back "Advance, you are recognized, and we will help you load." The two Marines and our G.I.s loaded the truck to the brim in less than half an hour and we were on our way back to base.

As evening approached, we arrived at our camp and the loot was distributed amongst the enlisted and officer personnel. The "Ten and One" rations from the Marines were absolutely outstanding. The first thing I opened was a huge can of boneless chicken. We sat around a small table, ladled succulent morsels of chicken onto slices of bread and munched. Words cannot describe how good this tasted. The four of us consumed the can of chicken in no time at all—not a drop of juice was wasted and the chicken was finger-licking good! This ration was supposed to feed ten men for a day and we consumed the whole thing in less than 15 minutes, licking the ooze off our fingers. The meal far surpassed the previous chicken that I had in Leyte, which consisted of a native bird which I ran down, plucked, and grilled over an open fire for 20 minutes, and then ate it—ugh!

The trip to the Marine dump gave us a little peek at our next base, at Tanauan, which was about ten miles south of Tacloban. This was to be the new home of the group, and was under construction 24/7. The strip was just a little over 5,000 feet long, with the ocean at the north end and a mountain at the south end. This would mean one-way traffic no matter which way the wind was blowing—oh joy, such good planning. There would be no such thing as an aborted landing go around. If one had to go around, one would have to dodge the mountain.

The majority of the strips we flew from were about 5,000 feet long.

Personally I used about 3,500 and made it a practice to try to touch down within the first two feet. I also made three-point landings a habit. It seems that nearly all our runways were adjacent to the ocean where we had an on-shore or off-shore wind to contend with. I had difficulty stateside (with crosswinds) where one always landed into the wind. I have no idea of the crosswind component limit of the Jug, but it was very heavy with great stall characteristics. You could approach with a big crab angle and flip out at the last second before the stall. It would plunk down like a speedy turtle.

In early December, I received my last Jug. It was a Razorback P-47D-23-RA equipped with a 13-and-a-half-foot paddle-blade propeller with square tips, which could bite a huge chunk of air. The turbo-supercharger had a top speed of 23,000 rpm, which greatly enhanced the service ceiling. It was equipped with a 60-gallon tank for water and alcohol carburetor injection. This gave it a takeoff power of 2,300 hp versus 2,000 hp on earlier models. This particular model was probably the finest produced by Republic Aviation—this is a consensus of Jug pilots. We later switched to P-51's in April of 1945, so we never saw a Jug with a bubble canopy in our squadron.[1]

The first time I saw the black trim on natural metal finish on a Jug it was on Bill Dunham's personal aircraft. It was shiny, natural metal polished aluminum, with no ugly brown paint. We had two of these late-model Razorbacks; one for Bill Dunham and the other for me to replace my worn-out one. The olive drab camouflage paint of old was phased out in late 1943. Shedding all that paint increased the top speed of the Jug.

I drooled at having so little paint to slow me down, but that was really secondary compared to the paddle prop, water-alcohol injection and the turbo that could turn at a higher rate. These attributes equaled a super-performing Jug. With the Lindbergh fuel economy technique, I could reduce fuel consumption from 30 to 35 gallons per hour, depending on the load. Compare this to the standard fuel consumption on Windy City Kitty of 60 gallons per hour. Believe me, I was in hog heaven with that aircraft and my fellow pilots stood in line to fly it.

These two planes were the last two replacement Jugs we received, I think. My squadron tail number was 121 and my aircraft serial number was one digit higher than Dunham's plane. Mine was flown up to Luzon later and eventually ended up back at Leyte, after I went stateside. It was destroyed by someone running it off the end of the runway at Tanauan and into San Pedro Bay. What a horrible fate for such a wonderful aircraft.[2]

Other changes were rapidly taking place in Leyte. The Japanese were still bent on reinforcing their hold on Ormoc Bay and the area directly north of the bay. Their air attacks were limited to night raids, due to diligent patrols by the 460th Fighter Squadron. Although I had not seen any enemy aircraft on my patrols, overall the squadron had many contacts, shooting down planes frequently.

THE ORMOC VALLEY FIGHT *Troops and supplies, brought in chiefly under cover of bad weather as well as darkness, continued to pour into Ormoc whence they were marched to the NE corner of the valley a few miles south of Limon. Here US artillery, tanks and infantry men, from their advantageous positions in foothills and northwestern slopes of Mt. Cabungagan, concentrated their superior power and pushed slowly and crushingly into the stream winding up from the south. . . . Flooded rice paddies, land slides, and foxholes turned into small cold wells by the worst rainy season in many years, added to the difficulties. Tracked vehicles were immobilized in many places, but US soldiers continued slowly and uncomfortably to advance.*—History of the 460th Fighter Squadron, December 1944

My missions in early December were diverse. On December 2, I flew a glide bomb and strafing mission to little Pacijan Island, to the south of Ormoc Bay.[3] Two days later, on December 4, I covered a PBY rescue mission in the Ormoc area after a dustup between American and Japanese naval forces the night before. The destroyer USS *Cooper* was sunk and the Catalina seaplanes went in during daylight to rescue her survivors.[4]

Some more variety arrived on Leyte about that time. The few Navy planes that were stranded at Tacloban had left when they ran out of starting cartridges, but the Navy wasn't long in moving a Marine fighter group in to reinforce the beachhead. Marine Air Group (MAG)-12 was the group, four squadrons of F4U Corsair fighter planes which came in on December 3.[5] This was the first time we had seen these fighters and we were impressed with the big gull-winged aircraft. We love the USMC dearly. We would have been in deep trouble without the way they came in to help at Leyte, which makes me grateful to them. They immediately started patrols over the beachhead, giving us a much-needed rest and time to catch up on over-due aircraft maintenance.[6]

LEYTE AIRFIELD PROVES A REALLY BUSY PLACE

Leyte Air Base, P.I. (AP)—The pilots, ground crews and airstrip workers have been so busy fighting the air war against the Japanese that they have just discovered this is the busiest single strip combat airdrome in the Pacific—possibly in any theater.

Lt. Col. James Pettus of St. Louis, Mo., the acting airdrome commander, estimates that until recently the strip averaged be-tween 600 and 700 daylight take-offs daily. It hit the peak Dec. 7 when 894 take-offs and landings were recorded—more than one every 45 seconds.

Army, navy and marine planes have used the strip.
—*The Milwaukee Journal*, December 20, 1944

One thing I don't think I've stressed enough was the remarkable air-craft maintenance I enjoyed in my tour of combat. It's incredible to realize I never had one sortie snafu in my whole tour. This was due to the care and diligence of the men who kept us flying under the worst conditions possible. Maintenance officer, armament officer, line chief (a master ser-geant), crew chief per aircraft (sometimes more than one aircraft), radio mechanics, armorers and general helpers. I never had enough good things to say about these dedicated enlisted Airmen that took such good care of their pilots and planes.

HERCULEAN EFFORTS *The armament, ordnance and engineering sections operated throughout this period with an understaffed air echelon; a bare skele-ton of the force authorized for a fighter squadron. Yet this small detachment was responsible for the maintaining of at least 10 additional airplanes to the normal strength, as well as loading 184-1/2 tons of bombs. In view of the fact that . . . a medium bombardment squadron that in a month's period of average operations they loaded approximately only 160 tons of bombs, the tonnage record established by 13 men in a period of 20 days, less five days during which weather curtailed bomb operations altogether, appears prodigious.*—History of the 460th Fighter Squadron, December 1944

In the Pacific combat zone things were very different than stateside or Europe in regard to maintaining aircraft. There were no back shops or areas for repair that I was ever aware of. The crew chief was the boss and person responsible for the aircraft. The other mechanics serviced planes as directed by the line chief who oversaw everything necessary to keep the planes operational. We had men with specialties like metal work, painting, Bendix brakes, etc. No such work was performed by group-level personnel. Pilots also lent a hand by keeping their crew chiefs informed of any deficiency on the aircraft, in detail. My crew chiefs seemed to sense everything about the aircraft that could go wrong. They had eagle eyes and never left anything to chance. I had remarkably good men working with me in both squadrons I flew in. I liked them and they liked me, which made for good flying. We had great respect for each other. Many of them said they would love to go with me on a mission, which of course was impossible in the single-seat Jug. Sadly, they are all gone now, but not in my memory.

PREVENTIVE MAINTENANCE *Investigation of fires in the accessory sections of two of this squadrons planes resulted in the addition of another check item in the daily maintenance inspection . . . In P-47 models which have the water injection system installed at the factory, there is a tendency for the soldered joint on the balance line from the carburetor to the water injection regulator to crystalize under vibration, and to break, thereby emitting raw gasoline into the accessory section. It is believed this fault accounted for the two fires mentioned. No corrective measure for this fault has been devised other than the constant check, and immediate removal for repair of the defective joint.—* 460FS Combat Evaluation Report, 11 January 1945

The first day the Marines started flying their Corsairs at Tacloban, they were taking off from north to south. As they were retracting their landing gear, they would make a violent turn to the left, immediately over our planes and our ready shack where pilots kept themselves out of the sun while on standby alert. We didn't stand alert on the ground for any ground support missions with bombs attached to the plane as I recall. We had a ready tent for standby alert, as it was too hot in the sun to hang around the plane, the metal of which was untouchable due to the intense sun.

This Marine Corps flying maneuver was very dangerous and unnerving for our pilots and ground crews. We immediately dispatched a delegation to the Marines HQ to find out why they were performing this unnecessary maneuver. They told us they were practicing avoiding downdrafts, which were experienced when taking off from a carrier. After much negotiation, they agreed to stop this practice. Apparently this complaint did not sit too well with the Marine cadre because the next thing I knew, my jeep was missing. A short search revealed it was in the hands of some Marine personnel and getting a new paint job to make it look like a Navy vehicle. We laid claim in no uncertain terms and drove it away half painted. It remained that way until I left for the States. I can't remember how we got the jeeps in our squadron, but we had about six of them and one was assigned to me for transportation of my flight members. Normally, as a flight leader, one worked with five or six pilots. But due to the fluid situation, flight members were all mixed up for reasons unknown and I found myself working with 15 to 20 different pilots, though not all at once.

Base operations decided that we would have a joint mission with the Marines on their foray beyond Leyte. The mission was assigned to me, and consisted of eight of our planes and eight more from the Marines. The flight was to Mindanao to disable a Japanese airstrip. Each plane was to carry two 500-pound bombs to destroy the runways. We briefed together and it was very simple—we were to lead the mission and attack first while the Marines flew top cover. After dropping our bombs, we would climb back up to the cover position while the Marines dropped their bombs.

Upon arriving at the target, my flight attacked first, and as I pulled up, the second flight dropped their load and then we all climbed up to the cover position. As soon as we had sufficient altitude, I called for the Marines to attack, which they did, all at the same time. Four planes flew from one direction and four from another. Unfortunately, two planes collided right over the target, killing both pilots. It was sad, as the mission left numerous gaping craters in the runway and the remnants of two Corsairs. I had no more contact with the Marines after that. Another unfortunate thing about the operation was that the Japs would have the airstrip operational in a few days unless it was continuously bombed, which with our limited resources, was not practical.[7]

The rest of our group was moving rapidly to Leyte, with the exception of the airplanes, which were awaiting a place to land. There was no room left at Tacloban because of what we had there already, and the fact that air-craft were taking off and landing all the time. Night operations were pro-hibited because of Japanese raiders who operated all night. We did have two twin-engine night fighters that were doing a fine job, but there were only a pair of them.[8]

THE ROUGH AND TUMBLE OF LEYTE *November had effected a fair assur-ance of Yankee air force survival in the islands. The air bridgehead at Tacloban had been established, and the worst that the enemy had been able or willing to hurl against it from the air had been repulsed by the Forty Niner Group and the 348th's Black Ram Squadron. December saw the initial development of the skillful frustration of Jap air, sea, and ground strategy which was finally to bring about their swift military downfall in the Philippines. November had been a time for tenacity, December was a time for audacity.*—348th Fighter Group History, December 1944

By the end of the first week in December, the squadron had flown sev-eral missions to plant 500-pound bombs on a challenging target in the Ormoc Valley; the target was located in a ravine with steep ridges extending east and west. It was the focal point of the north-south highway and was heavily fortified by the Japs, who held up our Army forces and caused heavy casualties.

I was assigned a mission against this target on December 6th, and eight P-47s were to be used as ground support for the infantry. Intelligence com-plained that we had not been effective in destroying this target, so I met with Lloyd Cuneo, our armament officer, to see if he had any suggestions as to what we could do to wreck the target. His answer was, "Bigger bombs." Out came my pencil and paper to figure how much I could carry with the P-47, considering I could get off the ground with two 165-gallon tanks of gasoline and 5,000 rounds of ammunition. I calculated that if we reduced the ammo to half, in order to lighten the gross takeoff weight, to about 17,500 pounds, I could possibly get airborne with two 1,000-pound high explosive bombs. We haggled with the engineering officer in charge of the ground crews and he finally agreed. The use of 1,000-pound bombs was a Black Ram first at Leyte, cooked up by Cuneo and me.

We got the bombs from the Navy ammo dump. The problem of getting away from the big bombs before they exploded was solved by putting a 15-second delay fuse on them. I was able to take off from Tacloban lugging two 1,000-pound bombs, airborne in 4,000 feet.

We got permission from the high brass to go on the mission, so on the 6th of December we launched eight P-47s with two bombs each, for a total of 16,000 pounds of high explosive TNT. As we approached the target area, I called the controller for a target designation, telling him we had a big surprise for the enemy and to be sure to cover their ears when we dropped our load. The controller had the artillery drop a smoke shell to mark where they wanted the load dropped. The shell landed right in the middle of the road in the gap between the ridges. We fanned out abreast in tight formation in a glide bombing run and zeroed in on the smoke shell at treetop level. Everybody triggered on my drop so that all the bombs hit the target at the same time. We did this at a relatively slow speed to ensure accuracy. When I dropped them, I was terrified when I looked off my left wing to see one bomb flying in formation with me, arming itself!

All the bombs went off within a few seconds of each other and the explosion was gigantic, obscuring everything on the ground in the target area. The controller immediately wanted to know what we dropped, and told us they had ear problems already from the noise of the blast. The target was totally destroyed and our troops advanced through the enemy strongpoint immediately after the strike with no problem.

General Krueger, in charge of our ground forces, later told us that they were immediately able to penetrate the Jap's strongpoint after the bombing without any losses, and was able to secure the area for our troops. We never had to go near that area again and General Krueger stated that he wanted only those pilots for ground support.[9]

HEADQUARTERS 77TH INFANTRY DIVISION
Office of the Commanding General
APO 77, c/o Postmaster
SAN Francisco, Calif.
24 December 1944
Merry Christmas to the stout fellows who so capably supported us in the capture of Valencia and Palompon. Your bombs and fire killed and chased many a Jap in our front. Your support not only

aided us in the defeat of the enemy but materially increased our morale especially when units were making wide encircling movements and felt alone until our air arrived on the scene.

May we serve together on future operations.

Sincerely,

A.D. BRUCE, Maj. Gen., USA.

Commanding.[10]

As we continued the battle for Leyte, our replacement pilots and extra support people had been moved to an airfield construction area at Burauen, a quagmire of mud from the typhoon, about 20 miles south of Tacloban. Late on December 6th, the Japanese made a parachute invasion of the area around where these personnel were camped, by Bayug, Buri and San Pablo airfields. We lost two enlisted men who were on guard duty there, from the 341st Fighter Squadron, my old outfit. One of our pilots killed an attacking paratrooper in his tent with his .45-caliber side arm. The infantry quickly rounded up the small Japanese force with few casualties.[11]

On Pearl Harbor Day, December 7, 1944, I did not fly but the day saw a big air-sea battle in Ormoc Bay as US forces made an amphibious landing, even as the enemy was attempting to send in yet another convoy to the same area.

ORMOC BAY MADNESS *On the seventh of the month—Pearl Harbor Day— it seemed to those on Leyte that everything that could possibly happen took place at the same time. The 77th Division, with the 7th and 11th on its heels, landed at Ormoc Bay, upsetting by an hour or so a scheduled Jap landing in the same harbor. Both convoys were protected by air cover, and in the ensuing melee it would have been difficult to determine which side was covering what, and who was bombing whom. The Jap convoy at one point was so close to the US surface forces, that at times pilots of both sides did not dare taking a chance attacking, fearing they might sink one of their own ships.*—History of the 460th Fighter Squadron, December 1944

It was an outstanding day for our squadron commander, Bill Dunham, as he racked up four more aerial victories, and others shot down about a dozen more enemy aircraft.[12]

DUNHAM EARNS A DISTINGUISHED SERVICE CROSS

Major WILLIAM D. DUNHAM, Air Corps, United States Army. For extraordinary heroism in action near San Isidro Bay, Philippine Islands, on 7 December 1944, Major Dunham was lead pilot of a flight of nine fighter planes whose mission was to engage, disperse and destroy aerial cover provided for the enemy for their shipping convoy lying in San Isidro Bay. While enroute to the objective at 18,000 feet, he sighted a formation of nine enemy fighters coming in from the northern end of Cebu, and immediately ordered an attack. Followed by his squadron he closed on the enemy in a diving turn and destroyed the lead plane. Observing an enemy fighter attacking one of his comrades from a position of temporary advantage, he dived after it and shot it down. During this action his squadron destroyed five additional enemy aircraft, after which the remaining enemy fled. Major Dunham then proceeded toward the squadron's rendezvous point over San Isidro Bay, and enroute thereto was joined by another plane which flew wing position for him. As these two planes circled over the bay, Major Dunham observed four more enemy fighters about two thousand feet above them. He directed his wingman to accompany him in attack, closed on the enemy in a climbing turn, and with a short burst destroyed his third enemy plane. He then flew to a point directly astern another enemy plane, pursued it through a maneuver, and brought it down in flames. The wingman meanwhile destroyed one enemy plane, while the other fled and escaped. Major Dunham's extraordinary flying skill, gallant leadership and heroism made it possible for our bombers to attack enemy shipping in San Isidro Bay unhampered by enemy interception.

By command of General MacArthur
HQ US Army Forces in the Far East,
General Orders No. 28, 11 February 1945[13]

PEARL HARBOR DAY AERIAL VICTORIES *This day was the climax of the campaign for members of the 460th. As the flights peeled off over the tower at Tacloban, roll after roll brought cheering, prancing enthusiasm from all its members on the ground who were able to watch.*—History of the 460th Fighter Squadron, December 1944

The next day I flew an afternoon mission to glide-bomb at San Isidro, a little port town on the northwest coast of Leyte, where an enemy convoy had landed troops. A dozen P-47's lugged two dozen 500-pound bombs and obtained good results: "All bombs landed in general target area destroying buildings," as recorded in the squadron's Weekly Status and Operations Report.[14]

December 9th was a down day for us, a chance to catch our breath and accomplish needed maintenance after many demanding combat missions. But we were at it again promptly the next day.

On December 10th I flew two missions. The first was cover for some C-47s. In the later mission I was assigned to patrol over the Ormoc area, and led a flight of four Jugs with J.J. Smith as my wingman. The four of us went out on patrol looking for any enemy airplanes coming in. We were climbing through the 20,000 foot area flying west, when two Japanese Army Air Force Tony fighter planes appeared suddenly on a northeast course, passing at very high speed about 2,000 feet above us, right over our heads. Unfortunately, we were on a slight southwest tack so had to perform a 180-degree turn to give chase. By the time we got turned around, the Japanese had also reversed course and were escaping toward Negros.

We continued our turn, now 360 degrees, at full military power, barely keeping the Japanese fighters in sight as we flew west of Leyte. They opted to escape by outrunning us in a very shallow descent and were now slightly below our elevation. This was a bad move for them because the P-47 operated its best in this kind of maneuver. I think they thought they were getting away, and probably weren't aware that we were closing so fast, maybe 500 mph IAS (add altitude for true airspeed). Within a few minutes it became obvious that we would overtake them.

It took about five minutes for us to close the gap; as we approached closer, the Japs split, with one going south and one going west. I immediately instructed my element leader to take his two ships and follow the one going west that split to the right and I bored in on the one going south.

My guns were prepared to shoot as I drew into range. The Jap grew rapidly in the 100-mil sight, so rapid I got off only a very small burst of fire because I was flying much faster than the Tony fighter. I could see that I scored a hit, but the plane was not disabled. The Kawasaki Ki-61 Tony was similar to the German Messerschmitt 109 and was a very good warplane. My wingman moved in to take a shot but missed, while I quickly maneuvered for a second shot at a much slower speed.

As I closed in again, I fired a two-second burst and the converging cone of fire from my guns blew the engine completely off the airframe. I must have also hit the pilot because there was no parachute from the falling plane. I looked around to see the other three planes of my flight right with me. Apparently the element leader did not hear my instruction to get the west-flying Tony, which escaped. We reported the incident to the air controller and continued our patrol.[15]

I would not give the enemy pilots a good score on this engagement because they chose to run instead of fight. Running from a P-47 was not a good idea. Neither the Zero nor the Tony could compete with a P-47 in the chase game. Apparently the Jap S-2 was not aware of this or did not inform their pilots intentionally, in my opinion.

Reflecting on the Tony kill I had made, I recalled how the first two Japs I shot down off New Guinea had caused me lots of problems of conscience. I wondered about their families and loved ones, as well as them. Not so at this later stage in my tour of duty. I felt nothing but regret that one apparently got away due to poor radio transmission. But our ground crews were joyous that we had warded off a Japanese attack and shot down one of the raiders.

JAPANESE FIGHTER TACTICS *Nip fighters have been most often encountered in two plane elements. In maneuvers, they continue to use the split-ess and tight turn, generally to the left. In recent combat, the Nip has shown a tendency for the head on pass. Zeke 32's predominate among the Nip fighters found in this area. Enemy pilots seem experienced, and have shown an aggressiveness and willingness to fight, even when outnumbered.*—460FS Combat Evaluation Report, 11 January 1945

The Japanese command had made persistent attempts at reinforcing their garrison in Leyte, with limited results. In mid-December, not long after we landed troops in Ormoc Bay, they made another move which proved to be their final attempt to stave off defeat in Leyte. They amassed from somewhere a force of 12 vessels; transports loaded with supplies, troops, and ammunition, with a select escort of destroyers. The 460th

Fighter Squadron was invited to participate in the attack on the Japanese task force on December 11th. Two missions were flown covering shipping strikes against them, and I flew on one of them. But there was no significant aerial opposition; only three Zekes were sighted on the first mission and two of them got away in the clouds.[16] This proved to be the final attempt by the Japanese forces to hold Leyte; shortly after this last convoy battle, General MacArthur declared Leyte secure.

We sure experienced a wide variety of mission types at Leyte, which was another hedge against boredom, if not exhaustion. On the afternoon of December 12th, I flew a 90-minute combat mission with four P-47's to cover four of our C-47 transports making an airdrop to our ground troops between Cabulan and Kananga. The squadron's weekly report recorded that the drop was successful, with the parachutes landing in an area 200 yards in diameter, on this otherwise uneventful mission.[17]

Upon return to Tacloban, I had little time for rest as I was scheduled for a patrol over the Dulag area. So it was up into the air again, for a combat mission of two and a half hours duration. We were cruising around 25,000 feet as I anxiously awaited my relief to take over and the air controller's word to descend. When the controller finally told me to come down, I peeled off in a tight spiral right over the strip to make the most rapid descent possible. It took only a few minutes to enter the traffic pattern; we had a green light to land immediately, as fighter planes had number one priority in landing. My landing was successful.

At the debriefing the head of operations stormed into the ready room completely unglued, wanting to know who that officer was who had just set off an alert, diving right over the airstrip. "I guess that was me!" I replied. I added, "I am sorry; but things have been a bit dull, and I was in a hurry to land for personal reasons." This set off another tirade and he promised to liven up my day as soon as possible. The base operations officer was a bomber pilot—enough said! After the indignant colonel left, I was the laugh of the ready room.

The bomber pilot's revenge on me came before too long, and I was summoned to the base commander's office for a briefing. I was selected for an "anti-boredom mission" as his revenge for my previous remarks subsequent to my fast letdown over Tacloban airstrip. Back on the 10th of November, a Japanese heavy cruiser was damaged in Ormoc Bay by our bombers. That was our first day in the Philippines. The cruiser, bigger than some of our battleships, was last seen heading west on fire.

The Japanese commander apparently visualized his ship in danger of sinking, and headed for Cebu Island where he drove it onto a sand bar so it would not sink. There she rested, still able to make steam and operate all her guns. Even though she couldn't go anywhere, merely having power and the ability to shoot at aircraft over long distances meant she was still a menace to all aircraft flying anywhere near. The colonel in charge of the Tacloban airstrip was a bomber pilot, and it had been resolved that the cruiser had to be neutralized. The colonel deemed this might provide me with some excitement, so I was selected for the job.[18]

Pilots were selected for the mission and assembled for a briefing in the late afternoon. The colonel said we would be armed with .50-caliber API ammo and 500-pound bombs. The mission was to take place next morning, and he further expected that we would hit the target in close formation at masthead altitude at 250 mph. You could have heard a pin drop in the briefing room. The colonel asked if we had any questions and I immediately replied, "No, sir!" before any of my pilots could pose a response.

As soon as we retired from the briefing and were out of earshot of the colonel, the guys started moaning about attacking like bombers do, at such slow speed and against such a deadly flak tower as this cruiser. The beefing from the guys was so strenuous I couldn't get a word in edgewise. Back at the line we contacted our armament officer, Lloyd Cuneo, and ordered up the bombs with one-second delay fuses and the gun ammo, to be ready to take off at the first sign of light.

We then started our own briefing as to how we would conduct the mission. The plan was to be near the target just as the sun made its appearance on the horizon. We would be at 25,000 feet east of the target. At this time, we would come to tight formation and make a maximum speed letdown to the surface of the ocean with the planes directly between the sun and the cruiser.

Prior to daybreak, we were all in our planes ready to go as soon as it got light enough to see the end of the runway. On signal, we started our engines and took off in an orderly fashion. The haul to Cebu only took 25 minutes and we were ready as the sun popped up. The letdown went according to plan and we had ample time to finely tune the aircraft to accommodate the high-speed approach. As the target grew in our gunsights we began to get some flak, but they were shooting blind because of the morning sun. It was all over a few seconds later with 16 direct hits on the target. It was possibly the fastest decommissioning of a ship of all time.

No one was hit on our side. At the debriefing, we congratulated the base commander on his "mission planning" and left it there. He was happy and so were we, and the Jap cruiser was no longer a threat.

Things seemed to be quieting down a bit after the last big Japanese push to reinforce Leyte, and we had help in the form of the Marine Corsairs and other squadrons of the 348th Fighter Group that now arrived. But quiet was hardly the case in the other nearby parts of the Philippines. In fact, the 348th Fighter Group's best day in action against the enemy was December 14, 1944, protecting the task force heading for the Mindoro Island invasion, a precursor to the big landing on Luzon. That day we shot down five aircraft, destroyed 76 on the ground and damaged 20 more on Negros Island, where the Japanese had concentrated a lot of their air forces to go into action against us at Leyte. I flew a combat mission intended to glide bomb Silay Airfield in northwestern Negros on that day, though we ended up hitting an alternate airfield target due to weather.[19]

MOVING UP IN THE ISLANDS *The task of Fifth Air Force, in protection of this bold stroke (Mindoro), was apparent. The Jap air force had to be kept from the air, primarily, and in the second place had to be destroyed whenever airborne. Jap suicide pilots were the most feared of enemy potentialities. Every plane available to the Fifth was committed to the accomplishment of this end. A twofold tactical campaign was carried out. The Jap airfields in the Visayas were bombed and scrutinized for serviceability as never before. The convoys plying west and north were constantly covered, except for but a few short intervals when intervening weather fronts prevented, by American fighters—Thunderbolts, Corsairs, and Lightnings.*—348th Fighter Group History, December 1944

Around this time, a little more than a month from when we first arrived in the Philippines, we prepared for our next squadron move, to a new airfield at Tanauan, the one with the mountain at the south end of the runway. By the end of the 14th, the squadron was once again assembled in one location and our Tacloban operation came to a close.

The next day, December 15, our forces landed on Mindoro as Mac-Arthur continued the Philippine campaign. I flew in a three-flight formation (12 P-47's total) assigned to cover the beachhead in the midday hours, from about 1100 into the afternoon. It was a quiet mission, four hours in duration, which reflected in part the results of our previous day's efforts against enemy air forces on Negros.[20]

HEADQUARTERS
308th BOMBARDMENT WING (H)
APO 72
AG 201.22—26 December 1944
SUBJECT: Commendation
TO: Commanding Officers, all Army Air Force and Marine Air Force units, 308th Bombardment Wing (H), APO 72.

1. On the 15th of December, 1944, the operational control of Army Air Force and Marine Air Force units by the 308th Bombardment Wing (H) in the Leyte area ended—our mission completed. From the 22nd of October, 1944, the day the first units of the Fifth Air Force returned to the Philippines after an absence of nearly three years, until the 15th of December 1944, we received the maximum cooperation and support of every unit under us.

2. The success of the operation is proof of your ability and determination to surmount obstacles so the enemy could be hit time and time again by every plane at our disposal. It made no difference whether the obstacles confronting you were typhoons, tropical downpours turning camp areas, roads and airstrips into quagmires, or enemy air attacks during which men and equipment were lost: they were met and overcome. Regardless of the task given you by this Headquarters, regardless of the long hours and extra work involved, you and your officers and enlisted men have conducted themselves in a manner that is a credit to the finest traditions of the service.

3. I proudly commend you for the jobs you have so efficiently and willingly performed and it is my sincere desire that we may on

future operations have you and your men under our command once again.

> D.W. HUTCHINSON
> Colonel, Air Corps
> Commanding[21]

NOTES

1. Jim Curran's flight records show he flew his first mission in a P-47D-23 on December 2, 1944, on the Pacijan Island mission (see footnote 3 below). The ultimate Razorback Thunderbolts, the P-47D-22-RE (Republic) and P-47D-23-RA (Evansville, Indiana factory) blocks, featured a 13-foot paddle-blade propeller, either a Hamilton Standard Hydromatic 24E50-65 or Curtiss Electric C542S, which enabled the aircraft to make full use of additional power provided by water injection. With this larger propeller, there was only six inches of clearance between the blade tips and the ground during takeoffs and landings. But this added 400 feet per minute to the climb rate. The Block 22 and 23 P-47Ds also had a jettisonable cockpit canopy. To release the canopy the pilot pulled a ring, after which the hood would be pushed backward and the slipstream would pull the canopy free of the plane. The last Razorbacks also had a bulletproof windshield and increased internal fuel capacity.

   Baugher, Joe, "P-47D/G Thunderbolt," http://www.aerofiles.com/JBrepub-p47dg.html

   "Major P-47 Thunderbolt Variations, Serial Numbers, & Production," http://www.368thfightergroup.com/P-47-2.html

2. Jim's last P-47, a D-23, serial number 42-27885, was transferred to the 58th Fighter Group in March 1945, when his squadron converted to the P-51 Mustang, so the aircraft's demise does not appear to be at the hands of a 348FG pilot.

   History of the 460th Fighter Squadron, Chapter Nine, (1 March 1945–31 March 1945).

3. There were two 460FS missions to the Pacijan Island area on December 2, 1944. Mission 3-189, 2 December 1944, Bomb & strafe Esperanza Town on Pacijan Island, TOT 1130I. Fourteen P-47's dropped 26 500-lb GP bombs, with these results: "6 bombs landed in target area. 6 bombs landed in water. 12 bombs missed. 2 bombs failed to release. 1 plane did not carry bombs."

   460FS Weekly Status and Operations Report (Form 34), (Report for Period 1 Dec to 10 Nov 44 Inclusive).

   The other Pacijan Island sortie that day was Mission 3-190, 2 December 1944, Bomb shipping in Ormoc Bay. Secondary Target: Palompon and Pacijan Island,

TOT 1715I. Sixteen P-47's dropped 32 500-lb GP bombs. "3 bombs landed in water. 18 bombs hit in target area. 11 bombs were unobserved. Target was heavily strafed."
Ibid.

Curran's December 1944 flight record shows he flew a "Cover PBYs, Ormoc" combat mission on December 4. This mission is not reflected in the squadron's weekly report (Form 34). The only tasking shown on 4 December 1944 is Mission 3-197, Bomb shipping at Palompon. Secondary target: Kananga Town, TOT 1730I, with 16 P-47's carrying 500-lb bombs. "Nil sightings primary target. 16 bombs landed on target. 16 bombs were unobserved. Target was thoroughly strafed." The reason for this difference between flight record and Form 34 is not clear.
Ibid.

4. The USS *Cooper*, DD-695, was an *Allen M. Sumner*-class fleet destroyer. It was sunk by a Japanese torpedo during a short, sharp naval battle on the night of December 2–3, 1944, when US Navy Destroyer Division 120 (USS *Allen M. Sumner*, DD-692, USS *Moale*, DD-693, and USS *Cooper*, DD-695) were sent into Ormoc Bay to intercept Japanese convoy TA-7. The Japanese lost the *Matsu*-class destroyer escort *Kuwa* in the battle that night, while it was participating in TA-7's unloading of men and materiel at Ormoc City. Of *Cooper*'s crew of 359 men, 191 were lost. Some survivors made it to shore and received help from Filipinos. Most survivors were rescued from the waters of Ormoc Bay between 1400 and dusk on 3 December 1944. Five PBYs from VPB-34 and one Army OA-10A (possibly from the Dulag-based 3rd Emergency Rescue Squadron) were sent to rescue them, and Army fighter planes covered the successful daylight operation. Given the time available to locate survivors and the proximity of enemy forces, the PBY crews threw out all the excess weight they could and gathered as many survivors as they could haul in—reports indicate one carried away 56 men, a record, while another Catalina carried 48 survivors, both of these loads exceeding previous rescue records. On December 4, another PBY was sent to pick up men who had made it to shore and were helped to safety by Filipinos. It appears that this Catalina, which rescued one officer and twenty-two men, was escorted by Jim Curran and a flight of the 460FS Black Rams.

Knott, Richard C. *Black Cat Raiders of WWII*. Annapolis, MD: The Nautical and Aviation Publishing Company of America, 1981, pages 180–181.

"The Battle of Ormoc Bay, December 2–3, 1944," http://www.dd-692.com/ormocbay.htm

"Squadron History: VP-34," http://www.daveswarbirds.com/blackcat/hist-34.htm

"VPB-34 History," http://www.history.navy.mil/avh-vol2/chap4-3.pdf

"563 RESCUE GROUP (AFSOC)," http://www.afhra.af.mil/factsheets/factsheet.asp?id=10271

5. Marine Air Group 12 arrived at Tacloban on December 3, 1944 with four squad-

rons of F4U Corsairs (VMF-115, VMF-211, VMF-218 and VMF-313 with 85 Corsairs) after flying all the way from Emirau and Green Island.
Boggs, 29–31.
6. MAG-12's contribution to the Leyte campaign was significant.

For its achievements in the first half of the month, the Group received the following citation from the Army it was supporting:

The Marine Fighter Squadrons 115, 211, 218 and 313 are cited for outstanding performance of duty in action in the Philippine Islands from 2 to 15 December 1944. During this period, at a critical stage in the operations on Leyte, first battleground in the campaign to liberate the Philippines, these Marine fighter squadrons not only carried out their primary mission of providing aerial cover, but also gave close support to our ground troops and intercepted large and heavily escorted enemy convoys.

The gallantry and fighting spirit of the Marine pilots and the skill and tireless fidelity to duty of the ground personnel, who so well carried out their arduous task of maintaining and servicing the aircraft under the worst possible conditions, constituted a major contribution to the success of the Leyte operations and initial American victory in the Philippines. The achievements of the Marine Fighter Squadrons 115, 211, 218 and 313 are in keeping with the highest traditions of the armed forces of the United States.

War Department, General Order #123, dated 18 October 1946"
Ibid, 45.
7. 460FS records do not indicate an attack on an airfield in Mindanao in this early December 1944 period, but the squadron conducted four airfield attacks north and west of Leyte on 5–6 December 1944. The squadron struck Legaspi Airdrome and Talisay Airdrome on 5 December, and attacked Silay Airfield on Negros twice on 6 December, likely as part of an effort to prepare for the American landings in Ormoc Bay on 7 December. There is no mention of any joint mission with Marine Corsairs in the squadron history.

Mission 3-199, 5 December 1944, Bomb Talisay Airdrome, Bomb and Strafe Legaspi Airdrome, TOT 0930I. Eight P-47's with 16 500-lb GP bombs. Results: "Direct hits were scored on barracks and other buildings. One bomb would not release. Four (4) enemy aircraft were destroyed on the ground, 2 Betty's, 1 Dinah, and one unidentified. 1 P-47 crash landed at Bayug. Pilot was uninjured."

Mission 3-202, 5 December 1944, TOT 1345I. Eight P-47's with 16 500-lb GP bombs. Results: "1 bomb failed to release. All bombs landed on strip and taxiways. Strip was left unserviceable."

Mission 3-205, 6 December 1944, Bomb and Strafe Silay Airdrome, TOT 0915I. Eight P-47's with 16 500-lb GP bombs accomplished the following: "4 bombs would not release. 12 bombs landed in general target area with results unobserved."

Mission 3-206, 6 December 1944, Bomb Silay Airdrome Negros Island, TOT 1330I, when eight P-47's with 16 500-lb GP bombs struck the airfield; "one bomb would not release. Six bombs were unobserved."

There was, however, a mission in late November 1944 that did strike Valencia Airdrome. Starting out as Mission Number 3-155, "Bomb Azagra, San Fernando, Romblon, Pulo ng Sibuyan [Island], primary target" on the afternoon of 25 November, it was incomplete due to weather, and the 12 P-47's diverted to accomplish Mission Number 3-155a, "Bomb Bitoon Harbor [possibly the Bitoon just north of Iloilo City, Iloilo Island]. Secondary target," with four P-47's while the other eight accomplished Mission Number 3-155b, "Bomb Valencia Airdrome, tertiary target." In the 1530I attack at Bitoon Harbor, "3 bombs dropped 50 yards west of 4 Sugar Charlies and straffed [sic]." At the 1545I attack on Valencia Airdrome "2 bombs hit bldgs East of Valencia Airdrome and straffed [sic]. 4 bombs dropped on Valencia area. 2 bombs jettisoned; 1 bomb dud; A/A at 9000 ft."

460FS Weekly Status and Operations Report (Form 34), (Report for Period 1 Dec 1944 to 10 Dec 1944 Inclusive), page 1–2.

460FS Weekly Status & Operations Report (Form 34), (Report for Period 21 Nov 1944 to 30 Nov 1944 Inclusive), page 3.

Jim Curran's flight record for December 1944 shows he flew a local mission of 20 minutes duration on 5 December, and a mission against Valencia on 6 December 1944. It does not indicate whether this was the Valencia on Leyte, north of Ormoc, or Valencia Airfield on Mindanao. However, squadron records indicate that Mission 3-204, 6 December 1944, "Bomb Bridge at Valencia and strafe Valencia Town," TOT 0955I was clearly against the Valencia on Leyte, north of Ormoc, and not Valencia Airfield on Mindanao. Eight P-47's carrying 16 500-lb GP bombs achieved the following results at Valencia: "4 bombs landed in target area. 12 bombs were unobserved. Town was strafed, some buildings left burning."

There being no mention here or in the squadron's narrative history for any joint mission with MAG-12 Corsairs, it is difficult to find any confirmation of such a joint Army-Marine Corps air mission and related Corsair collision mishap. It may have occurred at some other time during the Leyte campaign, though review of the records does not provide any information. This does not necessarily mean that the events did not occur, but perhaps they did, separately.

An alternate explanation might be that Jim Curran recalled a Corsair mid-air collision in a separate event from an airfield attack, something that may have been talked about around the airfield. For example, on 6 January 1945, when the 460th Fighter Squadron and the Corsairs of MAG-12 were based at Tanauan, the MAG-12 War Diary for 6 January 1945 reported on page 12 the following: "First Lieutenant John M. Wolf and First Lieutenant Edwin G. Robinson, both of VMF-313, disappeared in a cloud over the north tip of Burias Island on the way to the Calumpit Bridge target. The cause of the accident is unknown, although it is believed they collided. Planes Bu. # 57544 and 57547, are lost." The Calumpit bridges, railroad and highway, are northwest of Manila on Luzon Island. Burias Island is southwest of Luzon between Luzon and Masbate islands. First Lieutenant John M. Wolf remains missing in action, and is remembered on the Tablets of the Missing at the Manila American Cemetery, Manila, Philippines. He was awarded the Purple Heart and the Air Medal with Gold star for his service and sacrifice. First Lieutenant Edwin G. Robinson is buried at Plot L, Row 17, Grave 77 at the Manila American Cemetery. He too received the Purple Heart and the Air Medal with Gold Star.

The MAG-12 War Diary for 7 January 1945 reveals a second twin loss by VMF-313 on page 13: "Ten Corsairs of VMF-313 went on a strafing mission of airfields in Southern Mindanao and Negros. They strafed Dalwangan, Malaybalay, and two strips at Maramag. They shot up and set afire eight to ten barracks at Malaybalay. This strip is in good condition, is well revetted and has slit trench emplacements, but there are no aircraft located there. Fields at Dalwangan and Maramag contained nothing of importance but several huts not previously destroyed were strafed with unobserved results. They returned by way of Dumaguete airfield and saw no aircraft. They also flew low over the Turburan strip on Cebu, but saw nothing to report."

"VMF-313 sent out three planes in a search for Lts. Wolf and Robinson. They searched the Burias Island area for three hours with negative results."

"First Lieutenant Kenneth S. Sherwood and First Lieutenant Charles E. Brooks, both of VMF-313, apparently struck a mountain while flying between two peaks north of Malimono, Mindanao. They are reported missing in action. Their planes, Bu # 14445 and # 57547, was [sic] lost." These pilots were part of the ten aircraft that flew to Southern Mindanao, according to the VMF-313 War Diary for 7 January 1945. First Lieutenant Kenneth S. Wood is buried at Plot H, Row 12, Grave 93 of the Manila American Cemetery. He received the Purple Heart and the Distinguished Flying Cross with Gold Star for his service and sacrifice. The author is unable to find out any additional information about First Lieutenant Charles E. Brooks.

There were several other occasions during the Leyte campaign in which MAG-12 squadrons lost multiple Corsairs on the same day, though not necessarily on the same mission or in the same formation. These dates include December 6, 7, 11, 13, and 22, 1944, as well as January 3, 6 and 20, 1945, according to data in the Aviation Archaeological Investigation and Research (AAIR) website.

"Aviation Archaeological Investigation and Research website, US Navy Losses, December, 1944, and January, 1945," http://www.aviationarchaeology.com/src/ USN/LLDec44.htm and http://www.aviationarchaeology.com/src/USN/LLJan 45.htm

MAG-12 War Diary, December 1944, January 1945 and February 1945.

VMF-313 War Diary, January 1945

American Battle Monuments Commission, Burials and Memorializations database,

http://www.abmc.gov/search-abmc-burials-and-memorializations
8. Swift Japanese single-engine fighter bombers proved a challenge for twin-engine
   USAAF P-61 Black Widow night fighters to contend with, as compared to slower
   bomber aircraft. As a result, a notable joint service swap out was arranged. Marine
   Night Fighter Squadron VMF(N)-541, with a dozen F6F-5N Hellcats, arrived at
   Tacloban from Peleliu on the morning of December 3. In return the P-61s were
   sent to Peleliu, where they could still provide a useful defense against longer-ranged
   bomber-type aircraft.
Chapin, . . . *AND A FEW MARINES*, 4–5.

For their work, the Bateye Squadron received the following Letter of Commendation from the Fifth Air Force and V Fighter Command:

> The outstanding performance of your organization during its operations
> at Tacloban, Leyte Province, Philippine Islands, from 3 December 1944
> to 6 January 1945, deserves the highest praise and commendation. Op-
> erating under difficult conditions on missions of all types, the coordina-
> tion and skill as exemplified by your combat pilots was exceptional. The
> maintenance of the combat status of aircraft by your ground crews has
> also been carried out with exceptional proficiency.
>
> At a critical stage of the Leyte campaign, your organization moved in
> and made an important contribution to the control of the air that is now
> assured our forces, and in preventing reinforcements of enemy positions.
> In the attacks you continually carried out, your organization destroyed
> approximately twenty-three (23) enemy planes in the air and participated
> in more than two hundred (200) sorties under the most hazardous con-
> ditions and weather elements.
>
> It is desired to pass on to you the highest commendation, as well as
> the personal appreciation of the members of this command for your co-
> operative spirit and outstanding performance during this period.

General MacArthur also wanted to pass on his evaluation of VMF(N)-541's
performance. Shortly before its departure he sent the following message to Admiral
Nimitz:

> With your concurrence plan to relieve 541 Marine Night Fighter Squad-
> ron from Operations at Leyte and recall the 421 Night Fighter Squadron
> from Palau on or about 9 January. If this plan has your concurrence, re-
> quest you advise this headquarters with information to Commander,
> Allied Air Force and Commander Fifth Air Force. Your night fighter
> squadron has performed magnificently repeat magnificently during its
> temporary duty in this area and your assistance in furnishing the squad-
> ron is appreciated.

Message from GHQ, SWPA to CINCPOA, sgd MacArthur, 1 Jan 45.
Boggs, 46.

9. The description of this mission most resembles that of Mission 3-207, 6 December 1944, "Bomb and Strafe Kananga Town," TOT 1615I. Kananga is a town about four miles north of Valencia, Leyte, at the north end of the Ormoc Valley. Eight P-47's carried pairs of 1,000-lb GP bombs, although the report also indicates 500-lb bombs were employed without specifying a number, so it is unclear about the mix in the 16 bombs carried and expended. Thirteen bombs landed in the target area, while three were unobserved, and 6,000 rounds of .50 caliber ammunition were expended.

460FS Weekly Status and Operations Report (Form 34), (Report for Period 1 Dec 1944 to 10 Dec 1944 Inclusive), page 2.

This mission is the only readily identifiable mission to use 1,000-pound bombs in review of the 460FS Weekly reports for November and December 1944, though this size of bomb was employed in other missions performed by the squadrons of the 348th Fighter Group in the Leyte campaign.

Of note, despite great strides in the development of close support for ground forces in the Pacific, the Leyte campaign proved one of great frustration for both ground forces and air forces regarding direct support, and not due to any lack of aircrew skill. The reasons for this are complex, related to the limited air assets on Leyte due to basing constraints, and the demands in operational priorities for air cover, interdiction of enemy convoys to Leyte, etc., from these limited air assets. For a full discussion of close support in the Leyte campaign, see *Close Air Support in the War Against Japan*, Chapter VI, The Philippines: Leyte through Luzon, pages 217–225.

10. History of the 341st Fighter Squadron, Chapter XIV, December 1944, Inclosure 10, "Letter of Commendation and Greeting from Major General Bruce, Commanding 77th Infantry Division and Colonel Hutchison, Commanding 308th Bombardment Wing (H)," 25 December 1944.

11. In early December 1944, the Japanese executed Operation WA, part of which dropped Japanese paratroopers on the American airfields on Leyte. Two enlisted men of the 341st Squadron, Jim Curran's former unit, were killed by the Japanese as they stood perimeter guard on the night of 6/7 December 1944. They were Corporal Daniel V. Maurello, of Chicago, Illinois and Corporal Milton Sova, of Brooklyn, New York.

"The History of the 348th Fighter Group, December, 1944," http://www.ww2f. com/topic/37324-history-of-the-348th-fighter-group/

Taylan, Justin, "Operation Te-Go, Japanese Paratrooper Attack on Leyte December 7 1944," http://www.pacificwrecks.com/airfields/philippines/san_pablo/12-07-44/index.html

12. The US Navy expressed its appreciation for the help Fifth Air Force gave for the 7 December 1944 landings in Ormoc Bay. On 9 December 1944, Maj. Gen. Ennis C. Whitehead, Commander of Fifth Air Force, conveyed a commendation from

the Commander, Task Group 78.3 (Rear Admiral A.D. Struble, probably received the previous day, 8 December), the Ormoc Attack Group, to all Fifth Air Force unit commanders, which read:

"THE AIR COVER PROVIDED BY THE FIFTH AIR FORCE FOR THE OPERATION YESTERDAY UNDER DIFFICULT FIGHTER DIRECTION CONDITIONS AND AGAINST STRONG ENEMY ATTACKS WAS AN EXCELLENT PERFORMANCE. SEVERAL OUTSTANDING ACTS OF VALOR BY PILOTS PURSUING JAP PLANES IN THE FACE OF SHIPS GUN FIRE WERE NOTED. THE TASK GROUP COMMANDER AND ALL PERSONNEL GREATLY APPRECIATED YOUR OUTSTANDING HELP."

History of the 341st Fighter Squadron, Chapter XIV, December 1944, Enclosure 9. "Letter of Commendation from Major General Whitehead, Fifth Air Force, 9 December 1944."

13. History of the 460th Fighter Squadron, Chapter Eight, (1 February 1945–28 February 1945), Inclosure 1, "General Orders Number 28, Headquarters USAFFE," 11 February 1945.

14. Mission 3-213, 8 December 1944, Bomb and Strafe San Isidro Town, TOT 1635I. Of the 24 bombs dropped by 12 Thunderbolts, 23 released as desired, but one bomb would not release. 460FS Weekly Status and Operations Report (Form 34), (Report for Period 1 Dec 44 to 10 Dec 44, Inclusive), page 2.

San Isidro was probably a target due to the 7 December landing of Japanese troops from Leyte reinforcement convoy TA-8. This convoy was destined for Ormoc but was preempted by the American landings earlier the same day. Instead, it diverted with orders for the troop and cargo-carrying ships to run themselves aground at San Isidro, some 30 miles northwest of Ormoc. The four merchant ships and one naval transport carrying 4,000 troops of the 68th Brigade reached San Isidro but were all subsequently attacked and sunk by aircraft. Most troops made it to shore (though some 350 casualties were noted), before the air attacks sank the transports; hence the follow-on attacks on facilities in the landing area. Nevitt, "The TA Operations to Leyte, Part III."

15. Japanese Tony fighters were very active on 10 December 1944. There were four Imperial Japanese Army Air Force Kawasaki Ki-61 Hien (Allied codename TONY) fighter units that participated in the Philippines campaign of 1944–1945, which included the 17th, 18th, 19th and 55th Hiko Sentais. In December 1944, the 17th Sentai was based at La Carlota, Negros Island; the 18th and 55th Sentais were at Bacolod, also on Negros. The 19th Sentai had been at La Carlota early in the Leyte campaign, but returned to Japan in November after suffering heavy losses. Two Ki-61 Hien pilots known lost over the Leyte area on 10 December 1944 were 2nd Lt. Kingo Shiozaki and Lt. Koshichi Iwaya. Both were from the Bacolod-based 18th Sentai. However, as a total of five Tony fighters were claimed shot down by

the 348th Fighter Group on 10 December 1944, it cannot be confirmed if one of these two pilots was the man Jim Curran shot down in his engagement.

Of note, Jim Curran's element leader on this mission, Ed DeMeter, was also credited with a Tony victory on December 10, 1944, at the same time as Curran, 1145 local time. The Tony that Jim Curran shot down crashed about four miles northwest of Camotes Island whilst the Tony that Ed DeMeter claimed crashed into the ground on the extreme north tip of Cebu island, about 40 miles away, indicating quite a chase occurred. A third Tony appeared just after DeMeters' victim crashed, made a brief attack on DeMeter's element and then fled west, possibly for Negros Island. DeMeter pursued and obtained some hits before he ran out of ammunition. The Tony was last seen heading for northern Negros trailing smoke and white vapor, and a probable kill was claimed. For a full recap of this flight's engagement see the 460FS Unit Narrative Combat Report for Mission 3-217, 10 December 1944 at Appendix 8.

At 1210 local time on 10 December 1944, 2nd Lt. John E. Mastilock of the 341st Fighter Squadron, on the way back from a glide bombing mission to Lomonon on the west coast of Leyte (just north of Palompon), was credited with destruction of another Tony in the vicinity of Apale Point, Ormoc Bay.

In addition to this, 1st Lt. George A. Davis of the 342nd Fighter Squadron was credited with two Tony victories on the afternoon of 10 December 1944. Davis and his squadron were escorting troop transports moving from Baybay to Ormoc Bay, and at around 1630 local time they were attacked by four Ki-61 Tony fighters at 7,000 feet. Davis quickly maneuvered and gained altitude to 15,000, using the sun to ambush a pair of Tony fighters below. He pursued them as far as Cebu Island, where he closed to within 75 yards of the pair before destroying the first, nearly flying into the wreckage as it exploded; he damaged the second as it attempted to dive for cover in a cloud. A parachute was seen to emerge beneath the base of the cloud and Davis received credit for a kill. Of note, Davis became an ace in WWII (7 victories) and later an ace in Korea (14 victories). He posthumously received the Medal of Honor after he was killed in action during a combat mission on 10 Feb 1952.

Feredo, Tony, email to Terrence G. Popravak, Jr., Subject Ki-61 Pilots, 10 January 2014.

Francillon, René J., *Japanese Aircraft of the Pacific War,* Annapolis, MD, Naval Institute Press, 1987, page 116.

"George Andrew Davis, Jr.," http://en.wikipedia.org/wiki/George_Andrew_Davis,_Jr.

Hata, Ikuhiko, Izawa, Yasuho and Shores, Christopher, *Japanese Army Fighter Aces, 1931–1945,* Mechanicsburg, PA: Stackpole Books, 2012, page 310.

"Imperial Japanese Army Air Force Units in WWII," http://www.asisbiz.com/IJAAF-Units.html

"Mastilock, John E.," http://www.cieldegloire.com/fg_348.php

Stanaway, *Kearby's Thunderbolts*, 127, 183.

History of the 341st Fighter Squadron, Chapter XIV, December 1944, p. 7.

16. On 9 December 1944, Japanese convoy TA-9 left Manila and made a "do or die" effort to reinforce the Japanese forces at Ormoc, with three merchant ships carrying 4,000 soldiers, food and ammo, and two naval transports carrying 400 naval troops with some amphibious tanks, escorted by three small destroyers and two sub-chasers. Another naval transport headed for Cebu with two midget subs as cargo. The vessels reached Leyte late on 10 December with a merchant ship going to Palompon and the naval transports to Ormoc. Two of the merchants, two of the small destroyers and one of the naval transports were sunk and the other ships damaged from a gauntlet of American forces, including aircraft, PT boats, a destroyer, and at Ormoc, even US Army artillery, mortars and tank destroyers, in this last desperate convoy to Leyte.

Nevitt, "The TA Operations to Leyte, Part III."

17. Mission 3-225, 12 December 1944, Cover (4) Transports on dropping mission between Cabulan & Kananga Town, TOT 1430I. Four P-47's served as escort for the transports. Results: "Parachutes landed in an area 200 yards in diameter."

460FS Weekly Status and Operations Report (Form 34), (Report for Period 11 Dec. 1944 to 20 Dec. 1944, Inclusive), page 1.

18. This Japanese "heavy cruiser" on Cebu may actually have been a Japanese DD, the HIJMS *Hayashimo*, a large fleet destroyer of the modern Yugumo-class. She was damaged during the Battle of Leyte Gulf in October 1944, then grounded and sank in shallow water southeast of Mindoro, not off Cebu but off Semirara Island (12-50 N, 121-21 E). The ship experienced sporadic air attacks and salvage efforts continued until the last of the crew finally abandoned the vessel on November 12, 1944. The abandoned destroyer remained upright, although it settled aft to the top of turret No. 3. The wreck was shelled briefly and set afire by US Navy destroyer USS *Walke* (DD-723) on the afternoon of December 15, 1944, during the Mindoro invasion. There is no indication from historical records of any Japanese heavy cruiser beaching in the Visayas in the November–December timeframe. It would seem the utility of such an anti-shipping mission, which Jim Curran describes, would be in preparation for the American landing on Mindoro, but it is unclear from 460FS squadron records when this attack described by Jim Curran occurred. It was possibly Mission 3-276, flown on 27 December 1944, which was tasked to "Glide Bomb near Mindoro." But further details of this mission are not readily available due to illegibility of much of the mission data in the historical record for the squadron obtained on CD from the AF Historical Research Agency.

460FS Weekly Status and Operations Report (Form 34), (Report for Period 21 Dec 1944 to 31 Dec 1944 Inclusive), page 3.

"IJN Hayashimo: Tabular Record of Movement," http://www.combinedfleet.com/hayash_t.htm

19. It is unclear from squadron records which mission to Silay Jim Curran flew on December 14, as the 460FS executed two missions against this airfield on Negros Island. Silay was the main base for Japanese bombers and fighters on Negros. The first was Mission 3-241, Bomb Silay A/D, with 12 P-47's carrying two 500-lb bombs each, with instantaneous fuses. Two planes returned early and jettisoned their bombs. The primary target was obscured by cloud cover, so the aircraft diverted to the secondary target and bombed Alicante A/D, in northwestern Negros, at 1045 local time. Primarily a fighter base, Alicante was home to the IJAAF 200th Sentai at the time, a Nakajima Ki-84 Hayate fighter unit (Allied codename for the Ki-84 was FRANK). One bomb landed on the target; five bombs landed in water, 14 bombs were unobserved. At 1445 hours, Msn 3-245, 11 P-47's with the same type of bombload made another effort to "Bomb Silay." Instead, they attacked Talisay Airdrome on northwestern Negros, on the instructions of the Tacloban controller. Results: "8 direct hits scored on strip. 9 bombs landed in target area. 5 bombs unobserved. 4 parked T/E (twin-engine) A/C (aircraft) destroyed by bombing, 7 other by strafing. Fuel dump set afire."

    460FS Weekly Status and Operations Report (Form 34), (Report for Period 11 Dec. 1944 to 20 Dec. 1944 Inclusive), page 3.

    "Alicante Airfield," http://www.pacificwrecks.com/airfields/philippines/alicante/index.html

    "Silay Airfield," http://www.pacificwrecks.com/airfields/philippines/silay/index.html

    "Talisay Airfield," http://www.pacificwrecks.com/airfields/philippines/talisay/index.html

20. Mission 3-246, 15 December 1944, Cover Beachhead, TOT 1100I. Twelve P-47's were assigned to this mission in a combat air patrol at 8,000 feet. No contact with the enemy occurred. One plane did not return to base from this beachhead protection mission when a broken gas line forced it down. The pilot successfully bailed out and was rescued.

    460FS Weekly Status and Operations Report (Form 34), Ibid.

21. History of the 341st Fighter Squadron, Chapter XIV, December 1944, Enclosure 11, "Letter of Commendation from Colonel Hutchinson [sic], Commanding 308th Bombardment Wing (H)," 25 December 1944.

Chapter Eleven

TANAUAN

S HORTLY AFTER MY AERIAL VICTORY OVER THE TONY, WE
moved to our new airfield at Tanauan.[1] It was one-way traffic
at the new field because the south end of the strip was occupied by a sub-
stantial mountain. Upon landing, jeeps with our ground crews directed us
to our new revetments which offered some protection for the aircraft from
bomb attack. We filled out our Form 1's and debriefed, then went to see
our new housing.

Dick Searles, Wally Harding, Bill Cooley, and I shared a new tent
erected on a bamboo frame with a floor four feet off the ground. The frame
was built by our houseboy, a contractor, who did no work himself, having
relatives do all the work for which he got paid handsomely. The quarters
were elegant by New Guinea standards. Our footlockers, bedding, and personal effects were all in our tents. It was great to have my bed linens again,
acquired in Sydney, and to have hot showers with one less Jap to worry
about. So our squadron was again all together; we had mess halls to eat in
and screened-in huts for recreation with lights and fans, not bad at all!

TANAUAN CAMP *On 14 December, for the first time since its activation,
the bulk of the entire squadron was billeted in the same area when the
Tacloban echelon moved down to operate from the Tanauan strip. This camp
site was thought by the majority to be one of the most attractive ever occupied
by the Group since its arrival overseas. It was situated along the high bank of
a branch of the Guinarona River, just off the highway near a little gathering
of Nipa huts called Kabuynan, about two miles south of Tanauan. The ground*

*in most places was sandy enough to remain solid in the rain provided it was not mashed by continuous traffic. For this reason the number of vehicles allowed in the area was cut down to medical Department and Mess units only.—*History of the 460th Fighter Squadron, December 1944

By now, our initial fears about being able to stay on the island dissolved with the destruction of the enemy forces trying to reinforce themselves on Leyte. The roads had finally dried out and stabilized so there was no transportation problem. Our reinforcements had arrived in place and were able to operate. The mail was finally catching up with us and we were happy to hear that our parents finally knew where we were courtesy of Walter Simmons, the *Chicago Tribune* war correspondent. We now had thousands of new support troops unloaded at Leyte, including WACs. This was exciting news to everyone because the only American females seen for months were an occasional evacuation nurse, and they were too busy to say hello.

Tanauan itself was a very small village, mostly a place for the local farmers and fishermen to meet and trade. There was a Catholic church built by the Spaniards hundreds of years ago which was in good condition. Those of us who were Catholic got to services for the first time in months. Others also came to mass, out of curiosity to see how it was conducted in a Philippine community. All things considered, life was good at Tanauan.

The move to Tanauan, with the reunion of the squadron and our group, took a lot of pressure off us. Normal meals and sleep did wonders for our morale and physical stamina. I even put on a few pounds. We had more free time to compose letters to home and our incoming mail revealed that our people at home finally realized where we were. My mother constantly admonished me to be careful. My dad also communicated by mail, which was a first for him, though my mom did most of the writing. Hearing from home was very important for us, and daily mail call was the high point of our day.

TIME TO TROUBLESHOOT ORDNANCE *Release failures of bombs and tanks caused by fatigued bomb shackles was satisfactorily corrected by the Engineering section through the insertion of a 5/16" bolt between the topmost section of the bracket and the first bridge of the shackle. By actual measurement it was discovered that when the bomb shackle is subjected to its load the two*

*parallel stainless steel sides of the shackle draw together 3/32nds of an inch,
thereby restricting the free movement of the release lever. The insertion of the
bolt described above prevented this restricting effect. Since adoption it is estimated that 95 percent of bomb and tank release failures have been eliminated.*—460FS Combat Evaluation Report, 11 January 1945

The buildup of shipping in the harbor was so noticeable that we started
to speculate about what was going to happen next. It turned out to be a
landing on Mindoro Island, not too far from Luzon. Apparently Mindoro
was not heavily defended by the Japanese, so it became a target for Mac-
Arthur's forces to establish a beachhead in the western Philippines, bypassing
Negros Island, which had many airfields and a great network of roads built
by the Corps of Engineers prior to the war. On the 15th and 19th of December we got part of the assignment to cover the landings at Mindoro.
This was a piece of cake because the Japanese air force did not show up
during the two missions of about four hours duration each, with nil sightings of enemy aircraft.[2] The landings were a huge success and the move was
on to do more things as soon as another task force could be assembled.

SUPPRESSING JAPANESE AIRPOWER *The 348th shared in the achievements which made the Mindoro strategy a success. Thirty times, formations
of its Thunderbolts flew to dive bomb and strafe airdromes on Cebu, Panay,
Negros, and the Mindanao strips that lay below the southern belly of our attempted shipping route . . . It might be of interest to mention here that 23 of
the missions flown during December resulted in aerial combat, or one in every
twelve. . . . In a scant three weeks, beginning with the first of December, an
offensive against the Visayan Jap air force had been developed and consum-
mated. The stage was set for the great sky borne blows against Luzon air
strength. No time was lost.*—348th Fighter Group History, December 1944

Soon after we moved to Tanauan, our esteemed commander, Major
Dunham, earned his return to the States, and on December 18, Captain
Bill Carter became the squadron commander. Carter's tenure was brief,
however, and by the end of the month he too was headed for the States.
Captain Richard Frost assumed command on December 30.[3]

Strange things happened in combat zones. As the battle for Leyte continued in December 1944, we had a company of truck drivers located nearby who worked for the Quartermaster Command. Their assignment was to take ammunition to the infantry on the west side of the island, frequently under fire. One day they mounted a serious complaint about being shot at by the Japanese forces, finally ending in a strike—they refused to drive their trucks to the front line. The brass decided to have military police arrest the whole company and evacuate them to Dulag, about ten miles south of Tanauan. The whole company was billeted in an engineer ammo supply dump, since camp space was at a premium due to the ravages of the recent typhoon. A lone Japanese bomber attacked in the night, dropping a bomb in the dynamite dump where the company was billeted. The explosion was so powerful that many of us were jarred out of bed ten miles away. The loss was total. Disciplinary action on the strikers was no longer an issue because there were no survivors to punish. End of story, but not quite! Due to this loss in transportation capacity, there were now more interruptions of supplies getting to where they were needed.[4]

MINDORO DIVIDEND *Five days after the landing in the San Jose area of southern Mindoro, American planes were operating from its strips, making possible a more thorough cover for the western Visayan convoys, and thus releasing Leyte fighters for escort duty with the B-24's which then began to strike the greatest Japanese air center in Luzon, Clark Field.*—348th Fighter Group History, December 1944

As the month transpired, the 348th Fighter Group had its best day of the war in aerial combat on December 24, 1944, in a mission escorting B-24 Liberator bombers to Clark Field on Luzon. The Jap fighters let us all come in, but attacked as we were leaving.

FIGHTER COVER TACTICS *An advance two plane element well ahead of the bomber top cover proved highly effective in the recent cover missions flown by this squadron to Luzon airdromes. The use of this advance element permitted relay of the latest disposition of potentially airborne and airborne enemy aircraft back to the bomber top cover with the result that the bombers could plan the most advantageous course to the target, while the covering planes were cued for the most effective defense against enemy elements, the advance top* *cover element served to confuse their identification system. In the recent strike against Clark Field in which the 348th Group accounted for 32 enemy planes and 2 probables, the advance top cover element provided information which was declared by participating pilots to have been of the utmost value in the ensuing combat.*—460FS Combat Evaluation Report, 11 January 1945

It was estimated that 100 Japanese fighters rose to the occasion; the 348th mixed it up with the Japs, scoring many victories—32 were shot down, seven probable, and the balance dispersed.

FIRST CLARK MISSION KUDOS

MY PERSONAL HEARTIEST CONGRATULATIONS TO YOUR GROUP WHICH CARRIED OUT THE MAGNIFICENT STRIKE ON CLARK FIELD TODAY. FROM WHITEHEAD ARROW. THIS OPENS THE BATTLE FOR AIR SUPREMACY OVER LUZON. —COMFITERCOM FIVE message to COFITGR THREE FOUR EIGHT, 222110/I December 1944[5]

Christmas was almost upon us, though we had no particular plans for a celebration. But on Christmas Eve, several of us drove up to Tacloban to see our friends at Dr. Pascual's home, where we celebrated until about 2300 hours. Christmas in the Philippines was a different deal compared to New Guinea the year before. Dr. Pascual and his family were devout Catholics and we got to attend Christmas mass.

On the way back to Tanauan, a red alert took place and we had to stop our vehicle and douse our lights. All we could do was sit and wait because it was impossible to drive without lights. It was a very dark night and very still with no wind, and nothing moved at all. As we sat and waited, the faint drone of an aircraft could be heard.

As the noise grew louder we identified it as "Washing Machine Charlie," a Japanese night raider. This name was coined by our G.I.s because it sounded like a gasoline motor-powered washing machine, popular in rural areas of the US at that time. As the plane neared, a lone searchlight turned on. After a brief sweep, it zeroed in on the raider who appeared to be at about 15,000-feet of altitude. The searchlight held steady on the plane, but no anti-aircraft guns fired, much to our amazement.

Suddenly, close by, the stillness of the night was shattered by the bark of a 90 mm anti-aircraft cannon, firing a single shot. As soon as the blast subsided, we could hear the eerie sound of the projectile it fired, diminishing as it went aloft. After a suspenseful few seconds the shell exploded directly under the Jap raider, which exploded, immediately lighting up the whole sky with a beautiful pyrotechnic display. The roar of the people around us, plus our own cheers, was as astounding as what we just witnessed. The alert was over and we proceeded home, overjoyed with the Christmas present the anti-aircraft crew had furnished us. Until the day after Christmas, all we could talk about was the great shot we had seen.

Christmas Day, 1944, I was assigned to cover PT boats in Ormoc Bay. This was in support of a rescue mission which was designed to pick up military personnel who had been rescued by the local Filipinos. It went well and several of our people were returned to safety.[6]

Also on Christmas, General MacArthur declared the island of Leyte secure. The press release was just that, a press release. The ground fighting proceeded at a great pace on the west side of the island, and we received recognition from the soldiers fighting there who appreciated our help.[7]

On December 30, while leading a flight of four P-47's, I got to see the first part of the massive convoy that would be heading north for Luzon. Our mission was to cover a convoy assembled off Dulag, and as we flew, we could see a tremendous buildup of warships in San Pedro Bay. It was evident that the battle for the Philippines was about to escalate big time. This was deduced from personal observation, not from anything we heard.[8]

Unfortunately, a member of my flight, George Grace, experienced a sudden problem with his aircraft. From the Missing Aircrew Combat Report which followed the incident, my eyewitness statement was thus: "I was flight leader of the flight in which Lieutenant Grace was flying number 4 position. As we went into a right bank at about 10,000 feet, I noticed that Lieutenant Grace's plane was trailing white smoke and that he had lost about 1500 feet in altitude. This was at 1600/I hours. I radioed him and he replied 'Roger, I think I'll have to bail out.' This was the last radio contact with Lieutenant Grace. I watched his plane from that time on and never lost sight of it. For about 10 seconds after he radioed, his plane flew straight on, left wing down. It then went into a spiral of 3 turns and hit the sea at a vertical angle and disappeared. The spiral began at an altitude of 7/8000 feet. At about 7000 feet I saw what appeared to be confetti in the wake of the plane. After the crash I spent 45 minutes searching over the entire area. There were small native boats in the water, but they showed no signs of unusual activity. A destroyer came over from the convoy and circled the area. I did not see any sign of Lieutenant Grace. It is possible that Lieutenant Grace could have bailed out without me seeing him as there was a formation of white clouds against the mountains near shore which could have prevented me from seeing his chute." (Lt. Grace was never found.)[9]

The last day of December 1944, for my 17th and final combat mission of the month, I was chosen to lead the entire group, all four squadrons, on a nearly five-hour long mission to bomb Clark Field. This was the most significant honor ever bestowed on me in my tenure of military service. I led the 460th, as Colonel Rowland, the group C.O., flew my wing, which was a total surprise, even to my squadron C.O. Bill Dunham. The honor was never explained to me, but I surmised it might have been due to my navigating skill, as I was known to never get lost in the islands of the Pacific. After the near-catastrophe back at Tsili Tsili, New Guinea, I always made it a primary task to know my exact location at all times. Flying in the islands could be very confusing to even the most experienced pilots.

We had close cover escort on the B-24 bombers hitting the airfield. Our sister squadron, the 342nd, went ahead of the strike to engage any Japanese fighters. The 341st had high cover and the 340th was the last in, postured to extract the bombers.

The purpose of the mission was to destabilize Clark Field to the point where even the Jap engineers couldn't fix it. This was in preparation for the Luzon landing at Lingayen Gulf, which was still secret, even to us. Our mission was to protect heavy bombers of the 13th Air Force, consisting of the most B-24 Liberators I had ever seen at one time. They had so many planes they had trouble finding their Initial Point, which is the terminology for the starting point of the bombing run. The B-24s ran us low on gas with delays, so only the 340th was able to stay with the bombers when they finally dumped their bombs on the target.

SECOND CLARK STRIKE *The second strike on Clark Field, 31 December, was not as successful as the first due to weather and the type of bomber approach which was from far to the northwest of the target, causing the fighters* *to use up an amount of fuel prohibitive to combat and return to base. No interception was met by the fighters.*—History of the 460th Fighter Squadron, December 1944

We in the close cover did not see any enemy airplanes—the drubbing we gave the enemy at Clark the week before must have hurt them bad. Anyway, the mission was a success and the Japs couldn't use Clark Field.[10] But that didn't end the air threat. Like on Negros, the wily Japs just turned the highways into temporary airstrips and the fight was still on, so we had to be on guard.[11]

A PHILIPPINE NEW YEAR'S EVE *The new year literally opened with a bang. At Tanauan those gathered for what celebration could be eked from the limited night life facilities and even those relaxing in their bunks were alerted just before midnight for the coming of the New Year by the cawop, cawop, cawop of the 40 mm anti-aircraft guns. . . . Shortly after the alert an enemy bomb acted as a starter's gun for all manner of wartime noise . . . Rangers and infantry cut loose with BAR's and sub-machine guns, while the Air Corps and service troops belatedly tried to keep pace with pistols and carbines. Occasionally heavier, louder explosions, thought to be hand grenades by a few suspicious objectors, resounded up and down the beach road. The cacophony was topped by whops of heavy artillery in the distance and the anti-aircraft tracers which crossed the sky like a huge, phosphorous spider web.*—History of the 460th Fighter Squadron, January 1945

So much for 1944 and my 23rd year. Considering what was to come in the battle for the Pacific, I developed a new slogan for January 1, 1945. It was: "Home alive in '45!!"

LEYTE SETTLES DOWN *The month closed with routine and the organization at last coming unto its own. The cooks began to go on regular shifts, meal hours became stabilized, clothes were salvaged, and usually worn dry and clean. Neat rows of tents stood under the cool shade of the palm grove. A loud speaker system announced the latest news and played music to the entire camp; movies were shown several times each week.*—History of the 460th Fighter Squadron, December 1944

As I mentioned, the buildup of surface vessels in San Pedro Bay told us something big was afoot. Rumors had it there would be a massive effort to capture all of Luzon, but where the attack would take place, no one had any idea. The Japs had Corregidor Island, strategically located in Manila Bay, and Fort Drum, an island fortress with big guns. "The Rock" and concrete battlements fortified by artillery ruled out a frontal attack on Manila.

During a four-hour convoy cover mission on January 3, 1945, I got my first look at the fully assembled task force that was to attack Luzon. Some of the task force was assembled in San Pedro Bay; whence the rest came from is unknown to me.[12]

Minesweepers lead the way clearing a path for all ships, and set the pace of the entire task force. All the other ships had to stay behind the minesweepers, and when they entered Surigao Strait, they slowed to the pace of the minesweepers and the carriers could not launch their planes. This unfortunate necessity kept the naval flyers grounded because the carriers could not launch or land aircraft under these conditions. That meant land-based Army Air Force fighter planes would be the main defense for the convoy. This convoy covering job became the main event for our group in January and was an awesome responsibility.

With ten P-47's, we covered the massive convoy from south of Siquijor Island and onward as it sailed for the Strait of Mindoro on the passage to Luzon. We were about 25,000 feet over the convoy, which was so long that it took ten minutes to fly from one end to the other. It consisted of everything we had in our naval arsenal.

CONVOY COVER *Ninety combat missions marked the month with sorties totaling 538. Convoy cover occupied top spot in attention of the squadron as Leyte based aircraft provided a constant blanket of protection over the diverse convoys plowing into San Pedro Bay, pushing supplies and reinforcements to Mindoro, and carrying invasion forces for the Lingayen Gulf landing. Convoys of LST, LCI, LCM, tanker, liberty ship, DD, DE, PC, SC, YMS—almost every transport and escort vessel known—stretched in an undulating ribbon from Leyte Gulf, below the Visayas to Mindoro and Luzon. The squadron flew 47 missions of cover for surface vessels in convoy or anchored in Leyte harbors.*—History of the 460th Fighter Squadron, January 1945

Immediately west of Siquijor was the island of Negros; it had many military airfields and became the paramount staging base for the Jap air forces. From this position just north of the gigantic armada of Allied vessels, the enemy was determined to attack our task force at all cost. Our job was to keep them away at all cost. Through the massive effort of the Corps of Engineers and the Seabees, we now had plenty of airfields and planes, between Leyte and Mindoro, for our fighters. So we were better able to perform our air cover over the task force mission from before dawn to after dark.

JANUARY'S EFFORT *The 348th was largely concerned, in one way or another, with getting our convoys safely through Visayan Waters to the Mindoro Area, where other Air Force Fighters escorted them up the W[est] coast of Luzon. It was December's role all over again, but contact with the enemy dwindled away to scarcely more than a possibility.*—348th Fighter Group History, January 1945

As the task force came south of Negros, the Japanese moved all available planes under cover of darkness to Negros. Intelligence became aware of this development through lookouts scattered throughout the Philippines. The Fifth Air Force had a maximum effort to counteract this threat. For our part of the effort, we carried 500-pound bombs and maximum ammo to Negros, many times in the dark. We bombed the runways and then hunted up and down highways for planes to strafe that were parked under trees; it was a mammoth turkey shoot. We didn't have any high cover when we went down to strafe. Hundreds of planes were destroyed on the ground thanks to great intelligence.

On January 4, we ran three different four-ship fighter sweeps over Negros, shooting up all the Japanese airfields after the bombers dropped their bombs.[13] On January 5, I was back overwater and had the dusk-to-dark coverage of the convoy, a mission lasting over three hours.[14] Our four P-47's assigned altitude was 30,000 feet and we cruised from east to west and vice versa along the north edge of the convoy. This late flight was scary for me because it would involve landing at night for the first time since Transition Training in 1943. I was flying my most favorite aircraft, a brand-new P-47D-23-RA, of which we had only two at the time, mine and Bill

Dunham's. As it became dark, we did not turn on our navigation lights because that would be a dead giveaway to any possible Jap intruder. We flew by the glow of the exhaust ports and turbo-supercharger, which also had a dull rosy glow. The controller released us when the afterglow of the sunset finally disappeared. We headed for home in a very shallow letdown and were close to our home base very quickly.

As we approached Tanauan, we contacted the base for landing instructions. Much to my dismay, I was informed the entire area was on red alert for another night raid by the Japanese, and no lights were allowed. We were ordered to stall for time, but we were already getting close to critical on fuel. I immediately had visions of having to bail out of my beautiful new airplane in the dark. This was the pits and frightening beyond imagination; pleas to the controller to turn on the runway lights fell on deaf ears.

Finally a voice came on over the radio from a Navy controller at Guiuan Airfield, across Leyte Gulf on Samar Island, saying he would get us on the ground and to follow his instructions without a radio response. I had no choice, so I agreed. He spread us out on his radar screen, instructed me on a vector at low airspeed, and required me not to acknowledge any more instructions by radio.

From my compass heading, I realized he had me on a downwind leg. Suddenly he instructed me to lower landing gear and flaps, and to reduce speed to 150 mph. Next, I was put on a single needle-width, 90-degree left turn. Next was another turn to the left and start down; then reduce speed to 120 mph. I watched my altimeter gradually approach sea level when the command came through to cut the throttle. Bump, I was on the ground, decelerating from 100 mph. Finally coming to a halt in total darkness, I suddenly saw a flashlight waving to my right, and there was a Navy crew chief, (a plane captain in Navy parlance) pointing instructions on where to go. He got me to safety off the runway. The controller got us all down safely; I do not believe to this day that it was possible with our primitive radar, but I swear this really happened. I never got to find out who the Navy controller was, but I am forever grateful to him. I made a night landing on this field with no lights at all, courtesy of that naval controller who put four P-47s safely on the ground. Positively no light at all, ground or aircraft.[15]

LUZON LANDINGS *On the 9th of January Luzon was invaded by American forces which landed on the beaches at Lingayen. The initial landing operation was rapidly developed into a stabbing advance inland down the San Fernando Valley—the road to Manila. The relative ease with which the invasion was effected again was a reflection, in large part, of good use of air power. Clark Field strikes at the turn of the month had slashed fatal gaps in the Japanese air strength that remained on Luzon.*—History of the 460th Fighter Squadron, January 1945

My new P-47 was a dream plane and I was glad to get it through that night-landing nightmare. I loved this plane and so did everyone who flew it. My crew chief kept it spotless, and, in appreciation, I decided to organize a party for all the enlisted members of the squadron. I donated several bottles of gin out of my supply and got the flight surgeon to give a five-gallon can of medical alcohol; we scrounged up some beer also. For entertainment purposes we contacted the WAC group in Tacloban to see if they had any volunteers to come to the squadron dance, with refreshments as an inducement. These preparations were occupying a lot of my spare time. When the night of the party finally came to be, we sent vehicles to Tacloban for the WACs and wished all the enlisted men a great time, with absolutely no officers to spoil their fun.[16]

With the party underway, I retired in my new red parachute pajamas which our houseboy had his female relatives make for me out of nylon cargo drop chutes. Each of us in our tent got a pair of pajamas; all bright red, with the natives keeping the rest of the material for themselves in exchange for sewing the pajamas. About midnight I was awakened by a group of our enlisted men demanding I come to their party. I tried to deny them, but they insisted I come for at least one drink. With that they hauled me off bodily in my red pajamas to the party which was in full swing. There had been four or five fights but no one hurt seriously. The WACs were a huge success and I closed my eyes to all that was taking place and begged to get back to my tent because I had to fly the next day. I don't know how the party ended, but heard no complaints from anyone the following day. It was fun for us to do a little for the enlisted men who did so much for us and never complained about anything. We were a solid organization from the C.O. on down.

COMMENDATION TO ALL FIFTH AIR FORCE UNIT
COMMANDERS, 15 JANUARY 1945

The past year has been an extremely successful one for the AAF on all fronts, and it must be gratifying to you to know that you have had a considerable share in those successes.

The valuable part your command has played in knocking out the Jap bases one after another along the way to the Philippines, your long-range strategic operations over Borneo and Java, and the recent cooperation in the Sixth Army landings on Leyte made 1944 a brilliant year for the Fifth Air Force.

I have full confidence that these achievements will not only be equaled but surpassed by you during the coming year. Accept my most cordial wishes for success and please transmit them to the men in your command.

By command of Major General WHITEHEAD
History of the 341st Fighter Squadron, January 1945

Reflecting on my aviation career and war in the Pacific, back in flying school, prior to Primary Flight Training, we were taught the functions of various aircraft in the military. A bomber's function was to carry the war to the enemy. Fighters were to protect Allied forces from the enemy. Reconnaissance planes were to gather information. Other aircraft could be used to transport individuals and supplies. As the war progressed, other specialties developed, like small planes spotting for artillery, which was a function of aircraft in Europe during World War I.

Our fighter group's main assignment in 1943 was protecting transport planes from enemy fighters, which we were very successful at doing; our primary function was defense, the same function of the RAF in the Battle of Britain in 1940. Gradually our mission altered with the injection of the fighter sweep, where we carried the attack to the enemy, but our main objective remained to protect. In 1944 we transitioned into an offensive posture, and began to use our fighters in a fighter-bomber role. This trend abruptly changed back to protection in January of 1945. The Navy had all their eggs in one basket in traversing the waters up to Luzon. The pressure was on for us to protect the task force. Success of the war effort was on us, and failure was not an option.

In meeting our objective, the main tactic I remember in aerial combat was simply getting a chance to shoot at the Japanese. My personal chances were very few, and seeing an enemy aircraft was the most important occurrence.

In combat we did not steeply climb or turn with Japanese fighters. Shallow, high-speed climbs and high-speed approaches from above were advised, which worked for me in the P-47. My limited time in the "Spam Can" completely left me out of the air-to-air picture; I never saw a Japanese plane while I flew a P-51. I really only had two opportunities to shoot at enemy planes—with those two Navy Zeros in 1943 and that one Army Tony in 1944. The Tony was confirmed but the Zeros were not, even though they both tumbled out of control. However, I was without mutual support in that 1943 engagement, so had no witnesses to confirm those claims.

The rest of my opportunities for aerial combat were curtailed by flight leader mistakes where I couldn't break formation. I was very self-disciplined about following my flight leader. For example, once while flying number 16 position, I spotted a large group of enemy bombers flying under a broken overcast. The leader did not respond to my radio alert and I would not go off on my own, which resulted in the loss of a huge opportunity. The 475th Fighter Group got them a few minutes later and had a turkey shoot of unprecedented proportions while we went home without firing a shot—tough luck!

As we contemplated our responsibilities, a dirty enemy emerged to hamper our efforts. In November and December of 1944, our bathing facilities were practically non-existent. I used a hand-dug well near the beach and rinsed in the ocean and then rinsed again in the well water. My procedure was to lather up next to the well in the super soft water, shave and then wash off the soap in the ocean, then rinse off the salt in the soft well water.

Other members of the squadron opted to bathe in a stream which came from the interior of the island. The local farmers used carabao, the Philippine tractor, to till their fields and the animals often defecated in the stream. In their droppings was a fluke worm that could bore through one's skin and cause debilitating infections. The bug took up residence in the host's intestinal tract and spread parasites throughout one's body. By the time the malady was diagnosed, we had numerous casualties, affecting our ability to get enough pilots to man all our planes. Being averse to entering tropical streams might have saved my life. One of my wingmen had to have brain surgery after the war as a result of contracting Schistosomiasis in the streams of Leyte. When I returned stateside, I wasn't cleared to leave Hamilton Field, California, until I had been cleared of the disease by stool examination.[17]

So our mission was now back to 100% defense, and the entire month of January 1945 was dedicated to protection of the task force and the following resupply convoys, creeping through the waters of the Philippines. I flew a total of nine convoy cover missions in the month, on 3, 5, 6, 7, 8, 12, 13, 14 and 21 January, south of Siquijor, Negros and Bohol. As a convoy passed to the south of Negros, we smothered that island with fighter planes from dawn to dark. When we weren't covering the task force, we were strafing anything that moved and didn't move on Negros. The Japs were not able to get any planes into the island during the day, but were able to land at night and park on highways and roads under the trees. I flew a total of five missions reconnoitering and strafing Negros during the month, on 4, 15, 16, 22 and 23 January.

AIRFIELD DECOYS *The Nip has also been reported by our pilots to be using dummy aircraft dispersed throughout the revetment areas together with serviceable and unserviceable aircraft.*—460FS Combat Evaluation Report, January 1945

On January 21st, I flew in a flight of four P-47's to the task force in the dark, on hand to prevent any intrusion from kamikaze fliers.[18] The next day, intelligence spotters in Luzon reported a massive number of Jap planes moving to Negros in the night. We knew there would be a big attack if we didn't stop them from taking off in the morning, and Fifth Fighter Command ordered every plane available to stop this effort by the Japs. One of our squadrons took off in the dark and covered Negros. The rest of us took off at the first sign of light and were over Negros a short time later. The Japs had their planes hidden along the roadways; flying at treetop level we were able to spot them. It was a turkey shoot—we zipped up and down roads, destroying a few enemy planes. The entire island of Negros was peppered by the time we headed home with empty ammunition bays.[19]

JANUARY MISSIONS *Armed recco of Visayan, Mindanao and SE Luzon airdromes and installations was, second to convoy cover, the predominant duty of 348th Group fighters. 81 such missions were flown in January, of these . . . 22 [were flown] by the 460th.*—348th Fighter Group History, January 1945

The squadron experienced another change in command on January 22nd, when Captain Frost was relieved for return to the States by First Lieutenant DeWitt R. Searles. The next day, January 23rd, I flew my 14th and last combat mission of the month, which was my last combat mission from Tanauan. It was a Negros repeat, only it was harder to find any targets left to shoot at.[20]

Beginning in late January, the squadron began movement from Leyte north to our next base in the Philippines, at San Marcelino on Luzon. That area is north of Subic Bay; much of it is now buried by the lava flows from Mount Pinatubo that occurred in the 1990s.

BLACK RAM MOVEMENT TO LUZON *The water echelon, headed for Luzon, broke camp and loaded on LST 999 at San Roque 21 January. As always, the rising tide washed away the hasty ramp of sandbag abutments filled by chugging bulldozers, and workers had to shift from the dust of heavy traffic on the beach to the spray of the waves as they repaired the essential causeway over which their vehicles rolled equipment. As the sun began to set two days later, the convoy of 32 LSTs, 36 Liberty ships and cargo vessels and innumerable smaller craft threaded out of anchorages at Tacloban, San Roque, and Dulag.*—History of the 460th Fighter Squadron, January 1945[21]

LAST R&R IN AUSTRALIA

The flight surgeon decided it was time to fatten me up again, so I was packed off to Sydney, Australia for R&R. The distance from Leyte to Sydney fell a few miles shorter than going to Chicago. I would have gladly walked the difference.

I had lots of time to think on the long flight down under. I surmised it would be my last visit to Sydney, a town I had grown to love. I had to make up my mind what to do about my lady friend, Kathy. She wanted to get married in the worst way, but I had misgivings about a commitment to a gal so far from home, and she had a little personal baggage that my family might disapprove of.

On arrival in Sydney, many changes were apparent. There were very few American military personnel. The visitor shop in Kings Cross was no longer functioning. Our potables were now sold by bootleggers exclusively, which was no problem for us. I spent lots of time at Bondi Beach and the racetrack. Of course, much time was spent eating goodies which were now plentiful because of the dearth of Americans.

There were four squadron members on R&R at our beautiful 460th Fighter Squadron house on Rose Bay, and all the girls who dated our members were around constantly. We didn't know what to do with them all. We could skinny dip inside a fence that kept us protected from sharks right off the patio.

Time passed quickly and I finally packed all my gear, including the stuff I had stored with Kathy before. On the last day, she said she didn't think we would ever see one another again, and I nodded in agreement. It was a very emotional adieu and I think we both cried. We continued writing for a few years before our correspondence came to a halt.

ARRIVAL AT SAN MARCELINO *The squadron's ground echelon traveled by air and sea to San Marcelino. Those embarked on an LST landed at Subic Bay 2 February. The echelon left at Tanauan moved forward by air via C-46 transports on the fourth, fifth and sixth of February. The squadron's fighters arrived on the afternoon of the sixth.*—History of the 460th Fighter Squadron, February 1945

NOTES

1. Dates vary in different sources for the precise date the complete move of the 460FS from Tacloban to Tanauan, from as early as 12 December to 14 December. A group history mentions that by 15 December the group's planes began to operate from Tanauan. Also at Tanauan were Marine Corsairs, an A-20 Bomb Group and an advance echelon of the 345th Bomb Group (M) for handling its B-25s staging there from Morotai.

   History of the 460th Fighter Squadron, Chapter Six, (1 December 1944–31 December 1944).

348th Fighter Group History, December 1944.

460FS Weekly Status & Operations Report (Form 34), (Report for Period 11 Dec. 1944 to 20 Dec. 1944, Inclusive), pp. 3-4.

2. The 460FS flew two missions to cover the Mindoro Beachhead on 19 December 1944, 3-254 and 3-255, each with four P-47's and TOT's of 1145I and 1235I, and at 13,000 feet/230mph and 9,000 feet/220mph, respectively. There were nil sightings on these patrols. But just the day before, on Mission 3-249, Cover Mindoro Beachhead, TOT 1125I, a 460FS patrol of nine P-47s, at 15,000 feet/360mph, engaged enemy planes before they entered the beachhead area. A pair of this patrol came across a JUDY dive bomber while en route to Mindoro, got it after a 15-minute chase, but had to return to Tanauan as they had dropped their wing tanks in order to pursue the speedy JUDY. The remaining aircraft, a flight of four and a flight of three, reached Mindoro at 1125. At 1220 the first flight engaged a SALLY bomber and shot it down. Fifteen minutes later the two flights were jumped by five ZEKE 32's and after evading them, managed to shoot down one ZEKE. Some 6,000 rounds of .50-caliber ammunition were expended on this mission.

460FS Weekly Status and Operations Report (Form 34), (Report for Period 11 to 20 Dec 44 Inclusive), page 4.

460FS Unit Narrative Combat Report for Mission No. 3-249, 18 December 1944.

3. The Tanauan Enlisted Men's Club featured artwork by several gifted artists in the unit, including some painted on the sides of the walls by Sergeant Albert Leidigk. In addition to amusing depictions of Army life overseas, he ". . . inserted a slightly satirical jab here and there at 'Wewak Willie,' a secondary nickname for the P-47 of the commanding officer, Major William D. Dunham . . ." The 460FS started December of 1944 under Dunham's command with 54 pilots, eight ground officers and 238 enlisted men for 300 personnel total. By the time Capt. Frost took over the reins at the end of the month, however, nine pilots were lost in action or had departed, leaving 45, with nine ground officers and 246 enlisted men for a total of 300 personnel.

History of the 460th Fighter Squadron, Chapter Six, (1 December 1945–31 December 1945), page 10.

History of the 460th Fighter Squadron, Chapter Seven, (1 January 1945–31 January 1945), page 7.

4. Co-author research discovered an incident which may correspond to this Quartermaster recollection by Jim Curran. At nightfall on 25 October 1944, a Japanese aircraft dropped incendiary bombs which fell into a quartermaster area on Leyte and set off an ammunition dump which "exploded continually for 9 hours and intermittently after that until about 1430 on the 26th." Casualties in the 7th Quartermaster Company were 13 dead and 50 wounded. At this point in the war, a US Army division's quartermaster company was authorized 193 men; although 1/3 casualties would not necessarily render a given unit destroyed such as Jim Curran

described, it could certainly incapacitate a unit for some time, especially given any accompanying equipment losses.

Stauffer, Alvin P., *The Quartermaster Corps: Operations in the War Against Japan.* Washington, DC: US Army Center of Military History, 1990, page 275. http://history.army.mil/html/books/010/10-14/CMH_Pub_10-14.pdf

Forty, George, *US Army Handbook 1939–1945*. New York, NY: Barnes & Noble Books, 1998, page 73.

5. The 348th Fighter Group flew three missions against the Clark Airfield complex in late December 1944, on the 22nd, 24th and a mission Jim Curran flew lead on that took place on the 31st. These missions were a necessary part of efforts to defeat Japanese airpower that remained in the Philippines prior to the Luzon landings slated for early January 1945.

348th Fighter Group History, December 1944, page 5.

History of the 340th Fighter Squadron, Chapter 16, (1–31 December 1944), Inclosure 8, "Letter, VFC, re Clark Field strike," 22 December 1944.

6. Mission 3-269, 25 December 1944, Cover PT Boats to Ormoc Bay, TOT Four P-47's Four P-47's Results: "1 plane early return due to gas fumes in cockpit."

460FS Weekly Status as Operations Report (Form 34), (Report for Period 21 Dec 1944 to 31 Dec 1944 Inclusive), page 2.

7. General MacArthur declared all organized resistance had ended on Leyte on 25 December 1944, after elements of the 77th Division had captured Palompon from the enemy. Mop-up operations against isolated groups of Japanese soldiers continued into the spring of 1945. Cannon, M. Hanlin. *Leyte: Return to the Philippines.* Washington D.C.: US Army Center for Military History, 1993, Chapter XXII, pages 361–370.

8. The US Navy's Seventh Fleet was tasked to conduct the landings on Luzon Island, 9 January 1945, supported by the fast aircraft carriers of the US Third Fleet. US Army Air Forces aircraft supported the landings in various ways, such as providing air cover for convoys passing through waters of the central Philippines, neutralizing enemy airfields, overwater searches, etc. The Seventh Fleet alone was a massive organization. Mission 3-283, 30 December 1944, "Cover Convoy out of Dulag," by four P-47's, TOT, difficult to discern due to poor CD quality, possibly 1420 to 1640I, results illegible. Mission 3-284 was the same, by four P-47's, with a TOT of (possibly) 1630 to 1945I, and results of "Nil Sightings."

460FS Weekly Status and Operations Report (Form 34), (Report for Period 21 Dec 1944 to 31 Dec 1944 Inclusive), page 3.

Reports of General MacArthur, The Campaigns of MacArthur in the Pacific, Volume I. Washington DC: US Army, 1966. Chapter IX, The Mindoro and Luzon Operations, pp. 251–260.

9. The MACR stated that Lt. Grace went down while orbiting a convoy out of Dulag bound in the general direction of Ormoc, approximately two miles northeast of

Taytay Point, Leyte Island. It also states that Navy PBYs from Austere Controller at Tanauan Airfield were dispatched to search the area, with nil results. 2nd Lt. Leon W. Cottrell of the 460FS also filed a statement on the incident: "Our flight of four victors was in a right bank at about 10,000 feet. Lieutenant Grace was flying number 4 position. As he was behind and crossing under me, I could not see him, but I heard him call in and say he was going to bail out. By the time I could turn around, his plane, trailing white smoke was spiraling toward the water. I saw it go straight into the water and disappear. I did not see Lieutenant Grace bail out nor did I see the confetti Lieutenant Curran reported in his testimony. I did not see any trace of Lieutenant Grace in the vicinity of the crash. A destroyer came over, went right through the oil slick, circled the area in search and then rejoined the convoy."

George R. Grace, Missing Air Crew Report 12194

10. Mission 3-285, 31 December 1944, "Cover Mike Strike on Clark Fld. A/D's," TOT for B-24 bomber escort from 0705 to 1120I (possibly, difficult to read from CD), with fifteen P-47's. Results are illegible on CD copy of the Form 34 used as reference.

   460FS Weekly Status and Operations Report (Form 34), (Report for Period 21 Dec 1944 to 31 Dec 1944 Inclusive), page 4.

11. In December of 1944, the full combat power of the 348th Fighter Group was brought to bear in the Philippine liberation campaign. The group's narrative history for December 1944 captures the vital statistics of the unit for that month, which may be interesting to compare with other USAAF fighter groups in action during WWII: "During December, 348th Thunderbolts flew 5864 combat hours in 2213 combat sorties. The average sortie lasted a few minutes over 2-1/2 hours. Aside from these, 700 hours were consumed in flying 275 non-combat missions, an average mission, again of better than 2-1/2 hours. 540,858 gallons of gasoline were consumed, and 45,972 quarts of oil. The gasoline burned in this one month, had it been of lower octane, would have taken a Ford around the world 432 times, with fuel left over for side excursions. 346,991 rounds of .50 calibre ammunition were expended in combat. 186 X 1000 pound, 752 X 500 pound bombs were dropped in strikes against enemy targets. 98 Jap planes were destroyed in the air. (Statistics furnished by the Group Statistical Office.)"

12. Mission 3-294, 3 January 1945, "Cover Convoy S. of Siquijor Island and recco to Del Monte," with ten P-47's, TOT 0940–1120I. The P-47's flew at 5,000 feet and at 190mph on a mission of 4.6 hours duration. Results are illegible on CD copy of Form 34.

   460FS Weekly Status and Operations Report (Form 34), (Report for Period 1 Jan 1945 to 10 Jan 1945 Inclusive), page 2.

13. Mission 3-301, 4 January 1945, "Fighter Sweep & Recco over Negros Island," TOT 1505–1520I. Four P-47's at 7,000 feet/190 mph. Results: "Large fire seen

. . ." then becomes illegible on CD copy of Form 34.

Ibid.

14. Mission 3-304, 5 January 1945, "Cover (unintelligible due to poor CD quality) S of Siquijor Island," TOT (possibly) 1945–2105I. Four P-47's. Results: "Nil Sightings."

Ibid, page 3.

15. Guiuan Airfield (also known as Samar Airfield), lies on the southeast part of Samar Island. Guiuan is called Magellan's Gateway to the East. It is about 50 miles east of Tacloban or Tanauan across Leyte Gulf. Airfield construction at Guiuan by the 61st and 93rd Seabee battalions began on 6 December 1944. The airstrip was built over a swamp area and required much filling, but by New Year's Day, fighters and medium bombers arrived and Guiuan opened for combat operations. Guiuan Airport remains today, and US Marine Corps aircraft returned briefly in November, 2013, for Typhoon Haiyan relief operations.

"Guiuan Airfield (Samar Airfield)," http://www.pacificwrecks.com/airfields/philippines/guiuan/index.html

"Guiuan, Samar, The Philippines, Navy Base 3149," http://www.seabees93.net/MEM-SAMAR-index.htm

"Efforts in Guiuan shift from relief to recovery," http://www.dvidshub.net/news/117316/efforts-guiuan-shift-relief-recovery#.U8xdWrEuR4N

16. With the improved living conditions and operational tempo at Tanauan, the "Black Rams Enlisted Men's Club" was established at Tanauan, beginning in late December 1944. It took some time to build a clubhouse. Far East Air Force Headquarters, six or seven miles down the road at Tolosa, was reportedly heavily staffed with WACs, and a dance at the new club was planned for early January 1945. "The first dance was a success and was followed by another two days later to which all of the Filipinos living nearby were invited. The club was thronged. As an additional (attraction) there appeared several WACs who showed the local gay blades the latest dancing styles from the US. On learning about the coming move (to San Marcelino) an emergency dance was called for two nights later, which went off as well, if not better, than the first one." For more on the role of the Women's Army Corps in World War II including the Southwest Pacific Area, see Judith A. Bellafaire's *The Women's Army Corps: A Commemoration of World War II Service.* Washington, DC: US Army Center of Military History, 1993.

History of the 460th Fighter Squadron, Chapter Six, (1 December 1944–31 December 1944), pp. 8-9.

History of the 460th Fighter Squadron, Chapter Seven, (1 January 1944–31 January 1944), p. 8-9.

17. Schistosomiasis, also known as bilharzia, is a disease caused by parasitic worms. Although the worms that cause schistosomiasis are not found in the United States, more than 200 million people are infected worldwide. In terms of impact this dis-

ease is second only to malaria as the most devastating parasitic disease. The parasites that cause schistosomiasis live in certain types of freshwater snails. The infectious form of the parasite, known as cercariae, emerge from the snail, hence contaminating water. You can become infected when your skin comes in contact with contaminated freshwater.

"Parasites—Schistosomiasis," http://www.cdc.gov/parasites/schistosomiasis/

18. The squadron history shows three missions for 21 January 1945, Numbers 3-350, 3-351 and 3-352, and all were to "Cover Hoodlum Base off S.W. tip of Panay," from 0650 to 0835, 1200 to 1430 (possibly) and illegible, probably before 2000 hours, with four, eight and four P-47's flying missions of 4.1, 4.6 and 3.3 hours duration, respectively. Results were nil sightings for the first mission. Second mission: "One silver Mike was sighted could not be identified. Last seen (09-50 N) 122-28E) 4 planes returned early 1.4." The last mission, possibly the one Jim Curran flew on, noted results of: "One unidentified plane was sighted over Tanon Strait (between Cebu and Negros)."

460FS Weekly Status and Operations Report (Form 34), (Report for Period Jan 21 1945 to Jan 31 1945 Inclusive), page 2.

19. At this time, the US Navy's Third Fleet had just completed a major operation against enemy forces in the South China Sea and along the Indochina coast, and had passed around the north of Luzon in order to strike enemy bases in Formosa. It is possible that whatever Japanese aircraft were left in Luzon flew to the Visayas to escape this rampage. In any event, the kamikaze threat to our shipping in the Philippines was a serious cause for concern, and the 460FS flew four separate missions against Negros on 22 January 1944; it is unclear which one Jim Curran flew on. Mission 3-353, Recco & Strafe Targets of opportunity. Negros, Cebu, Masbate. Four P-47's Results: "La Carlota and Bacolod were strafed with unobserved results." Mission 3-355, Recco & Strafe targets of opportunity on Negros, Cebu, Panay, Bohol. Three P-47's obtained these results: "2 serviceable aircraft destroyed at San Jose A/D. One other hit." Mission 3-356, same as 3-355, three P-47's got these results: "one 30ft. covered barge sunk in Cebu harbor. 1 (P-47) returned early." And Mission 3-357, same as 3-355, four P-47 "Victors strafed San Jose A/D with unobserved results."

Morison, Samuel Eliot. *History of United States Naval Operations in World War II, Volume XIII, The Liberation of the Philippines, 1944–1945.* Boston: Atlantic, Little & Brown, 1959. Chapter VII, Third Fleet Cuts Loose, 10-27 January 1945.

460FS Weekly Status & Operations Report (Form 34), (Report for Period Jan 21 1945 to Jan 31 Jan 1945 Inclusive), page 2.

20. This was likely Mission 3-359, 23 January 1945, "Recco & Strafe all A/D's on Panay, Negros, & Cebu," TOT 1150 to 1253I, with four P-47's expending over 1,000 rounds of .50 caliber ammunition. Results: "Target of strafing was appx 12

dummy a/c in dispersal area." The airfield strafed was not identified.

460FS Weekly Status and Operations Report (Form 34), (Report for Period Jan 21 1945 to Jan 31 1945 Inclusive), page 3.

21. 460th Fighter Squadron Nolan Machen described the Black Ram preparations for the move up to Luzon in the 20 January 1945 entry in his War Diary: "Nothing much has happened lately right here. But now something big is up. We don't know yet just where to but it's something big we know because we are taking 15 days boat ration & 25 days field rations. Several barrels of gas (about 200), 500 boxes of cal .50 ammo and much other equipment that we have never taken with us before. I packed yesterday & tore down our tent this morning and traded it for a new one. After that I helped haul sugar to the beach (180 lbs short of two tons). Oh, yes—other than packing yesterday, I worked hauling full gas drums down to the beach. We are taking close to 200 wing tanks. All this we will load as soon as the LST docks . . . The rumors are as wild as ever. They range as differently as 'We are going to invade the island of Japan itself,' to 'We are going to invade somewhere on the China coast,' [and] 'We are to make another beachhead on Luzon.' No matter what it is, we [the 348th Fighter Group] are ready to go in & start operating. And we are all hoping that it is a move that will get us all home quicker . . . We have all done this same thing before, so many times that no one shows any feeling of excitement. Instead everyone acts as if they don't give a damn & I guess that's true with me too."

War Diary of Nolan Machen, pages 8–9.

Chapter Twelve

SAN MARCELINO

MANILA BURNS *Manila fell, officially, early in the month but intense fighting raged at the end of the month. Lt Col William M. Banks, deputy CO of the 348th Group, and Captain DeWitt R. Searles, after a recco reported that the entire city seemed in flames with black smoke rising countless thick columns and spreading over the bay to form a murky, solid overcast. The Japs, realizing they could not hold the city had set fire to full city blocks. Some personnel travelled to Manila to see the devastation and charred remains of the 'Pearl of the Orient.'*—History of the 460th Fighter Squadron, February 1945

On February 15th, 1945, I was promoted from First Lieutenant to Captain; on February 18th, I resumed my combat flying at our new base in Luzon. It was named San Marcelino after a nearby town.[1]

SAN MARCELINO AIRFIELD *San Marcelino airstrip, built by USAFFE for use as an emergency landing ground before the invasion of the Japanese, was developed by the enemy into an operational drome of at least 500-plane capacity with widely-dispersed revetments and plans for hangars and a personnel housing project. Before evacuating the field, the Nips burned or demolished all installations and grounded airplanes. Immediate work by American engineers lengthened the strip, topped with hard clay, to 6,000 feet and stretched two rows of hardstandings roughly parallel to the runway.*—History of the 460th Fighter Squadron, February 1945

It was on a flat alluvial plain north of Subic Bay and just southwest of

Mount Pinatubo, a restless volcano. It was very hot and dusty, like Texas in the summer. The South China Sea was visible off to the west from a few hundred feet above San Marcelino.

SAN MARCELINO CAMP AREA *The camp area, planned by Lt. Edwyn C. Niederhofer, AUS, adjutant and First Sergeant George Houlton, was as convenient as at Tanauan, posing only problems of dust from the dry, sandy valley and lack of water for bathing. Group initiated a project to supply water and construct shower facilities for all squadrons and headquarters. From a well which was dug nearby on the banks of a river, a quarter of a mile of pipe was laid to the shower site, located in a sloping gulley in the 460th area. Once in operation, the system made water continually available . . . The camp was set on a flat, sandy plain, sliced by dry stream beds. The sparse vegitation [sic] of short grass, dotted with a few stunted trees and bushes along stream beds, became a little more verdant near the flowing river. The dust problem remained unresolved although every preventative measure was taken. The proximity of the camp to a main road from the airstrip to service and quartermaster organizations kept it in a continuous cloud of dust and prevailing winds sent swirls of sand across the river. A 5-mile per hour speed limit was enforced by two MP's posted at either end of the area and trucks with water sprinkler made almost hourly patrols, but sun, wind and traffic prevented complete control.*—History of the 460th Fighter Squadron, February 1945[2]

I was back in my P-47D-23 escorting PT boats in Manila Bay, an easy mission; they usually ran from two to four boats on a mission. We carried 500-lb bombs in case the PT's ran into trouble. Although I can't recall the details, we were probably on guard against small Japanese surface vessels hiding in coves along the coastline. The Japanese used motorized barges extensively at night to move men and supplies. They were small, usually powered by a six-cylinder Chevrolet truck engine modified for marine use. These barges were similar to our landing craft.[3]

FEBRUARY OPERATIONS *Although overshadowed by the more spectacular ground support work, local patrols were flown, covering San Marcelino, convoys destined for or leaving Subic Bay and Lingayen Gulf, and the amphibious landings at Mariveles Bay and Corregidor. From Tanauan, before coming to*

Luzon, the squadron performed convoy cover and fighter sweeps to Carolina and Dumaguette airdromes, Negros Island. In the month's operations no enemy interception was met and anti-aircraft was encountered on only eight occasions, just once causing damage.—History of the 460th Fighter Squadron, February 1945

Next day was convoy cover in the morning and then a checkout in a P-51 in the afternoon.[4]

MUSTANG ARRIVAL IN THE 348TH FIGHTER GROUP *The 341st Squadron flew its first P-51 mission on 6 January 45. Conversion to P-51 operations broached no simple problems. There were very real difficulties for all departments. Training soon became a paramount concern. The over-all conversion in the group was planned to be a squadron by squadron process, during which time there were to be no operational demands other than for orientation and training. However, scarcely a week after the P-51's were delivered, operation orders began to arrive placing 341st P-51's on regular combat schedules. Pilots, little more than checked out in P-51's if one considers the P-47 training they enjoyed before flying combat in that type, were required to fly regular convoy cover, escort, and armed recco missions . . . The problem was further aggravated by a relatively sudden and complete turnover of pilot personnel. After January, with almost all veteran fliers home or enroute home, a situation was to exist wherein green pilots were being trained by almost equally green flight leaders.*—348th Fighter Group History, January 1945

We were told the squadron was changing from P-47s to P-51s, and I had an hour-long local flight the next day, 20 February, as part of this transition. I did not welcome the change, especially after flying the P-51 and not being enthralled with the new aircraft for many reasons. I just didn't feel as safe in the Mustang as I did in my reliable Thunderbolt. At 5' 11" and 135 pounds it was a tight fit in the P-51 cockpit with all the survival gear. Also, I was giving up two .50-caliber machine guns because the P-51 only had six. I didn't get enough hours nor have very many combat missions in the Mustang to love it. Cooley and I held on to our Jugs as long as possible, to the very last. This transition that began in the Black Rams in February 1945 was a very slow process.

For the next four days we pounded the island bastion of Corregidor with 500-pound bombs and wing drop tanks loaded with napalm. With the napalm, we hit targets such as Fort Drum and caves entrances on Corregidor.[5]

NAPALM EFFECT *The napalm bombs, if they did not always kill Japs in the area, were psychologically effective by frightening the enemy into forsaking his relatively safe position to run in terror, thus exposing himself to ground fire. One POW captured on Corregidor told interrogators he was so terrified by a napalm strike that he could neither eat nor sleep for four days and finally decided to surrender. In addition, the napalm charred off thick cover of vegetation and exposed the Jap positions . . . During February 152 wing tanks, each containing 150 gallons of napalm, were dropped by the squadron.*—History of the 460th Fighter Squadron, February 1945

The Japs were finally all killed on the tiny island fortress, but it took a lot of doing by all involved. The Navy brought up a destroyer and fired point blank into the Jap positions on the tadpole tail of the island.

Speaking of napalm, I also remember using it in a raid against the Japanese at Clark Field. At the time, our troops held the field, but the Japanese had all the high ground to the northwest quadrant of the area. We were loaded with 165-gallon drop tanks filled with low octane gas mixed with napalm additive, and large phosphorous detonators or igniters that activated on contact with any object.

NAPALM EMPLOYMENT *While greater accuracy can be achieved by dropping Napalm tanks from 300 feet down to tree top level, better results are obtained when they are dropped from 800 to 1,000 feet altitudes, since sufficient accuracy can be maintained and the resulting spread of fire greatly increased. An additional point is [sic] support of this level for the release of Napalm bombs is the tendency for the solid matter of the solution to settle toward the bottom after it has stood for several hours. Unless this state is changed the bomb's efficiency is appreciably affected. Consequently when the bomb is dropped from the higher altitude, the tumbling end over end motion of the falling bomb acts to remix the solution, restoring to a large extent its former effectiveness.*—460FS Combat Evaluation Report, 24 February 1945

Our initial point was the runway area of Clark. We made a ground-level approach to the box canyons of the target area, dropping our ordnance on the uptick. It was most scary having to fly up these narrow canyons occupied by Japanese ground troops. The effects of napalm were beyond belief. The heat was felt through the canopy when the stuff ignited. The flames were awesome; sometimes they came up right next to our wing tips. Napalm was a most devastating weapon; I am sure the Japanese dreaded these attacks. Personally, I didn't feel bad about it after seeing what the enemy did to helpless prisoners.[6]

LUZON OPERATIONS *Armament and ordnance received the brunt of the labor as flight after flight of eight or sixteen planes returned, only to be loaded with ammunition and bombs for another takeoff. The tactical situation necessitated rapid changes in mission plans so that sometimes after fitting the planes with wing tanks for napalm, the crews had to switch the load to 500-pound bombs, lugged from the dump just before takeoff. Objections were few, however, and morale would soar upon the return of a flight when pilots recounted their successful hits, raging fires, or liquidation of troop concentrations.*—History of the 460th Fighter Squadron, February 1945

MUSTANG TRANSITION *March saw the awaited transition, almost a mutation, from the P-47 to the P-51. At the end of the period, one lone and venerable Jug sat complacently on the 460th's hardstands, surrounded by 25 flashy, silver and black Mustangs. The P-47 was now a museum piece, highly revered by the pilots whom it took through attacks from Saidor toward the Jap stronghold of Wewak; from Wakde to the strange names of Dutch New Guinea; from Noemfoor to Ceram, Boeroe and the Moluccas; and from Leyte's Tacloban and Tanauan through the toughest tasks in the squadron's experience.*—History of the 460th Fighter Squadron, March 1945

In late February, after flying nine combat missions that month, I was put on detached service to the island of Biak for the purpose of selecting replacement pilots and some new P-51s for the group. About the 25th of February, Bill Cooley, Wally Harding, R.P. Smith, J.J. Smith, and myself boarded a C-47 bound to Leyte.[7] The flight was uneventful until we landed in Leyte, where the pilot of the C-47 made a very bad landing. He ground-looped the big plane and ran off the runway. This was very scary, but none of us suffered any critical damage. The plane didn't fare so well, however, so we had to wait to get transportation to our next stop at Peleliu, in the Palau Islands. These islands were directly north of Biak, which had become a major supply base for Fifth and Thirteenth air forces. We stayed in a USMC transient camp overnight at Peleliu. This was the place Charles Lindberg shot down a Jap aircraft on a fuel economy demonstration flight. The Japanese were still on other islands in the chain and the Marines took spoiled cans of beer and food to these outposts in landing barges. The Japs would eat the stuff and then crowd their latrines the next day. The local Marine fighter pilots would have sport shooting up the hapless Japs while they were using their sanitary facilities—gross!

The next day, we flew inward and arrived at Biak to see it up close for the first time. The signs of the fight that took place there were still evident everywhere. The casualties that occurred were some of the worst in the war, yet little of the battle was known to the public because the Army had no press club. We were met by a former member of the 460th Fighter Squadron who had been transferred to Biak from Noemfoor. He was a pilot but could not cut the mustard with Bill Dunham, our C.O. He wasn't the only pilot who got moved off for various reasons; we had one who was assigned to me who couldn't coordinate his plane on bombing runs. He had a Ph.D. in mechanical engineering, so I worked very hard to help him correct his flying shortcomings. He spent a lot of time with the mechanics on the line, and one day he came up with plans for a device to automatically control the coordination of the plane while on a low-level bombing run. We were all so impressed with his idea that we got it to the boss, Bill Dunham. It took no time at all for the brass to transfer this guy to a place where they could use his very bright brain.

While on Biak, we got to see the Jap defenses, or what was left of them, and marveled at their ingenuity. The central part of Biak was a coral atoll raised up by tectonic forces almost a thousand feet higher than the beaches. This made a natural fort where the defending Japs could pour fire down on the attacking Army forces. No amount of bombing or shelling seemed to have any effect on the fort. The Japs were too far underground in connecting caves and tunnels, with plenty of ammunition and supplies. I had covered the initial assault all of June 1944, from Wakde Island. Little did

I realize what a terrible battle was taking place below me and how many lives were being lost.

My first sustained experience with a Mustang was at Biak, where I was sent to help pick up 20 new P-51's. Of course I had to check out in the new aircraft; as usual the runway was cross-winded, as were most runways we used because they were built adjacent to the ocean. Crosswinds were a very small problem with the Jugs because of their great weight and excellent stall characteristics. Not so with the Mustang. It was a terror on takeoff due to propeller torque. Landing the beloved Mustang for the first time in a crosswind was a real challenge, but I survived, despite my impression that the plane was flying me instead of me flying it. After checking out in the P-51, we trained some pilots for the long flight to Luzon and were soon scheduled to take all available planes to San Marcelino.[8]

Finally on March 19, we got all of our new pilots and planes ready to go to the Philippines. We divided the planes into two groups. Wally Harding had 8 planes and Bill Cooley and I had 12. I was elected to be the leader and navigator for the flight. The first leg of the journey was flying to Morotai. We made Morotai in three hours and 15 minutes, a really fast trip in the shiny new P-51's. We remained there overnight, and it was a more pleasant stay than our previous one when we were first on the way to Leyte. We got everyone together in the morning and after some minor repairs, took off en masse for Luzon.

While traversing over Mindanao, for some reason beyond my ken, Wally Harding veered off west with his Mustangs and didn't respond to my radio pleas to get back into formation. I proceeded on to Mindoro as planned where we gassed up for the final leg of the journey to San Marcelino on Luzon.

When I got my remaining 12 planes on the ground at San Marcelino, I had to make excuses for losing the planes that Harding was in charge of. I got chewed out for this and could give no explanation; I didn't have the foggiest idea where they went. The next day, Harding showed up with all the planes. He stated he thought I was lost over Mindanao, and then he wound up lost over the Sulu Sea. Fortunately, he stumbled across Palawan Island where they all landed safely on an airfield under construction, nearly out of gas. He was very fortunate to make that landfall. A few miles north or south of Palawan and 8 pilots and planes would have been lost in the

South China Sea. After getting his directions straight, he was able to find San Marcelino the following day.[9]

Although I was forgiven by the C.O. and got a three-day pass to Manila, I was blamed for Harding getting lost. So I got an ass-chewing, and they made Harding the squadron's operations officer. Fortunes of war? I never did really understand all the decisions in the military. It was already March 20, and it was difficult to believe I had been gone from the squadron so long—so long that I had difficulty realizing how many new faces there were among the flight cadre.

MUSTANG ARRIVAL AT SAN MARCELINO *That night each tent in the camp area housed heated, loud, and lengthy discussions of the P-47 versus the P-51.*

"Why, with the Jug you can depend on getting home if some Hammo spits a couple rounds into you, but one hit on the coolant system of the 51 and you're through, Brother."

"The 51 will outrun the Jug on the deck anytime and as for getting hit you can come in at the target too fast. They aren't going to do much plugging at 600 mph."

"You can have that tin whistle on landings. Give me the old Jug everytime."

And on it went, not just the night but for days.

—History of the 460th Fighter Squadron, March 1945

My only base in Luzon was San Marcelino. It was an excellent airfield, but is now completely covered by ash from its local volcano, the ash giver, Mt. Pinatubo. Speaking of rugged terrain, I remember the time that I traversed Zigzag Pass in a jeep with a 500-gallon trailer while some of the pass was still in Japanese control. Our mission was to get beer from the San Miguel brewery (in Manila). As things turned out, it was a total success and we didn't have to fire a shot to accomplish our mission. Everybody in the squadron got a helmet of cold beer.

LIFE AT SAN MARCELINO *Here, as at Tacloban and Tanauan, Filipinos in need of food and clothing swarmed into camp offering to wash clothes, construct tent frames, and serve as houseboys. Such work was always gladly given* *and after squadron mess, all Filipinos were given the excess food . . . Recreation and an escape from the routine of camp was found in San Marcelino and Castillejos, two medium sized towns near the airfield. Many men made an evening trek to these bits of civilization attending parties and dances given by the townspeople and happily accepting their invitations to dinner. Roast pig, eggs, tomatoes, chicken, and a specially-fried sweet potato topped the menus.—* History of the 460th Fighter Squadron, February 1945

WITH THE INFANTRY

Our unit got a complaint once from an Army Regimental Combat Team (RCT) there in Luzon. The complaint was that we were strafing our own troops. Since the date of the occurrence was the date that Bill Cooley and I were leading sections on close troop support, we knew that we did not shoot our own troops. There were no casualties involved, but it seemed that our G.I.s were terrified by our close troop support, and we were sent as troubleshooters.[10]

LUZON OPERATIONS *Whether in the Thunderbolt or the Mustang, the month was one of ground support with the entire group tossing full loads at the cornered, desperate Japs on Luzon. The 460th carted 80 tons of bombs, AN-M64 #500, 222 Napalm bombs and 289,000 rounds of .50 calibre ammunition which they dumped, smashed and fired at the remnants of Yamashita's garrisons.—*History of the 460th Fighter Squadron, March 1945

So Bill Cooley and I were put on detached service and motored to the join this RCT on the front lines somewhere east of Clark Field. We went armed with our standard firearms and hard hats.

We met with their C.O. and explained that our mission was to solve their complaint. After a night with the infantry, we got the "con" as forward controllers for the close support by attacking fighter planes. We took over the forward controller's radio and were soon in radio contact with planes from our squadron, which came in for the first strike with demolition bombs and .50-caliber ammo. Their mission was to hit targets delineated by artillery smoke shells.

After contacting the flight leader, we gave him instructions to come in over our positions and deposit their bombs on a smoke marker from an artillery smoke shell that pinpointed the area to be attacked. We instructed the pilots to come in over our position and shoot from west to east. They did exactly that, and everything went according to plan; the P-51s came in roaring over our heads at very low altitude and started firing about 200 yards behind the front line. The roar of the engines and the noise of the Browning machine guns were deafening. As we crouched in the frontline trench and watched, we had to take cover as empty .50-caliber shell casings rained down on us, which was a little scary and created an atmosphere of terror. It did seem like we were in the line of fire but it was only empty casings. No wonder our G.I.s had misgivings from this saturation of brass. But that's what you get with close support.

We explained to the infantry officers that it was necessary to start shooting about five hundred yards from the target. This meant shooting started 300 yards behind our own lines. With this info circulated among the troops, their apprehension evaporated when they saw Bill and me standing in the open rooting for our planes. We stayed with the regimental team another night, telling them what a great job they were doing and how much we liked helping them.

GROUND SUPPORT IN EASTERN RIZAL PROVINCE *Toward the end of the month, then, emphasis was shifted to the new Yamashita line east of Manila where again the Jap had called terrain to his aid . . . Here the squadron piled trouble on artillery concentrations, road blocks, heavily travelled trails, villages and two churches which were housing supplies and ammunition. The Group served as a wedge, driving into the toughest Nip defenses so that the 43rd and 6th Divisions and Baldy Force, the 169th and 112th Regimental Combat Teams, could inch ahead.*—History of the 460th Fighter Squadron, March 1945

In the morning of the third day, we noticed some activity at the most forward post. Something was going on and there were two soldiers with their rifles pointed down the hill. Curiosity got the best of us so we edged up to the outpost to see what was happening. There at the bottom of the hill was a Jap waving a handkerchief. He would stand up, wave, and then take cover. We could hear him shouting. Finally, after popping up several times, waving his white handkerchief, he stood up. The G.I. in charge waved back at him, so the Jap started up the hill toward our position.

As he got closer we could hear him yelling in English, "Don't shoot!" As he got closer we could hear the word "Stanford." As he neared the G.I.s holding their Garands on him, he shouted, "Please don't shoot! I am from Stanford University!" He finally made it to the top without getting killed and explained that he was a Japanese American who was sent to Japan before the war by his parents for a vacation and was subsequently conscripted into service by the Japanese government. We didn't get to hear his debriefing, but I bet it was most valuable to our side. That was the end of the whole flap; everybody was happy, including the enemy officer who was alive and now in custody for the duration. We had a great time with the front line guys.

SUPPORT OF GROUND TROOPS *Our activity in connection with the support of ground troops frequently called for extreme accuracy, not only in bombing and strafing, but in determining the exact target area. Facilities for the latter have been inadequate. Our squadron was provided with a sufficient number of 1/1,000,000 AAF cloth charts, but had only one 1/30,000 detailed map, and one photograph of the target area. These maps were carried by the flight leader, and the missions were efficiently carried out as long as he stayed in the air. Fortunately, no difficulty was experienced in this respect. However, had he been compelled to return to base before reaching the target area, the mission could not have been completed without subjecting our ground troops to the hazard of an inaccurate determination of exact target area. Furthermore, after these maps were used several times they became soiled or torn, and the Photographs cracked. It seems inconsistent that the success of a mission which demands the utmost in close and accurate cooperation of the air arm, because of the property and lives involved, should be jeopardized because of the lack of a few dollars worth of maps and photographs.*—460FS Combat Evaluation Report, 24 February 1945

On April 2, I flew three combat missions; the first was with two flights of P-51s, eight aircraft, to bomb and strafe enemy positions east of the Mango River area, northeast of Manila, in mountains to the east of the La Mesa Reservoir. We were unable to reach the primary target due to weather, and went to the secondary in the Ipo area some ten miles to the north.[11]

CLOSE SUPPORT *Often the close support was just what the name implies, in one instance within 2–300 yards of friendly troops. The enviable record of inflicting no casualty on American forces was maintained, and often at the completion of the mission the controller would call for a buzz job. As the planes swooped over the waiting infantry the "paddlefeet" would wave helmets, rifles, handkerchiefs and even jump and shout in appreciation.*—History of the 460th Fighter Squadron, April 1945

The second was to bomb and strafe a sawmill at Mt. Kapatalin, southeast of Manila between Laguna de Bay and Lamon Bay. Six P-51's and a lone P-47 flew this mission, lugging pairs of 260-lb M81 fragmentation bombs.[12]

GROUND FIRE *Greatest hazard to pilots on these missions was anti-aircraft or small arms fire from well-concealed emplacements. The Japs frequently avoided using tracers so that the light fire gave no warning unless pilots observed the ground flashes, usually difficult to perceive. This ground fire or light ack-ack knocked down two of the squadron's planes.*—History of the 460th Fighter Squadron, April 1945

The last one was to bomb and strafe enemy concentrations, ammo and supply dumps at Gumian, east of Manila near Infanta, on the east coast of Luzon. Eight Mustangs with 500-lb bombs flew the mission.[13]

KUDOS FROM GENERAL KRUGER *From veteran Lieutenant General Krueger, 6th Army's stolid commander came word to Major General Ennis Whitehead of the Fifth Air Force, "I would appreciate your announcing to all ranks of your command my gratitude for their fine cooperation and effective results obtained in the support being rendered by units of the Fifth Air Force to Sixth Army during the vital Luzon campaign. It is superb and is assisting materially in the taking of our objectives and in holding our own battle casualties to a minimum.*—History of the 460th Fighter Squadron, March 1945

On landing from the third mission, my crew chief jumped up next to me as I was shutting down the engine and announced that my orders to go home were waiting for me. My joy knew no bounds! As I filled out

Form 1, I was informed that my plane had been hit by four .50-caliber bullets in the bottom of the fuselage. They could not figure out how the bullets miraculously missed any vitals, like the cooling pipes. "Irish luck!" I said.[14]

IMPROVING CLOSE AIR SUPPORT *After loss of two aircraft from small arms and medium anti-aircraft fire over targets east of Manila, the squadron evolved a procedure for bombing and strafing which provides mutual protection for all planes and allows maximum accuracy with a minimum time over the target.*

By placing the squadron in a string formation and approaching the target from 90 degrees for the bomb run, a process of variation in angle of approach can be achieved. Each pilot in the formation varies his run by 10–15 degrees from the aircraft in front of him, either swinging a little wide or cutting slightly inside his predecessor. This deviation prevents tracking of identical runs by anti-aircraft. This variation, with strafing during the bomb run, produces an effect of intense attack and discourages as well as hinders ground fire.

It has been found that a dive from 7,000 feet above the target at a 45–50 degree angle with nose placed directly on the target and pull out at 3,000 feet, produces best results.

At the completion of the bomb run the flight leader makes a wide 360 degree turn over enemy territory at high speed, as determined by the proximity of friendly troops, the same time avoiding all known or sighted anti-aircraft positions. Each plane then cuts off the man in front of him so he can individually check for hung-up bombs on the aircraft he is following. If any bomb hangs up, the pilot of the plane carrying the bomb calls the flight leader, then breaks out of formation to shake off the bomb over enemy territory. This course allows a hung-up bomb to fall or be shaken off without injury to American troops or installations.

When the last man in formation reports by radio that he has dropped his bombs, the flight leader is then in position to start his strafing pattern from the direction of original attack as instructed by the ground controller.

Praise of ground controllers and reports of destruction of pinpoint targets, along with the low loss of personnel and equipment, has proved the effectiveness of such procedure.

—460FS Combat Evaluation Report, April 1945.

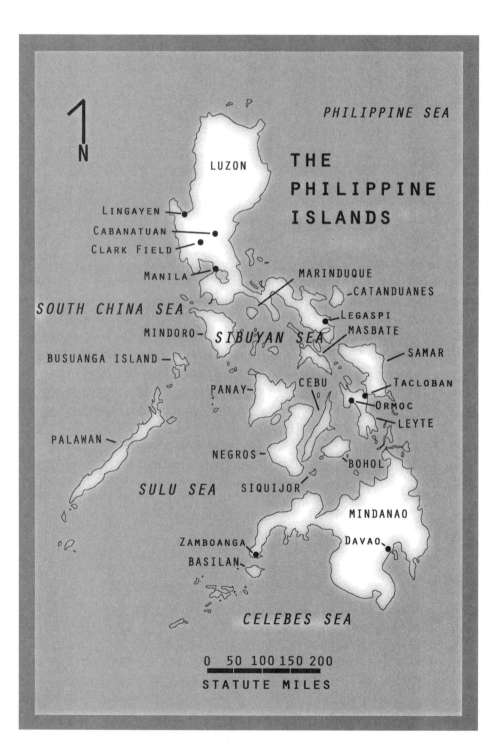

N

THE
PHILIPPINE
ISLANDS

PHILIPPINE SEA

LUZON

SOUTH CHINA SEA

Lingayen
Cabanatuan
Clark Field
Manila

MARINDUQUE
CATANDUANES
Legaspi
MASBATE

MINDORO
SIBUYAN SEA

BUSUANGA ISLAND

SAMAR

PANAY
CEBU
TACLOBAN
Ormoc
LEYTE

PALAWAN

NEGROS
BOHOL

SULU SEA
SIQUIJOR

MINDANAO
Davao

Zamboanga
BASILAN

CELEBES SEA

0 50 100 150 200
STATUTE MILES

NOTES

1. It is interesting to note that San Marcelino Airfield was initially secured by Filipino guerillas led by Capt. Ramón Magsaysay, who became President of the Republic of the Philippines in December 1953, until his untimely death in an aircraft accident in March 1957.

   "San Marcelino Airfield," http://www.pacificwrecks.com/airfields/philippines/san_marcelino/index.html

   "Ramon Magsaysay," http://en.wikipedia.org/wiki/Ramon_Magsaysay

2. The dust problem at San Marcelino was not confined to the camp areas of the 348th Fighter group. The 341FS History for March 1945, describes this: "The local base area is inherently dusty and dirty. Particularly in the morning before the warm air currents have increased enough to cause a slight wind the dust stirred up by planes revving up and taking off just hangs limpidly and unstirring over the strip. No means has been found to satisfactorily exclude the dust from the aircraft, the equipment and the supplies in storage. Therefore, in spite of great precautions taken, the aircraft and equipment experienced more than usual wear and tear."

3. Mission 3-437, 18 February 1945, "Cover P-T boats in Manila Bay," TOT 1330 to 1530I, from the deck to 2,000 feet at 240 mph. Four P-47's with eight 500-lb bombs. The aircraft appear to have expended their eight bombs, but the results do not indicate a particular target, but do appear to read: "One or two smoke fires were seen at Corregidor . . . Other Sightings Nil."

   This mission occurred shortly after the combined American airborne and amphibious landings on Corregidor of 16 February 1945. It took twelve days to defeat enemy forces on Corregidor. Earlier in the month, on 3 February 1945, American PT boats became the first Allied vessels to enter Manila Bay since the surrender of Corregidor in May 1942. (Bulkley, *At Close Quarters,* pages 423–424). Although the carriage of 500-lb bombs on this mission to escort PT Boats may seem unusual, it should be noted that the Japanese employment of "Shinyo" explosive motorboats was a known danger in the Manila Bay area. Early on 16 February 1945 a group of 30 Shinyo attacked US Navy amphibious assault vessels at the port of Mariveles, on Bataan. LCS(L)(3)-7, LCS(L)(3)-26 and LCS(L)3)-49 were sunk; LCS(L)(3)-27 beached to avoid sinking. Seventy-three sailors were killed and another 49 men wounded in this attack. The PT boats were likely hunting for these craft and the P-47's provided top cover against any Japanese air attack as well as backup firepower for any lucrative surface targets discovered.

   460FS Weekly Status & Operations Report (Form 34), (Report for Period Feb 11/45 to Feb 20/45 Inclusive), page 5.

   Bulkley, Robert J., Jr. *At Close Quarters: PT Boats in the United States Navy.* Washington, DC: Naval History Division, 1962, pp. 423–424.

Hackett, Bob and Kingsepp, Sander, "Shinyo! Explosive Motorboats based in the Philippines 1944–1945, Revision 8," http://www.combinedfleet.com/PhilippinesEMB.htm

Meister, Harry, and Demeter, David, "A Brief History of USS LCS(L)(3) 7," http://www.navsource.org/archives/10/05/050007h.htm

4. 19 Feb 45, "Cover Convoy in China Sea," Missions 3-441, 3-443, 3-445, 3-447, kept a patrol of four P-47's up at around 7,000 feet and 195 mph from about 0935 through the day to past 1800 (Mission 3-445 was only three P-47's). Results for all: "Nil Sightings."

460FS Weekly Status and Operations Report (Form 34), (Report for Period Feb 11/45 to Feb 20/45 Inclusive), pp. 6–7.

Jim Curran's flight record for February 1945 indicates that on 19 February he checked out for an hour in a P-51K-10 and flew the same type aircraft again for an hour-long local flight on 20 February.

5. Jim Curran flew four or five missions against Corregidor in this time, depending on interpretation of his flight records against the squadron history. These included clearly one mission each on 21, 22 and 23 February, and either one or two missions on 24 February. The poor quality of the Form 34 for this period as reproduced on the CD precludes provision of much detail, and none of the results. It is thus unclear which of the multiple Corregidor missions the squadron flew each day in this timeframe were the particular ones Jim Curran flew on. But these Corregidor missions by the 460FS appear to include the following, if not more:

21 February 1945, "Bomb Corregidor," Missions 3-450, 3-451, 3-452

22 February 1945, "Bomb Corregidor," Missions 3-455, 3-456

23 February 1945, "Bomb Corregidor," Mission 3-467

24 February 1945, "Bomb Corregidor," Mission 3-468, 3-470

24 February 1945, "Napalm Bomb Corregidor," Mission 3-469

460FS Weekly Status & Operations Report (Form 34), Report for Period 21 Feb 1945 to 28 Feb 1945 Inclusive) pp. 1–3.

It is not clear to the author when napalm was first used in the Philippine campaign, but the 341FS History for December 1944 on page 9 does mention that five aircraft of this squadron used the incendiary weapon, loading up at Tacloban Airfield for a mission to Palompon, Leyte, on 23 December 1944. The target was the southeast corner of town and the coconut grove southeast of the town, which were successfully attacked in treetop level deliveries by elements of three and two aircraft each, spaced ". . . 30 to 40 seconds apart to allow the hot currents of air sent up upon ignition of the bombs to settle down." Stanaway, *Kearby's Thunderbolts*, page 131, states this was the first recorded use of napalm by a unit of the V Fighter Command.

6. The 460FS Form 34 for this period shows Mission 3-471, 24 February 1945, "Napalm bomb W. of Stotsenburg," TOT 1620 to 1715 local time, 1.5 hour sortie

duration, 8 P-47s that flew between the deck and 5,000 feet at 240 mph. Results are illegible on the poor quality CD copy of the Form 34. As an example of the feedback which sometimes came back to the 348FG after close support missions flown for the ground forces, "Eight bombing and strafing missions were flown during the first week of March in the area west of Ft. Stotsenburg and the following message was received from 17 SAP: 'It is a pleasure to notify you that missions flown by 12 P-47s of the 460th Squadron and 8 P-51s of the 340th Squadron 5 March 1945, on ground support targets west of Ft. Stotsenburg are officially credited with killing 574 Nips.'—message from 17 SAP with XI Corps dated 9 March 1945."
460FS Weekly Status & Operations Report (Form 34), (Report for Period 21 Feb 1945 to 28 Feb 1945 Inclusive), pp. 1–3.
"The History of the 348th Fighter Group, March, 1945," http://www.ww2f.com/war-pacific/47729-history-348th-fighter-group-3.html

7. The 460FS History for March 1945 indicates "The trek to Biak to ferry P-51's to San Marcelino was begun March 6 when 18 pilots, muttering about giving up their Jugs; Captain Elmer C. Stewart . . . engineering officer; and a handful of ground crew members packed into the Group war-weary C-47 turned 'fat cat' for the hop 1100 miles to the Southeast. Damage to the C-47 which overshot the Tanauan strip and hit a small ditch slowed the journey by four days."
History of the 460th Fighter Squadron, Chapter Nine, (1 March 1945–31 March 1945), page 1.

8. The 460FS pilots who assembled at Biak accomplished their check out of the new Mustangs at Mokmer Airfield on Biak. The transition flying went well except for one accident when 2nd Lt. Thomas Stenger had a landing accident and suffered head cuts and a possible skull fracture. Ibid, p. 2.

9. The 460FS History for March 1945, states that 20 Mustangs, flown by 17 squadron pilots plus three other pilots from the unit on their way back from an R&R in Sydney, departed Biak for Morotai on a three hour and fifteen minute flight on 19 March 1945. There they rested overnight. Two aircraft experienced minor mechanical difficulties and did not proceed on the rest of the journey the next day, 20 March 1945. The 18-plane formation, led by Capt. Wallace Harding, operations officer, and flight leaders Willis Cooley and James Curran, brought the aircraft up from Morotai on a four hour hop to a refueling stop at Mindoro. After refueling, the 18 aircraft formation completed the mission with a one hour flight, and ". . . zoomed across the strip and soon filled the hardstands with the new Mustangs," arriving on the afternoon of the first day of spring at San Marcelino. There is no mention of any part of the group becoming lost along the way. On 22 March, six more pilots led by 1st Lt. George Della flew their well-used P-47's to Biak to trade them in to a service organization for new Mustangs, while other pilots flew there by C-47.
Ibid, pp. 2–3.

10. The air support provided to ground forces in the Luzon campaign of 1945 was the greatest in quantity and quality seen in the entire Pacific War, and the most successful insofar as air-ground coordination and cooperation. Many factors contributed to this favorable situation including basing, units, experience gained in the Leyte campaign and lack of enemy air opposition. USMC aircraft again played an important role in this campaign, with two groups of SBD-5 Dauntless dive bombers (Marine Air Groups 24 and 32) which provided perhaps the best, most accurate support of all the air units in the campaign. For a detailed discussion of close support in the Luzon campaign, including detailed descriptions of the processes to request and provide such air support, see *Close Air Support in the War Against Japan,* Chapter VI, The Philippines: Leyte through Luzon, pages 227–295.

Part of the reason for the quality of the air support was due to the effective and frequent liaison between air and ground forces, which promoted mutual understanding and trust. Jim Curran's visit to the front lines on Luzon was not uncommon, according to an excerpt on pages 259–260 of the above study: "Of even greater importance to mutual understanding as well as to the morale of the ground troops were the visits by pilots to forward ground units. This practice, apparently begun by Marines from Dagupan, became widespread before the end of the campaign. Ground commanders were enthusiastic in their approval."

Improvements in close support were constantly affected. Indeed, by the end of the Philippine campaign, as preparations were being made to invade Japan, page 295 of the above study indicated that: "Far East Air Forces (FEAF) commanders realized that the methods used during the Luzon and southern Philippines campaigns were not suited to large-scale operations in a restricted area where air opposition was probable. At the end of the war Fifth Air Force was in the process of organizing tactical air commands on the European model. These commands, designed to control masses of aircraft in the support of mass ground operations, were intended to function after Allied troops invaded the home islands of Japan."

For the Marine Corps perspective on aviation in the Luzon Campaign, see Boggs, Chapter 3, Luzon Campaign, pp. 56–106.

11. Mission 92-D-16, 2 April 1945, "(Primary) B/S enemy positions E of Mango River 60 miles from T.O.P." Eight P-51's took off at 0855. Results: "Unable to reach target due to weather." The mission then rolled to an alternate target. Mission 92-D-16 (Secondary) B/S IPO area 55 miles from T.O.P. TOT 0930–1010I. Eight P-51's with 12 M64A1 500-lb bombs. The aircraft expended 12 bombs and 1,696 rounds of .50 caliber ammunition on the target. Results: "2 early, 1 escort. 4 bombs dropped safe between Mt. Haponong [Mt. Hapanong-Baloy] & Mt. Pamitian [Mt. Pamitinan] by early returns. 4 strafing passes made hitting 3 staff cars, 5 trucks & 5 other light M/T, setting one truck on fire. 4–6 small caves along road in same area strafed twice starting a black smoke fire in mouth of the cave on S. side of road. Other sightings nil." 460FS Weekly Status and Operations Report (Form

34), (Report for Period 1 April 1945 to 10 April 1945 Inclusive), page 2.

12. Mission 92-D-19, 2 April 1945, "B/S Kapatalin Sawmill 80 Miles from T.O.P.," TOT 1125-1230I. Six P-51 with 12 M81 and one P-47 with two M81. (Note: The AN-M81 was a 260-lb fragmentation bomb.) All bombs expended as well as 5,004 rounds of .50 caliber ammunition on the target. Results: "Sawmill suffered one direct hit and one directly along side. 6 strafing passes thoroughly covered area including officers quarters, camp & garage. One strafing pass at sawmill brought spurt of orange flame which died out quickly. One truck strafed and left unserviceable. Two Japs seen running S.W. from sawmill, strafed with results unobserved. Entire area covered with Fox holes and shows evidence of activity." Ibid.

13. Mission 92-D-26, 2 April 1945, "B/S enemy concentrations, ammo & supply dumps at Gumian, 75 miles from T.O.P.," TOT 1625 to 1650I. Eight P-51's with 12 M64A1 500-lb bombs. Results from the expenditure of 12 bombs and 3,036 rounds of .50 caliber ammunition are largely illegible on the poor quality CD copy of the Form 34 except for ". . . A 120 ft long warehouse on n. side of road with metal roof strafed on 3 passes starting fire of undetermined size inside." Ibid, page 3.

14. According to Jim Curran's flight records for April 1945, he flew a fighter plane one last time in the Philippines before returning stateside. On 15 April 1945, he flew a P-51K-10 on a 30-minute, non-combat, local test flight, which completed his flying activity in the combat zone.

Although Jim Curran was lucky on this last mission and didn't have to bail out of his damaged aircraft, a sign of the continuous improvements in USAAF aircrew equipment was noted regarding evasion and escape materials. The History of the 341st Fighter Squadron, Chapter XVII, (March 1945), noted on page 3 the following: "A noticeable increase in the quality and quantity of escape aids during the month permitted a satisfactory system to be established in the squadron. Captain Charles D. Hildebrand, squadron Intelligence Officer, was appointed squadron Rescue Officer. The theory behind such an elaborate system of rescue and escape aids is simply that so many thousand dollars are spent on pilot training, it is worth a few more dollars to equip the pilots with the most convenient and comprehensive aids possible—as Chinese flags for safe conduct, pointie talkie booklets, small burning glasses, miniature compasses, ocean currant charts, and vinylite map cases. This vinylite map case is one of the most important and most useful. As long as the other aids are kept small enough to fit within its 4" by 5" dimensions, it makes a conveniently compact case to be carried in the shirt pocket. The vinylite composition is sweat resistant and keeps the contents perfectly dry. One suggestion is that the pointie talkie booklets be reduced in size and shape to fit into the vinylite case with the other aids. At present this booklet is 4-1/2" wide and 5" long and so does not fit into the case. If 1" were taken off the width, this valuable booklet could be included in the map case and not have to be carried separately in the pocket."

PART THREE

PACIFIC AFTERMATH

Chapter Thirteen

GETTING HOME

A COUPLE OF DAYS AFTER MY LAST COMBAT MISSION, ON April 4, the commander of V Fighter Command, Brigadier General Frederic H. Smith, Jr., pinned medals on a number of the group's officers and enlisted men for accomplishments in the recent campaigns we participated in. I was one of ten Black Ram pilots who received awards, along with three of our enlisted men, two of which were awarded the Purple Heart. I was presented with the Second Oak Leaf Cluster to the Air Medal.[1]

After the award ceremony, I found myself with time on my hands while awaiting orders to return to the Zone of the Interior. On one of those days in Luzon, I sat in a folding chair and got my teeth cleaned. The chair was in a squad tent with the side flaps rolled up. Not a big deal, but it was the first time I had my teeth attended to in three years.

BLACK RAM PARTY *As the sun began to set 10 April jeeps and weapons carriers filled with officers started down the rough, dusty roads to San Narcisco. There at a "night club" preparations had been made for a Black Ram party. The barren frame building with cement floor had been converted by Filipinos to a reasonable facsimile of a cabaret. On a raised wooden terrace, white covered tables, topped with flowers, and a motley collection of chairs were quickly filled by invading officers. A few Filipino girls, bright in their immaculate print dresses, a smattering of bamboo wall decorations, and the uncertain light of the gas lanterns hung from nails in the rafter beams lent a festive, if not plush, atmosphere.*

271

Platters of chicken, still crackling from the deep fat in which it had been fried, were carried in, to be followed by dishes of roast pork, tomato and onion salad, crisply cooked Camotes, and a strange sort of Philippine bread which tasted like chalk. In the vaguely remembered civilization of plates, glasses, cups and table service the food disappeared like money in a pay-day crap game.[2]
—History of the 460th Fighter Squadron, April 1945

At last, with orders from FEAF dated 23 April, and some from the 348th Fighter Group dated 29 April, I finally had authority to proceed with my return to the States on/about April 30, 1945, which I expeditiously did. I made the evening flight to join the return pool in Leyte with little time to say goodbye to my friends. The C-47 waddled its way to Tacloban, Leyte, P.I., and when I arrived I was directed to the returnee transient camp for people like me and the ambulatory wounded. The camp facilities were very spartan, to say the most! Exhausted, I had no trouble going to sleep after a hectic day of events.[3]

The next morning, I reported for travel and was informed I had a very low priority to fly home and that a ship would be my best choice, with a wait of two to three weeks for passage, plus another four weeks at sea on a miserable troop transport. This news was the pits so I went to Tacloban and got drunk. With a big hangover from drinking the local stuff, I began a long wait.

Happily, I was soon joined at Tacloban by Willis Cooley, who also received orders stateside after 24 months overseas. This was very fitting since we started out together in San Antonio, at Brooks Field in 1943 as aviation cadets. But he was very unhappy with the waiting situation. I was a little more pragmatic, accepting the Army way of "hurry up and wait." I quickly got into the routine of bugging the people who handled the manifests of the planes returning stateside. It was a thankless task but they got to know me by my first name. The wounded got first pick on air travel, and the C-54 four-engine transports were loaded accordingly. The days were long and miserable, and the nights even longer.

One night, Cooley and I went to the outdoor movie because they were supposed to have a Hollywood celebrity. Hoping it would be some gorgeous starlet, we sat in the rain, watching a D movie that we had seen six times previously. At the end of the movie the entire crowd of G.I.s booed to show their disgust. Then the guest appeared, a man called Joe E. Brown. He got a small hand from the crowd, and then proceeded to berate us for booing the movie. This went over like a lead balloon. No one laughed sitting there in the rain. The poor guy just didn't get it.

There was little to like in the camp. The chow was so bad that I started to lose weight rapidly, and was now about 135 pounds, down from my normal of 180. Cooley went AWOL and I was without anybody to talk with that I knew except the people at the airport, which I now haunted.

Time began to drift; finally on May 6th, 1945, I got a break. A C-54 arrived and the pilot was put into the hospital. His crew consisted of a navigator, crew chief and flight officer co-pilot. When it was determined that the pilot was not getting out of the hospital they asked for a pilot with a commission to sit in the co-pilot's seat, and I was called on. I agreed to fly with them, so on May 8th we loaded the C-54 to capacity with ambulatory wounded G.I.s and took off for Palau. The co-pilot ran me through the checklist several times and assured me he had plenty of time operating the plane. Somebody had to sit in the right hand seat so I volunteered, which was almost a final mistake. The plane handled better than a C-47 and the autopilot worked fine. The flight officer did all the actual flying. With only two days of training I was airborne with a flight officer and 30 wounded men. Since the C-54 was not pressurized, we had to stay under 12,000 feet and it was bumpy; every tiny bit of weather was a problem. We had to steer around any rough-looking clouds, and were limited to daylight flight.

About halfway to Palau, we had an engine shut down and limped along on three engines. The co-pilot, now captain, told me the plane was ready for engine replacement at the end of the journey at Hamilton Field, California. As we were making our final approach to Palau, we had to feather another propeller and landed on two engines—very scary. The mechanics worked all night on the engines, so in the morning we were off to Ulithi Atoll. It was almost a repeat of the day before, but we made it down in one piece. Again, loaded up as it grew light in the east, we took off for Oahu, some 4,000 miles distant.

The long flight from Ulithi ended at Hickam Field, on two engines again. We pleaded with base engineering to give us another plane but they refused, and we were loaded up again with maximum fuel load for the last leg of the journey stateside. On takeoff from Hickam, we struggled to get airborne and were able to retract the landing gear but couldn't get enough altitude to milk up the flaps. When this plane took off you had a flap setting of about 30 degrees. If the aircraft is in a nose up attitude at very low altitude, raising the flaps too fast might cause the plane to lose its ability to fly and sink to its doom. The aircraft was loaded to the max, 70,000 pounds, if my memory serves me well. Underpowered due to mechanical problems, the plane could not gain enough speed to get altitude or a normal flying configuration. The flaps being in the takeoff position made it difficult to attain a good attitude to gain altitude. After literally skimming the wave tops for many minutes, the air speed increased to a point that the plane could gain enough air space to make a gentle, climbing turn to get back to Hickam Field.

We realized that we were in a bit of trouble with this timeworn aircraft. After about 35 miles, we finally got the nose down enough that we gained enough altitude to get the flaps up and turned around to head back to Oahu. As we got closer to the island, one engine failed and we feathered the prop. We called operations for clearance to come back and land. They refused us clearance, saying we had too much fuel on board and were afraid we would collapse the landing gear with so much weight, so we circled at full rich mixture in order to burn off fuel so we could land at an acceptable weight.

Finally, after three hours, another engine started to give out so we called for emergency clearance to land. They couldn't stop us this time so we plopped the plane on the ground. The gear held and we parked. There I filled out Form 1 and put the aircraft on a big red "X." As we disembarked, I grabbed my Val pack and swore I would never get in that airplane again.[4]

A few hours later, I boarded a brand-new C-54 bound for San Francisco. I attempted to sleep as it got dark, and though this plane had night radar capabilities, sleep would not come. I fretted all night; in the morning, the navigator informed us that we were nearing the coast of California and invited me to the pilot's office for a look. As the light of dawn started, I saw the most beautiful sight of my life. There, directly over the nose of the plane, were two towers sticking up out of the fog, the Golden Gate Bridge. The long journey across the Pacific was about to end!

The long flight from Luzon to California ended with a beautiful, greased-in landing in the fantastic new C-54. As we departed the plane, I shook hands with the entire flight crew and thanked them for a wonderful flight. The Army greeting people immediately took over. As soon as we gulped some coffee we were ushered to the reception center where our orders were perused. I was released to proceed home: "Officer will provide transportation." But first, there was a little matter of the medical inspection.

By 0700, I was in the base infirmary, buck-naked, for a short arm inspection. Next, they listened to my heart and lungs to see if I was alive. They weighed my sack of bones at 126 pounds. Next, they had to determine if I was carrying any Schistosomiasis flukes. This was determined by taking a stool sample with an instrument that resembled a one-inch pipe. While the laboratory was assaying the sample my orders were cut to go home for 30 days, not including travel; then, to report to Santa Ana Army Air Base in southern California. Rail transport was authorized. Although I weighed 126 pounds upon arrival, I started to gain about a pound a day for a long time after.

The next stop was the paymaster where they loaded me up with three months back pay, plus allowances. I was informed that I could leave as soon as I got lab clearance. While waiting for the lab work, the bus for San Francisco left, with the next bus scheduled for late in the p.m. This was sad; three G.I.s and I were stranded for the day because of late lab results.

As we sat in the transportation office with our gear, sipping coffee and lamenting about the lab work, I noticed a memo on the bulletin board about field grade officers being entitled to limousine transportation. A huge light bulb lit up in my head. I removed my captain bars from my collar and phoned the livery pool, explaining to the operator that I was Colonel J.C. Curran and that me and my staff had just landed and needed to get to San Francisco A.S.A.P. for a meeting. The results were astounding. In a few minutes, a Packard limo arrived with a courteous military driver who asked "Where to, sir?" I replied, "Take us to the Alexander Hamilton Hotel, we have an urgent meeting to attend." And we were off across the Golden Gate Bridge. At the hotel, I signed for the transportation, and duked the driver ten dollars.

As soon as the limo disappeared, I said goodbye to the three G.I.s who abetted me. I then approached the desk in the hotel with my Val pack and briefcase in tow. I told the clerk my name and said I had a reservation made in 1943. After a few moments, he announced that I would have the same room. The bellboy grabbed my gear and I got my room where I called Chicago to inform my parents I was coming home. My mother was almost impossible to talk to because she was hysterical at hearing my voice. I finally gave up trying to converse with her and called my dad at work. He was dumbfounded when I identified myself, and all he could say was, "How soon do you think you will get to Chicago?" I told him as soon as I could get reservations.

The next call was to my Aunt Bessie who worked for Western Union and lived with her husband at the Alexander Hamilton Hotel where I was staying. She took the rest of the day off from work and came to the hotel immediately. I hadn't yet bathed when she got there, and I had ordered the biggest salad on the menu for breakfast. While I gobbled the salad, washed down with cold beer, we visited as fast as possible. She was aghast at my appearance because I weighed 180 pounds when she last saw me in 1943. Also, I had a sickly yellow cast under my deep tan that was very unappealing. I explained that this was due to the Atabrine medication I took to keep from getting Malaria, which I never got.

About the time I got all the salad down, I told Aunt Bessie I was going to be sick and promptly threw up everything I had eaten. I was so weak after this episode that I collapsed in bed and slept until 1900. When I awoke, Aunt Bessie and her husband, Whitman Prentice, and the young lady who had entertained me in 1943, were all on hand. My clothes were all unpacked, cleaned, and pressed, thanks to Aunt Bessie. I showered, shaved, got dressed and ordered a pitcher of Martinis from room service. Aunt Bessie was astounded at how much I had recovered from my morning sickness. Whitman asked if I wanted to eat, to which I replied, "I could eat a horse!" With that, we were off to Fisherman's Wharf, where I ate a one-pound horse steak. Beef wasn't available for neither love nor money. We reveled until midnight when Aunt Bessie and Whit gave up because they had to work the next day. I finally gave up some time prior to sunup and hit the sack until 1400.

After a late breakfast, I started the search for transportation to Chicago. Flying was not an option because of the wait for reservations, so I booked on the Union Pacific for the first available space, about a ten-day wait. Next stop was a military uniform shop where I blew myself into some new clothes, because all the rest of my gear was in a sad shape. The service of the shop was outstanding, so by cocktail hour I looked like a new man with a new uniform that fit.

I informed my aunt that I would be in San Francisco for at least a week more. I responded to real food so well that by the third day I was full of energy that I hadn't felt in months. Whitman was employed in defense work as an executive in a huge shipyard. He took me there on a tour to introduce me to his business associates, to whom he introduced me as his favorite nephew. Perhaps this was because I was his only nephew, I later learned. He also dragged me to his exclusive men's club to meet his pals there. The name of the club was a misnomer for a men's club—it was called the Family Club of San Francisco. One thing I do remember about the club was the quality of the food. It was positively the best treat on the west coast.

San Francisco was a blast. I renewed my visits to the Top of the Mark at the Mark Hopkins Hotel, which had become the hangout for military fliers visiting San Francisco. One night as I approached the bar at the Top, I was surprised to see Bill Dunham sitting there with a bunch of flying officers. When I walked up to him, he was equally astounded to see me. We spent the next several hours hashing over news. He was on his way back to the V Air Force and was to take up a position in the V Fighter Command. He immediately put the bite on me to return to the Pacific and offered me the 460th Fighter Squadron command or to come to headquarters with him as an inducement. I told him it would be an honor after I got some rest. I hadn't got my breath yet but would give it serious thought. He was leaving for the Orient the next day so we bid adieu. The war ended a short time later and that was that for any return to the Pacific. Little did I know that it would be 40 years before I would see him again.

I had a super time in San Francisco; it was still a great town at that time. But like all good things, my stay finally came to an end and I boarded the Union Pacific train bound for Chicago, a ride of 39 hours and 45 minutes.

NOTES

1. History of the 460th Fighter Squadron, Chapter Ten, (1 April 1945–30 April 1945), page 18.
2. 10 April 1945 Black Ram party continued: "Dinner music provided by a four-piece

ensemble, whose forte was tempo and volume, raced into 'Bugle Call Rag,' 'Margie,' and the inevitable 'You Are My Sunshine' to lure the dancers to the cement floor. The weird combinations of jitterbugging, the rhumba and the reliable fox trot kept the Filipino partners in continual state of apprehension as to what the unpredictable officers would do next.

"All went smoothly, however, and dancing, conversation and harmonization of incomparable squadron ballads continued until the orchestra's inspired rendition of 'God Bless America' signaling closing time, and jeeps and weapons carriers once again jounced toward camp." Ibid, page 14.

3. Jim Curran finished his combat tour in April 1945, just as the 348th Fighter Group began to implement a mandatory Headquarters V Fighter Command-pilot training program. It was an additional burden on the unit and the men, as the schedule was ". . . already heavily loaded with tactical missions . . ." But it may have reflected concerns over the loss of many experienced personnel and the need to bolster the operational training of new replacement pilots. Certainly this was a period of preparation for the last great planned operation of the war, the invasion of the Japanese home islands. In any event, it showed the lessons learned in combat across the South Pacific in the experience of pilots like Jim Curran, and the importance of aircrew proficiency training, even in an active combat zone.

HEADQUARTERS V FIGHTER COMMAND
APO 710
8 March 1945
AG 353.00–E
SUBJECT: Training Program.
TO: Commanding Officer, 85th Fighter Wing, APO 72.
    Commanding Officer, 86th Fighter Wing, APO 70.

1. Operational commitments at this time have decreased to a point where it will be possible to inaugurate a training program within this Command.

2. It is suggested that the missions outlined below serve as a guide to group commanders when setting up their training program. Missions which must be flown will have the word MANDATORY in parentheses after them. Group commanders may make any additions to the program outlined below, which they decide will benefit their pilots.

MISSION	TIME PER MONTH PER PILOT
INSTRUMENT FLYING (MANDATORY)	4 hours
NIGHT FLYING (MANDATORY)	4 hours
AERIAL GUNNERY (MANDATORY)	4 hours
CAMERA GUNNERY	2 hours
DIVE BOMBING	1 hour

SKIP BOMBING	1 hour
INTERCEPTION	2 hours
GROUND GUNNERY	2 hours
GROUP FORMATION	1 hour
SQUADRON FORMATION	1 hour
AEROBATICS	1 hour
SIMULATED COMBAT	1 hour

3. It is expected that a certain percentage of the above missions will be flown under ordinary operational commitments. Full credit should be given the pilots who perform any of the above missions while on an operational flight.

4. A ground training schedule will be set up by the Fighter Group as TRAINING AIDS become available. The time each pilot will be able to spend on the ground training will be governed by Operational and Training Air Commitments, but the figures set forth below are suggested as minimum.

LINK TRAINER	2 hours per month
SKEET	2 hours per month
MOBILE TRAINING UNITS	As available
FILMS	As available
*DITCHING PRACTICE (simulated)	1 hour

*An improved water tank or the ocean may be utilized for this practice. A frame, parachute harness, boat, etc. should be used to approach as closely as possible the actual experience of ditching.

5. A report on the average number of hours and average percent of training completed per pilot will be forwarded to this headquarters monthly. The first report will be due 30 days after the program has been put into effect. This program will go into effect upon notification from this headquarters.

This training program was implemented in the 348th Fighter Group by order of Group Commander Colonel Rowland in a 15 April 1945 letter from the group S-3, Subject: "Training," addressed to the Commanding Officer of each of the four fighter squadrons in the group, the 340th, 341st, 342nd and 460th. The pertinent paragraphs read as follows:

1. It is directed that the training program as set forth in V Fighter Command letter, file AG 353.00E, Subject: "Training Program," dated 8 March 1945, be inaugurated as of 16 April 1945.

2. In addition to the report called for in aforementioned letter, the following information will be included:

   a. Average number of aircraft required daily for combat missions.

   b. Average number of aircraft available for training.

   c. Average number of aircraft employed for daily training.

3. Squadrons will submit original copy of report to this headquarters and

retain duplicate for file. Report will be forwarded monthly, the first report due thirty (30) days after program goes into effect.

History of the 342nd Fighter Squadron, Chapter XVIII, (1–30 April 1945), pp. 8–9, and Enclosure 2, "Training Program," 8 March 1945.

4. The Val pack was a standard GI issue suitcase for officers made of olive drab canvas with lots of zipper compartments. Said Jim Curran, "It was considered carry-on luggage, but too large to fit into the compartment in a P-47. I normally used my parachute bag for travel in the combat zone, like going on R&R to Sydney." Source: Jim Curran email to Terrence Popravak, 24 April 2009, Subject: "Feedback on Chapter 42."

Chapter Fourteen

HOME FROM THE WAR

THE UNION PACIFIC PASSENGER TRAIN ARRIVED FROM THE west coast to Chicago on time, almost to the second. As the train pulled into the station, the porter got my stuff and said he would have it waiting for me at the terminal gate, so I was hands free. My father had long ago instructed me on how to get along on passenger trains. His sage advice was to duke the porter as soon as you met him and the rest of the trip would be trouble-free. So it was on this trip.

As soon as the train rolled to a stop, I exited to the platform into the arms of my mother. Tears streamed down her cheeks and all she could utter was "Look at how thin he is!" My dad was all smiles and didn't seem to notice anything but my new Eisenhower jacket and silver captain bars. After lots of hugs, we ambled toward the gate. I collected my gear and got another hug from the porter.

It was still early in the day and my mother started to inquire if I was hungry. I had already had a hearty breakfast on the train, so my answer was no. We proceeded to the parking area where I was surprised to see my old 1937 DeSoto five-window coupe. It was clean but had a lot of dings. We loaded my gear into the trunk and headed for South Prairie Avenue where my parents lived.

As we drove south to home, I marveled at how things had not changed and how good it was to see Chicago again. When we got home, I put my gear in my room and headed to the kitchen for a beer. As I sat at the kitchen table a huge meatloaf suddenly appeared. Meatloaf was one of my favorites. The munching began and with the appearance of an apple pie, I could see that my mother would be fattening me up for the next 30 days.

As we were sitting in the kitchen talking blue streaks, a very touching thing happened. I heard a scratching noise coming from the back door. When I looked out on the porch, there was Duke, a German Shepherd that belonged to Dick Kenney who lived across the alley from us. I used to play ball with Duke for years prior to the war. Somehow he knew I was home and came to visit, climbing up two flights of stairs to greet me in his old age. It was a gargantuan effort for him to make the climb.

The phone commenced to ring with all kinds of people wanting to greet me. One call was from Mary Jane Condon whom I had casually dated once in 1941. She was a pen pal while I was in the service, which was the thing to do in those days. She was also the target of a buzz job at Lakeland, Florida while I was in Transition Training at Dale Mabry. She asked to come over with her girlfriend Jayne Zidek, and was welcomed by my dad who was manning the phone between Budweisers. The two ladies arrived shortly thereafter and overwhelmed me with unexpected kisses upon entering the front room. Mary Jane announced to all present that I was her exclusive property for my entire leave, no ifs, ands, or buts. Her girlfriend Jayne was the only one to demur, saying she was also on the scene. So my leave began with celebrations on the agenda.

My father finally explained to me why he was using my old DeSoto. It seems that he was celebrating something one day after work and had the misfortune to run his 1940 Pontiac into a truck, totaling it. There were no replacements available so dad had to use my old jalopy to get around.

The next day, my dad insisted I go to his office with him to meet all his fellow workers. This was the start of answering thousands of questions. Usually the first was, "Did you fly the plane?" Next it was, "Who shot the guns?" Followed by, "Who navigated and dropped the bombs?" It was difficult to explain that these chores were all done by me in the P-47. The next most popular question was, "How many missions did you fly?" When I replied 221, they wanted to know why I didn't come home after 25. I met John F. Cuneo, president of Cuneo Press, Inc., where my father was employed, as well as Jack Stewart, vice-president, and a host of other people. I told Mr. Cuneo that our squadron's ordnance officer was Lloyd Cuneo, but he said he was not related.

After a grueling day with my dad, we finally came home to a delicious dinner prepared by my mother. Mary Jane had been on the phone calling for me all day, so after dinner I called her. She said she would pick me up in 15 minutes, and that a party was in progress for me at the Bamboo Room cocktail lounge. I went in spite of being full, and so the fun began.

The first week of being home went so fast I could scarcely catch my breath. There were lots of young ladies, but a scarcity of male contemporaries. After two years of close companionship with fellow soldiers, I found this to be a little disconcerting. Mary Jane Condon kept me very busy meeting lots of people.

The second week of my leave brought sad news of the demise of my close friend, John Peter Fardy.[1] We were friends from fifth grade grammar school and four years at Leo High School. John was a Marine Corporal in the First Marine Division. I tried to visit him in 1944 at Cape Gloucester, New Britain, when I was at Finschhafen, but the Army would not let me fly over there to land. Keeping in touch was difficult, so we didn't correspond much. John was killed in Okinawa while on patrol with his squad. Cause of death was a Japanese hand grenade. He shielded his comrades with his body when a grenade was tossed into their foxhole. John was posthumously awarded the Medal of Honor by the President of the United States, Harry S. Truman. The award was presented after the war in Chicago and I was in attendance. The award cited John as Squad Leader who covered the grenade with his body, saving his buddies. Two of those buddies were present for the award and I spoke to both. It was very sad for all.

There were other reminders of the sacrifice of the war. Another Marine, my first cousin, Flory Barret, was killed in another incident. His brother, Frank, was killed in the Battle of the Bulge, where I lost another school chum, Jay Kapple.[2] Hearing of these fatalities had a chilling effect on me. I also visited the parents of a squadron member who lost his life while on patrol with me at San Pedro Bay off Leyte. That was a most difficult day for me.

My dates with Mary Jane took on seriousness as the days progressed, and it became apparent she was very serious about getting married. Time flew by and before I knew it, it was time for me to report to Santa Ana Army Air Base in Santa Ana, California, for assignment and duty with the 1040th AAF Base Unit. I rode the Sante Fe Super Chief to Los Angeles, where I was met by my mother's youngest sister, Thelma Solyom—and who else, but Clare Larkin Brophy, my high school sweetie who had sent me a "Dear John" letter when I was in basic training. Small world. Her husband was in the Corps of Engineers someplace and she was living in L.A. It was nice to see people I knew, and Clare had a car that she loaned to me in order to report in at Santa Ana.

NOTES

1. Corporal John P. Fardy was a squad leader in Company C of the 1st Battalion, 1st Marine Regiment of the 1st Marine Division. He participated in the landings at Cape Gloucester in 1943, Peleliu in 1944 and Okinawa in 1945. He was mortally wounded on May 6, 1945 and died the next day, at age 22. The Medal of Honor was presented to Corporal Fardy's parents in Chicago on September 15, 1946. "John P. Fardy," http://en.wikipedia.org/wiki/John_P._Fardy

2. Jim Curran's cousins were Marine Sgt. Florance "Florrie" Barrett (1919–1944), who died on 16 Dec 1944 in Guadalcanal, of leukemia at the age of 25. He was an aviation mechanic and saw action in the Guadalcanal campaign of 1942. Florance reportedly knew that he was ill, even came home stateside on leave, but chose to return to Guadalcanal. He was reburied 13 Jan 1949 in the National Memorial Cemetery of The Pacific, Honolulu, Hawaii, at Plot C 1623. Private First Class Francis P. "Frank" Barrett, Jr. (1917–1945), US Army, died in Germany on 17 Apr 1945 during the last days of World War II (V-E Day was 8 May 1945). He was 28 years old, and left his wife Marie behind. Francis was a member of the 38th Infantry Regiment of the 2nd Infantry Division. His cousin Kathleen Barrett Price said that, "He was walking down the street after the war was over and was shot by a sniper." He is buried in the Netherlands American Cemetery, Margraten, Netherlands, buried at Plot B, Row 21, Grave 31.

   These two brothers are remembered today by Barret Brothers Park in St. Louis, Missouri. It is a 13-acre park in the Wells Goodfellow Neighborhood, and was dedicated to their memory in 1947.

   Private Jay P. Kapple, US Army, was a soldier in the 393rd Infantry Regiment, 99th Infantry Division, and was killed 31 January 1945. He is buried in the Henri-Chapelle American Cemetery, Henri-Chapelle, Belgium, and is buried at Plot C, Row 15, Grave 55. He was awarded the Purple Heart.

   "Barrett Brothers Park," http://www.stlouiscitytalk.com/2013/06/barrett-brothers-park.html

   "Francis P. Barrett, Jr." and "Jay P. Kapple," http://www.abmc.gov/search-abmc-burials-and-memorializations

Chapter Fifteen

FLYING AGAIN

W HEN I ARRIVED AT THE BASE, I WAS PROMPTLY PRO-
grammed for exhaustive physicals and also psychiatric
evaluation. The latter took more than one day, much to my surprise. It
seems they were looking for post-combat anomalies that some of the re-
turnees were experiencing. After a week of this, on June 26th, I was ordered
to Foster Field, Victoria, Texas for regular duty. They furnished transportation so I was off for Texas again in the middle of summer.

On arrival at Foster Field on July 2, I was assigned for duty to the
2539th AAF Base Unit and resumed regular and frequent AT-6 flights in
a refresher-training course. I was assigned to some mundane ground classes
and housed in the BOQ. It seemed that they did not know what to do
with me until July 25th, when I received orders for duty as a Transition
and Fixed Gunnery Instructor. But I knew absolutely no one on the base,
so I was very lonely and I just hated being in Victoria. This probably has-
tened me to dwell on Mary Jane Condon. We talked on the phone almost
daily, so plans to get married were hatched and a date of August 2nd was
suggested. I checked with my commanding officer and it was no problem
since they had little for me to do, so following that I received orders author-
izing 19 days leave of absence.

I flew to Chicago at the end of July in time to get the required blood
tests and license. My dad assisted me in finding a place on the north side
to buy a car. It was a 1940 Chevrolet coupe, Office of Price Administration
ceiling price, $900.00. I had to shell out $300.00 under the table to get it,
and was told by everyone it was a good deal.

On August 2, 1945, I married Mary Jane Condon at St. Clotilde Catholic Church at 8400 Calumet Avenue, Chicago, Illinois. We were married there, which was my parish, because Mary Jane's church had no times available. My lifetime friend, Hank Woessner, a captain in the USMC stationed temporarily at Great Lakes Naval Base, was my best man, and Jayne Zidek stood up for Mary Jane.

We had our reception at the South Shore Country Club which lasted all afternoon. I invited the wedding party to the Blackstone Hotel for dinner which lasted too late. Mary and I finally exited for the Edgewater Beach Hotel where Betty Dewey, the daughter of the hotel owner, made reservations for us. We got there late, our room had been let out and no more were available. This was a very important night and I started to raise hell. When the management found out who made the reservations, they got us the Peacock Suite at the Medina Hotel on Michigan Avenue. This was a really elegant accommodation and cost us nothing but the room service.

The day after the wedding, preparations were made to report back to Foster Field. On August 4, we started the long drive to Texas in the 1940 Chevy and a new life in the Army Air Corps. The tires were recaps with adequate tread, but very old, so I had to drive at a very moderate speed to avoid tire failure. This made the trip to St. Louis long and tedious, but safe. We stayed at my paternal grandmother's house and visited with relatives who came en masse to see me and my new bride.

On the fifth of August, we made it to the Ozark Mountains, but the roads were so bad I had two tire failures. Stopping in a small town, we shopped for a tire replacement but were not able to find any auto tires. They just were not available. At a Goodyear dealer, I pleaded my case with the manager, telling him I had to report for duty in Texas. He suggested I mount four implement tires on the car. The tires were brand new, but had implement tread which made driving very difficult, but possible.

The next morning when I was gassing up my Chevy, the attendant topped off the tank and told me to keep my gas ration coupons. The war was over—they'd dropped a bomb so big it blew up a whole city. With that bit of news we restarted for Texas again.

TIME RUNS OUT FOR THE EMPIRE *An overwhelming succession of crushing blows fell on the Japanese nations early this month. The Soviet Union's entry* *into the Pacific war; the shelling of the Homeland by United States Navy Units; the stepped up air offensive, and lastly, and probably the decisive factor, the "Atomic" bomb, caused the Japanese cabinet to change their earlier attitude, "To fight to the bitter end in accordance with previously established policies."*—History of the 341st Fighter Squadron, August 1945

I was all over the road with the new tires, but made good time driving about 50 mph, tops. We made it into Texas, found a place to eat and sleep and hear the news. Hiroshima had been bombed with a secret, new weapon that destroyed the city. I knew the squadron was not too far from there. I wondered what is was all about.

We made Victoria the next day and I reported for duty. The air base was agog with all the news and we wondered what the consequences would be. We busied ourselves with looking for a place to live because there were no accommodations available on base. We found a bedroom apartment in a mansion, with private bath, but no kitchen facilities. All meals had to be purchased out. This was expensive, but our options were non-existent.

It was hot and muggy, so we spent as much time as possible at the base Officer's Club which was air-conditioned. Mary Jane did not like anything at all about Texas and life in the military. She complained vigorously, but there was little I could do.

END OF THE WAR

Another bomb was dropped on Nagasaki and the war came to a sudden, screeching halt. I was making inquiries as to a future assignment away from Texas without much success. The main reason for doing so was to get Mary Jane to some place like Florida where she would be happy.

COMMENDATION TO FAR EAST AIR FORCES FROM GENERAL ARNOLD

THE FOLLOWING MESSAGE FROM
COMGENAIR TO BE PASSED TO
ALL UNITS UNDER YOUR COMMAND:
THE BRILLIANT OFFENSIVE OF THE FAR EAST AIR FORCES
UNDER YOUR INSPIRING LEADERSHIP WAS AN OUTSTAND-
ING FACTOR IN JAPAN'S DEFEAT. LOOKING BACK TO THE

HEROIC OPERATIONS OF THE EARLY WAR IN WHICH, GRAVELY OUTNUMBERED AND UNDERRESUPPLIED YOU AROSE FROM THE DUST OF THE PORT MORESBY STRIPS TO STOP THE AUSTRALIA-BOUND JAPS IN THEIR TRACKS, IT MAY BE TRUTHFULLY SAID THAT NO AIR COMMANDER EVER DID SO MUCH WITH SO LITTLE. ALL THAT YOU HAVE DONE SINCE HAS MADE AIR HISTORY. THE ARMY AIR FORCES HONOR YOUR FIGHTING SPIRIT, TO WHICH WE SO LARGELY OWE TODAY'S SPLENDED TRIUMPH. SIGNED ARNOLD.

—HQ Fifth Air Force Message to All Fifth Air
  Force Unit Commanders, 20 August 1945[1]

August slipped into September, then October when I was assigned to duty as a P-47 Transition Instructor. Finally, I was asked if I would like to go to Muroc Army Air Base (Edwards AFB today) in Muroc, California. I brought the news to Mary Jane and she liked the idea, but that night she discussed Muroc with some of her newfound lady friends at the Officer's Club, and got an earful of life in the Mojave Desert. She put her foot down on the prospective move. No way would she live in the desert; she wanted to return to Chicago immediately, saying she had enough of Texas and the Army.

This was enough, so I opted to separate from the service. On October 22, 1945, orders were cut for me releasing me from assignment and duty in the 2539th AAF Base Unit. I was ordered to report to the Separation Center at Chanute Field, in Rantoul, Illinois, on October 27, 1945, and we were off to Chicago. I dropped Mary Jane off at her mother's apartment and proceeded to the separation base.

At Chanute Field things went smooth and I was guided and processed by an old sergeant major who seemed to take a personal interest in me. Being a single-engine fighter pilot there was no way for me to get a discharge. My only options were rank—being retained in reserve status was not an option, as I was required to stay in the reserve. He suggested I freeze my rank at captain, his reasoning being that if there was another war, they would have to call me back as a major. This was sound advice and I opted to keep my temporary rank. This later kept me out of the Korean conflict.

My active duty service terminated in January 1946. When I separated from active duty, it was as a Captain in the reserve, which later became the US Air Force Reserve. My total flying time was recorded as 1,034 hours and 30 minutes. My pay and allowances went on well into 1946, because they did not charge me for any of the leave time that I had spent.

POSTWAR

When I separated from active duty I presumed I would be flying for United or American Airlines, but they weren't interested in fighter pilots at all, suspecting us of being hot dog pilots. So it took me about three and a half months to get hired. I took a job with *Family Circle* Magazine as a sales representative, which I was totally unqualified for, and tried to get back into civilian life. It wasn't easy and turned out to be a bum deal, but I had fun. What was not fun was when my wartime marriage ended, but life goes on.

A few years later the Korean fiasco erupted. I found myself on 24-hour alert for a couple of years, but was never called up due to my rank. The Air Force's Table of Organization was always being filled for majors. This was planned by my separation sergeant major, an old timer who knew the ropes. Old Enlisted Men know what they are doing.

However, I have a lot of buddies buried in Korea, some with a J47 turbojet engine for a headstone. If it hadn't been for that old NCO, and my rank keeping me from being called up, I might have had a J47 for a headstone too, or would have been court-martialed for investigating the terrain north of the Yalu River.

In 1955, Congress decided to get rid of all the inactive reservists, so a law was passed requiring all reserve personnel to be discharged unless they were participating in military programs. They sent me a notice that I met this qualification and was given the opportunity to continue or become a full-time civilian. I chose the latter without regret and was finally honorably discharged from the Air Force Reserve July 29, 1955, when they got rid of thousands of us for not taking their money. Thus ended my military career, which spanned 13 years.

On the down side, I received no benefits from the government for military service because I had no service-connected disabilities that I could prove. This is regrettable financially, but I again say no regrets.

Also in 1955, I got my footlocker back that I shipped prior to going overseas in 1943. The hasp was still in place though it had been sawed apart. The box was completely empty and the government reimbursed me for the loss at 1943 prices. All my memorabilia could never be replaced.

I fooled around in sales for ten years and then went back into the building trades as a pipe fitter. I was a boilermaker prior to the war, and joined Local Union 597. L.U. 597 members were the only pipe fitters in northern Illinois and Indiana, but were many in number. L.U. 597 is the biggest local in the country. At this time, I moved to the Country Club Hotel on South Shore Drive. My last residence in Chicago was 1130 South Michigan Avenue, overlooking Grant Park. I lived in Chicago until 1971, and then moved to Hinsdale, Illinois, just west of Chicago. I was happy in this work and stayed there until retirement in March of 1987.

I met my latest companion and loving wife, Mary Jean Toppett, in 1979 and we were married on June 20, 1986 in Wheaton, Illinois. The years together have been the most wonderful and joyous time one could have, with many happy memories. A few years after retirement, we moved out west to Trail, Oregon. My mother had a sister who resided in Trail, and I visited her in 1970 and fell in love with the Rogue River and her ranch, which had 600 feet of frontage on that beautiful water. Lost Creek Dam was in the talking stage as well as Elk Creek Dam, which was adjacent to my aunt's property. Boating and fishing were one of my dreams.

James and Mary Curran smile for the camera at a Black Ram Reunion in October, 2010, in Branson, Missouri.
—courtesy Mary Jean Curran

We made several trips to Oregon. When my aunt passed away in 1985, she left me sole heir to the property, having no children of her own. So I retired there in 1988 with my wife, but she couldn't hack the boonies and the damp winters, so we moved to Las Vegas in 1991 where the climate is a little friendlier for my wife's arthritis. My son John moved from Ohio to Trail and we gave him the property, which he still maintains and enjoys.

Having homes in Trail, Oregon and Las Vegas, Nevada, became difficult to maintain, especially traveling back and forth every six months. So we decided to make Sun City Summerlin, in Las Vegas, Nevada, right across the valley from Nellis AFB, our permanent residence in 1991, which enabled me to continue my favorite sport, fishing. I brought my boat with me so I could use it in Lake Mead, to which the Colorado River flows through. A beautiful place it is.

In Las Vegas we have enjoyed our retirement, staying busy with hobbies, bridge, music, watching sports, traveling, gambling and all other Las Vegas activities. I loved the military, but was always a civilian at heart. I suffered no trauma for my military experience. I think all Americans should have a hitch in the military so they can appreciate what protecting our country is all about.

I am reminded of the military from time to time, like when we got buzzed by a B-52 in Northwestern Nevada on Route 140. He almost blew us off the highway—what a thrill that was! I found out later that they were conducting low-level attack procedures. Also, I've stayed very active with the 460th Fighter Squadron Association. The squadron's reunions have kept war memories alive for me, through such activities as viewing military museums, tours of air bases and attending airshows, which all bring back memories of my "old flying days."

My involvement in squadron reunions began in 1984, while living in Hinsdale, Illinois. I was reading a veterans magazine when an article caught my eye about a 460th meeting being held in Oak Brook, Illinois, with a host by the name of Jack Mullins. He was a flyer I had met in the service. By the time I made contact with him the reunion was over, but I was very excited at the prospect of getting together again with my squadron buddies. So this was the beginning of our many adventures in future squadron reunions. The first squadron reunion took place in 1982, hosted by Herb and Nora Cass in Anaheim, California. So far there have been a total of

30 reunions, with the 31st to be held in Monterrey, California in 2012.

In 1995, I had the whole 348th Fighter Group reunion here in Las Vegas with 144 attendees. We arranged a tour and luncheon at Nellis AFB. The personnel that assisted me told me the base was named after a deceased P-47 pilot, killed in the crash of a Jug.[2] The reunion was held at the Tropicana Hotel.

Our enlisted and commissioned people have been a significant part of our reunions, but you must remember our ages. Many of the pilots were really young compared to the enlisted members. So we have lost all of the enlisted members due to age attrition. The number of pilots has shrunk dramatically in the last few years. Alas, our offspring are filling the gaps of those departed, and they contributed in 2008, for the first time, as hosts and will do so again next year in Southern California. Last year we had 38 people in Seattle with no enlisted members. I have hopes of attending the 2012 reunion in Monterey, California.

The A-10 Warthog pilots at Nellis once expressed interest in joining the P-47 Pilot's Association, but since then, the Jug pilots disbanded, as did the 340th and 341st squadrons of the 348th group. In the not too distant future, the 460th will probably do the same.

One reunion in particular that stands out most vividly was the September 2001 event held in Montauk, Long Island, New York. We decided to travel by auto, as we wanted to visit with family and friends along the way. As we were passing through Omaha, Nebraska, the radio broadcast was interrupted by a special bulletin, telling about the attack by planes on the twin towers of New York City, and that all airline flights were to be halted or grounded. We were going to turn back for home, but decided to continue on. Arriving two days later we came upon a very confused, devastating mess. We could only see the terrible black smoke in the distance, outside of getting lost and turned around. We did arrive at Montauk Manor, Long Island, but many squadron members were unable to arrive due to the airports being shut down. This was a very sad day for all of us, to think that our nation had come under such an attack.

We did continue on with our everyday lives. As the old saying goes, "one day at a time," which I guess has helped me get through each day. We may not have many reunions left to go to, but all the joyous and precious memories shall never be forgotten.

I still fly occasionally with friends, but no longer hold a license.

NOTES

1. History of the 341st Fighter Squadron, Chapter XXII, (August 1945), Inclosure 4, "Letter of Commendation," 20 August 1945.
2. Nellis Air Force Base in Nevada is named after 1st Lt. William H. Nellis, a P-47 Thunderbolt pilot in the 513th Fighter Squadron, 405th Fighter Group. After completing 70 combat missions and being shot down three times, he was killed in action during the Battle of the Bulge on December 27, 1944, during an attack on a German vehicle column in Luxembourg.

    "Nellis, William H., 1st Lt," http://airforce.togetherweserved.com/usaf/servlet/tws. webapp.WebApp?cmd=ShadowBoxProfile&type=Person&ID=116575

EPILOGUE

J AMES CHANDLER CURRAN PASSED AWAY ON JUNE 3RD, 2012, before he could attend what turned out to be the last 460th Fighter Squadron Association reunion in September 2012, in Monterey, California, and before his account of his war across the Pacific could be finished. But his contributions to America's freedom and military heritage are written in the liberty we enjoy today as well as the record of his combat squadrons and the 348th Fighter Group.

Jim's combat group, the 348th Fighter Group, fought its way to Japan and was on Ie Shima at the end of the war. The group moved to Itami Air Base, near Osaka, Japan and participated in the occupation until it was inactivated on May 10, 1946. Two weeks later it was redesignated as the 108th Fighter Group and allotted to the State of New Jersey as part of the postwar buildup of the Air National Guard.

Today it is designated as the 108th Air Refueling Wing, flying the KC-135R Stratotanker at Joint Base McGuire-Dix-Lakehurst (JB MDL), NJ.

Photo of James Curran late in life, taken by his grandson, Brad.

For its service in WWII, the 348FG received three major decorations: the Distinguished Unit Citations for operations in New Britain, 16-31 December 16–31, 1943, and the Philippines Islands, 24 December 1944, as well as the Philippine Presidential Unit Citation. It also received credit for participation in eight campaigns during the war.

His first combat squadron, the 341st Fighter Squadron, followed the path of its parent group, to include a redesignation on May 24, 1946, as the 141st Fighter Squadron and allotment to New Jersey. Today, the squadron is the 141st Air Refueling Squadron and operates the KC-135R Stratotanker at JB MDL. The squadron received the same major decorations as the 348th Fighter Group, and credit for participation in nine WWII campaigns.

Jim's second combat squadron, the one he helped found, the Black Rams of the 460th Fighter Squadron, went on from the Philippines to the island of Ie Shima, next to Okinawa. From there they flew combat missions against the Japanese home islands and other points in the waning days of the Japanese Empire. J.J. Smith remembered what happened on August 9, 1945: "We were up on August 9th and saw the one go off at Nagasaki. I don't think there was any way to see the earlier one as the distance was too great."

When the war ended, the 460th became part of the occupation force in postwar Japan, and in November of 1945, flew up to Itazuke Air Base on Kyushu to participate in the occupation of Japan. The squadron lost 11 men in combat, including ten flying officers and one sergeant who was killed on Leyte. On February 20, 1946, the squadron inactivated, having earned the Distinguished Unit Citation in the Philippine Islands, 24 December 1944, the Philippine Presidential Unit Citation and credit for nine campaigns in World War II.

On March 18, 1955, the squadron activated again as the 460th Fighter-Interceptor Squadron at McGhee-Tyson Airport, Tennessee with the F-86 Sabre fighter. On August 18 of the same year, it moved to Portland Air Force Base, in Portland, Oregon, as a fighter-interceptor squadron assigned to the Air Defense Command. The squadron then flew the F-89 Scorpion and later transitioned to the F-102 Delta Dagger. It received the Air Force Outstanding Unit Award at least three times, for distinguished service from March 1954 to July 1959, 8 June 1960 to 30 April 1962 and 1 May 1962 to 31 July 1963. The 460th won the F-102 category

The men of the Black Ram squadron gather for a picture at their 1989 reunion in Issaquah, Washington. William D. Dunham, Brigadier General, USAF (Retired) leads from the front again. He passed away less than a year later, on March 3, 1990. Jim Curran is standing at the extreme right of the group in white jacket and holding his hat.—courtesy Mary Jean Curran

of the 1959 William Tell Worldwide Weapons Meet, and 460FIS pilot Capt. Fredrick H. England was the F-102 Top Gun of the competition.[1] In 1966, the squadron inactivated, but in 1968 it was reactivated once more, at Oxnard AFB, California, equipped with the F-106 Delta Dart fighter-interceptor. In November 1969 the squadron moved to Kingsley Field in Oregon. In April 1971, the squadron moved yet again to Grand Forks AFB, Montana where it continued to operate the F-106. The squadron won Top Unit honors in the F-106 category at William Tell 1972.[2] It inactivated again on July 15th, 1974.

In its most recent era of existence, the 460th was activated again January 15th, 1982 as a Fighter Interceptor Training Squadron at Tyndall AFB, Florida. It was inactivated again on October 15th, 1982, and remains so until this day.

On May 20, 1991, 460FS Association members met at Wright Patterson AFB, OH for a reunion. They dedicated a 460FS memorial in honor of those squadron members lost in the war: Lt. Adrian A. McLendon; Lt. Kenneth F. Saunders; Lt. Floyd H. Stone; Lt. Perry A. Tubre; Lt. Randall

U. Tuttle; Lt. Paul F. McMath; Lt. Walter A. Abraham; Lt. Gerald Economoff; Lt. David T. McMahon; Lt. Bernard P. Kane, and Sgt. Richard N. Van Nostrand.[3]

In October 2012, the Black Rams of the WWII 460th Fighter Squadron Association held their last formal reunion in California, where they remembered Jim Curran and the other Black Rams who were lost during the war and in the years after. Seven members attended and made the decision to inactivate the organization. At the end of the reunion, they broke out the squadron tontine and drank a salute to their comrades who have flown west. There was a 460FS website for many years, but it went off-line in 2013; hopefully it will be revived and endure to help tell the story of the Black Ram's part of the air war in the Pacific.

NOTES

1. "William Tell 1950's" http://www.mcchordairmuseum.org/REV%20B%20OUR%20HISTORY%20UNITS%20MISC.%20%20WT%201950%27S.htm
2. "William Tell 1970's" http://www.mcchordairmuseum.org/REV%20B%20OUR%20HISTORY%20UNITS%20MISC.%20%20WT%201970%27s.htm
3. "A Brief History of the 460th Fighter Squadron," http://www.ottocarter.com/thunderbolt/html/searles.htm

APPENDIX 1 *USAAF Pilot's Issue Flying Gear, From Chapter 3*

As for what else we were issued as pilots, here is the list of items I had from my A.A.F. Form 121, Individual A.A.F. Issue Record:

022100 Bag, flyers clothing, type B-4

401520 Helmet, flying sum, type ANH

595905 Mask, Oxygen, Type A-14

336050 Goggles, flying, Type B-8

792030 Suit, flying summer

590800 Protractor, semi-circular

62-084760 Computer, type D-4

2B838 Headset, HS-38

2B1660.1 Midrophone, ANB-M-C1

022200 Bag, flyers kit, Type A-3

298880 Gloves, flying, Type A-11

298313 Gloves, flying, Type B-3

456000 Gloves, Insert, Rayon

396000 Helmet, flying, Type A-11

720850 Shoes, flying, Type A-6

470710 Jacket, flying, Type B-10

878610 trousers, flying, Type A-9

290400 Glasses, flying, sun

336010 Goggles, assy, Type B-7

Jacket, flying, Type A-2

Vest, flying, Type C-2

6200-480400 Watch, nav, Type A-11

Pistol Cal (45 No Model 1911/A1 (Ordnance issue)

APPENDIX 2 *Pidgin English Phrases used in the Southwest Pacific Area (SWPA)*

PIDGIN ENGLISH PHRASES

The following Pidgin English phrases which may be useful to pilots stranded in New Guinea or New Britain Territory are set forth below.

I AM AMERICAN	ME BILONG AMERIKA
I AM FRIENDLY	ME PREN BILONG YOU PELLA
I FELL FROM A PLANE	ME FALL DOWN LONG BALUS
MY PLANE CRASHED	BALUS BILONG ME E BUGARAP
BRING ME FOOD—BANANAS, SWEET POTATO, PIG	TARO YOU BRINGEM ME SOME PELLA KAI KAI BANAN, TARO, KAUKAU, PIG
ARE THE JAPANESE NEAR?	JAPAN E SITOP CLOSE TO?
ARE THE AMERICANS NEAR?	AMERIKA SOLDIER E SITOP CLOSE TO?
ARE THE JAPANESE COMING?	JAPAN E COME?
YOU MUST HIDE ME IN THE BUSH	YOU MAS HAITEM ME LONG BUSH BILONG
CAN YOU TAKE ME TO THE AMERICANS?	YOU KAN BRINGEM ME LONG ALTOGETA AMERIKA?
YES, I CAN TAKE YOU	ME KAN BRINGEM YOU
YOU MUST NOT TAKE ME TO THE JAPANESE	YOU NO KAN BRINGEM ME LONG JAPAN
I AM VERY SICK. ALL THE NATIVES MUST CARRY ME	ME SIK TIMAS. ALTOGETA KANAKA E MAS LIFTIMUP ME
WHERE IS THE ROAD TO THE AMERICANS?	WHERE SITOP ROD BILONG ALTOGETA AMERIKA?
I HAVE COLLAPSED FROM ILLNESS	ME BUGARAP LONG LONG PELLA SIK
YOU MUST LOOK AFTER ME	YOU MUST LUKAUTIM ME
I CAN PAY	ME KAN PAY
I CAN PAY LATER	ME KAN PAY BEHIND
IF YOU BRING ME TO THE AMERICANS I CAN CAN REWARD YOU WELL	SIPOS YOU BRIGEM ME LONG AMERIKA ME KAN PAYIM YOU GOOD

SEND A NATIVE TO TELL THE AMERICANS I AM HERE IN THE BUSH	YOU SEND HIM ONE PELLA KANAKA BILONG TOKIM ALTOGETA AMERIKA ME SITOP LONG BUSH
I WANT TO STAY IN A NATIVE HOUSE	ME LAIK STOP LONG HAUS KANAKA
I WILL WRITE A LETTER YOU BRING IT TO THE AMERICANS	ME RAITIM PASS YOU BRINGEM ID PELLA PASS LONG TO AMERIKA
LIGHT A FIRE	YOUR WORKIM PIRE
GET ME SOME WATER	KESIM LIL LIK WARA

VOCABULARY

PLANE — BALUS

IS (ARE) — SITOP

AM — BILONG

WATER — WARA

FOOD — KAI KAI

FIRE — PIRE

NATIVE — KANAKA

REWARD — PAYIM

Note: Correct Pidgin English spelling has not been used in the above phrases. This has been done in order that the sentences may be more easily understood.

Enclosure 6, "List of Pidgin English Phrases," from History of the 342nd Fighter Squadron, Chapter III, (July 1, 1943 to January 31, 1944).

APPENDIX 3 *Credit for Destruction of Enemy Aircraft, 25 October 1943*

341ST FIGHTER SQUADRON
348TH FIGHTER GROUP
APO 929 / AG 373
25 October 1943
SUBJECT: Credit for Destruction of Enemy Aircraft.
TO: Commanding General, Fifth Air Force, APO 925 (Thru Channels).

1. Request official confirmation for the destruction of one (1) enemy airplane, type ZEKE, in aerial combat near Finschhafen, New Guinea, on 23 October, 1943, at 1040L, by 2nd Lieutenant JAMES C. CURRAN.

2. On 23 October, 1943, at 1040L, while on a patrol mission to Finschhafen, New Guinea, at an altitude of 21,000 feet, our formation of 14 P-47 type airplanes encountered an enemy formation of approximately 14 fighters. In the ensuing engagement, I dove in shooting down one (1) of the enemy fighters.

   I dove on a ZEKE and shot it, he suddenly did a half snap, stalling out up side down, then spun down apparently out of control. Lieut. DELLA observed this enemy plane going down out of control.

JAMES C. CURRAN, 2nd Lt., Air Corps.

WITNESS: I was a member of the formation in the above communication and saw 2nd Lieut. JAMES C. CURRAN, shoot down the enemy ZEKE type aircraft at the time, and under the circumstances outlined above. I saw the ZEKE 2nd Lieut. Curran, shot down spinning out of control.

GEORGE DELLA
2nd Lt., Air Corps.
1st Ind.

Headquarters, 341st Fighter Squadron, APO 929, 25 October, 1943.
TO: Commanding Officer, 348th Fighter Group, APO 929.
Approved
SAMUEL V. BLAIR, Capt., Air Corps.
Commanding.

Original Copy in James C. Curran's 201 Personnel File

APPENDIX 4 *348th Fighter Group Air Combat Intelligence Report, 2 February 1944*

HEADQUARTERS 348TH FIGHTER GROUP
OFFICE OF THE INTELLIGENCE OFFICER
APO 322 / 2 February 1944

The following information has been taken from Individual Combat Reports.

ENEMY TACTICS—The most common tactics used by the enemy fighters are:
1. Steep climbing turns—both to the right and left with majority of the turns to the left. This is especially true of the Zeke.
2. Split "S"—this evasive action is almost invariably taken by the Tony.
3. Tight Luftberry—This is not as common as the above mentioned maneuvers, but has been used by the enemy several times—usually to the left.
4. Dives have been used occasionally, especially by the TONY, and to a lesser degree by the Val.
5. Enemy Bombers usually stay in formation and the only change they make in their formation, when attacked, is to tighten it.

OWN TACTICS
1. Get all possible altitude advantage.
2. Use tremendous diving speed of the P-47 to full advantage.
3. Attack enemy fighters from stern, if possible, and from a dive. Pilots try to attack from 4 O'clock and 8 O'clock positions, in case of enemy bombers.
4. No attempt is made to dog fight. Usually make one pass and keep going. This has been especially true of the 4 ship flights to WEWAK.
5. Head-On attacks are occasionally necessary and it has always been noticed that the Jap has no stomach for such attacks, and is always the first to break away.

Our pilots regard the TONY as by far the best enemy fighter plane, and the BETTY as the best enemy bomber, of those that we have encountered.

Another interesting fact is that we have never had a report from our pilots of having ever been fired at by the rear gunners of the VAL. In one case a pilot reported that he was able to see in the VAL, and that there was no rear gunner in the plane, and that the guns were sticking straight up into the air. We are of the opinion that the VAL's we have encountered have had no rear gunners.

JOHN M. MILLER, Capt. Air Corps, Group Intelligence Officer

COMBAT OPERATIONS

Operations of the P-47 type airplane with 305 gal. fuel internal tanks; 200 gal. fuel external belly tanks

PATROL MISSIONS (4-4 1/4 hrs) 16 or more airplanes.

1. Climb 18,000' 33" Hg — 2300 RPM — 170 mph — 500'/min
2. Climb 18,000–25,000' 36" Hg — 2450 RPM — 170 mph — 500'/min
3. Climb above 25,000' 38" Hg — 2500 RPM — 165 mph — 500'/min
4. Level cruise to 25,000' 30" Hg — 2000 RPM 200 mph 1AS
5. Level cruise above 25,000' 31" Hg — 2000 RPM — 190 mph 1AS
6. Climb to 20,000' on straight line at above setting will take formation approximately 150 miles from base in 45 minutes.
7. Average gasoline consumption (auto-lean above 8,000')
   a. Climb to 25,000 125–150 gal/hr
   b. Level cruise 80–100 gal/hr
   c. Average for mission 100–110 gal/hr
8. Radius of 300 miles maximum, allowing for 20 min combat and reserve of 50 gals.

ESCORT MISSIONS (3–3 1/2 hrs) 16 or more planes.

1. Same settings as above only formation has to weave constantly after leveling off to stay with bomber formation.
2. Over target, air speed is increased to 250 mph -35" and 2450 RPM, continually weaving and changing altitude within 1000–1500' to off set enemy anti-aircraft fire.
3. Gasoline consumption is increased slightly, averaging 110–120 gal/hr.
4. Radius of 300 miles maximum, allowing for 20 min combat and reserve of 50 gals.

PATROL MISSIONS (4–4-1/2 hrs) 4 ship flight.

1. Same settings as 1
2. Gasoline consumption averages 95–105 gal/hr
3. Radius of action of 300 miles gives 45–60 min. over target.

History of the 348th Fighter Group, http://www.ww2f.com/topic/37324-history-of-the-348th-fighter-group/page-3

APPENDIX 5 *341st Fighter Squadron Statistical Data for May 1944*

A.   Strength

    (1) Personnel, commissioned and enlisted.   Flying   Ground

	Flying	Ground
(a) At beginning of period	45	254
(b) Net increase during period		3
(c) Net decrease during period	1	
(d) At end of period	44	257

    (2) Airplanes.

        (a) At beginning of period, by types:

P-47 D11	3
D11M	1
D15	2
D15M	1
D16	1
D16M	12
D21	1
D21M	5
Total —	26

        (b) Net increase or decrease during period, including:

            1. No. lost through combat, by type: 1 P-47 D16M

            2. No. lost on ground through enemy action, by type: None

            3. No. lost by accident, by type: None

Net increase during period: P-47 D15	1
Net decrease during period: P-47 D16M	1

        (c) At end of period, by types:

P-47 D11	3
D11M	1
D15	3
D15M	1
D16	1
D16M	11
D21	1
D21M	5
Total —	26

B. Number of sorties

    (1) Reconnaissance   4

    (2) Bombing

        (a) Number   256

        (b) Ton-miles flown   19,500

(3) Bombing cover   4

(4) Interception   8

(5) Fighter sweep   6

(6) Other: patrol   172

     cross country   96

C. Bombs dropped and ammunition fired.

   (1) Bombs dropped

(a) Tons, by types	M57 (250#)	29.5 tons
	M64 (500#)	15.0 "
	M31 (300#)	10.5 "
	M30 (100#)	7.0 "
	M43 (500#)	6.0 "
	Total —	65.0 tons

     (b) Results—good

   (2) Ammunition fired   65,082 rds .50 cal

     (a) Rounds, by size

     (b) Results—good

D. Aerial attacks by enemy on our ground installations: None

E. Ground battles engaged in by unit: None

F. Messing

   Bully Beef Dehydrated Spuds Dehy Eggs

   (1) Food consumed during period: 2,484 lbs / 3,600 lbs / 300 lbs

   (2) No. Meals when fresh meat served during period: 7

   (3) No. manhours spent on K.P.: 3,224

History of the 341st Fighter Squadron, May 1944, pp. 1–2.

APPENDIX 6 *Notes from Charles Lindbergh Lecture on P-47 Operations*

ENCLOSURE 2
THREE FORTY SECOND FIGHTER SQUADRON
OFFICE OF THE OPERATIONS OFFICER
APO 565 UNIT 1 / 18 August 1944
MEMORANDUM / TO: ALL CONCERNED.
TACTICS ON OPERATING P-47

Efficient cruising airspeed
— 195 to 200 with tanks and full gasload.
— 185 to 190 without tanks (decrease with lighter wing loadings)
Best climbing airspeed
— varies from 185 mph with full external tanks to 170 without tanks.
— 165 with internal gas and/or ammunition partially expended.
— It is better to stay on the high side of these figures as efficiency
drops rapidly at low speeds.
Normal climbing power — 42" Hg and 2250 rpm.
Maximum auto lean settings — 36" Hg and 2300 rpm. (In formation the leader
will use 34" to allow for variations in the plane).
Maximum range setting —
(1) Auto Lean
(2) 34" Hg
(3) Minimum rpm necessary to hold efficient cruising airspeed. Do not
go below the following rpm:
Standard Prop. — 1650 rpm
Semi-paddle Blade — 1600 rpm
Props on D23s and D25s — 1400 rpm
(4) After the minimum rpms have been reached, hold speed down to efficient cruising by reducing manifold pressure.
(5) The rpm settings will increase with altitude in order to hold efficient
speed. Tests have been run up to 15,000 feet which show that the range
is not affected however, due to the increased true airspeed derived.

For Maximum Range:
1. Do not climb. Hold the altitude at which you left target. There are
exceptions to this and it is sometimes advantageous to seek a tail wind
or a stable layer of wind.

2. If it is necessary to climb due to weather or terrain, do so at maximum auto lean setting and best climbing airspeed.

3. When nearing home base, utilize excess altitude in a 200 ft. descent, holding efficient cruising airspeed and maximum range settings. However, little will be gained by reducing manifold pressure below 30–32" to hold efficient cruising airspeed.

4. For most long-range flights it is best to stay below 8000 ft.

Best Procedure for Squadron Missions

1. Take-off with 15-degree flaps and water injection (58" max.)

2. Climb to 8000 at maximum auto lean settings.

3. Proceed on course at maximum range settings and efficient cruising airspeed.

4. Prior to entering target, the formation will climb at either maximum auto lean settings or normal climbing power depending upon the situation and the altitude to be reached.

5. The advantage gained by going to target at 8000 feet are:

   1. Pilot comfort and ease of formation flying.

   2. Increased range at that altitude.

6. All pilots will keep formation by changing rpms rather than manifold pressure. This will prevent exceeding the maximum auto lean settings and prove to be very effective.

7. If all members of the squadron hold the same manifold pressure and change rpms to hold formation, each individual plane will be operating at its own maximum efficiency, regardless of the higher rpm for slower ships.

For Absolute Maximum Range Returning from Target

1. Drop tanks.

2. Fire all ammunition.

3. Use 36" and sufficient rpms to hold 185 to 190 mph and 200 ft, minimum descent until 3000 to 5000 is reached. Reduce manifold pressure to maintain speed after minimum rpms have been reached.

4. Using the mixture control in the manual lean range has proven to be of very little value.

5. There is still question as to the efficient cruising airspeed under varying load conditions, but the present figures will be used until tests have been run.

It is suggested that all patrol missions, fighter sweeps, and cross-country flights be accomplished in accordance with this Memorandum.

Pilots will take notes on speed, altitude, distance, and fuel consumption on all such flights and turn them into Operations for comparison.

ROBERT H. KNAPP
1st Lt., Air Corps
Asst. Operations Officer.

History of the 342nd Fighter Squadron, Chapter X, (1–31 August 1944), Enclosure 2, Operations Memorandum, 18 August 1944, Subject: Tactics on Operating P-47.

APPENDIX 7 *460th Fighter Squadron*
Monthly "A" to "L" Report for November 1944

SQUADRON—460TH FIGHTER
GROUP—348TH FIGHTER
APO 248 / SUBJECT: Monthly "A" to "L" Report.
TO: Commanding General, Fifth Fighter Command, APO
(Attention Statistical Officer) / Month of November, 1944

A.	Total Combat Flying Hours		1817:00	
	Total Non-combat Flying Hours		68:30	
B.	Combat Sorties		885	
	Non-combat Sorties		49	
	Combat Missions		146	
	Non-combat Missions		27	
C.	Gasoline Consumption (gal)		184730	
	Oil Consumption (qts.)		21625	
D.	Ammunition expended:			
	Combat —.50 Cal.		229250	
	Training —.50 Cal.			
E.	Bombs Expended—Type		Number	
		500 lbs.	GP 786	
F.	US Aircraft Losses:			

Type	Serial No	Combat	Operational	Trans. To Serv. U.
P-47D21	42-25414	1		10th Serv Gp
"	42-25401	1		59th Serv Gp
"	42-25397	1		59th Serv Gp
"	42-25416	1		59th Serv Gp
"D23	42-27868	1		96th Serv Sq
*"	42-27637	1		59th Serv GpNo
"D21	42-25399	1		59th Serv Gp
"	42-25398	1		96th Serv Sq
"	43-25637	1		342nd Fitr Sq
"	43-25624	1		342nd Fitr Sq
"	43-25485	1		342nd Fitr Sq
"	42-27706	1		96th Serv Sq
"	42-27853	1		96th Serv Sq

* Shot down by friendly plane.

G. Enemy Aircraft Destroyed:
   Fighter   Bomber
   a. Definite: 10 a. Definite
   b. Probable   b. Probable

H. Shipping sunk (include barges) Tonnage   50,000
I. Average number of pilots present for duty   42
J. Number of Pilots assigned on last day of month   51

Source: 460FS History, November 1944

APPENDIX 8 *Unit Narrative Combat Report, 10 December 1944*

FOUR SIXTIETH FIGHTER SQUADRON
348TH FIGHTER GROUP
APO 72 / UNIT NARRATIVE COMBAT REPORT

MISSION NO. 3-217 / DATE: 10 December 1944
460TH FIGHTER SQUADRON 348 Fighter Group / BASE: Tacloban

4 Victors
TASK: Patrol Ormoc Area
TAKEOFFS AND LANDINGS: 4 took off 1050/I — TOT 1100/I–1145/I
1 landed 1215/I out of ammunition. Alt: 10,000–12,000 feet
3 landed 1300/I
WEATHER: Enroute and on return: Scattered cumulus, 6,000–10,000
                                              feet, 9/10ths covered.
              Over target and Camotes: Scattered cumulus, 6,000–10,000
                                              feet, 5/10ths covered.
AIR COMBAT: The Victors were at 12,000 feet circling the Ormoc area, when two TONYS were sighted flying NW over CUATRO ISLAND, at an altitude of 12,000 feet. The Victors pursued and intercepted the TONYS over the CAMOTES ISLANDS. The Victors attacked at 1145/I. The flight leader's element attacked the TONY on the left, the second element attacked the TONY on the right. The flight leader closed on the left hand TONY and fired three long bursts from astern which brought hits but which did not stop the enemy plane. He (the flight leader) broke off and his wingman then attacked the TONY with one pass, which scored hits but did not apparently do serious damage to the enemy plane. Then the flight leader closed to within 50 yards and fired another burst. The TONY burst violently into flames and crashed about 4 miles NW of the CAMOTES ISLANDS.

The element leader made several passes on the TONY which he attacked, getting hits but not deterring the enemy plane seriously in its flight toward northern CEBU. The element leader's passes were from the stern and various stern angles. Finally the element leader made a pass from dead astern just as the TONY was reaching the coast of CEBU. There were numerous hits all over the wings and fuselage of the TONY, and it crashed on the extreme N tip of CEBU ISLAND, trailing smoke as it dived to the ground. Just as the second TONY crashed, the Victor element leader was attacked by a third TONY which dived on him from somewhere above. The Victor was at 2,000 feet. The Victor did an uncoordinated skid to the right and the TONY overshot. Then the Victor gave chase and the TONY went into a shallow dive toward N. NEGROS. The Victor pilot shot his remaining ammunition at him, then broke off and returned home. The TONY was hit several times, and when last seen was still in a shallow high speed dive heading toward N NEGROS, trailing white vapor and smoke.

The first two TONYS appeared to be heading back toward CEBU after a flight over LEYTE. Whether or not the third TONY was in any way associated with the first two was undetermined. It would appear that the first two TONYS were experienced in evasive action, but unwilling to press aggressive combat, while a hit and run attitude was reflected in the action of the third.

OUR LOSSES: Nil
ENEMY LOSSES: 2 TONYS definitely destroyed.
1 TONY probably destroyed.
AMMUNITION EXPENDITURE: 2,800 x 50 cal.

JOHN R. WHITNEY
1st Lt, Air Corps, S-2.

APPENDIX 9 *Press Release by Fifth Air Force to All Correspondents, Circa May 1945*

"FIFTH AIR FORCE, PHILIPPINES . . . . FOR THE FIRST TIME IN THIS WAR A FIGHTER GROUP HAS DROPPED A GREATER TONNAGE OF BOMBS DURING A SINGLE MONTH THAN ANY SINGLE HEAVY BOMB GROUP.

THE RECORD-SHATTERING OUTFIT IS THE FIFTH AIR FORCE FIGHTER COMMAND'S 348TH FIGHTER GROUP. DURING THE PAST MONTH (APRIL, 1945), P-51 MUSTANGS OF THIS JAP BLASTING FIGHTER GROUP DROPPED 2091 TONS OF BOMBS, OF WHICH 2068 TONS WERE CHECKED OFF AS DIRECT HITS ON THE PIN-POINT TARGETS.

THE 348TH, WHICH DURING ONE PERIOD SHOT DOWN 251 JAP AIR-CRAFT FOR A COMBAT LOSS OF ONE PILOT, HAS BEEN CREDITED BY GROUND FORCES INTELLIGENCE WITH THE DESTRUCTION OF 10,000 JAPANESE BY BOMBING AND STRAFING DURING THE PAST MONTH.

DOING THEIR BOMBING "ON THE DECK" IN CLOSE SUPPORT OF THE INFANTRY DIGGING THE JAPS OUT OF LUZON, THE 348TH'S PI-LOTS DID SUCH OUTSTANDING WORK, OFTEN AS CLOSE AS 50 YARDS IN FRONT OF AMERICAN LINES, THAT THE GROUP HAS BEEN OFFI-CIALLY COMMENDED BY THE COMMANDING GENERALS OF THE 38TH INFANTRY DIVISION AND 112TH CAVALRY.

FLYING AS MANY AS 200 SORTIES A DAY, THE MUSTANG PILOTS FIRED NEARLY 2,000,000 ROUNDS OF FIFTY CALIBER AMMUNITION DUR-ING THE PAST MONTH. THEY STRUCK AT EVERY CONCEIVABLE TYPE OF TARGET—CAVES, ENTRENCHMENTS, GUN EMPLACEMENTS, TROOPS, VEHICLES, FACTORIES, WAREHOUSES, BARGES, SHIPPING AND ANY-THING ELSE THAT WAS JAP. THEY DID THE JOB WITH THE LOSS OF A SINGLE PLANE, AND THE PILOT OF THAT ONE WAS RESCUED.

THE 348TH FIRST ESTABLISHED ITS REPUTATION AS A "GO DOWN AND BLAST 'EM" SCOURGE OF JAP SHIPPING. IT RAN UP A RECORD TOTAL DURING THE LEYTE CAMPAIGN AND DURING ONE THREE WEEK PERIOD THIS YEAR ITS PILOTS SANK ONE TENTH OF THE JAP SHIPPING CREDITED TO THE ENTIRE FIFTH AIR FORCE."

History of the 340th Fighter Squadron, Chapter 20, (1-31 May 1945), Inclosure 9, "Press Release from Fifth Air Force."

APPENDIX 10 *Awards and Decorations of James C. Curran*

According to documents in James Curran's 201 File he was authorized a number of awards and decorations for his service in World War II. He received credit for participation in the New Guinea, Bismarck Archipelago, S. Philippines and Luzon campaigns.

James Curran was awarded the Air Medal with six Oak Leaf Clusters for meritorious achievement while participating in aerial flight. The oak leaf cluster signifies an additional bestowal of this decoration. His first award of the Air Medal for operational flight missions from 26 August 1943 to 1 November 1943 included this citation: "For meritorious achievement while participating in twenty-five operational flight missions in the Southwest Pacific Area, during which hostile contact was probable and expected. These operations included escorting bombers and transport aircraft, interception and attack missions, and patrol and reconnaissance flights. In the course of these operations strafing and bombing attacks were made from dangerously low altitudes, destroying and damaging enemy installations and equipment. Throughout these flights outstanding courage, ability and devotion to duty were demonstrated."

In addition to campaign credits and awards, James Curran was entitled to several unit decorations. The first two were the 348th Fighter Group's Distinguished Unit Citations (now called Presidential Unit Citations). The DUC/PUC is awarded to units of the US Armed Forces, and those of allied countries, for extraordinary heroism in action against an armed enemy on or after 7 December 1941. A unit must display such gallantry, determination, and esprit de corps in accomplishing its mission under extremely difficult and hazardous conditions so as to set it apart from and above other units participating in the same campaign.

NEW BRITAIN, 16–31 DECEMBER 1943

The 348th Fighter Group is cited for outstanding performance of duty in action from 16 December to 31 December 1943. In the middle of December 1943, the 348th Fighter Group was designated to help provide fighter cover for troops engaged in landing operation at Arawe and Cape Gloucester, New Britain, and for bombers striking at enemy installations. The airplanes of this group flew the first mission in this important assignment on 16 December 1943, the day of the initial landings, and they were continually in the air over Arawe and Cape Gloucester for the remainder of December. Seeking out and attacking enemy aircraft of all types, often in adverse weather, they completely dispersed hostile bombers and dive-bombers attempting to attack our ground and naval forces and, although often outnumbered two or three to one, fiercely out-fought protecting enemy fighter planes. The gallantry displayed by these pilots, many of them heretofore inexperienced in combat, in flying these hazardous missions everyday, and the tireless devotion to duty of the ground crews in working day and night to keep their aircraft in top fighting condition enabled the 348th Fighter Group, in a period of 16 days, to destroy 79 enemy aircraft in the air with a loss of only 2 of its own, a ratio of almost 40 to one. The combat prowess of this organization was a formidable factor in the capture of Arawe and Cape Gloucester and made an important contribution toward the neutralization of the enemy in the Bismarck Archipelago. The courage and devotion to duty displayed by the personnel of the 348th Fighter Group are in keeping with the highest traditions of the Armed services of the United States.

PHILIPPINE ISLANDS, 24 DECEMBER 1944

The 348th Fighter Group is cited for outstanding performance of duty in action in the Philippine Islands on 24 December 1944. On that day, four P-47 squadrons of the group were assigned to provide protection for twenty-two B-24 aircraft making a raid on Clark Field, Luzon, then one of the principal Japanese strongholds in the Philippine Islands. Taking off from an airstrip on the island of Leyte, the airplanes of the 348th Fighter Group rendezvoused over Masbate with the bombers, which were flying from Palau. Two of the P-47 pilots, dispatched to make a preraid reconnaissance, reached the target area 25 minutes ahead of the main striking force without being detected. Finding the air filled with Japanese airplanes at altitudes of from 10,000 to 16,000 feet, they unhesitatingly dived into the nearest enemy formation and, in the ensuing battle, destroyed 3 enemy aircraft and damaged another. Then, before the remaining Japanese could close in on them, these pilots radioed full information to the main American force on the number and disposition of the enemy formations, the weather, and possible targets. As the American bombers approached Clark Field under a cover of P-47 aircraft at 20,000 feet, enemy fighters began to attack. Soon, a series of fights between elements and flights of P-47's against 2-airplane flights and single aircraft of the enemy raged at altitudes of 2,000 to 20,000 feet for 10 to 15 miles on either flank of the Liberators' approach. Despite increasing antiaircraft fire, two of the Thunderbolt squadrons provided close protection for the bombers, engaging the enemy fighter aircraft only when they broke through the cover to attack the bombers. In a 45-minute battle, the P-47 pilots destroyed 32 hostile fighters and probably 2 others, or more than half of the airborne Japanese fighters, and thereby enabled the American bomb squadrons to destroy grounded aircraft, large hangars, extensive supply dumps, and repair installations without suffering a single casualty. Of the Thunderbolts which participated in this perfectly coordinated strike, four were lost, with one pilot crash-landing safely. Credit for the outstanding success of this mission must be given not only to the pilots of the group but also to the maintenance, operations, and intelligence personnel who readied the airplanes and airmen for the flight. In helping to deal a smashing blow at the center of Japanese air power in the Philippines and thereby pave the way for the invasion of Luzon some weeks later, the personnel of the 348th Fighter Group brought great honor on themselves and the United States Army Air Forces.

PHILIPPINE PRESIDENTIAL UNIT CITATION

James Curran was also entitled to a decoration from the Republic of the Philippines. It was awarded to certain units of the United States Armed Forces and the Philippine Commonwealth military for actions in World War II. The award of the Philippine Presidential Unit Citation was for personnel assigned to and present for duty in the Philippine Islands with the 348th Fighter Group and other units of the Armed Forces of the United States in recognition of participation in the war against the Japanese Empire during the period 17 October 1944 to 4 July 1945, inclusive.

APPENDIX 11 *A Brief History of the 460th Fighter Squadron*

A BRIEF HISTORY OF THE 460TH FIGHTER SQUADRON
PRESENTED DURING THE MEMORIAL
DEDICATION CEREMONY AT
THE UNITED STATES AIR FORCE MUSEUM,
WRIGHT-PATTERSON AIR FORCE BASE, OHIO, 20 MAY 1991

The unique fighting organization which we honor today was conceived some 47 years ago in the midst of combat, to blaze briefly but brightly, across the skies of Southeast Asia and Japan. Less than 14 months elapsed between its inception at Nadzab, New Guinea on 14 July 1944 until V-J Day, 2 September 1946. And the total active life-span of this 300-man, 25 plane unit was less than 20 months.

The squadron was born out of organizations, aircraft, equipment and people that could be made available because combat attrition had been less than anticipated. The ground echelon came from the 1st Airborne Squadron at Gusap, New Guinea. The initial cadre of pilots was drawn from the three squadrons of the 348h Fighter Group then based at Wakde Island on the New Guinea coast. Additional pilots were assigned from the Combat Replacement Training Center at Port Moresby. The aircraft, the Republic P-47 "Thunderbolt," the famous and beloved "Jug," came from excess theater resources.

The personal bonding that made this aggregation of men and machines unique began at Noemfoor Island in September 1944 and was strengthened through inspirational leadership, camaraderie and combat during successive moves to Tacloban, Tanauan and Floridablanca in the Philippines; Ie Shima Island, just off Okinawa in the Ryukyus; and finally to Itazuke airfield near Fukuoka, Japan.

Of necessity, this is a brief and selective account of the 20-month history of the 460th Fighter Squadron. No two members of the squadron would choose to highlight the same events. A vivid memory for one might be only dimly remembered, or forgotten entirely, by another. But here are a few of the things that will probably be remembered by all.

First, and most important, was the inspirational, follow-me leadership of the squadron's first commander, Major (later Brigadier General) William D. "Dinghy" Dunham. He came to the 460th from the 342d Fighter Squadron. He reveled in combat, and he led us into it with zestful enthusiasm for the first five of those 14 combat months.

All should remember 8 October 1944 on Noemfoor Island when we experienced our first air raid. A single Japanese bomber dropped one stick of bombs that caused more consternation than damage.

Not to be forgotten also were the long, long flights from Noemfoor across Geelvink Bay to Ambon and Ceram. Fuel requirements prevented carrying much of a payload. And while anti-aircraft fire was a hazard, weather was our worst enemy. It could change completely during the long hours between takeoff and landing. Those early combat missions taught us much about our airplane and about each other.

Then came the first real test. Dinghy was successful in convincing Fifth Air Force to select the 460th as the 348th Fighter Group's lead squadron into the Philippines. On 10 November 1944, only 21 days after MacArthur waded ashore at Leyte, the squadron launched from Morotai as top cover for a B-25 strike against a Japanese naval convoy in Ormoc Bay attempting to land troops on the west side of Leyte. For the B-25's it was their bloodiest day of the war. More than half the strike force was shot down by naval gunfire as we watched in dismay while flying top cover for an air attack that never came. When we landed at Tacloban the engineers were still laying pierced steel planking at both ends of the runway.

Whoever selected the 460th camp area did so in a hurry. We pitched our tents in a rain filled depression only a few yards back from White Beach, crowded between a gasoline dump on one side and an ammunition dump on the other. Tacloban was receiving day and night air raids. A well-placed stick of bombs could have done for us all.

A nightly occurrence was to drive back from the airstrip in a blackout, crowded into a single weapons carrier. Pilots, ground officers and enlisted men dined in the dark on cold "C" rations right out of the can while standing in ankle deep mud, cracking jokes, laughing and enthusiastically rehashing the events of the day.

Two days later, on 12 November, we received our first taste of air-to-air combat. Captain Dick Frost scored the squadron's first victory when he shot down a Zeke 32 over Leyte Gulf. Nine more enemy aircraft were downed by the end of the month. Then the air war intensified. Thirty-eight enemy aircraft were downed in December followed by only three in January when Japanese resistance from the air virtually ceased. Seven long months would pass before we scored another air-to-air victory when flying out of Ie Shima in August 1945. In all, the 460th shot down a total of 54 enemy aircraft with 38 of those destroyed during December 1944 when Japan made an all out effort to drive us from Leyte into the sea. The memories and hand-flying yarns from that month alone are more than could be recounted today.

None of us will forget December 7, 1944, third anniversary of the Japanese attack on Pearl Harbor. For us, it was one of the strangest days of the war. A US convoy carrying the 77th Army Division, with the 7th and 11th Divisions close behind, landed at Ormoc Bay on the west side of Leyte only an hour or so in advance of a Japanese troop convoy that steamed into the same harbor. Two troop convoys, both protected by naval warships and strong air cover, and both were zeroing in on the same landing beach. It was wild. In the confusion it was hard to determine who was attacking whom. The 460th engaged enemy air cover in the morning and enemy shipping in the afternoon with notable successes in each. Of the 76,000 tons of shipping sunk by the squadron throughout the war more than half was sunk in the month of December.

A final bizarre note was added on the evening of December 7, just at dusk, when the enemy launched a paratroop attack on San Pablo airfield directly across the road from Group Headquarters. The Group lost contact with all four of its squadrons. Two 341st Squadron sentries were killed by Japanese troops wielding sabers. Fortunately, Army ground troops reacted to the attack in time to nullify its success. Still, it was a nip and tuck day.

On 14 December the 460th moved to a new airstrip at nearby Tanauan. The camp area appeared to be ideally located on a palm-dotted grassy plain along the banks of the beautiful Guinarona River, but we suffered more from that river than we ever did from the enemy. It was infested with a tiny liver fluke that transmitted a pernicious disease called Schistosomiasis. A number of our people were infected before we discovered the cause and banned swimming in the river. Some of those stricken are still being treated today, more than 50 years after immersion in that deadly stream.

The move to San Marcelino on the Island of Luzon took place in February 1945 along with a major change in our combat mission. We became primarily a fighter bomber squadron and all that month provided close air support to the 37th Infantry and 1st Cavalry Divisions as they raced down the central Luzon plain and invested Manila. Japanese air resistance had disappeared. Manila fell. The 460th provided air cover for the paratroop attack on Corregidor [sic] and then bombed and strafed ahead of the troops until the enemy was driven from the island fortress. The American Army once again entered the bunker that had sheltered Douglas MacArthur and his wife and son some four years earlier.

In March 1945 came the transition from the gallant old "Jug" to the North

American P-51 "Mustang" and the arguments are still being made as to which was the better aircraft. They were both superb. Every pilot in the squadron would jump at the chance to fly either of them again.

The 460th officers were unanimous in agreeing that our enlisted men were unsurpassed. Every section of the squadron was strongly manned. One of the best examples of the magnificent support they provided took place on 14 April 1945. On that date we launched 20 perfectly maintained and armed P-51s from San Marcelino 650 miles across the China Sea to the Hong Kong/Canton area covering a B-25 bombing mission. There was not a single abort. Four of our twenty aircraft were spares. Not one was needed. All 20 aircraft made it to the target area and returned. According to the group commander, Colonel Dick Rowland, "The China mission on 14 April is unparalleled in the maintenance record for the group."

We received the same kind of support from our armament people. During May 1945, the 460th Fighter Squadron dropped more than 2000 tons of bombs, a record for bomb tonnage dropped by a fighter squadron.

In May came the move to Floridablanca with strikes against Luzon and Formosa (Taiwan) and the continuation of ground support and patrol and escort missions during the mopping up operations in the Philippines.

Relentless pressure against the Japanese continued. In July, the squadron moved forward again, this time to Ie Shima, just off the coast of Okinawa, and only 350 miles from Japan's southernmost island of Kyushu. From Ie Shima we flew missions to China and launched our first strikes against the enemy's homeland: fighter sweeps, bomber and rescue escort missions, dive bombing and strafing missions against a great variety of targets in southern Kyushu. On 29 July 15 of our P-51's covered A-26's on a strike at Nagasaki. No air opposition was encountered on any of these missions. Obviously, the Japanese were conserving what airpower they had in anticipation of an allied invasion of the home islands.

Of course, as we now know, such invasion never took place.

August 6: Hiroshima.

Then, less than a month from the end of the war, on the night of 7/8 August, the squadron suffered its worst ever loss to enemy action. A single bomb dropped from a lone enemy aircraft over Ie Shima, exploded in the midst of the 460th aircraft parking area. Fire spread rapidly. Five planes were immediately destroyed. In the morning two more were found to be non-reparable and ten others were damaged.

August 9: Nagasaki. A flight of P-51's from the 460th was airborne at the time and saw the huge atomic cloud created by the second and last atomic bomb dropped during World War II.

On 12 August, Lieutenant Kermit Allen shot down a George II fighter over Kyushu to account for the squadron's last air-to-air victory of the war.

August 30: US Navy warships steam into Tokyo Bay.

September 2: V-J Day. Peace accords were signed aboard the battleship Missouri. The war was officially ended.

The 460th remained active for another five months. The excitement of combat gave way to routine reconnaissance missions and training. Squadron strength dropped from a total of 260 to 166 personnel as many pilots and support personnel were sent home. In October our pilots began to fly excess P-51's to Clark Air Base in the Philippines for shipment back to the States.

A monster typhoon with torrential rains and 132 mile-per-hour winds struck Ie Shima on 8 October 1945. Virtually all squadron tents were blown away. While still recovering from the damage, the squadron was ordered to move to Itazuke airfield near the city of Fukuoka on Kyushu, Japan. This final squadron move began on 17 October.

The flow of personnel to the States continued and by 24 November we were down to 131 total personnel. All officers were assigned secondary and tertiary duties. Strength dropped to less than 100. Flying almost ceased. Nearly all the veteran pilots had returned to the States. Second lieutenants were serving as flight leaders.

Then, on 3 February 1946, General Order #25, Headquarters, Fifth Air Force, deactivated the 460th Fighter Squadron effective 20 February. The remaining personnel, aircraft and equipment went stateside or were transferred to other units.

Despite deactivation, the 460th continues to live.

It lives because there was an undefinable mystique surrounding the organization that cannot be captured by a chronology or by operational statistics. It had to do with the happy accident that brought together a very skilled and dedicated group of people, in a remote part of the world, and under conditions made memorable by the shared experience of combat. Nothing like this has happened to any of us before or since. That is why our wartime experiences in the 460th remain so vivid in our memories and why we have continued to meet with each other at annual reunions for the past ten years. That is why we are here today, some 45 years later, to dedicate this memorial.

(Here, unveil the memorial)

Ladies and Gentlemen.

This memorial is dedicated to the following members of the 460th Fighter Squadron who now survive only in our memories: Lt. Adrian A. McLendon; Lt. Kenneth F. Saunders; Lt. Floyd H. Stone; Lt. Perry A. Tubre; Lt. Randall U. Tuttle; Lt. Paul F. McMath; Lt. Walter A. Abraham; Lt. Gerald Economoff; Lt. David T. McMahon; Lt. Bernard P. Kane and Sgt. Richard N. Van Nostrand. Also indicated in this dedication are those members of the squadron who died after the war.

For the living, this memorial commemorates our continued devotion to freedom and to our great nation. We entrust it now to the United States Air Force Museum for the benefit and knowledge of those who will visit here from around the world.

On behalf of the 460th Fighter Squadron we are pleased to present officially this memorial to the Air Force Museum.

Prepared by DeWitt R. Searles

"A Brief History of the 460th Fighter Squadron," http://www.ottocarter.com/thunderbolt/html/searles.htm

APPENDIX 12 *460th Fighter Squadron Combat Losses in World War II*

No one ever dies, as long as they are remembered. Retelling stories and sharing experiences of our generation, keeps all our lost friends and loved ones alive, even though we may have moved on long ago.
—Dee Rodrigues, widow of Ensign John W. Brock,
  VT-6 Devastator pilot lost at Battle of Midway

November 10, 1944, 2nd Lt. Adrian A. McClendon in P-47D-23-RA 42-27637 was last seen by pilots of his flight over the Mindanao Sea heading directly for Tacloban with engine trouble. It was discovered later that he had been shot down by a friendly P-38 whose pilot had mistaken this plane for an enemy. Missing in Action. He is remembered on the Tablets of the Missing at Manila American Cemetery, Manila, Philippines. Lt. McClendon was awarded the Purple Heart and Air Medal. MACR 11295

November 14, 1944, S/Sgt Richard N. Van Nostrand, a crew chief, died of shrapnel wounds received at Tacloban Airfield, Leyte, during an air raid from one of the hundreds of small, hand-grenade-like anti-personnel bombs the Japanese were noted for using during this time. He entered military service at Utica, NY in 1941.

November 30, 1944, 2nd Lt. Perry A. Tubre was killed on the first pass by six enemy Oscar fighters that jumped the squadron from behind during a mission to Port Carmen on the east coast of Cebu Island. Many hits from enemy fighters were seen to strike in and around the cockpit. He is remembered on the Tablets of the Missing at Manila American Cemetery, Manila, Philippines. Lt. Tubre was awarded the Purple Heart and Air Medal.

December 24, 1944, 2nd Lt. Kenneth F. Saunders did not return from the Clark Field mission. His plane was hit by an enemy fighter, and while on the way home, his ship slid away from his escort's wing and plunged into the water near Burias Island. The escorting pilot saw no parachute, but could not be positive that Lt Saunders did not clear his plane before it dove in. He is remembered on the Tablets of the Missing at Manila American Cemetery, Manila, Philippines. Lt. Saunders was awarded the Purple Heart and Air Medal.

December 30, 1944, 2nd Lt. George R. Grace. Flew P-47D-21-RA 43-25493 crashed 2 miles north of Taytay Point, Leyte, Philippines after his plane's engine caught fire and the aircraft went into a spiral and crashed in flames in the water. He was not seen to bail out and was believed killed. He is remembered on the Tablets of the Missing at Manila American Cemetery, Manila,

Philippines. Lt. Grace was awarded the Purple Heart and Air Medal. MACR 12194.

January 7, 1945, 2nd Lt. Randall V. Tuttle was reported missing after a strafing pass at Opon airdrome which stretched along the Northwest coast of Mactan Island, opposite Cebu City. Although his P-47 was not seen to crash, members of his flight expressed belief that he had been hit by small arms fire. He is buried at Arlington National Cemetery, Arlington, Arlington County, Virginia, at Section 12, Site 5965.

January 12, 1945, 2nd Lt. Paul F. McMath was lost in action when he crashed 10 miles northeast of Plaridel landing ground in Luzon's central valley, after catching direct hits from light anti-aircraft fire. He is buried at the Wood-lawn Cemetery in Leslie, Ingham County, Michigan at Section 4, Plot C, Lot 7.

January 29, 1945, 2nd Lt. David T. McMahon died in the hospital from burns received when he cracked up on a pre-dawn takeoff three days before. He is buried at Plot F, Row 5, Grave 57 at Manila American Cemetery, Manila, Philippines. Lt. McMahon was awarded the Purple Heart and Air Medal.

April 11, 1945, 1st Lt. Walter A. Abraham, while strafing an enemy concentration 200 yards south of Metropolitan road and 1500 yards east of Santa Maria River fork, was seen to pull up to 3000 feet at the completion of the bomb run. Suddenly his P-51 went into a spin, crashed into the side of a hill, and burned. Other pilots saw the canopy fly off just before the plane crashed but reported Lt. Abraham did not bail out. He is remembered on the Tablets of the Missing at Manila American Cemetery, Manila, Philippines. Lt. Abraham was awarded the Purple Heart and Air Medal.

May 23, 1945, 1st Lt. Gerald Economoff flying (possibly) P-51D-20 44-63320, "was killed when his airplane disintegrated in mid-air and crashed on Rizal Hill just east of Manila. Flying wingman to Captain George Della on a two-plane weather recco over WAWA, he was on his way back to base after completing the mission. They dove their planes over Rizal Hill at an estimated speed of 475 miles per hour. When Captain Della leveled out he had lost sight of his wingman and could not make radio contact with him after that time. Eyewitnesses stated that they saw Lieutenant Economoff's plane level out after the dive at approximately 3,000 feet whereupon it suddenly seemed to disintegrate, then crashed on Rizal Hill." He is buried at Plot L, Row 5, Grave 27 in Manila American Cemetery, Manila, Philippines. Lt. Economoff was awarded the Distinguished Flying Cross with Oak Leaf Cluster, Purple Heart, and Air Medal with Oak Leaf Cluster.

June 10, 1945, 1st Lt. Floyd H. Stone, "one of the original pilots of the squadron who was active in the fighting over Ormoc, Cebu, Negros, and with one Zeke to his credit over Clark Field, Luzon, was killed when his plane collided with that of 2nd Lt. James A. Hamilton, Jr., in mid-air over San Julian, Luzon, Philippine Islands. Lt. Hamilton's propeller and right wing-tip hit the tail assembly of Lt. Stone's ship, shearing off his elevator and rudder. Though Lt. Hamilton was able to parachute safely to the ground, Lt. Stone was killed as his plane immediately crashed." He is buried at Plot F, Row 9, Grave 92 in Manila American Cemetery, Manila, Philippines. Lt. Stone was awarded the Purple Heart and Air Medal with three Oak Leaf Clusters. The 460FS history for June 1945 indicates two combat losses for the month involving P-51D-20-NA 44-64126 and P-51D-20-NA 44-63304, likely the two aircraft involved in this mid-air mishap.

July 28, 1945, 1st Lt. Bernard P. Kane, flying (probably) P-51D-20-NA 44-64114 was covering B-25's and A-26's and dive-bombing Kanoya East Airdrome, Kyushu, Japan. While on the bomb run at 8,000 feet, he went into a somersault as the right wing of his airplane came off at the root over Kanoya Town. No parachute was seen to open, and the cause was presumed to have been an anti-aircraft hit. Lt. Kane was listed as killed in action. He is buried at the Golden State National Cemetery, San Bruno, San Mateo County in California, at Section C, Site 204-A.

August 6, 1945, 1st Lt. Richard J. Miller, was flying P-51D-20 44-63205 during an escort mission for B-25's which were conducting a shipping strike on Tsushima, developed a coolant leak. He bailed out after the coolant was gone at approximately 32-00N, 129-05E, (about 66 miles southwest of the city of Nagasaki, on Kyushu) and appeared alright in his dinghy with dye-marker out. Lt. Walton S. Reed circled for twenty minutes vainly attempting to contact rescue aircraft, but was forced to return to the base after buzzing Lt. Miller at 100 feet because of fuel shortage. The following day while providing cover for rescue aircraft a flight of the 460th overheard a radio call at 0630/I from another flight that they were strafing an empty life raft. The 460FS planes were over Danjo Island (32-00N, 128-23E) (about 42 miles west of the reported bailout position) at the time, but radio contact could not be made with rescue craft, air or sea. Rescue aircraft with fighter escort searched for Lt. Miller on 7 and 8 August but did not find him. He is remembered at the Courts of the Missing, Court 7, Honolulu Memorial, National Memorial Cemetery of the Pacific, Honolulu, Hawaii. Lt. Miller was awarded the Purple Heart and Air Medal. MACR 14887

"A Brief History of the 460th Fighter Squadron," http://www.ottocarter.com/thunder-bolt/html/searles.htm

History of the 460th Fighter Squadron, wartime chapters.

American Battle Monuments Commission, Burials and Memorializations database, http://www.abmc.gov/search-abmc-burials-and-memorializations

Stanaway, *Kearby's Thunderbolts*.

History of the 348th Fighter Group, http://www.ww2f.com/topic/37324-history-of-the-348th-fighter-group/

GLOSSARY

AAF — Army Air Forces

ATC — Air Transport Command

BOQ — Bachelor Officers Quarters

CinC — Commander-in-Chief

CO — Commanding Officer

DFC — Distinguished Flying Cross

FEAF — Far East Air Forces (not to be confused with the earlier Far East Air Force in the Philippine campaign, 1941–42)

HF — High Frequency

IAS — Indicated Air Speed

IJAAF — Imperial Japanese Army Air Force

LST — Landing Ship, Tank

MP — Military Police

PBY — Navy amphibian patrol bomber; P=Patrol, B=Bomber, Y=letter designating Consolidated as the manufacturer

PT Boat — US Navy motor torpedo boat; P=Patrol, T=Torpedo

QM — Quartermaster

RAAF — Royal Australian Air Force

RCT — Regimental Combat Team

RDX — Research Department Explosive, an explosive compound more powerful than TNT

R&R — Rest and Recuperation/Relaxation

RAAF — Royal Australian Air Force

SE — Single Engine

SWPA — Southwest Pacific Area of military/naval operations

TAC — TAC officer—Teach Assess Counsel, i.e. a training officer

TDY — Temporary Duty

UHF — Ultra High Frequency

USO — United States Overseas service organization

VHF — Very High Frequency

WAC — Women's Army Corps

BIBLIOGRAPHY

BOOKS AND BOOKLETS

Air-Sea Rescue, 1941–1952, US Air Force Historical Study No. 95, Maxwell AFB: USAF Historical Division, Air University, 1953.

Anderson, Charles R. *Leyte: The US Army Campaigns of World War II (Pamphlet), CMH Pub 72-27.* Washington, DC: US Army Center of Military History, 1994.

Bell, Dana. *Air Force Colors Volume 3, Pacific and Home Front, 1942–1947.* Carrollton, TX: Squadron/Signal Publications, 1997.

Bellafaire, Judith A. *The Women's Army Corps: A Commemoration of World War II Service.* Washington, DC: US Army Center of Military History, 1993.

Birdsall, Steve. *Flying Buccaneers: The Illustrated Story of Kenney's Fifth Air Force.* New York, NY: Doubleday & Company, Inc., 1977.

Bulkley, Robert J., Jr. *At Close Quarters: PT Boats in the United States Navy.* Washington, DC: Naval History Division, 1962.

Boggs, Charles w., Jr., Major, USMC. *Marine Aviation in the Philippines, USMC Monograph.* Washington, DC: Historical Branch, G-3 Division, Headquarters, US Marine Corps, 1951.

Cannon, M. Hanlin. *Leyte: Return to the Philippines.* Washington, DC: US Army Center for Military History, 1993.

Chapin, John C. *A History of Marine Attack Fighter Squadron 115.* Washington, DC: History and Museums Division, Headquarters US Marine Corps, 1988.

Chapin, John C., Captain, USMC. . . . *AND A FEW MARINES: Marines in the Liberation of the Philippines, Marines in World War II Commemorative Series.* Washington, DC: Marine Corps Historical Center, 1997.

Close Air Support in the War Against Japan, USAF Historical Studies: No. 86. Maxwell AFB, AL: USAF Historical Division, Research Studies Institute, Air University, February 1955.

Cooling, Benjamin Franklin, Editor. *Case Studies in the Achievement of Air Superiority.* Washington, DC: Center for Air Force History, 1994.

Craven, Wesley F and Cate, James L., Editors. *The Army Air Forces in World War II, Volume VI, Men and Planes.* Chicago, IL: University of Chicago Press, 1955.

Davis, Ronald L. *Duke: The Life and Image of John Wayne.* Norman, OK: University of Oklahoma Press, 1998.

Development of the South Pacific Air Route, Army Air Forces Historical Studies No. 45. Arlington, VA: AAF Historical Office, February 1946.

Fletcher, Gregory G. *Intrepid Aviators: The True Story of USS Intrepid's Torpedo Squadron 18 and its Epic Clash with the Superbattleship Musashi.* New York, NY: New American Library Caliber, 2012.

Forty, George, *US Army Handbook 1939–1945.* New York, NY: Barnes & Noble Books, 1998.

Francillon, René J. *Japanese Aircraft of the Pacific War.* Annapolis, MD: Naval Institute Press, 1987.

Garand, George W. and Strobridge, Truman R. *History of U.S. Marine Corps Operations in World War II, Volume IV, Western Pacific Operations.* Arlington, VA: Historical Branch, G-3 Division, Headquarters, US Marine Corps, 1971.

Hata, Ikuhiko and Izawa, Yasuho, translated by Gorham, Don Cyril. *Japanese Naval Aces and Fighter Units in World War II.* Annapolis, MD: Naval Institute Press, 1989.

Hata, Ikuhiko, Izawa, Yasuho and Shores, Christopher. *Japanese Army Fighter Aces, 1931–1945.* Mechanicsburg, PA: Stackpole Books, 2012.

Hess, William N. *P-47 Thunderbolt at War.* New York, NY: Doubleday & Co., Inc., 1976.

Higham, Robin and Williams, Carol, editors. *Flying Combat Aircraft of the USAAF-USAF, Volume 2.* Ames, IA: Iowa State University Press, 1978.

Holmes, Tony, Compiler. *'Twelve to One' V Fighter Command Aces of the Pacific, Osprey Aircraft of the Aces Special 61.* Oxford, Great Britain: Osprey Publishing Limited, 2004.

Howmet Corporation, The World of Materials, News from the Department of Materials Science and Engineering, Vol. 3, No. 2. Blacksburg, VA: Virginia Polytechnic Institute and State University, Fall 1998.

Johnson, Frank D. *United States PT-Boats of World War II, In Action.* Poole, United Kingdom: Blandford Press Ltd., 1980.

Kenney, George C., *General Kenney Reports.* New York, NY: Duell, Sloan and Pierce, 1949, reprinted by Office of Air Force History, Washington, DC, 1987.

Kernan, Alvin. *The Unknown Battle of Midway: The Destruction of the American Torpedo Bomber Squadrons.* New Haven, CT: Yale University Press, 2005.

Knaack, Marcelle Size. *Post-World War II Fighters, 1945–1973.* Washington, DC: Office of Air Force History, 1986.

Knott, Richard C. *Black Cat Raiders of WWII.* Annapolis, MD: The Nautical and Aviation Publishing Company of America, 1981.

MAG-12 War Diary, December 1944, January 1945 and February 1945.

Maurer, Maurer, Editor. *Air Force Combat Units of World War II.* Washington, DC: Office of Air Force History, 1961.

Maurer, Maurer, Editor. *Combat Squadrons of the Air Force, World War II.* Maxwell AFB, AL: USAF Historical Division, Department of the Air Force, 1969.

McDowell, Ernest R. *Thunderbolt: The Republic P-47 Thunderbolt in the Pacific Theater.* Carrollton, TX: Squadron/Signal Publications, 1999.

McFarland, Stephen L. *Conquering the Night: Army Air Forces Night Fighters at War.* Washington, DC: Air Force History and Museums Program, 1988.

Melson, Charles D., Major, USMC. *Condition Red: Marine Defense Battalions in World War II.* Washington, DC: Marine Corps Historical Center, 1996.

Monday, Travis. *Wings, WASP & Warriors.* Raleigh, NC: Lulu.com, 2005.

Morison, Samuel Eliot. *History of US Naval Operations in World War II, Volume VI, Breaking the Bismarcks Barrier, 22 July 1942–1 May 1944.* Boston, MA: Little, Brown and Company, 1950.

Morison, Samuel Eliot. *History of United States Naval Operations in World War II, Volume XII, Leyte, June 1944–January 1945.* Boston, MA: Atlantic, Little & Brown, 1958.

Morison, Samuel Eliot. *History of United States Naval Operations in World War II, Volume XIII, The Liberation of the Philippines, 1944–1945.* Boston, MA: Atlantic, Little & Brown, 1959.

Park, Edwards. *Nanette.* New York, NY: W.W. Norton & Company, 1977.

Park, Edwards. *Angel's Twenty: A Young American Flyer a Long Way from Home.* New York, NY: McGraw-Hill, 1997.

Reports of General MacArthur, The Campaigns of MacArthur in the Pacific, Volume I. Washington, DC: US Army, 1966.

Shaw, Henry I. and Kane, Douglas T., Major, USMC. *Isolation of Rabaul.* Washington, DC: Historical Branch, G-3 Division, Headquarters, US Marine Corps, 1963.

Smith, Robert Ross. *Triumph in the Philippines, United States Army in World War II, The War in the Pacific.* Washington, DC: United States Army Center of Military History, 1991.

Stanaway, John C. *Kearby's Thunderbolts: The 348th Fighter Group in World War II.* Atglen, PA: Schiffer Publishing, 1997.

Stanaway, John C. *Mustang and Thunderbolt Aces of the Pacific and CBI, Osprey Aircraft of the Aces No. 26.* Oxford, Great Britain: Osprey, 1999.

Standard Classes of Japanese merchant Ships, ONI 208-J (Revised), Supplement 3. Washington, DC: Division of Naval Intelligence, January, 1945.

Statistical Control in the Army Air Forces, Air Historical Studies No. 57. Maxwell AFB, AL: USAF Historical Division, Air University, January, 1952.

Stauffer, Alvin P., *The Quartermaster Corps: Operations in the War Against Japan.* Washington, DC: US Army Center of Military History, 1990 at: http://history.army. mil/html/books/010/10-14/CMH_Pub_10-14.pdf

Steinberg, Rafael. *Return to the Philippines.* New York, NY: Time-Life Books, Inc., 1979.

The Fifth Air Force in the Huon Peninsula Campaign, January to October 1943, US Air Force Historical Study No. 113 (Formerly Army Air Forces Reference History, Short Title—AAFRH-13). Arlington, VA: AAF Historical Office, Headquarters, Army Air Forces, January, 1946.

The Fifth Air Force in the Conquest of the Bismarck Archipelago, November 1943 to March 1944, Army Air Forces Historical Studies No. 43. Arlington, VA: AAF Historical Office, Headquarters, Army Air Forces, January, 1946.

Tillman, Barrett. *Hellcat: The F6F in World War II.* Annapolis, MD: Naval Institute Press, 1979.

Wiggins, Robert Peyton. *Jungle Combat with the 112th Cavalry: Three Texans in the Pacific during World War II*. Jefferson: McFarland & Co., 2011.

Wolf, William. *US Aerial Armament in World War II, The Ultimate Look, Volume 2: Bombs, Bombsights, and Bombing*. Atglen, PA: Schiffer Military History, 2010.

Yenne, Bill. *Aces High: The Heroic Saga of the Two Top-Scoring American Aces of World War II*. New York: Berkley Caliber, 2009.

ARTICLES

"A Brief History of the 460th Fighter Squadron, presented during the Memorial Dedication Ceremony, at the United States Air Force Museum, Wright-Patterson Air Force Base, Ohio, 20 May 1991," on Otto Carter website, accessed 24 July 2014 at: http://www.ottocarter.com/thunderbolt/html/searles.htm

"Barrett Brothers Park," 29 Jun 2013 posting on St. Louis City Talk blog, accessed 24 July 2014 at: http://www.stlouiscitytalk.com/2013/06/barrett-brothers-park.html

"Charles Augustus Lindbergh helps the 5th Air Force during WW2," on Oz at War website, accessed 24 July 2014 at: http://www.ozatwar.com/ozatwar/lindbergh.htm

Hackett, Bob and Kingsepp, Sander, "Shinyo! Explosive Motorboats based in the Philippines 1944–1945," Revision 8, posted on combinedfleet.com at: http://www.combinedfleet.com/PhilippinesEMB.htm

Nevitt, Allyn D., "The TA Operations to Leyte, Parts I, II and III," http://www.combinedfleet.com/lancers.htm

Taylan, Justin, "Operation Te-Go, Japanese Paratrooper Attack on Leyte December 7 1944," on Pacific Wrecks website, accessed 24 July 2014 at: http://www.pacificwrecks.com/airfields/philippines/san_pablo/12-07-44/index.html

"The Battle of Ormoc Bay, December 2–3, 1944," on the USS Allen M. Sumner DD-692 website, accessed on 30 July 2014 at: http://www.dd692.com/ormocbay.htm

Shindo, Hiroyuki, "Japanese air operations over New Guinea during the Second World War," Journal of the Australian War Memorial, No 34, June 2001, accessed 24 Feb 2014 at: https://www.awm.gov.au/journal/j34/shindo.asp

UNPUBLISHED SPECIAL STUDIES

340th Fighter Squadron, Official histories for World War II. Maxwell AFB, AL: Air Force Historical Research Agency Reel A0777, on CD, 1942–1946. Includes Weekly Operations and Status Reports (Form 34) and Combat Evaluation Reports for the unit.

341st Fighter Squadron, Official histories for World War II. Maxwell AFB, AL: Air Force Historical Research Agency Reel A0777, and Reel A0778, on CD, 1942–1946. Includes Weekly Operations and Status Reports (Form 34) and Combat Evaluation Reports for the unit.

342nd Fighter Squadron, Official histories for World War II. Maxwell AFB, AL: Air

Force Historical Research Agency Reel A0778, on CD, 1942–1946. Includes Weekly Operations and Status Reports (Form 34) and Combat Evaluation Reports for the unit.

348th Fighter Group, Official histories for World War II. Maxwell AFB, AL: Air Force Historical Research Agency Archives, including July 1943, November 1944, December 1944, January 1945, September 1945.

460th Fighter Squadron, Official histories for World War II, Maxwell AFB, AL: Air Force Historical Research Agency Reel A0777, on CD, 1944–1946. Includes Weekly Operations and Status Reports (Form 34) and Combat Evaluation Reports for the unit.

Curran, James C. Individual Flight Records (AAF Form 5), 13 October 1942–22 October 1945

Curran, James C., Personal 201 File

Curran, James C., Pilot Log, 10 August 1942–30 June 1943 (Training)

Final Report on Comparative Combat Evaluation Trials of Japanese Tony I Type 3 Fighter, US Navy Project Ted No. PTR–1115, undated, accessed 24 March 2013 at: http://www.wwiiaircraftperformance.org/japan/Tony-I.pdf

Grace, George R., Missing Air Crew Report 12194, HQ Far East Air Forces, 31 Dec 1944

Machen, Nolan, War Diary, 8 May 1944–2 January 1946

McClendon, Adrian A., Missing Air Crew Report 11295, HQ Far East Air Forces, 13 Jan 1945

Porter, R.C., Jr. *War record of the USS Reid (DD369), Narrative of.* 31 December 1944.

USS *Barnes*, ACV 20 War Diary, June and July 1943

USS *Nassau*, CVE 16, War Diary, May and June 1944

USS *Reid*, DD 369, War Diary, October 1943

USS *Saratoga*, CV 3, War Diary, July 1943

VMF-218 War Diary,

VMF-313, War Diary, January 1945

ON-LINE RESOURCES

17 Mile Drome (Durand, Waigani), entry on Pacific Wrecks website, accessed 24 July 2014 at: http://www.pacificwrecks.com/airfields/png/17-mile/

"563 RESCUE GROUP (AFSOC)," Lineage and Honors Fact Sheet, Air Force Historical Research Agency, accessed 31 July 2014 at: http://www.afhra.af.mil/fact sheets/factsheet.asp?id=10271

American Battle Monuments Commission website, at: http://www.abmc.gov/

Arlington National Cemetery, at: http://www.arlingtoncemetery.mil/

Baugher, Joseph F., Homepage, accessed 24 March 2013 at: http://www.joebaugher.com/

Baugher, Joseph F., "USASC-USAAS-USAAC-USAAF-USAF Aircraft Serial Numbers–1908 to Present," accessed 24 March 2013 at: http://www.joebaugher.com/

usaf_serials/usafserials.html

Baugher, Joseph F., "US Navy and US Marine Corps Aircraft Serial Numbers and Bureau Numbers—1911 to Present," accessed 24 March 2013 at: http://www.joe baugher.com/navy_serials/navyserials.html

Greinert, Robert, "Donation of P-47 Tail Section and Machine Gun from Neel Kearby's Thunderbolt to USAF Museum, article updated 18 February 2014 on Pacific Wrecks website, accessed 9 November 2014, at: http://www.paci ficwrecks.com/aircraft/p-47/42-22668/donation.html

History of the 348th Fighter Group, accessed 24 July 2014 at: http://www.ww 2f.com/topic/37324-history-of-the-348th-fighter-group/

"Imperial Japanese Army Air Force Units in WWII," Games—IL2 page on the Asisbiz website accessed 25 July 2014 at http://www.asisbiz.com/IJAAF-Units.html

Imperial Japanese navy webpage, http://www.combinedfleet.com/

"Major P-47 Thunderbolt Variations, Serial Numbers, & Production," 368th Fighter Group website, accessed 24 July 2014 at: http://www.368thfightergroup.com/P-47-2.html

"Mastilock, John E.," aerial victory credit, on 348th Fighter Group page of the Ciel de Gloire (Sky of Glory) website, accessed 25 July 2014 at: http://www.cielde gloire.com/fg_348.php

McChord Air Museum, http://www.mcchordairmuseum.org/

"McMath, Paul F.," grave information at: http://www.findagrave.com/cgi-bin/fg. cgi?page=gr&GSln=McMath&GSiman=1&GSst=24&GRid=85570834&

Meister, Harry, and Demeter, David, "A Brief History of USS LCS (L) (3) 7," posted on navsource.com at: http://www.navsource.org/archives/10/05/050007h.htm

Nevitt, Allyn, "AKIZUKI Class Notes," http://www.combinedfleet.com/akizuk_n. htm

Oz at War, http://www.ozatwar.com/

Pacific Wrecks, http://www.pacificwrecks.com/

P-39F-1-BE Airacobra Serial Number 41-7128, entry on Pacific Wrecks website, accessed on 24 July 2014 at: http://www.pacificwrecks.com/aircraft/p-39/41-7128.html

"Republic P-47 'Thunderbolt'," posted on the 456th Fighter-Interceptor Squadron website, accessed 9 November 2014, at: http://www.456fis.org/P-47.htm

"Squadron History: VP-34," Dave's Warbirds website, accessed 30 July 2014 at: http://www.daveswarbirds.com/blackcat/hist-34.htm

Together We Served, http://www.togetherweserved.com/

"Tuttle, Randall V.," grave information at: http://www.findagrave.com/cgi-bin/fg.cgi? page=gr&GRid=49329766

US Navy Cruise Book, USS Baltimore (CA-68), 1946, page 220, on Fold3 website, accessed 24 July 2014 at: http://www.fold3.com/image/#301704719

USS Reid, History, on the USS Reid Association webpage, accessed 10 November 2014 at: http://www.ussreid369.org/History.htm

USS Reid, Wikipedia entry, accessed 10 November 2014, at: http://en.wikiped
ia.org/wiki/USS_Reid_%28DD-369%29

Veterans Administration, National Cemetery Administration, Nationwide Gravesite
Locator (sans Arlington) for military cemeteries, accessed 11 November 2014, at:
http://gravelocator.cem.va.gov/

VMF/VMF(AW)/VMFA-115 Reunion Association Homepage, accessed 24 March
2013 at: http://115marinereunion.com/

VP-54 History, US Navy Patrol Squadrons website, accessed 17 October 2014 at:
http://www.vpnavy.com/vp54_1940.html

"VPB-34 History," Dictionary of American Naval Aviation Squadrons, Volume 2,
Chapter 4, pp. 453–457, Accessed 30 July 2014 at: http://www.history.navy.
mil/avh-vol2/chap4-3.pdf